The Analects of Dasan, Volume 1

The Analects of Dasan, Volume 1

A Korean Syncretic Reading

Translated with Commentary by
HONGKYUNG KIM

UNIVERSITY PRESS

Oxford University Press is a department of the University of Oxford. It furthers
the University's objective of excellence in research, scholarship, and education
by publishing worldwide. Oxford is a registered trade mark of Oxford University
Press in the UK and certain other countries.

Published in the United States of America by Oxford University Press
198 Madison Avenue, New York, NY 10016, United States of America.

Library of Congress Cataloging-in-Publication Data
Names: Chong, Yag-yong, 1762-1836, author. | Kim, Hongkyung, 1959–
translator, writer of added commentary.
Title: The analects of Dasan, Volume 1 : a Korean syncretic reading / Hongkyung Kim.
Other titles: Nono kogumju. English
Description: New York : Oxford University Press, 2016.
Identifiers: LCCN 2016010464 | ISBN 9780190624996 (hardcover : alk. paper) |
ISBN 9780190625016 (epub) | ISBN 9780190625023 (online)
Subjects: LCSH: Confucius. Lun yu.
Classification: LCC PL2471.Z6 C536 2016 | DDC 181/.112—dc23
LC record available at https://lccn.loc.gov/2016010464

9 8 7 6 5 4 3 2 1
Printed by Sheridan Books, Inc., United States of America

Dasan composed *Plum and Birds*, the artwork on the cover, to encourage his daughter to be loyal to her family-in-law. It was 1813, the thirteenth year of his eighteen-year exile, when he completed *Noneo gogeum ju*. The poem in its entirety (including the part obscured in the design of the cover) reads:

Two birds, fluttering, rest on a plum tree in my garden
They flew in, mesmerized by its permeating fragrance, and
Would stay and nestle here to please your family
Full-blown flowers should lead to an abundance of fruit

According to Dasan's explanation of the image, the "canvas" he painted it on was made out of a faded red silk skirt that his wife, Lady Hong, sent to him one day in the midst of his exile. This image was provided by the Korea University Museum.

This project of publishing *Noneo gogeum ju* in English was supported by an Academy of Korean Studies (Korean Studies Promotion Service) grant funded by the Government of the Republic of Korea (Ministry of Education) (AKS-2013-KCL-2230002).

CONTENTS

ACKNOWLEDGMENTS

My research project on *Noneo gogeum ju*—or *The Analects of Dasan*, as it is referred to in this book—was resumed when I received a grant from the Academy of Korean Studies in 2013. It was part of their series of One Hundred Korean Classics. In fact, *Noneo gogeum ju* was not initially included among the books in this series probably because it is so voluminous and complex. I suggested that it be included, and the Academy accepted my suggestion. The grant proposal stipulated that I finish the translation of the entire text with my commentary in six volumes over six years. This book, its first volume, is the result of my work in the first year. I am humbled by the fact that my research on Dasan's interpretation of the *Analects* could only be completed after gaining financial support from the Academy. It would be shameful to pretend that it was only my love for Dasan that made this publication possible. So it is with great humility that I express my respect for him here, and how great a pleasure and inspiration it has been to read his *Analects* and attempt to understand his thought.

Besides the generous support from the Academy of Korean Studies, I also received various kinds of help from Ms. Lucy Randall, a member of the Oxford University Press. I met her in the 2015 American Philosophy Association Eastern Division Meeting in Philadelphia, where I presented an article on Dasan's *Analects*. It was my first contact with the publisher for this project, which was followed by much fruitful correspondence. The anonymous peer reviews also proved productive, whose authors deserve my many thanks as well. Douglas Hong has been my personal editor since the first year of the project, serving even now in that role as I continue to work on the third volume of the *Analects of Dasan*. He is in the Cultural Studies doctoral program at Stony Brook University and extremely talented. Without his support, this project would undoubtedly have proceeded at a snail's pace. Also, I would like to mention my colleagues who read my manuscript to correct my errors and provide supplementary information that has helped bring this book closer to the vision that inspired it. They include: Eon-jong Kim from Korea University, Hong-sik Park from Daegu Haany University, Yeong-ho Kim from Youngsan University, Seon-hui Kim from

Ewha Womans University, Min-jeong Baek from Catholic University of Korea, Han-sang Kim from Myongji University, Bong-gyu Yi from Inha University, So-yi Jeong from Sogang University, and Mark Setton from University of Bridgeport. Back in 2003, I acknowledged in one of my books my wife's steadfast presence throughout all of the hardships we experienced by saying, "I want to share with my wife everything that I can share." I am happy that these same words hold true today.

The Analects of Dasan, Volume 1

| Introduction

1

Dasan 茶山, "a tea mountain," was the pen name of the Korean Confucian scholar whose reading of the *Analects* provides the subject of this book. To follow the old Confucian style of introducing a highly respected person: he was a member of the twenty-third generation of the Jeong 丁 family, whose ancestral seat was Naju 羅州 (originally Aphae 押海), and the two characters *yak* 若 and *yong* 鏞 constituted his personal name. His full name was Jeong Yak-yong (1762–1836). He is also remembered by various pen names besides Dasan, including Yeolsu 洌水, Sammija 三眉子, Yeoyudang 與猶堂, Tak-ong 籜翁, and Sa-am 俟菴. Yeolsu, "the Yeol water," refers to the Han River, in whose upper region he was born and interred. Sammija, "the master with three eyebrows," suggests how he was distinguished from others, not only by a scar that smallpox left him with but also by his talents. Yeoyudang, "a hall of hesitation," attests to his awareness of certain dangers during a stage of his life that caused him to confine himself, as it were, in hesitation. Tak-ong, "an old man on a bamboo mat," may signify the abject conditions in which he lived. Finally, Sa-am, derived from a passage in *Constant Mean*,[1] connotes his confidence in understanding people.

All the pen names paint a picture of Dasan's life. He was born into a family of the Southerners faction that, generation after generation, lived in the vicinity of the capital around the Han River and with which he was affiliated for the entirety of his life.[2] He was undoubtedly an outstanding scholar. He

---

[1] Two passages in *Constant Mean* pertain to the character *sa* 俟 (to wait). The line pertinent to it in the first passage reads: "Therefore, the noble person stays calm, waiting [俟] for the appointments of Heaven" (*Zhong yong zhangju* 中庸章句, 9b); The line in the second passage reads: "The noble person is not bewildered, even when he waits [俟] for one hundred generations for sages to come. This shows that he understands human beings" (25a).

[2] The scholars of the Southerners faction constituted an important wing of the Silhak 實學 (Practical Learning) movement, including Yu Hyeong-won 柳馨遠 (1622–1673) and Yi Ik 李瀷 (1681–1763). Yi Ik was successful in forming his own school in the Ansan 安山 area, from which many great scholars in the movement of Practical Learning emerged, such as An Jeong-bok 安鼎福 (1712–1791), Yi Ga-hwan 李家煥 (1742–1801), and Gwon Cheol-sin 權哲身 (1736–1801). Dasan once stated that he was deeply inspired by the works of Yi Ik, who expressed wishes to carry on the legacy of Yu's scholarship. Meanwhile, Yu Hyeong-won revered Heo Mok 許穆 (1595–1682), whose master was Jeong Gu 鄭逑 (1543–1620), one of the major disciples of Yi Hwang 李滉 (1502–1571).

was targeted by his rivals and victimized in the first grand-scale persecution of Joseon Catholics in 1801, as a result of which he was banished. He must have endured a scarcity of resources, especially right after his banishment.[3] Despite all of the hardships he had to face, he was confident that he was passing down his understanding of the Way to the next one hundred generations. However, he is usually remembered by the pen name Dasan, because most of his major works, including his *Analects*, were either drafted or finished during his eighteen-year exile, for ten years of which (1808–1818) he stayed in a "grass hut" by a small mountain full of tea trees.[4] Ironically, he rarely used this pen name to identify himself, probably because it brought up memories of pain and frustration that he experienced from the deaths of loved ones, the ruin of his family, political atrocities, widespread poverty, and unrealized dreams. Thus the world is still harsh to him because in its memory, it forces him to remain in exile.

The following chronology of Dasan's life will aid in reading my entire translation and commentary on his *Noneo gogeum ju* 論語古今註.[5]

> June 1763: Dasan was born to a family that belonged both to the class of Confucian bureaucrats and to the Southerners faction, which was deeply involved in the factional strife of the seventeenth and eighteenth centuries in Joseon. His father, Jeong Jae-won 丁載遠 (1730–1792), had retired just before Dasan's birth from a low-level government post to express his grief over the tragic execution in May of the crown prince, Sado 思悼 (1735–1762), by his own father, King Yeongjo 英祖 (r. 1724–1776). Dasan's mother was a descendant of the Haenam 海南 Yun 尹 family, which was honored for the accomplishments of Yun Seon-do 尹善道 (1587–1671), a great master of Korean literature and a key participant in the factional strife. When Dasan was born his father had just returned to his hometown, so he gave Dasan the childhood name Gwinong 歸農: "returning to the farming area."
>
> 1768: It is said that Dasan started composing poems in this year and that his early poems were later compiled into *Sammija jip* 三眉子集 (*Collected Works of the Master with Three Eyebrows*), a title associated with a scar on his eyebrows.
>
> 1770: Dasan's mother, lady Yun, passed away. Since Dasan was her youngest son, his eldest brother's wife, lady Yi 李, began to take care of Dasan like a mother. Yi Byeok 李蘗 (1754–1786), an ardent Catholic who introduced Catholicism to Dasan, was her younger brother.

---

[3] During the first five years of his exile, Dasan stayed in a small inn near the east gate of the town Gangjin 康津.

[4] Dasan is regarded as one of the founders of Korean tea culture.

[5] Secondary sources in English on Dasan's life include Mark Setton, *Chŏng Yagyong: Korea's Challenge to Orthodox Neo-Confucianism* (Albany: State University of New York Press, 1997), 53–66, and Choi Byonghyon, *Admonitions on Governing the People* (Berkeley: University of California Press, 2010), xvi–xxvi.

1776: Dasan received an adult name, Yak-yong, following the capping ceremony reserved for all sons of bureaucratic families. He married a girl from the Pungsan 豊山 Hong 洪 family.

1777–1782: Dasan studied the Confucian classics, literature, and history, while receiving indirect or direct instruction from eminent scholars in the Southerners faction, including Yi Ik, Gwon Cheol-sin, and Yi Ga-hwan.

1783: Dasan entered Seonggyungwan 成均館, the national Confucian academy. He also had an audience, for the first time, with King Jeongjo 正祖 (r. 1776–1800), the son of the executed Sado and Dasan's "forever-lord," after he passed the literary licentiate examination.

1784: Dasan dedicated to King Jeongjo *Jungyong gang-ui* 中庸講義 (*Discussions on the Meaning of* Constant Mean), which later developed into *Jungyong gang-ui bo* 中庸講義補 (*Supplementation of the Discussions on the Meaning of* Constant Mean, six rolls), in response to the king's request. In April, Dasan learned about the tenets of Catholicism for the first time from Yi Byeok at a memorial service for the fourth anniversary of the death of his eldest brother's wife. He started reading about Catholic teachings.

1785–1789: Achieving many minor successes in the academy, Dasan continued to study at Seonggyungwan until he passed the national civil service examination in March 1789. Afterward he was invited to join a group of specially selected civil officers for in-depth study of Confucian statecraft and literature. He also transcribed his dialogues with King Jeongjo about *Great Learning*, later compiled into *Daehak gang-ui* 大學講義 (*Discussions on the Meaning of* Great Learning, one roll). In addition, Jeongjo gave special recognition to his proposal to build a boat-bridge across the Han River for the royal procession.

1790: Dasan experienced exile for the first time, though very briefly, due to his confrontation with the Patriarchs faction, the dominant faction at the time.

1791: Dasan's *Sigyeong gang-ui* 詩經講義 (*Discussions on the Meaning of* Classic of Poetry, later finalized into twelve rolls) was praised greatly by Jeongjo. In the winter the so-called Jinsan 珍山 Incident occurred, in which two Confucian Christians in the county of Jinsan burned and buried their ancestors' spiritual tablets, in compliance with the pope's order that all Christians should disobey the Confucian ancestral rituals. The incident triggered the first wave of persecution of Joseon Catholics. One of the two offenders was a nephew of Dasan's mother. In later writings, Dasan recollects that he was appalled by their aggressive actions and thus severed his ties to Catholicism this year.

1792: Obeying the Confucian ritual protocols, Dasan resigned from his position in order to mourn his father's death. He continued, however, to help materialize Jeongjo's plan to restore prince Sado's honor by submitting to him his designs for the Hwaseong 華城 fortress, a commemorative monument for Sado, along with a blueprint of a stationary crane to be used for its construction.

1794: Dasan returned to the court after fulfilling his ritual duties for his deceased father. Months later, Jeongjo sent him to Gyeonggi 京畿 province to inspect the atrocities of the local governor and magistrates. Dasan's bold censure of the province's inhumane administration led to the discharge of its governor, Seo Yong-bo 徐龍輔 (1757–1824).

1795–1799: Dasan served the dynasty primarily as a main third-rank official in various offices within the court, when he was not prevented from doing so, or as a local magistrate, when suspicions and criticism against him arose.

1800: Early in the year, Dasan stepped down from his office because of imminent dangers he could sense. On June 28, the demise of Jeongjo was announced. At the conclusion of the weeping period for the deceased king, Dasan returned to his hometown. He then named a study hall the "Hall of Hesitation."

1801: In January, Dowager Jeongsun 貞純 (1745–1805) issued a royal edict to ban the "wicked teaching"—Catholicism. In the same month, Jeong Yak-jong 丁若鍾 (1760–1801), Dasan's third older brother, was caught by the authorities when he tried secretly to remove books and letters related to activities of the Joseon Catholics from his house. In February, Dasan was arrested and interrogated by high officials, including Seo Yong-bo. He was eventually punished with exile to Janggi 長鬐; his second older brother, Jeong Yak-jeon 丁若銓 (1758–1816), was banished to Sinji 薪智 Island. Jeong Yak-jong was executed. In October, Dasan and Jeong Yak-jeon were again summoned to the court for another round of interrogation in connection with the arrest of Hwang Sa-yeong 黃嗣永 (1775–1801), a son-in-law of Dasan's eldest brother, who had dared to write a letter to a bishop in China requesting a dispatch of the French navy to show off their military power to the Joseon court. In November, Dasan was banished to Gangjin, a small provincial town, where he would stay for the following eighteen years, while Jeong Yak-jeon was sent to Heuksan 黑山 Island.

1802: Although he had written Yi-a sul 爾雅述 (An Exposition of Er ya) and compiled local proverbs into Baek-eon si 百諺詩 (Poems of One Hundred Proverbs), which later developed into Idam sokchan 耳談續纂 (A Sequel to The Stories Heard by Ears), in 1801 when we was in Janggi, this year he began to conduct scholarly research and to write on a large scale, according to his recollections.

1803: Dasan concentrated his research on the Confucian mourning rituals, which resulted in the writing of a crucial part of Sangrye sajeon 喪禮四箋 (Four Commentaries on the Mourning Rituals, fifty rolls).

1804: The Gapja 甲子 edition of Juyeok sajeon 周易四箋 (Four Commentaries on Changes of Zhou, eight rolls) and Ahak pyeon 兒學編 (A Text for Children's Learning) were completed.

1805: In the summer, Dasan completed "Jeongche jeonjung byeon 正體傳重辨" (Discourse on Legitimacy in Royal Succession, three rolls), which advocated the Southerners' stance in the Rites Controversy under the reign of King Sukjong 肅宗 (r. 1674–1720). In the winter, Dasan was able to move from a small inn to the Goseongsa 高聲寺 temple, thanks to his acquaintance with the Buddhist monk Hyejang 惠藏 (1768–?). The revised Eulchuk 乙丑 edition of *Juyeok sajeon* (eight rolls) was completed there.

1806: In the fall, Dasan moved to the home of one of his local students in the town of Gangjin. He completed part of *Sangrye sajeon* and the revised Byeong-in 丙寅 edition of *Juyeok sajeon* (sixteen rolls).

1807: Dasan completed *Sangrye sajeon* and the revised *Jeongmyo* 丁卯 edition of *Juyeok sajeon*.

1808: In the spring, Dasan moved to a house near the Dasan (Tea Mountain) provided by Yun Dan 尹博 (1744–1821), a descendant of the Haenam Yun family. Dasan completed the Mujin 戊辰 edition of *Juyeok sajeon* (also known as *Juyeok simjeon* 周易心箋, twenty-four rolls) and *Yeokhak seo-eon* 易學緒言 (*Initiatory Words on the Studies of Changes*, twelve rolls).

1809: Dasan completed *Sangrye oepyeon* 喪禮外篇 (*Outer Compilation of the Mourning Rituals*, twelve rolls). *Sigyeong gang-ui* (twelve rolls) was finalized.

1810: Dasan completed *Sigyeong gang-ui bo* 詩經講義補 (*Supplementation of the Discussions on the Meaning of* Classic of Poetry, three rolls), *Gwallye jak-ui* 冠禮酌儀 (*Protocols of Offering Wines in the Capping Rituals*), *Garye jak-ui* 嘉禮酌儀 (*Protocols of Offering Wines in the Rituals of Royal Weddings*), and *Sohak jucheon* 小學珠串 (*Threaded Beads for Lesser Learners*), as well as *Maessi Sangseo pyeong* 梅氏尚書平 (*Fair Discussions on* Documents *of Mei Ze*, nine rolls) and *Sangseo gohun* 尚書古訓 (*Ancient Meaning of* Documents, six rolls).

1811: Dasan completed *Sangseo jiwon rok* 尚書知遠錄 (*A Record of* Documents' *Understanding of the Ancient Affairs*, nine rolls) and *Abang gangyeok go* 我邦疆域考 (*Investigations on the Territory of Our Country*, ten rolls).

1812: Dasan completed *Minbo ui* 民堡議 (*Discussions on the People's Fortress*, two rolls) and *Chunchu gojing* 春秋考徵 (*Veritable Investigations of* Spring and Autumn, twelve rolls).

1813: Dasan completed *Noneo gogeum ju* 論語古今註 (*Old and New Commentaries on* the Analects, forty rolls).

1814: Dasan completed *Maengja yo-ui* 孟子要義 (*Essential Meaning of* Mencius, nine rolls), *Daehak gong-ui* 大學公義 (*Fair Discussions on* Great Learning, three rolls), *Jungyong jajam* 中庸自箴 (*Self-Admonition of* Constant Mean, three rolls), *Jungyong gang-ui bo*, and *Daedong sugyeong* 大東水經 (*Critical Waters in the Great Eastern State*, two rolls).

1815: Dasan completed *Simgyeong milheom* 心經密驗 (*Esoteric Examination of* Classic of Mind-Heart, one roll) and *Sohak ji-eon* 小學枝言 (*Complementary Words on* Lesser Learning, one roll).

1816: Dasan completed *Akseo gojon* 樂書孤存 (*Sole Preservation of the Books of Music*, twelve rolls).

1817: Dasan completed *Sang-ui jeolyo* 喪儀節要 (*Essential Summary of the Protocols of Mourning*, six rolls). He also started writing *Bangrye chobon* 邦禮草本 (*Drafted Edition of the Rites of Our Country*, later published as *Gyeongse yupyo* 經世遺表, forty-four rolls), and *Mongmin simseo* 牧民心書 (*Treasured Book of Nurturing the People*, forty-eight rolls).

1818: In the spring, Dasan completed *Mongmin simseo*. In the summer, he completed *Gukjo jeollye go* 國朝典禮考 (*Investigations on the Cardinal Rituals of Our Dynasty*, three rolls). On September 30 he was released from exile, and he returned to his home the following month. In the winter, he and his students formed the Society of Tea and Letters [茶信契].

1819: Dasan completed *Heumheum sinseo* 欽欽新書 (*New Book of Judicial Prudence*, thirty rolls) and *A-eon gakbi* 雅言覺非 (*Realization of the Errors in the Everyday Terminologies*, three rolls).

1820–1832: Dasan enjoyed the most leisurely period in his life, composing poems, having scholarly discussions with colleagues, and traveling. In 1822, he wrote two versions of "Self-Written Epitaph [自撰墓誌銘]" in celebration of his sixtieth birthday: the shorter one for burial and the longer one for the collection of his writings.

1833: *Sangseo gohun* and *Sangseo jiwon rok*, 1810 edition, were compiled into *Sangseo gohun*, twenty-one rolls. *Maessi Sangseo pyeong* was also revised.

February 22, 1836: Dasan passed away. The date marked the sixtieth anniversary of his marriage. His body was buried behind the Hall of Hesitation.[6]

2

Dasan is one of the most revered cultural heroes in Korea today. Not only have streets, buildings, and parks in Korea been named after him, but the provincial government in Dasan's hometown has also recently announced that it will build "a green environment-friendly new city following the ideas of Dasan," to be named Dasan. Taking advantage of his reputation, the local government plans to sell numerous apartment units to Korean citizens. The city of Seoul also operates a municipal service for "answering all questions" that is named

---

[6] This chronology is based on Gyu-yeong Jeong, *Sa-am seonsaeng yeonbo* 俟菴先生年譜 (Seoul: Jeongmun sa, 1984). It was initially published in 1921 in traditional book binding and recently translated into Korean. See Gyu-yeong Jeong, *Dasan-ui han pyeongsaeng: Sa-am seonsaeng yeonbo* trans. Jae-so Song (Paju si, Changbi, 2014).

the Dasan Call Center, because Koreans tend to regard Dasan as the most knowledgeable individual of traditional Korea.

Dasan's reputation, however, is relatively modern. Although two major works of sociopolitical analysis by him, *Heumheum sinseo* and *Mongmin simseo*, were printed during the imperial age of Korea under the auspices of Emperor Gwangmu 光武 (r. 1863–1907, King Gojong 高宗 prior to 1897) in 1901 and 1902, respectively,[7] he remained underestimated by the majority of Korean scholars until the 1930s because he lacked philosophical appeal to either the mainstream Confucian scholars or the rising tide of young intellectuals: he criticized mainstream Confucians for sacrificing so much to defend the legitimacy of neo-Confucianism, but he was one of those same Confucian scholars in the eyes of the young proponents of the modernity projects in Korea.

The historical context changed significantly in 1931, when Singan hoe 新幹會, the unified pan-Korean organization struggling for independence, disintegrated. Afterward a certain nationalist group that dissociated itself from leftists responded to an urgent need to restore the nation's dignity by proving the eminence of Korean history and culture, in order eventually to regain national sovereignty. It was a Korean reaction to the aggressive efforts of Japanese imperialists to degrade Korean tradition, which was later dubbed the Joseon studies [朝鮮學] movement. The leading scholars in this movement—including An Jae-hong (1891–1965), Jeong In-bo (1893–?), Baek Nam-un (1894–1979), and Mun Il-pyeong (1888–1939)—did not wish to link Korea's intellectual tradition so closely with neo-Confucianism, so they naturally turned their attention to cultural and scholarly accomplishments made by "outsiders" to Joseon academia. Dasan's works attracted their interest.

In 1938 a Korean publisher, Sinjoseon sa 新朝鮮社, finished printing a multivolume set of Dasan's writings in their entirety, under the title *Yeoyudang jeonseo* 與猶堂全書 (*Entire Works of Yeoyudang*), four years after the first volume was printed. This achievement would not have been possible without the assiduous dedication of the owner of the company, Kwon Tae-hwi.[8] This monumental and inspiring Sinjoseon sa edition of *Yeoyudang jeonseo* (Sinjo edition hereafter) consisted of 154 volumes in seven collections, which were published in seventy-six books in modern book binding (a collection of poetry and essays

---

[7] During this period, three more of Dasan's works were printed, including *Idam sokchan* in around 1902, *Daehan gangyeok go* 大韓疆域考 [我邦疆域考] in 1903, and *Ahak pyeon* in 1908. In 1914, the last part of Dasan's trilogy on sociopolitical reformation, *Gyeongse yupyo* (*A Bequeathed Treatise on Government*), was printed. Prior to the publication of his major works, manuscript copies were made of selections from his works for preservation and reading. The first compilation of Dasan's entire oeuvre must have been completed under his direction even before his death, although it is unclear whether it contained every one of his works.

[8] Much of Kwon's life is unclear. What we do know is that he was a student of An Jae-hong and later joined a Korean communist organization. Kim Han-kyeong, a descendant of Dasan's maternal family, was also an active member of this organization. He and Choe Ik-hwan later established a branch office of the Korean Communist Party in Japan. Kim Seong-jin, Han-kyeong's father, was in charge of the publication of *Yeoyudang jeonseo*. See Bo-reum Kim, "*Yeoyudang jip* seongnip e gwanhan gochal," *Dasan hak* 18 (2011): 197–235.

in twenty-six volumes; a collection of writings on Confucian classics in fifty volumes; a collection of writings on rituals in twenty-five volumes; a collection of writings on music in four volumes; a collection of writings on administration and laws in thirty-nine volumes; a collection of writings on geography in eight volumes; and a collection of medical studies in six volumes). Readers were excited about this "new excavation" and hoped to hear from experts about how Dasan contributed to the distinction of Korea's long intellectual tradition. The responses of leading scholars of the Joseon studies movement to this demand were in agreement with Jeong In-bo's claim that "our research on the one man Dasan definitely represents our research on the history of Joseon and on Korean near-modern thought."[9] In 1936, amid the ongoing publication of Dasan's works, these scholars began to shed much-needed light on Dasan's life and philosophy. Following the completion of the publication, Choe Ik-hwan (1897–?) wrote a series of interpretative essays on *Yeoyudang jeonseo*, sixty-five in total, which were later integrated into the publication of the first modern monograph on Dasan.[10] His essays provide crucial information on the collection: that the structure of *Yeoyudang jeonseo*, in which Dasan's poems and essays appear first, before his commentaries on the Confucian classics, mirrors neither that of "Self-Written Epitaph" nor that of "the Complete Table of Contents of *Yeolsu jeonseo* [洌水全書總目錄]," which was attached to the final drafted edition of *Yeoyudang Jeonseo*; in line with this, Dasan apparently opted for "Yeolsu," his pen name associated with his hometown, as the title of the collection; and the base manuscript was marked with the title *Yeoyudang jip* 與猶堂集, not *Yeoyudang jeonseo*.[11] Notwithstanding the textual disputes surrounding the Sinjo edition, scholarly research on Dasan continued, owing to the Sinjo edition's merits.

At the early stages of research in Korea on Dasan, the understanding of Jang Jiyeon (1864–1921) of Dasan's scholarship was definitive.[12] In his book *Joseon Yukyo yeonwon* 朝鮮儒敎淵源, Jang distinguished Dasan (along with Yu Hyeong-won) from mainstream neo-Confucian scholars for his expertise in matters of government and people's welfare. Although Jang also recognized

---

[9] In-bo Jeong, "Yu-ilhan jeongbeopga Jeong Dasan seonsaeng seoron (1)," *Dong-A ilbo*, September 1934, 10. Also see In-bo Jeong, "Dasan seonsaeng ui saeng-ae wa sasang," in *Damwon gukhak sango* (Seoul: Mungyo sa, 1955), 70–108.

[10] Ik-hwan Choe, *Silhak pa wa Jeong Dasan* (1955; reprint, Seoul: Cheongnyeon sa, 1989).

[11] Ik-hwan Choe, "*Yeoyudang jeonseo* reul dokham (15)," *Dong-A Ilbo*, February 1939, 3. Also see Choe, *Silhak pa-wa Jeong Dasan*, 450–455. Some argue that *Yeoyudang jeonseo* should be revised so that it follows either the structure of "Self-Written Epitaph" (Seong-eul Jo and Mun-sik Kim) or that of "Complete Table of Contents of *Yeolsu jeonseo*" (Dong-u Jang). See Seong-eul Jo, Yeoyudang jip *ui munheonhak jeok yeongu—siyul mit jammun ui yeondae gojeong eul jungsim euro* (Seoul: Hye-an, 2004); Mun-sik Kim, "*Yeoyudang jeonseo* gyeongjip cheje ui geomto," *Dasan hak* 5 (2004): 385–411; and Dong-u Jang, "*Yeoyudang jeonseo* jeongbon sa-eop eul wihan pilsabon yeongu—gyeongjip eul jungsim euro," *Dasan hak* 7 (2005): 251–289.

[12] Yong-ha Sin accentuates Jang's contribution to the "excavation" of Dasan. See Yong-ha Sin, "19 segi mal Jang Ji-yeon ui Dasan Jeong Yak-yong ui balgul," *Hanguk hakbo* 29, no. 1 (2003): 2–21. Alongside Jang Ji-yeon, Hyun Chae (1856–1925) and Yi Geon-bang (1861–1939) belong to the earliest group of scholars who excavated Dasan.

Dasan as an established scholar in Confucian classical studies and literature, what set him apart, for Jang, were his views on sociopolitical issues.[13] The leading scholars of the Joseon studies movement also highlighted the practicality of Dasan's reformative ideas. While all these scholars adopted the notion *sil* 實 (practicality) in defining Dasan's scholarly achievements, Choe Nam-seon (1890–1957) used an existing term, *silhak* (practical learning), to describe the sociopolitical work of a larger group of scholars, including Dasan, who are now referred to as scholars of Practical Learning (Silhak).[14] All of the pioneering articles written by Yun Yong-kyun (1903–1931), Jeong In-bo, and An Jae-hong were dedicated to revealing the significance of Dasan's scholarship in the same context. The first monograph on Dasan, by Choe Ik-hwan, likewise focused on Dasan's trilogy on social reform rather than his other works, although it purported to be an integral introduction of Dasan and Practical Learning. As for South Korean scholarship, Hong I-seop opened a new horizon in 1959 by publishing a book on Dasan's political and economic thought, an elaboration of this pervasive understanding of Dasan's work.[15]

Although Han U-geun raised questions about the ambiguity of the term *silhak*, since it was used sometimes to refer to Confucianism itself,[16] no substantial argument was ever made against the perspective of Dasan's work as a crystallization of the movement of Practical Learning. Indeed, Dasan's readers were delighted by the even bolder suggestion of linking his ideas with modernity, proposed initially by Cheon Gwan-u in a public lecture in 1967,[17] since they sought a vernacular origin for modern establishments in Korea's philosophical tradition. Yi U-seong attempted to help people understand the complexity of the ideas of Practical Learning by placing the leading scholars in this intellectual movement in three different categories: the school of government and social merits, the school of economic development and betterment of people's lives, and the school of scholarly investigations of actual things.[18] In Yi's view, which has been adopted for Korean secondary education textbooks, Dasan made complete the ideas of the school of government and social merits. On the other hand, Yi Eul-ho uniquely focused on Dasan's research on the Confucian classics, including *Noneo gogeum ju*, in this period when Dasan's sociopolitical proposals were emphasized.[19] He should be given credit for starting the discussion of Dasan's interpretation of the classical texts, a discussion to which this book is more closely related. However, Yi Eul-ho, despite his

[13] Ji-yeon Jang, *Joseon Yukyo yeonwon* (Seoul: Hoedong seogwan, 1922), 128–129.
[14] Hong-sik Park, "Ilje ganggeomgi Jeong In-bo, An Jae-hong, Choe Ik-hwan ui Dasan yeongu," *Dasan hak* 17 (2010): 45–93.
[15] I-seop Hong, *Jeong Yak-yong ui jeongchi gyeongje sasang yeongu* (Seoul: Hanguk yeongu doseogwan, 1959).
[16] U-geun Han, "Yijo Silhak ui gaenyeom e daehayeo," *Jindan hakhoe* 15 (1958): 25–46.
[17] This lecture was later published in a book. See Gwan-u Cheon, "Joseon hugi Silhak ui gaenyeom jaeron," in *Hanguksa ui jaebalgyeon*, ed. Gwan-u Cheon (Seoul: Iljo gak, 1974), 107–185.
[18] U-seong Yi, "Silhak yeongu seoseol," in *Silhak yeongu immun*, ed. Yeoksa hakhoe (Seoul: Iljo gak, 1973), 1–17.
[19] Eul-ho Yi, *Dasan gyeonghak sasang yeongu* (Seoul: Eul-yu munhwa sa, 1966).

unique association with one of the branches of the study of Dasan's works, was like other scholars in that he wished to separate Dasan from the neo-Confucian tradition, characterizing Dasan's entire classical studies as a return to "the learning by Zhu-Si 洙泗 waters" (where Confucius taught his disciples). All in all, earlier Korean scholars agreed that the movement of Practical Learning (the only major intellectual current opposed to neo-Confucianism in Joseon's intellectual history) culminated in Dasan's writings, which impressively enriched the literature of the country.

As a matter of fact, it is truly challenging now to summarize Korean scholarship on Dasan precisely because there is an awe-inspiring number of monographs and articles about Dasan. Through them, scholars have attempted to convince readers of their new "discoveries" of various aspects of Dasan. The Foundation of Dasan's Scholarship and Culture, for example, provides a list more than eighty pages long of scholarly works on Dasan. Recent discourse on Dasan, however, seems to reflect three changes from early Korean scholarship on the topic. First, the conventional conception of Dasan's philosophy as exemplary of Practical Learning has faced counter-arguments from relatively young scholars. They tend to emphasize continuity and mutual influence among various philosophies in the late Joseon period. As a result of this challenge, it now seems crude to locate Dasan exclusively in the orbit of anti-neo-Confucianism or intellectual defiance of neo-Confucian orthodoxy.[20] Second, while Dasan's sociopolitical views still form the basis of his high reputation among readers, a growing number of scholars have found that his classical studies yield more insights about his philosophical inspirations than they originally anticipated. Given that a larger portion of Dasan's writings concerns Confucian classics, this trend will likely continue unabated, and a quantitative growth of articles and monographs dedicated to illuminating Dasan's classical studies is now evident. Third, today's researchers on Dasan have specialized in narrowly defined topics rather than drawing grand conclusions. This is only natural, given the circumstances in Korea, where widely available information on Dasan renders it easy to take one's overall familiarity with Dasan's works for granted. This book has been shaped by the new Korean scholarship, as is evident in my approach to Dasan's scrupulous studies of the Analects. My task will be to show how Dasan's works attempted to synthesize all past Confucian commentaries and the philosophical ideas contained therein.

3

The original title of Dasan's commentary on the Analects is Noneo gogeum ju, which translates to the Old and New Commentaries on the Analects. Ju 註 in the title appears as ju 注 in an earlier edition without bearing a different meaning.

---

[20] For example, see Yeong-u Han et al., Dasi, Silhak-iran muet-inga (Seoul: Pureun yeoksa, 2007).

In this book, I use the former ideogram because I have based my translation on the Sinjo edition, the first printed edition of *Noneo gogeum ju*.

Needless to say, there must have been at least one base manuscript for the Sinjo edition. In this regard, many accept Jeong In-bo's claim that the base manuscript for the Sinjo edition was the alleged "finalized" manuscript of *Yeoyudang jeonseo* that was preserved by Jeong Gyu-yeong 丁奎英 (1872–1927), Dasan's great-great-grandson, who was known to have risked his own life to save it from a flood in 1925, was the base edition for the publication.[21] The so-called finalized manuscript, however, seems to have later been owned by several people, who each had a different part.[22] It is unclear how closely these fragmentary manuscripts resembled the real "finalized one." Thus, it would be safer to say that scholars have not yet discovered the one that was actually used for printing the Sinjo edition.[23] As for the manuscript of *Noneo gogeum ju*, Kyujanggak 奎章閣 at Seoul National University is the only place in Korea that has it. The entire Kyujanggak edition of *Yeoyudang jeonseo*, including *Noneo gogeum ju*, is evidently the result of careful reflection on Dasan's revisions of the earliest manuscript. This is confirmed by a comparison of the Kyujanggak edition with an earlier manuscript that contains Dasan's marginal notes for revision.[24] In other words, the Kyujanggak edition of *Noneo gogeum ju* seems to be, in effect, a revision of the earliest manuscript, based on Dasan's instructions in his marginal notes. Another manuscript that includes a complete version of *Noneo gogeum ju* may be found in the Osaka Municipal Library in Japan, but scholars have conjectured that it might be a copy of the Kyujanggak edition. In addition to these manuscripts, *Noneo sucha* 論語手箚 (*Brief Notes on the Analects*) is worth mentioning since it is an abridged version of *Noneo gogeum ju*. It is currently preserved in two manuscripts, one in Kyujanggak and one in the Asami Collection at the University of California, Berkeley.

As already mentioned, it took the publisher four years to completely publish the Sinjo edition. Lacking adequate financial resources, the publisher was initially able to print only two volumes per month out of the full set of seventy-six. They could only acquire funds for publishing the next two volumes by selling the volumes they had just printed. This pattern recurred in four crisis-ridden years, including the year that compelled them to put the project on hold temporarily until they found a donor. Given the logistical challenges, it

---

[21] See In-bo Jeong, *Damwon munrok* 4 in *Damwon Jeong In-bo jeonjip*, vol. 5 (Seoul: Yonsei University Press, 1983), 376–377. More precisely, the Sinjo edition might have been directly derived from an edition that was made from a transcription of the finalized edition when an unknown person attempted to publish the *Yeoyudang jeonseo* in 1926.

[22] See Yeong-ho Kim, "*Yeoyudang jeonseo* ui *text* geomto," in *Jeong Dasan yeongu ui hyeonhwang*, ed. U-geun Han et al. (Seoul: Min-eum sa, 1985), 11–41.

[23] Four parties are believed to preserve parts of the earlier manuscript of *Yeoyudang jeonseo*: the Academy of Korean Studies, Kyujanggak (the royal library of Joseon dynasty), Danguk University Library, and Yeong-ho Kim. See Bo-reum Kim, "*Yeoyudang jip* eseo *Yeoyudang jeonseo* ro," *Jindan hakbo* 124 (2015): 207–234.

[24] See Dong-u Jang, "*Yeoyudang jeonseo* pilsabon e gwanhan gochal," *Dasan hak* 15 (2009): 119–138, and In Bang, "Danguk dae bon *Juyeok sajeon* yeongu," *Dasan hak* 17 (2010): 7–44.

was not surprising that the edition ended up having multiple editorial errors. In addition, as discussed earlier, it might not have correctly reflected the base manuscript in structure and content. As a matter of fact, at least a portion of *Yeoyudang jeonseo* has already been proven to be interpolations consisting of another scholar's writings.[25]

Efforts to rectify the errors and supplement the Sinjo edition thus began, in the hope of minimizing possible misunderstandings of Dasan's ideas that could be blamed on inaccuracies in the printed source. In 1960, *Minbo ui*, one of Dasan's indispensable works of sociopolitical analysis, was added to a new edition of *Yeoyudang jeonseo*; in 1962, *Sa-am seonsaeng yeonbo* was added to it in the same manner; in 1970, one volume of *Yeoyudang jeonseo boyu* 與猶堂全書補遺 (*Supplementary Collection of* Yeoyudang jeonseo), which was later supplemented with more of Dasan's writings, was published, consisting of writings that were previously unavailable to the general public; and in 2002 the Committee for Propagation of the Nation's Culture (later reorganized as the National Institution for Translation of the Korean Classics) printed a rectified version of *Yeoyudang jeonseo*. The most noteworthy was the project for the publication of the *Established Edition of Yeoyudang jeonseo*, which was propelled by the Foundation of Dasan's Scholarly and Cultural Heritages. That project, concluded in 2012, resulted in the publication of thirty-seven solid volumes. This edition reflects up-to-date textual scholarship on Dasan's works. On top of these new editions, Yi Ji-hyeong finished his translation of *Noneo gogeum ju* into Korean in 2010, suggesting numerous corrections of the editorial errors in the Sinjo edition. Since Yi Ji-hyeong was in charge of *Noneo gogeum ju* for the *Established* edition, many of the same corrections may be found there. The scholars involved in these efforts frequently referred to the Kyujanggak edition of *Noneo gogeum ju*. Contemporary research on *Noneo gogeum ju* thus depends on several editions: the Sinjo edition, the Kyujanggak edition, the Committee edition, Yi Ji-hyeong's edition, and the *Established* edition. One of the aims of this book is to contribute to the improvement of the text of *Noneo gogeum ju* by suggesting more necessary rectifications of the errors. I use brackets to indicate that the original wording enclosed within them should be corrected, but only when other editions do not note this, in order to avoid repetition and save space.

All relevant documents agree that Dasan finished writing *Noneo gogeum ju* in 1813, the thirteenth year of his exile. It appears that his unique interpretation of the *Analects* was informed by a deep knowledge of the Five Classics of Confucianism, and of history and culture—especially rituals—given that, according to his memoir, he started writing about the classics in 1802 and that all of his major works on them had been accomplished prior to the completion

---

[25] Eon-jong Kim, "*Yeoyudang jeonseo boyu* ui jeojakbyeol jinwi munje e daehayeo (1), (2), and (3)," *Dasan hak* 9 (2006): 123–175; *Dasan hak* 10 (2007): 305–331; and *Dasan hak* 11 (2007): 321–353.

of *Noneo gogeum ju*. Not only Dasan's knowledge but also his students, whom he accepted when he gained fame for his academic distinction in the rural area of Gangjin, assisted him in this project. One of his sons, on visiting his residence, witnessed how he managed to be productive during the period of his exile: he was dictating his interpretations to his students, who diligently jotted them down; some were searching the classical texts for passages that supported his arguments; others were making fair copies of what had been jotted down; still others were binding manuscripts into books.[26] His students Yi Gang-hoe (1789–?) and Yun Dong (1793–1853) especially contributed to the completion of *Noneo gogeum ju*, which contains numerous records of their comments. To recognize the students' contributions, scholars today use the term "the scholarly group of Dasan" for those who assisted him in his pursuits.[27] This is not intended to suggest, of course, that his works should primarily be identified with them.

Regardless of the recorded year of the completion of *Noneo gogeum ju*, Dasan's efforts to revise it seem to have continued. In his revisions, according to instructions found in his marginal notes, he tried to tone down his criticism of contemporary scholars, including Mao Qiling 毛奇齡 (1623–1713), and sometimes completely removed his original comments, for unknown reasons. Yi Ji-hyeong has argued that the students' comments that were recorded in *Noneo gogeum ju* might have been added to the main body later and that theories and comments unavailable to Dasan also appear in *Noneo gogeum ju*.[28] There is no evidence to suggest, however, that the basic structure and philosophy of the work was altered after its initial completion.

First published as forty rolls in traditional book binding, *Noneo gogeum ju* was later printed in ten volumes by Sinjoseon sa and in two volumes in the *Established* edition. The most unusual aspect of the structure of *Noneo gogeum ju* is a list of 175 "original meanings" of the *Analects*, titled "An Overview of the Original Meanings" [原義總括], which is placed at the very front of the work. The topics of the selected arguments vary: some concern culture and philosophy; others concern philology, history, and textual studies. Dasan must have believed that they would help readers correctly understand the teachings of Confucius. However, this list does not cover all of the creative readings and interpretations he offers in *Noneo gogeum ju*. *Sa-am seonsaeng yeonbo* says: "Since there are so many different ideas in *Noneo gogeum ju*, the 'Original Meanings' is specially placed in the book."[29] The number of arguments *Noneo gogeum ju* contains easily exceeds five hundred.

---

[26] See Gyu-yeong Jeong, Jae-so Song trans., *Dasan-ui han pyeongsaeng: Sa-am seonsaeng yeonbo*, 266–267.

[27] See Hyeong-taek Im, "Jeong Yak-yong ui Gangjin yubaegi ui gyoyuk hwaldong gwa geu seonggwa," in *Silsa gusi ui Hanguk hak*, ed. Hyeong-taek Im (Seoul: Changbi, 2000), 399–434 and Jae-so Song, "Dasan hakdan yeongu seoseol," *Dasan hak* 12 (2008): 7–24.

[28] Ji-hyeong Yi, *Noneo gogeum ju* (Seoul: Sa-am, 2010), 10–11. To supplement this argument, see my comment on 5.18.

[29] Gyu-yeong Jeong, Jae-so Song trans., *Dasan-ui han pyeongsaeng: Sa-am seonsaeng yeonbo*, 207.

In fact, Dasan never stated that he himself selected and made a list of the 175 "original meanings." *Sa-am seonsaeng yeonbo*, the only work that attests to the motivation for compiling "Overview of the Original Meanings," was written by Jeong Gyu-yeong approximately ninety years after Dasan's death. Although most of them certainly deal with crucial points in the *Analects*, some concern minor arguments; more important discussions of philosophical significance are missing from the list. Thus, in my view, it is debatable whether the creation of "Overview of the Original Meanings" should be attributed to Dasan or not. Certain arguments are currently missing in "Overview" that the author himself would surely have included had he prepared it himself. Unfortunately, no research materials are currently available to further this discussion. At the same time, it is also true that "Overview" impressed readers with what they took to be the creativity and contentiousness embedded in Dasan's *Analects*.

The title *Noneo gogeum ju, Old and New Commentaries on the* Analects, suits the content well because Dasan addresses all of the commentaries he had access to, both old and new. The major corpus of the "old commentaries" includes *Lun yu jijie* 論語集解, which was compiled by He Yan 何晏 (195–249); *Lun yu jijie yishu* 論語集解義疏 (hereafter *Lun yu yishu*) compiled by Huang Kan 皇侃 (488–545); and *Lun yu zhengyi* 論語正義 compiled by Xing Bing 邢昺 (932–1010).[30] Besides these major commentaries, Dasan seems to have regarded all of the commentaries produced before Zhu Xi 朱熹 (1130–1200) as "old commentaries." In harmony with the general understanding of the history of Confucian classical studies, Dasan acknowledged that Zhu Xi had opened a new era of research on the *Analects* by writing *Lun yu jizhu* 論語集註, a crucial new commentary in Dasan's view. Thus he regarded all commentaries after Zhu Xi as "new commentaries"—including *Lun yu jizhu daquan* 論語集註大全, which introduces the commentaries of scholars in Zhu Xi's school. In this respect, it is notable that Dasan also cited works of the Evidential Studies in Qing China and the Ancient Learning in Tokugawa Japan, especially the school of Learning of the Ancient Writings and Words. Although these works openly criticized neo-Confucian interpretations of the *Analects*, Dasan considered them "new commentaries," alongside Zhu Xi's commentary.

The title, however, conveys more than mere information on the scope of Dasan's references. In my understanding, it tells us about his research methodology and the goal of his commentary. In other words, what he truly wished to achieve through his commentary on the *Analects* was a synthesis of all transmitted Confucian ideas (methodology) and thereby the creation of a new Confucian philosophy (goal). He was an ambitious syncretist who claimed that he understood the original meaning of the *Analects*. Since according to Dasan no one had addressed the original meaning before him, his claim is equivalent to a declaration of a new Confucian philosophy. It seems that he hoped that

---

30 In *Siku quanshu*, *Lun yu jijie* and *Lun yu zhengyi* are compiled into *Lun yu zhushu*.

after his elucidation of the original meaning, three different kinds of commentaries on the *Analects* would exist: the old commentaries, the new commentaries, and his commentary, which synthesized both.

The main body of *Noneo gogeum ju* largely consists of two parts: grounds for Dasan's readings and arguments against various influential theories that he believed were invalid or interfered with "correct" understanding. Although "grounds" are not demarcated from "arguments" in the original text, in this book all grounds introduced in a chapter are placed under the heading "Grounds" and all arguments under "Arguments," even when only one argument is presented, in order to clarify the nature of the discussions in these two different categories.

To find his grounds, Dasan referred to a wide range of commentaries on the *Analects* and the classical texts. In this regard, he appears to have had no predilection for any post-Confucius school. For the most part, he disassociates Han-Tang Confucianism from Song-Ming Confucianism and, in turn, dissociates both of them from the intellectual movements that occurred during his time, Evidential Studies and Ancient Learning. He adopts comments sometimes from the old commentary, sometimes from the new, and sometimes from the works of his contemporaries, and he sometimes rejects them all. The grounds are usually supplemented by his own comment(s) following a phrase, *bo-wal* 補曰 ("I supplement as follows" in my translation), when he feels that the grounds are insufficient to reveal the true meaning of the passages: when he concludes that all transmitted comments fail to correctly explain a given passage, he supply his supplementary comment(s) only. Notwithstanding the fact that he respected Zhu Xi's scholarship the most, he only supports the comments by Zhu Xi that he believes are in harmony with his own understanding.

Since Dasan did not translate the original Chinese text of the *Analects* (which is sometimes difficult to read without comments) into Korean or more comprehensible forms, an examination of his arguments and refutations is necessary to understand how his interpretation differs from others'. He usually begins his argument by saying *bak-wal* 駁曰 ("I would refute this as follows" in my translation) except when he refutes comments by Zhu Xi or Cheng Yi 程頤 (1033–1107), in which cases he uses the more polite expression *jil-ui* 質疑 ("I question Master Zhu as follows" in my translation) to show, of course, his contemporary readers that he still maintains respect for the great leaders of neo-Confucianism. In my translation, his questions to Zhu Xi are not distinguished from those to Cheng Yi, and all questions phrased with *jil-ui* have been translated as though they address Zhu Xi's comments because Zhu Xi, in *Lun yu jizhu*, introduces and approves of those ideas of Cheng Yi that Dasan quarrels with.

Dasan's arguments are, more often than not, buttressed by textual evidence that he has "selected" from the classical texts and appear immediately after the expression *yinjeung* 引證 ("for a classical text that supports my argument here," or other similar expressions, in my translation). Since he relies on other classical texts to validate his interpretations, it is often necessary to translate his quotations completely. When his quotations are not indispensable to understanding his grounds and arguments, however, I merely note the location of the relevant lines of the classical texts in *Siku quanshu*, giving volume, page, and line numbers. In fact, Dasan arranged all of the classical texts in his mind in a hierarchy: the *Analects* itself was the most important and amenable to human understanding; the Five Classics of Confucianism were next; and pre-Qin texts (other than the Confucian classics), Han texts, and post-Han classical texts followed, in that order. He basically believed that the Confucian classics contained no errors and thus that what was recorded in the Confucian classics, for the most part, took precedence over what was recorded in other texts.

Like his contemporary scholars, however, Dasan was also aware that parts of the Confucian classics were compromised by interpolations, manipulation, and forgery. In his discussion of the "forged" *Documents* of the old scripts, which were "going viral," as it were, among his contemporaries, he endorsed Yan Ruoqu's 閻若璩 (1636–1704) view. Accordingly, in Dasan's view, chapters known to have been submitted by Mei Ze 梅賾 (fl. fourth century) from the Eastern Jin were considered forged; certain chapters of *Record of Rites*, such as "Li yun 禮運," were either interpolated or manipulated by later hands; the commentary on the historical records in *Zuo's Commentary* was added in the early Han to the ancient record of historical events. Dasan's suspicions sometimes extended to parts of other Confucian classics, such as *Changes*. As a result, the authority of these texts was sometimes denied by what was recorded in the later texts. He also contended that two texts solely dedicated to conveying Confucius's life and thought—*Kongzi jia yu* 孔子家語 and *Kong congzi* 孔叢子—were dubious. However, he seems to have had no skepticism about the earliest Confucian classics, such as *Poetry*, the untainted part of *Documents*, *Rites of Zhou*, *Protocols and Rites*, and the main body of *Spring and Autumn*, not to mention the main body of *Changes*. Thus the real tensions arose when these reliable sources contradicted one another. This was when Dasan used his criterion, which I will explain later, for selection. In his arguments he explores, besides the main arguments and his quotations of the classical texts, the textual differences in a few passages that begin with the expression *go-yi* 考異 ("I explore the textual differences as follows" in my translation).

During his eighteen-year exile, Dasan could not help but wallow in personal resentment because he was a victim of history. His family faced the great danger of total annihilation from the prestigious scholarly community. He was also ignored by "secular Confucians" due to his alleged involvement in the "wicked" Western teaching. Thus it is conceivable that one of his motivations in pursuing distinction in the study of the classics was to rid himself of resentment by proving how ridiculous it was to underestimate his scholarship and to persecute his family. Indeed, Sima Qian 司馬遷 (135–90 BCE) had a similar motivation for writing *Shi ji* 史記: "In the past, King Wen 文 dictated *Changes* when he was detained in the prison of Youli 羑里; Confucius wrote *Spring and*

Autumn when he was humiliated in the area between the states of Chen 陳 and
Cai 蔡; Qu Yuan 屈原 (c. 340–c. 278 BCE) composed 'Li sao 離騷,' when he was
banished.... All these people bore resentment in their minds and could not
get their Ways heard in the world. Thus they stated what happened in the past
and waited in expectation of the people to come." Sa-am, a pen name Dasan
wished to use for the entire collection of his writings, connotes this sense.
Indeed, in *Sa-am seonsaeng yeonbo*, Jeong Gyuyeong pointed out that Dasan
had intentions analogous to Sima Qian's.[31] Dasan's second older brother also
noticed that Dasan's misfortunes drove him to accomplish his brilliant rein-
terpretations of the Confucian classics: "If Miyong 美鏞 [i.e., Dasan], comfort-
ably enjoying honors and wealth, had assumed the high government posts
that were appropriate for him, he would have not been able to write a book of
this kind.... [T]herefore, it was fortunate for Miyong himself as well as for our
Confucian tradition that he did not have the opportunity to achieve his political
vision." By virtue of his perseverance, Dasan was successful in offering hundreds of creative readings of the *Analects*—a new source of inspiration in the
long exegetical history of the *Analects*.

4

I believe that it is necessary to add Dasan's *Noneo gogeum ju* to the list of must-
read commentaries on the *Analects*. First of all, his reading is quite independent. Although he was inspired by existing works on the *Analects*, his reading is
bold, critical, and creative. Beyond the 175 arguments in "Original Meanings,"
he dared to supplement the readings of his predecessors or to create entirely
new readings in almost every chapter. He was uncompromising whenever he
refuted the transmitted interpretations and provided new ones. On his tem-
perament, his second older brother once remarked, "My younger brother has
no shortcomings in personality. But it is a flaw that he is not tolerant."[32] Dasan
shares this comment in his own writings, acknowledging that his second older
brother is the one who really knows who he is. Fortunately, lacking tolerance
is a virtue for scholars. Dasan was not intimidated by any authority figures and
was brave enough to establish his own reading of the *Analects*. This spirit of
independence permeates *Noneo gogeum ju* from the first to the last chapters.

Dasan also dedicates a significant portion of *Noneo gogeum ju* to discussing
Confucian philosophy. In East Asia, from the seventeenth century onward,
philosophical defiance of neo-Confucian orthodoxy is evident in three countries: China, Japan, and Korea. In the wake of Manchu's emergence, Chinese
scholars embarked on a comprehensive reexamination of the Chinese

---

[31] Gyu-yeong Jeong, Jae-so Song trans., *Dasan-ui han pyeongsaeng: Sa-am seonsaeng yeonbo*, 187–188.
[32] Yak-yong Jeong, "Sin Hag-yu gagye 贐學游家誡," in *Yeoyudang jeonseo*, in vol. 281 of *Hanguk munjip
chonggan* (Seoul: Minjok munhwa chujin hoe, 1989–2011), 390d. In this book, I cite all of Dasan's writings from the *Yeoyudang jeonseo* in *Hanguk munjip chonggan*.

imperial system and sought a new paradigm that could substitute for neo-Confucianism, which resulted in the formation of the Evidential Studies. Similarly, Japanese scholars attempted to give local meanings to Confucian sociopolitical and ethical thought in defining the "ancient meaning" of the Confucian classics. They eventually drifted away from neo-Confucian philosophy. The Korean movement of Practical Learning paralleled these movements, in that it tended to focus on practical issues and critique neo-Confucian ideas. Scholars in this movement, like those in the Evidential Studies and Ancient Learning, also looked for concrete evidence for their theories and respected ancient Confucian lore.

However, the Korean movement should be distinguished from the radical reactions to neo-Confucianism that occurred in the other two countries. This is because it never totally severed its relationship with neo-Confucianism. Joseon was too thoroughly ruled according to neo-Confucian principles to support an aggressive movement for total detachment from them. The intellectuals were well disciplined in neo-Confucian ideology and truly accepted its values. Today's South Korean scholarship, taking for granted this distinctive trait that derived from the Korean reaction to neo-Confucian dominance, tends to eschew a clear-cut division between Practical Learning and neo-Confucianism.[33] Opening a debate on this issue, Yi U-seong stated that Practical Learning, especially the philosophy of Yu Hyeong-won, essentially derived from neo-Confucianism, and his theory was buttressed and complemented by the work of Kim Jun-seok.[34] In the same context, Ji Du-hwan asserted that until the emergence of Northern Learning [北學] in the eighteenth century, no scholar in Practical Learning abandoned neo-Confucian ontological, epistemological, and metaphysical discussions.[35] More recently, some young Korean historians, encouraged by Han Yeong-u and Choe Wan-su, have accounted for the formation of Practical Learning by using such concepts as the "ancient learning of the six classics," the "era of true view landscape," the "society of scholar-officials in Seoul," and the "scholars at Pavilion Chimryu."[36] Though their views differ on the origin of Practical Learning, these new approaches similarly relate Practical Learning to neo-Confucianism. In the West, James Palais contended that the reformative political suggestions made by proponents of Practical Learning were by no means innovative but instead derived from the theoretical Zhou 周 institutions.[37] Some specialists in Korean religion and philosophy, such as

---

[33] For example, see Gwon-jong Yu, "Jeong Yak-yong ui dgwa cheolhak sasang," in *Hanguk Yuhak sasang daegye*, vol. 3 (Andong: Hanguk gukhak jinheungwon, 2005), 385–398.
[34] U-seong Yi, "Chogi Silhak gwa Seongnihak ui gwangye," *Dongbang hakji* 58 (1988): 15–22; Jun-seok Kim, "Yu Hyeong-won ui byeonbeop gwa silliron 實理論," *Dongbang hakji* 72 (1995): 69–113.
[35] Du-hwan Ji, "Joseon hugi Silhak yeongu ui munjejeom gwa banghyang," *Daedong gojeon yeongu* 3 (1987): 103–148.
[36] See Yeong-u Han et al., *Dasi, Silhak-iran muet-inga*.
[37] James Palais, *Confucian Statecraft and Korean Institutions: Yu Hyŏngwon and the Late Chosŏn Dynasty* (Seattle: University of Washington Press, 1996), 3–21.

Donald Baker and Mark Setton, have also opposed the separation of Practical Learning from Joseon neo-Confucianism.[38]

The compromising aspect of Practical Learning is observable in Dasan's *Noneo gogeum ju*, too. He respected Zhu Xi's scholarship and never went too far in his criticisms of neo-Confucianism. This is especially evident when Dasan is compared with Dazai Jun 太宰純 (1680–1747) in terms of their differing attitudes toward neo-Confucianism. Throughout his interpretations of the Confucian classics, Dasan always honors Zhu Xi, calling him "Master Zhu," whereas Dazai frequently attempts to debase Zhu Xi's reputation by calling him by his personal name, Xi. Interestingly, when Dasan quotes a passage in which Dazai mentions Zhu Xi, he changes "Xi" to "Master Zhu," presumably because he cannot leave the master's personal name as it appears in Dazai's writing. Actually, the alleged core values of Practical Learning—criticism, practicality, and practical evidence—are more conspicuous in Dazai Jun's writings than in those of comparable Joseon scholars, including Dasan. A comparison between Dasan and Mao Qiling serves to bolster this distinction, for Mao's interpretation of the Confucian classical texts was solidly aimed at criticizing Zhu Xi's views, while Dasan's remained reverent to them.

Indeed, Dasan's esteem for "Master Zhu" is clearly illustrated in his criticism of Dazai's and Mao's attacks on neo-Confucianism:

> Master Cheng [Cheng Yi] said, "Why have filial piety and brotherly respect existed in human nature from the beginning?" This does not mean that there is no principle in human nature to enable people to practice filial piety and brotherly respect, but that they are accomplished in the outer world. However, Xiaoshan [Mao Qiling] intended persistently to oppose the theories ... [s]o his theories have become more distorted.[39]

> Notwithstanding that Dazai has no idea of what the moral principle is, he tenaciously opposed the theories of neo-Confucianism. How absurd this is![40]

These are denigrations of what Dasan saw as a radical attempt to uproot the foundation of neo-Confucian moral philosophy. Thus the perspectives of those who attempt to separate Dasan's philosophy from neo-Confucianism are hardly free from distortion.

Koreans' efforts to negotiate with neo-Confucianism in their reformative intellectual movement may be deemed indicative of the premodern elements that exist in traditional Korean philosophy. This view was initially suggested

[38] Donald L. Baker, "The Use and Abuse of the Sirhak Label: A New Look at Sin Hu-dam and His *Sohak byon*," *Gyohoesa yongu* 3 (1981): 183–254. Also see Setton, *Chŏng Yagyong*, 67–122.
[39] Yak-yong Jeong, *Noneo gogeum ju*, in vol. 282 of *Hanguk munjip chonggan*, 159a.
[40] Yak-yong Jeong, *Noneo gogeum ju*, 322c.

by imperial Japanese scholars but was also held by many "modernist" cultural analysts in Korea. The compromise Koreans made with neo-Confucianism is still a matter of debate, with significant historical implications. However, it appears self-evident that the legacy of neo-Confucianism could not be abandoned in the various discussions within Confucianism because it was a great synthesis of all Confucian traditions that had existed prior to its emergence. Neo-Confucianism undeniably endured throughout the most crucial Confucian era. In contrast to Qing and Tokugawa scholars, Dasan attempted to integrate this crucial component into his philosophy through the traditional Confucian framework.

This syncretic aspect of Dasan's thought, which allowed him to adopt any ideas he found convincing, may raise a question: what was the criterion for his adoption of ideas, if there was any? Indeed, one of the impressions readers may have while reading Dasan's *Noneo gogeum ju* is that judgments permeate his writings. Ethical judgments for discerning the good from the bad are unavoidable to any Confucian, since Confucianism itself is didactically judgmental. However, Dasan did not withhold judgment even in his investigations of philological meanings, provenances of words, historical events, figures pertinent to the given passages, details of Confucian rituals and institutions, and so on. Almost every time he raised a dispute, he tried to reach his conclusions by making judgments. When taking in this plethora of judgments, the reader may wonder what Dasan's criterial basis for making these judgments was, provided that the judgments were consistent with one another. On this subject, I would like to center on his frequent use in his writings of the concept *li* 理, which can be translated as "principle" or "reason."

To begin with, I will explain how frequently Dasan adopted this notion of *li* in his writings. According to my examination of the database of Korean classics provided by the Institution for Translation of Korean Classics, *Yeoyudang jeonseo* contains 2,042 pieces of writing in which the character *li* appears, regardless of the length, genre, and nature of the writing. After eliminating instances in which this character is used as a verb meaning "to control" or "to manage," more than seventeen hundred works by Dasan remain that contain the philosophical notion of *li*. The frequency with which it appears should be contrasted with that of other important concepts in Dasan's philosophy, such as *tian* 天 (heaven; appears in 3,028 pieces of writing in *Yeoyudang jeonseo*), *ren* 仁 (humanity; 878), *de* 德 (virtue; 1,599), *li* 禮 (ritual propriety; 2,733), *xing* 性 (human nature; 604), *xiao* 孝 (filial piety; 782), *zhong* 忠 (loyalty; 511), and *xu* 恕 (reciprocity; 192).[41] Only pieces of writing that contain the concepts *tian* and *li* (ritual propriety) outnumber those that contain *li* (principle). This is remarkable in consideration of the fact that the concept of "principle" has been

---

[41] In some of the writings enumerated here, the character for each concept discussed is sometimes used as part of a proper name. If these cases are removed, the number of writings containing each character, used in a philosophical sense, will certainly be reduced.

abandoned in common discourse about Dasan's philosophy, whereas "heaven" and "ritual" have been stressed as pivotal components of it.

In *Noneo gogeum ju*, Dasan uses the concept *li* (principle) 322 times. This fact is also remarkable when one considers the frequency of other important concepts in *Noneo gogeum ju: tian* (919), *ren* (849), *de* (513), *li* (ritual propriety: 1,382), *xing* (258), *xiao* (223), *zhong* (193), and *xu* (97). Although Dasan uses some significant concepts more frequently in *Noneo gogeum ju*, note that they are the ones Confucius himself discussed, whereas the concept *li* (principle) did not even emerge in Confucius's time. This examination, I believe, is sufficient to show that *li* (principle) is one of the essential notions in Dasan's interpretation of the *Analects*.

Dasan often combines in his writings this concept with other concepts to form an important notion, as in the following examples: moral principle [義理], principle in human relationships [事理], universal principle [公理], principle of Heaven [天理], investigations on principle [窮理], principle of things [物理], principle of the Way [道理], true principle [實理], right principle [正理], principle of human beings [人理], fundamental principle [本理], principle of order [條理], utmost principle [至理], and principle in mysterious function [妙理]. He sometimes also uses the concept *li* to refer to the "principles" in various sciences or disciplines. Examples of this include: principle in governing [治理], principles in farming [農理], principles in diseases [病理], principles of yang [陽理], principles in medicines [醫理], principles in management of living [生理], principles in geography [地理], principles in entertainment [歡樂理], principles in geomancy [風水理], and principles of comets [彗星理].

More important is the fact that this concept, "principle" or "reason," is categorical in Dasan's philosophical paradigm and criterial in his reasoning. His discussions can easily be thought of as examinations of the compatibility of given topics to "principle" or "reason." If he judges a given philosophical discourse, a political suggestion, or even a philological argument as compatible with "principle" or "reason," he regards it as valid; if not, it is invalid. Because of this, readers have often discovered in many of his arguments a recurrence of such expressions as "being compatible with principle [合理]," "basing our reasoning on principle [以理推之]," "in discussion of principle [論理]," "going against principle [非理]," "in light of principle [於理]," "in observance of principle [見理]," "understanding principle [知理]," "fitting into principle [中理]," "having no principle [無理]," "distorting principle [悖理]," "illuminating principle [明理]," and "in accord with principle [有理]." These expressions consistently play crucial roles in his discussions and in many cases are associated with his conclusions. Even when he discusses empirical and experimental issues, such as strategies for improving people's lives or the observance of ancient Confucian rituals, he often returns to his final judgment: are they harmonious with "principle" or "reason?" He seemed to feel that he could strengthen the validity of his arguments by doing so, probably assuming that the "principle" or "reason" was universal.

Of course, Dasan was not concerned with neo-Confucian metaphysical discourses on the relationship between *li* (principle) and *qi* (vital force), the mechanisms of human nature and sentiment, the subtle but distinctive conceptualizations of various perspectives on human nature, the structure of the mind-heart, epistemological possibilities and methodologies for understanding neo-Confucian principles, and so on. He seemed to avoid these complicated discussions because he believed they were unnecessary. He regarded these discourses as studies of "human nature and principle" [性理] and criticized them for their excessive inclination toward metaphysics. In his philosophy, however, "human nature and principle" make up one of the many possible combinations of a Confucian value and "principle," just as neo-Confucianism is one of several Confucian schools in the history of Confucianism. Therefore, the paucity of discussion in his work of conventional themes in neo-Confucian metaphysics should not be regarded as a rejection of the concept of "principle." He actually noted that this concept had been discussed in many classical texts, such as *Constant Mean*, *Record of Rites*, *Commentaries on the Changes*, *Mencius*, *Poetry*, *Zuo's Commentary on the Spring and Autumn*, *Changes*, *Huainanzi*, *Huangdi neijing*, and *Han shu*. After examining these sources with regard to the concept of "principle," he concluded: "[All these concepts] have been derived from either regularity of pulses [脈理] or regularity in governing [治理] or regularity of laws [法理]. Is there any trustful ground for the neo-Confucian assertion that directly relates human nature to principle?"[42] Consequently, he attempted to keep his distance from only excessive metaphysical discussions in the "studies of human nature and principle," while accepting and utilizing the concept of "principle."

In light of this academic orientation, I suggest that Dasan's philosophy be conceptualized as the "Learning of Practical Principle [實理學]" instead of Silhak (Practical Learning). Pre-Qin Confucian scholars emphasized practicality [實], and neo-Confucian scholars developed Confucian metaphysical theory by adopting universality—the principle [理]. What Dasan wished to achieve in his commentary on the *Analects* was to synthesize these Confucian legacies to create a new theoretical paradigm. Terming his scholarship Learning of Practical Principle credits him with attempting to integrate all transmitted Confucian philosophies into a syncretic or synthetic system.

In fact, the neo-Confucian theory of "principle" itself has two dimensions: a dimension consisting of "one principle [一理]" as a pure pronouncement of *taiji* 太極 and a dimension consisting of "diversified principles [分殊理]" as the embodiment of the one principle in specific beings. The one principle is substantial, abstract, and noumenal, whereas the diversified principles are always associated with phenomena. If they are associated with concrete human relationships, they are collectively called "principles in human relationships [事理]." In this respect, they are believed to mirror one of the two aspects of the

---

42 Yak-yong Jeong, *Maengja yo-ui* 孟子要義, in vol. 282 of *Hanguk munjip chonggan*, 139d.

principle—that is, principle as "deontological rule [所當然之則]." If they are associated with physical beings in nature, they are collectively called "principles of things [物理]." In this respect, they are believed to mirror another aspect of the principle—that is, principle as "ontological ground [所以然之故]." In their discussions of humanity, neo-Confucian theorists perceive that "human nature of original thus-ness [本然之性]" and "human nature of vital and physical forces [氣質之性]" match the one principle and the diversified principles and proceed toward more complicated discussions of the relationship between them and mind-heart, a concept of human subjectivity.

Among the concepts introduced in this brief explanation of the neo-Confucian theory of principle, those that Dasan most vehemently opposed were the one principle and human nature of original thus-ness:

> This is the so-called human nature of original thus-ness, but there is nothing more detrimental than this theory in betraying Heaven, neglecting the mandate of moral behavior, distorting principle, and bringing harm to the good.[43]

> Human beings have no dual natures. It is like the fact that rice in its nature favors water and has no other nature of favoring dryness. . . . [T]he theory of the original goodness of human nature is the real idea of the ancient sages and not an individual argument of a private school. Nevertheless, neo-Confucian scholars see it as incomplete. Is this contention in accord with principle?[44]

> If principle is truly one, how can it be diversified? I am afraid that the theory of one principle is not reasonable.[45]

As he denied the core idea of neo-Confucian metaphysics, he also disagreed with neo-Confucian applications of the *ti-yong* 體用 paradigm to the relationships between the one principle and the diversified principles and between the two different human natures. In his view, it was consistent with Buddhist and Daoist theologies to say that "[the Way of Confucius] begins with one principle, becomes diversified in myriad things in the midst of changes, and [is] eventually integrated into the one principle again."[46] Dasan's assessment of these neo-Confucian theories matches his criticism of the "studies of human nature and principle" because these theories were its main topics. However, while being critical of neo-Confucian indulgence in metaphysical discourses, he still approved of many "principles," as long as they were manifested in reality. In other words, he actively employed the concept of principle when his discussions arrived at the topic of the diversified principles, although he did not accept the distinction between the one principle and the diversified principles.

---

[43] Yak-yong Jeong, *Simgyeong milheom*, in vol. 282 of *Hanguk munjip chonggan*, 38a.
[44] Yak-yong Jeong, *Simgyeong milheom*, 38a.
[45] Yak-yong Jeong, *Maengja yo-ui*, 151a.
[46] Yak-yong Jeong, *Simgyeong milheom*, 45d.

However, questions still remain: what is the difference between the neo-Confucian "one principle" and that principle of Dasan that is variously referred to as "principle of Heaven," "universal principle," "fundamental principle," and "principle of the Way?" How does the neo-Confucian understanding of human nature, revolving as it does around "human nature of original thus-ness," differ from Dasan's understanding of human nature? If he denied the transcendental aspect of "principle," why did he frequently reduce his investigations on many topics to a deductive judgment in order to see if the opinions were compatible with principle? Such reductionism is premised on a single or much simpler cause of the universe, which is inevitably transcendental.

Dasan might have played the same game neo-Confucians did: pieces of prescribed Confucian norms were given, and he was expected to assemble those pieces to build the structure for a moral philosophy. And Confucianism's confrontation with Buddhism may perhaps have required philosophers at that time to build metaphysical and ontological grounds for morals. Even though Dasan refused to blindly accept the neo-Confucian structure because he had experienced the abusive effects of the neo-Confucian indulgence in metaphysical discourses, by and large he could not avoid working on the same project. He may have attempted to diminish the transcendental connotations of "principle of Heaven" when he stated that "the principle of Heaven means the humanity that has been accomplished with the utmost sincerity, commiseration, and compassion that have penetrated Heaven and Earth. They are the actual virtues observed when a filial son deplored his fate of having immoral parents [as in the case of King Shun 舜]."[47] Still, Dasan's principle is an ontological and categorical one, as suggested in his statement "if something is compatible with the principle of Heaven there is nothing wrong in it."[48] In his moral philosophy, he substituted the "one principle" with various notions of "principle," including the "principle of Heaven," "universal principle," "fundamental principle," and "principle in the Way." Despite Dasan's intent to shun metaphysical discourses, all these concepts played analogous roles in their respective moral philosophical contexts.

Just as he resisted "one principle," he also removed the concept of "human nature of original thus-ness" from his lexicon. However, this does not mean that he truly abandoned the philosophical implications of the concept—that is, the optimistic and idealistic understanding of the possibility for self-perfection. In the same manner as he dealt with the "one principle," he rejected human nature of original thus-ness, replacing it with another metaphysical concept: in this case, the concept of "Dao-mind [道心]." One of the better known propositions in Dasan's philosophy is "human nature is the mind-heart's natural tendency to favor something [性卽嗜好]." He suggested this because he thought it necessary to deny the neo-Confucian view of human nature, that is, "human nature is no more than principle [性卽理]," in order to

[47] Yak-yong Jeong, *Maengja yo-ui*, 129d.
[48] Yak-yong Jeong, *Maengja yo-ui*, 139d.

undermine neo-Confucian abuse of abstract notions. However, he tempered what was naturally favored by the mind-heart with a sense of disciplinarian censorship, reminiscent of on the notion of "commonality of human psychology [心之所同然]" in *Mencius*:

> In my examination, human nature is the mind-heart's natural tendency to favor something. Like vegetables favoring excrement and algae favoring water, human nature favors the good.[49]

> When it comes to the discussion of human nature, I would say that everyone is delighted with the good and ashamed of evil. Therefore when one behaves morally, her mind-heart becomes filled with delight; when one behaves immorally, her mind-heart becomes filled with self-dissatisfaction. . . . [B]ased on these examples, I know that the good is what the mind-heart is delighted with and evil is what the mind-heart is ashamed of.[50]

Dasan asserts here that the intrinsic psychology of human beings tends toward the good. He conceptualizes this intrinsic psychological tendency in his philosophy as Dao-mind: "Dao-mind always wants to practice the good and enables us to choose the good. If one continues to listen to what Dao-mind wants to do, it is called following human nature: following human nature is being compliant with the mandate of Heaven."[51] Actually, Dasan admits that Dao-mind is a metaphysical concept when he says, "the nature of Dao-mind is to have neither form nor substantial quality; it is ultimately subtle and ultimately elusive."[52] With this claim, Dasan's Dao-mind comes to overlap with Zhu Xi's human nature of original thus-ness.[53]

In Confucianism, it was neo-Confucianism that conceptualized the ontological foundation for the universality of Confucian morals as principle. Neo-Confucian scholars perceived that an awareness of reasonability in Confucian morality underlay all Confucian teachings, and with reference to Huayan 華嚴 philosophy and certain Confucian classics, they made "principle" pivotal in their philosophy. The goal of this activity was to strengthen, prioritize, and absolutize the Confucian norms. Dasan positively recognized this contribution, and his philosophy also posited a transcendental regularity to the world, which was often conceptualized in conjunction with notions of "principle." Although

---

[49] Yak-yong Jeong, *Daehak gang-ui*, in vol. 282 of *Hanguk munjip chonggan*, 26b.
[50] Yak-yong Jeong, *Simgyeong milheom*, 38a.
[51] Yak-yong Jeong, *Jungyong jajam*, in vol. 282 of *Hanguk munjip chonggan*, 47d.
[52] Yak-yong Jeong, *Maengja yo-ui*, 125d.
[53] One may argue that the difference can be found in the fact that Dasan clearly believed that the Dao-mind belongs exclusively to human beings, whereas in Zhu Xi's philosophy the human nature of original thus-ness can be universal among all beings, including animals. To some interpreters, however, Zhu Xi's idea also acknowledges that Dao-mind is only found in human beings. This was one of the fierce debates among Joseon Confucian scholars.

he might not have agreed that his principles were transcendental, it is evident that his philosophy presumed it.

The problem with neo-Confucianism, as Dasan saw it, derived from excessive emphasis on the metaphysical affirmation of Confucian norms. He pointed out that the defect of Song Confucianism was the imbalance between its metaphysical interpretation and relevant evidence. He claimed that this stemmed from its narrow speculation on principle, which brought about the enervation of practices.[54] Based on this estimation, Dasan attempted to integrate into his philosophy certain topics, such as social reform and modern science, that contemporary interpreters have considered predominant ideas in the so-called Practical Learning. However, as I have already suggested, it would be more accurate to designate his views on these topics the Learning of Practical Principle, because his suggestions for social reform were about "practical principles in human relationships" and his studies on the modern sciences were about the "practical principles of things."

In my understanding, the most outstanding tendency in Korean philosophy, evident in certain representative philosophers' works, is the pursuit of universality and emphasis on humanity. Even though the forms this combination vary and consequently have generated a diversity of thought, these two main themes permeated the thinking of these philosophers, who shared a premise that each human being represents universality. Over the course of constructing this characteristic, philosophers often adopted a syncretic approach to the existing theories, which they would synthesize and integrate into a new paradigm. Dasan's philosophy demonstrates this characteristic of Korean philosophy well: he tried to synthesize the old and new commentaries on the *Analects* and thereby paid tribute to the original *Analects*; he tried to synthesize the old Confucian teachings on practical issues and the neo-Confucian learning of principle to form the learning of practical principle; he tried to synthesize the moral principle and the principles of human relationships and things to suggest a new dimension of the philosophy of principle; and he tried to combine the new Confucian developments in China and Japan with the persistent Korean awareness of moral foundations. This sense of moderation or syncretism extends in *Noneo gogeum ju* to his efforts to bring balance between inner cultivation and social merit, between refined cultural expressions and natural substance, between ideals and reality, between textual investigations and contemplation, and between words and meaning. All these endeavors aimed at reconfirming universality—principles, reasonability, Dao-mind, and Heaven—in order to help promote humanity in his society.

---

[54] In contrast, Dasan thought that the fatal weakness of Han Confucianism was its lack of rational and insightful thinking, which engendered many unreasonable and formalized interpretations. This stemmed from its overreaching focus on the historical and philological "investigations for the evidence" and resulted in overlooking the essence of learning. See Yak-yong Jeong, *Noneo gogeum ju*, 169c.

Dasan was aware that his time required a new philosophy and perceived the responsibilities of the time.

> Since it is a time of decline and disorder, we cannot fastidiously criticize immoral deeds such as lords not acting like lords, subjects not acting like subjects, parents not acting like parents, and children not acting like children, in the same way as we might do in an age of purity and peace. Therefore, when the noble person chooses to act, he naturally considers the responsibilities of the time. These days, people always say that the sages were inclined to neither yes nor no, and thus they want to blindly practice the Way regardless of the circumstances. How can this be deemed as the words from those who understand the time?[55]

I believe that this remark succinctly presents the essence of Dasan's philosophy. As he said, in a time when "the Confucian scholars replied to the kings, who talked to us with a sense of urgency, only with the great principles and the great laws," he himself attempted to respond to the responsibilities of his time.[56]

5

As a result of Dasan's ambitious plan to synthesize all transmitted commentaries of the *Analects, Noneo gogeum ju* contains numerous names and titles of works. All historical figures mentioned in this book will be identified with their birth and death years when they first appear, unless the information is not available. Detailed introductions to their achievements, however, are omitted in this book to spare as much space as possible; simple online searches using the Chinese characters of their names that follow their Romanized names can provide enough information to those who wish to inquire further. Dasan mentions most of these figures because their views are worth quoting, for either endorsement or refusal. Although Dasan, in accord with the traditional citation practice in Korea, did not provide bibliographical details for his sources, I attempt in this book to provide all the sources, in compliance with the standards of modern scholarship. Exceptions are when Dasan quotes interpretations of renowned commentators on the *Analects*, who appear in *Noneo gogeum ju* quite frequently. Major commentators in this category include Kong Anguo 孔安國 (c. 156–c. 74 BCE), Bao Xian 包咸 (7 BCE–63), Ma Rong 馬融 (79–166), Wang Shu 王肅 (195–256), and He Yan 何晏 (c. 195–249), whose comments appear exclusively in *Lun yu jijie*. I refer any experts who wish to read their comments in the original text to any edition of *Lun yu jijie*. As for Zheng Xuan 鄭玄 (127–200), all of his comments on the *Analects* are found in *Lun yu Zhengshi zhu* 論語鄭氏註, while the majority of them also appear in *Lun yu jijie*. All of

---

[55] Yak-yong Jeong, *Noneo gogeum ju*, 347a–b.
[56] Yak-yong Jeong, *Noneo gogeum ju*, 272b.

Huang Kan's comments come from *Lun yu yishu*. And all of Xing Bing's comments come from *Lun yu zhengyi*. Most of Zhu Xi's comments, along with most of Cheng Yi's comments, may be found in Zhu Xi's *Lun yu jizhu*, although some of Zhu Xi's views are excerpted from Zhu Xi's other works, such as *Zhuzi yulei* 朱子語類 and *Jinsi lu* 近思錄. Dazai Jun's comments can also be easily found in relevant chapters of his *Rongo kogun gaiden* 論語古訓外傳. Although Dazai Jun published another commentary on the *Analects, Rongo kogun* 論語古訓, it is unclear whether Dasan directly made reference to it. The comments made by the other two Japanese scholars, Ito Koreshada 伊藤維禎 (1627–1705) and Ogyu Nabematsu 荻生雙松 (1666–1728), whom Dasan often quotes, may also be found in *Rongo kogun gaiden*. I have not been able to find an exception to this yet. Despite the fact that Dasan quotes from Mao Qiling more frequently than from Dazai Jun, Mao Qiling should be dealt with differently because his views are presented in various short essays in *Lun yu jiqiu pian* 論語稽求篇, *Sishu shengyan* 四書賸言, which includes *Sishu shengyan bu* 四書賸言補, *Sishu gaicuo* 四書改錯, and *Xihe ji* 西河集. I therefore supply information on the sources Dasan consulted for Mao's views. In the same manner in which I have provided citations for Mao, I have tried to provide them for the comments and opinions of scholars other than those of the major figures I have mentioned here, except when the source materials could not be identified.

For the purpose of establishing these sources I have relied on *Siku quanshu*, because it contains almost all pre-Qing classical texts and because there are again obvious merits in using online resources. The Wenyuange edition of *Siku quanshu* has been digitized and is available at major universities' libraries. Usually, I have enclosed sources in parentheses, along with relevant information: the title of the work, when it is not mentioned in related sentences in the main body; the roll number in the original book binding; the page number in the original book binding, which is separated from the roll number by a colon; and a letter, either *a* or *b*, that refers to one of the two halves of the page. When the original script extends beyond two pages, a dash is used to indicate the range of pages. Line numbers are usually not noted because it does no harm to read the original script. However, in cases in which I have omitted a translation of Dasan's quotation that would otherwise follow the expression *yinjeung*, I have provided line numbers so that the reader may know exactly what part of the source he quotes. Where he quotes passages from the *Analects* and *Mencius*, I have provided, for the sake of convenience, citations based on the numbering in Legge's editions of the classics, which were in turn based on Zhu Xi's division of chapters. Where it was necessary to provide a source for Dasan's writings , I have used the National Institute for Translation of Korean Classics edition of *Yeoyudang jeonseo* in *Hanguk munjip chonggan* because it is one of the most up-to-date editions and because it has been digitized. Scholars other than Koreanists, who may have limited access to the original version of Dasan's writings, will be able to read the original this way. Information on all other sources conforms to the normal practices of modern scholarship.

In line with this, I would like to note that Dasan's quotations of the classical texts do not precisely reproduce what appears in the extant editions of them. These discrepancies seem to have occurred via various routes: his practice of summarizing and abridging source texts, his limited access to them and concomitant reliance on his memory, and the possible existence of various editions available to him but not handed down to us. More important, scholars in the past were less bothered to provide exact citations. In any case, I do not detail the discrepancies, since doing so would only disrupt one's reading of *Noneo gogeum ju*, not help. It is quite a minor issue in *Noneo gogeum ju*. More significant might be that Dasan often requotes comments and views on the given passages from his major sources, such as Mao Qiling's and Dazai Jun's works, without informing his readers of that fact. This aspect has sometimes agonized scholars who want to understand the context of remarks that Dasan requotes, because it is challenging to locate the original sources. Even when researching a simple quotation of the definition of a term from, say, *Shuo wen jie zi* 說文解字, readers may face difficulties in finding the exact page in the original source. Due to this problem, I have provided secondary sources when I have not been able to locate the exact page of the original source. This recurrent practice of requotation hinders an understanding of the precise scope of Dasan's references. As more consideration is given to his practice, the number of references will surely be reduced, if not drastically. Given that he was banished to a rural town remote from the busy centers of Korean intellectual life and that the library he could freely access was owned by a local Confucian family, the claim that he did not have as many sources as appear in *Noneo gogeum ju* is persuasive. However, he surely did his best to refer to as many sources as possible, regardless of the number of works he had physical access to.

Since Dasan used footnotes to expand on his comments, all the footnotes in this translation are his. Within the footnotes or the main text, brackets set off my own brief notes clarifying the text; all material enclosed in brackets is mine. In the main text, after my translation of each chapter, I have placed (signaled by three asterisks) my broader explanations of the meaning of Dasan's discussions. In my view, these explanations are indispensable to an understanding of the nature of Dasan's philosophy, the creativity of his interpretations, and the exegetical implications of his reading, because a mere translation of *Noneo gogeum ju* cannot ensure even one's grasp of the subtleties that imbue his definitions of the various characters. For this book, I am certainly indebted to the existing Korean translation of *Noneo gogeum ju* by Yi Ji-hyeong. I am responsible for my translation, however, when it turns to have an error. Although I have found numerous errors in the Korean translation, as well as reliable information and renditions, I do not make any comments on them in this book.[57]

---

[57] Among many researches on *Noneo gogeum ju*, two doctoral dissertaions, which pioneered scholarly investigations of it, deserve a special note: Eon-jong Kim, *Jeong Dasan Noneo gogeum ju won-ui chonggwal gojing* (Taiwan: Xuehai chubanshe, 1987) and Yeong-ho Kim, *Jeong Dasan ui Noneo haeseok e gwanhan yeongu: Noneo gogeum ju reul jungsim euro* (Seoul: Sungkyunkwan University, 1994).

For Korean terminology, I have used the revised system because it is recommended by the Academy of Korean Studies; for Chinese terminology, I have used the pinyin system; for the titles of works authored by Koreans, I have used the same pronunciation of them as is used for the pronunciation of Korean proper names; for the titles of works written by Chinese or Japanese authors, I have adopted their pronunciations. I have not translated any of the titles of works, except for Dasan's works, into English, because doing so would be disruptive—at least to experts in this field. The definition of a Chinese character(s) or term(s) in parentheses, if enclosed in double quotation marks or single quotation marks, is the one Dasan adopted in *Noneo gogeum ju*. If the definition of a Chinese character(s) or term(s) is introduced without quotation marks, it is the common definition. The titles of the thirteen Confucian classics are provided in English, because the intended reader of this book should be familiar with them. I note names of ancient Chinese figures—including Confucius's disciples, whom *Noneo gogeum ju* introduces with certain honorifics, such as *zi* 子, *meng* 盟, *bo* 伯—in such a way as to distinguish the honorifics from their real (either personal or family) names. For example, in accord with Dasan's use of the honorific *bo*, Bo Qin refers to the eldest son (*bo*) of the Duke of Zhou, whose personal name was Qin; I use Zi Lu for a respected disciple (*zi*) of Confucius, Lu, whose name mysteriously appears in the Chinese sources either as Zhong You (the second son You) or as Ji Lu (the youngest son Lu); I use Zhuang Kang for the wife of Duke Zhuang of Wei (Zhuang), whose family name was Kang. In the main text, I give the names of people from East Asia in the order prescribed by tradition, with the family name first, followed by the personal name.

An Overview of the Original Meanings

1. The virtues of humanity, rightness, ritual propriety, and wisdom are accomplished through practices and not the principles that exist in one's mind-heart.[1] (1.2)
2. The phrase "I would call him learned" should be read in association with the passage headed "To learn extensively" in Book 19 "Zi Zhang 子張." (1.7)
3. A pause should be placed after "frugal," to make "Our Master is temperate, benign, respectful, and frugal" a separate sentence. (1.10)
4. As for the sentences "trustworthiness is close to rightness" and "respectfulness is close to ritual propriety," one should follow the old interpretations.[2] (1.13)
5. The sentence zhong xing gong zhi 眾星共之 means that all stars move together with the celestial axis and is not meant to convey a sense of nonaction. (2.1)
6. The expression er shun 耳順 means that people's words do not sound offensive to Confucius. (2.4)
7. With regard to the sentence "Even dogs and horses attend people," one should follow Bao Xian's 包咸 (7 BCE–65 CE) comment. (2.7)
8. Xiansheng 先生 and dizi 弟子 do not refer to parents and children.[3] (2.8)
9. The phrase "renewing the past learning and acquiring new knowledge" refers to one of the benefits of being a teacher. (2.11)
10. Yiduan 異端 does not refer to the ideas of Yang Zhu 楊朱, Mo Di 墨翟, Buddha, or Lao Dan 老耼. (2.16)
11. The phrase ju zhi 舉直 ("raise up the honest") means to raise up the worthies; the phrase cuo wang 錯枉 ("place them over the crooked") does not mean to abandon the wicked. (2.19)
12. The clamp and the collar-bar connect two different things in the same manner in which trustworthiness associates two different persons. (2.22)
13. Any state that succeeds the Zhou 周 will not change the rituals of the Zhou even a hundred ages hence. (2.23)
14. The theory that the Xia 夏, the Yin 殷, and the Zhou, respectively, prioritized wholeheartedness, natural substance, and refined expression is basically fallacious and derives from a discussion among scholars of apocryphal texts. (2.23)
15. The Ji family [季氏] was not the major chief descendant of the three families. (3.1)
16. "Having rulers in a barbaric state" means that a ruler preserves his position by adopting the ways of barbarians in a state. (3.5)

---

[1] This debate appears in the "Master You [有子]" chapter (1.2).
[2] Debates on the first four points appear in Book 1, "To Learn."
[3] This is related to the chapter that begins "Zi Xia 子夏 asked about filial piety" (2.8).

17. *Xia er yin* 下而飲 means that the contenders drink when they lose an archery match. (3.7)
18. I discussed the meaning of the Di 禘 sacrifice. (3.10)
19. The kitchen god and the inner room god are not among the gods of the five sacrificial rituals. (3.13)
20. The reason Confucius asked about everything when he entered the Grand Shrine was that the state of Lu 魯 violated ritual propriety in performing their rituals in the shrine. (3.15)
21. The saying "in ritual archery, hitting the mark is not emphasized" pertains to archery for greeting guests from other states and archery for official banquets. (3.16)
22. The sacrificial sheep for the announcement of the first day were reserved for serving the king's envoys. (3.17)
23. The phrase "it is sad but not hurtful" pertains to the Juaner 卷耳 ode. (3.20)
24. With regard to the phrase "Guan Zhong 管仲 married three women," one should follow Bao Xian's interpretation. (3.22)
25. The reason King Wu's 武 music was said not absolutely to yield the good lies in his incomplete merits, not his virtue. (3.25)

BOOK 1 | To Learn 學而

1.1 The Master said, "To learn and at times to exercise what one has learned, is that not also pleasant? To have a friend coming to visit you from afar, is that not also delightful? Not to be irritated even when unrecognized by people, is that not also being a noble person?" [This chapter opens the first roll of *Noneo gogeum ju* in traditional book binding and the first volume of it in the Sinjo edition, which corresponds to the seventh volume of the collection of classics of *Yeoyudang jeonseo*.][1]

子曰; 學而時習之, 不亦說乎? 有朋自遠方來, 不亦樂乎? 人不知而不慍, 不亦君子乎?

1.1.1 Grounds

1) Xing Bing commented, "Teachers are called 'Master.'[2] The reason for only mentioning 'The Master said' here is that everyone knows, even without specifying his family name, who he is, as his sacred virtue has become widely known and his exemplary deeds have been transmitted across generations."[3]

2) I supplement as follows: *Xue* 學 ("to learn") refers to receiving lessons; *xi* 習 ("to exercise") refers to becoming familiar with given responsibilities; *shi xi* 時習 ("at times to exercise") means to exercise what one has learned from time to time; *yue* 說 ("pleasant") is a state in which one's mind-heart remains sanguine.[4] In *Changes*, both hexagrams Dui 兌 and Guai 夬 have an

---

[1] This book contains sixteen chapters. According to Xing Bing 邢昺 (932–1010), "Since the first word that appears in this book is *xue* 學 ('to learn'), it eventually became its title."
[2] *Gongyang's Commentary* employs the term "Master Shenzi [子沈子]." On this term, He Xiu 何休 (129–182) commented, "Placing the character *zi* 子 before one's family name is to explicitly display that that person is one's teacher" (*Chunqiu Gongyang zhuan zhushu* 春秋公羊傳註疏, 3:30a–b).
[3] Ogyu Nabematsu 荻生雙松 (1666–1728) commented, "People of Confucius academy called Our Master [夫子: Confucius] 'the Master' within the academy [to avoid calling him by his name]. It is similar to the fact that in *Spring and Autumn*, the dukes of the state of Lu were just called 'the Duke.'"
[4] Huang Kan 皇侃 (488–545) commented, "It means that one's mind-heart is pleased and exuberant."

open line, representing *yin*, at the top. This may inform that the meanings of "pleasant [悅]" and "sanguine [快]" are close to one another.[5]

3) I supplement as follows: *Peng* 朋 ("friends") are those who follow the same way together.[6] Those "coming to visit you from afar" must be the dauntless, and those who are visited must be virtuous and brilliant. *Le* 樂 ("delightful") means deeply causing cheer;[7] *ren bu zhi* 人不知 ("unrecognized by people") means that people do not know that one's learning has been accomplished; *yun* 慍 ("irritated") means that one's mind-heart is entangled with agony.[8] *Changes* says, "Even if people do not see that I am on the right way, I have no anxiety" (*Zhou Yi zhushu*, 1:18b).[9]

4) I supplement as follows: *Junzi* 君子 ("noble person") is an appellation for those who have virtues. On the poem "Yu zao 玉藻," Zheng Xuan 鄭玄 (127–200) commented, "*Junzi* refers to classes of the great officials [大夫] and low-ranking officials [士]" (*Mao Shi zhushu*, 2:30b).[10] His annotation on "Shao yi 少儀" also says, "*Junzi* refers to ministers [卿] and great officials" (*Li ji zhushu* 禮記註疏, 30:19a).[11] I believe that the so-called *junzi* initially refers to offspring of the legitimate princes [大君] as though kings were called the Son of Heaven. In ancient times, only those who had virtues could assume higher positions so that, in later periods, the virtuous came to be called *junzi* even without such positions.

1.1.2 Arguments

1) Someone [Mao Qiling 毛奇齡] argued, "'To learn' in this chapter means to be committed to the Way."[12] I would refute this as follows:

"Xue ji 學記" of *Record of Rites* says, "Without learning, one would not understand the Way" (*Li ji zhushu*, 36:2a). Confucius also said, "At fifteen, I became resolute to learn" (*Lun yu jizhu*, 2:4). "To learn" may mean "to be committed to the Way" only in these passages. An explanation of *Shuo wen* 說文, "'To learn' means to become enlightened" (*Shuo wen jie zi* 說文解字, 3-B:20a), may also inform that "to learn" is a process in which those who are enlightened earlier enlighten those who are as yet to be enlightened.

---

[5] In *Changes*, "Tuan 象" in the hexagram Dui reads: "The king pleasantly [說] leads the people" (*Zhou Yi zhushu* 周易註疏, 10:1b).

[6] See the annotation on the hexagram Kun 坤 (*Zhou Yi zhushu* 2:1b).

[7] Master Zhu (Zhu Xi 朱熹, 1130–1200) said, "*Yue* (pleasure) is what is triggered in response to outer circumstances and then felt inside the mind-heart, whereas *le* (delight) is what is accumulated inside the mind-heart and overflows to the outside" (*Zhuzi yu lei* 朱子語類, 20:11b).

[8] "Hui feng 檜風," in *Poetry*, sings, "My mind-heart is entangled with agony" (*Mao Shi zhushu* 毛詩註疏, 13:8a).

[9] This is Master Cheng's quotation (*Lun yu jizhu* 論語集注, 1:1b).

[10] He also commented that *junzi* refers to the class of low-ranking officials or above.

[11] *Mencius* says, "Without people working in the fields, there is no way to feed *junzi*" (*Mengzi jizhu* 孟子集注, 3A:3).

[12] *Xin shu* 新書, by Jia Yi 賈誼 (200–169 BCE), quotes the lost *Rites*, which says, "In the Lesser Academy, one learns about the lesser Way; in the Great Academy, one learns about the great Way" (quoted in *Lun yu jiqiu pian* 論語稽求篇, 1:5a).

Although these examples demonstrate the primary definition of this character [學], the *Analects* is not grounded on this definition.

2) Huang Kan argued, "There are three timings in learning. First, there is a timing in learning in the course of one's life.[13] Second, there is a timing in learning in the course of a year.[14] Third, there is a timing in learning in the course of a day."[15] I would refute this as follows:

Shi xi ("at times to exercise") means "to exercise what one has learned from time to time."[16] To learn some codes of conduct, such as attending to the comfort of one's parents in the early morning and making their bed in the evening, assumes that one exercises these codes of conduct every day; to learn certain attitudes, such as being spirited in the daytime and being concerned about surrounding matters, implies that one exercises those attitudes every day; to learn ceremonial rituals implies that one exercises them; to learn village rituals implies that one exercises them;[17] to learn music implies exercise;[18] to learn recitation implies exercise; to learn archery and to drive carriages imply exercise in them;[19] to learn handwriting and calculation implies that one exercises these skills. All these instances of learning are ways to become familiar with given responsibilities. Learning is a way to understand things, and to exercise is a way to practice them. "To learn and at times to exercise what one has learned" is to improve one's knowledge and practice at once. However, in the later generations learning only focuses on learning without exercising. Because of that, there is no pleasure in learning.

3) Wang Shu 王肅 (195–256) argued, "'To learn' means at times to recite and master the classics." I would refute this as follows:

Merely reciting and mastering passages constitute the learning of the later generations. Rituals, music, archery, and driving carriages—one can learn all these things. How come learning is no more than recitation? A sentence in *Changes* reads: "I do discuss and, in doing so, master things with friends."[20] To "discuss" here means debating and arguing, the subjects of which are unlimited. In contrast, what one can recite is just *Poetry* and

---

[13] "Xue ji," in *Record of Rites*, says, "If a man starts learning after the due age, he would feel it agonizing, and accomplishments can hardly be made" (*Li ji zhushu*, 36:15a).

[14] "Wang zhi 王制" says, "In spring and autumn, *Rites* and *Music* are taught; in winter and summer, *Poetry* and *Documents* are taught" (*Li ji zhushu*, 13:3a).

[15] "Xue ji" says, "When a noble person is learning, there are times of embracing what one has learned in the mind, practicing it, taking a repose, and enjoying it" (*Li ji zhushu*, 36:10a). This sentence discusses what one has to do daily.

[16] This is Master Zhu's annotation [in *Lun yu jizhu*].

[17] For example, the protocols of having a cup of wine before ascending an archery platform or of arrow throwing are included in the village rituals.

[18] "Yue ling 月令" says, "In the early spring, the king orders the head official of music to teach ritual dances in the national academy. In the late fall, the king orders the head official of music to teach how to play the flutes in the national academy" (*Li ji zhushu*, 15:11a).

[19] In the early winter, "Yue ling" says, "One learns archery and driving carriages" (*Li ji zhushu*, 17:22a).

[20] See "Xiang 象" in the hexagram Dui (*Zhou Yi zhushu*, 10:2a).

Documents. Learning cannot be constrained within them. For a classical text that supports my argument here, see *Da Dai Li ji* 大戴禮記, 4:2a, 7.[21]

4) Bao Xian argued, "Those who are in the same academy are called 'friends.'" I would refute this as follows:

An annotation on *Gongyang's Commentary* says, "Those who are in the same academy are called 'friends'" (*Chunqiu Gongyang zhuan zhushu*, 25:26a).[22] An annotation on *Rites of Zhou* says, "Those who are learning from the same master are called 'friends.'"[23] Meanwhile, *Lun yu jizhu* says, "Those who are alike to one another are called friends" (*Lun yu jizhu*, 1:1b). Overall, "friends" are those who have the same ideas and intention. How does it necessarily mean people in the same academy?

5) He Yan 何晏 (190?–249) argued, "Even if people sometimes do not understand certain topics, the noble person feels no anger."[24] Someone [Mao Qiling] argues, "It is said that the Master has never felt exhausted in learning and never felt bored in teaching in his life. The passage under discussion duly mentions the Master's teaching. Therefore when Wei Wenjing 魏文靖 (1178–1273), teaching in Yushan 余山, met an audience who did not grasp what had been discussed and gave him a displeased look, he said, 'People do not understand on their own. For what reason do I become irritated?' He surely attained the meaning of this passage" (*Si shu shengyan* 四書賸言, 1:5a). I would refute this as follows:

This chapter deliberates on the entire structure of accomplishing one's virtues and accomplishing merits for the world. The first sentence sheds light on the matter of accomplishing one's virtue. Once it is accomplished, it is delightful when people recognize my accomplishments and follow me. However, even though people neither recognize my accomplishments nor respect me, I am not irritated. This illuminates the fact that the circumstances for accomplishing merits are not under my control. Xing Bing's theory of "given obtuseness" is not worth even introducing here.

* * *

This chapter reveals Dasan's perspective on learning. As seen in the definition he gives in his annotations, learning is an activity that consists of "receiving lessons." Lessons in this context, according to Dasan, can include many topics, from rituals and music to handwriting and calculation. However, he did not

---

[21] The relevant passage appears in "Zengzi li shi 曾子立事."

[22] This definition also appears in a comment on the hexagram Dui (*Zhou Yi zhushu*, 10:2a).

[23] This comment appears in "Da si tu 大司徒" (*Zhou li zhushu* 周禮註疏, 10:30a).

[24] Xing Bing said, "In ancient times, people learned for self-cultivation. They concealed their brightness within themselves so that only their inner world became bright. Thus, even if others did not recognize it, they did not get angry. The passage under discussion can also be explained as saying that the noble person does not become angry but forgives those who, with given obtuseness, do not intellectually understand certain topics."

accept the claim that the subject of learning is the Way, a metaphysical concept. While embracing all practical topics with which people can improve their practical knowledge, skills, and manners, he clearly rejected the neo-Confucian viewpoint that the goal of learning was to understand the Way. In contrast, Zhu Xi, in his *Lun yu jizhu*, explains "learning" in this chapter as follows: "The primary meaning of 'learning' is to emulate. Although human inborn nature is universally good, in the time of attaining enlightenment, people are different from one another. Thus, only when those who are to be enlightened emulate the deeds of the enlightened at an early stage, can they reveal the good and return to their inborn state" (*Lun yu jizhu*, 1:1a).

As a matter of fact, Dasan seems to be well aware, in this chapter, of Zhu Xi's annotation because he also discusses the matter of relating "learning" to "attaining enlightenment." Instead of directly criticizing Zhu Xi's interpretation, however, Dasan, focusing on the original source, insists that that interpretation cannot be applied to the passage under consideration. This manner of criticizing Zhu Xi pervades *Noneo gogeum ju*. Throughout the work, he shows respect for Zhu Xi and, simultaneously, appears cautious about the potential danger of overtly criticizing him in Joseon 朝鮮 society, where his neo-Confucianism prevailed.

Dasan's definition of "learning" here and his repudiation of the neo-Confucian attempt to link "learning" to the Way may confirm the conventional understanding of Dasan's philosophy: Dasan is a champion of Practical Learning, an intellectual movement challenging, in many of its aspects, the neo-Confucian orthodoxy. This impression is partially valid because Dasan criticized the neo-Confucian concentration on metaphysical concepts, as seen here. However, this should not be construed as meaning that Dasan intended to discard all neo-Confucian legacies. In short, while sometimes criticizing Zhu Xi's views, Dasan still respects Zhu Xi. As I will show, one of the eventual goals of "learning" in Dasan's philosophy is identical to that of neo-Confucianism: cultivating yourself to become a sage through an understanding of the Way. What Dasan was truly worried about was that students, by only paying attention to the eventual goal of learning, tended to become negligent of their practical responsibilities, such as learning proper manners, protocols, and the driving of carriages. In Dasan's view, this proclivity, hovering over Joseon Confucian academia, was not consistent with Confucius's teaching because Confucius made it clear that everyone should "try to reach up above by learning about matters below" (*Lun yu jizhu*, 14:35). Thus, what Dasan really objected to in neo-Confucianism was its adherents' imbalance: they were excessively inclined toward "reaching up above."

Meanwhile, Dasan also rebutted Wang Shu's definition of "learning" as reciting and mastering the classics. Wang's perspective on learning represented the academic fashion of the Han and Tang dynasties, such that one's knowledge of the classics held more importance than one's inner virtues. Song neo-Confucians detested this knowledge-first Han-Tang notion of learning and attempted to overcome it with a morality-first spirit. In this regard, Dasan would side with Song neo-Confucianism. Nevertheless, he always tried to synthetically absorb the transmitted intellectual traditions, maintaining a balance between these Confucian camps in a post-Confucius era. Even though Dasan did not accept Wang's point of view on "learning," it did not necessarily mean that he thought one did not need to "recite and master the classics."

1.2 Master You said, "Those who are filial to their parents and compliant with their elders hardly defy their superiors. Those who hardly defy their superiors but like to cause disorder do not exist. The noble person works on the root. Only when the root takes firm hold, will the Way grow. Thus, are filial piety and respect for elders the root of humanity?"

有子曰;其爲人也孝弟,而好犯上者鮮矣.不好犯上,而好作亂者,未之有也.君子務本,本立而道生,孝弟也者,其爲仁之本與?

1.2.1 Grounds

1) He Yan commented, " 'Master You' refers to Confucius's disciple You Ruo 有若."[25]

2) Master Zhu commented, "*Fan shang* 犯上 ('To defy their superiors') means to unexpectedly defy those who are in higher positions."[26]

3) I supplement as follows: *Zuo luan* 作亂 ("to cause disorder") means to trigger insurgencies through regicides and treacherous doings. In the Spring and Autumn period, many caused disorder of this kind, worrying the rulers of the time. The rulers did not know how to resolve the issue, however, so Master You addressed it in this passage.

4) Master Zhu commented, "*Wu* 務 ('To work') means to concentrate one's efforts; *ben* 本 ('the root') means the root of a tree."

5) I supplement as follows: [The literal meaning of] *dao* 道 ("the Way") is that through which people move. *Ren* 仁 ("humanity") signifies two people being together. In regard to serving one's parents, being filial corresponds to a form of humanity wherein a father and a son become the two who are together; in regard to serving one's elders, being compliant with them corresponds to a form of humanity wherein an older brother and a younger brother become the two; in regard to serving one's ruler, being loyal corresponds to a form of humanity wherein a ruler and a subject become the two; and in regard to nurturing the people, being merciful corresponds to a form of humanity wherein a magistrate and a commoner become the two. In all relationships between two people, including relations between

---

[25] According to "Dizi liezhuan 弟子列傳," in *Shiji* 史記, "You Ruo was forty-three years younger than Confucius" (*Shiji*, 67:23a). On this record, Zheng Xuan mentioned: "You Ruo was born in the State of Lu" (*Shiji jijie* 史記集解, 67:18b).

[26] He also commented, "Being irritable or disobedient even a bit falls under defying superiors."

husbands and wives and between friends, thoroughly fulfilling the Way guarantees humanity without exception. However, filial piety and respect for elders are the root.

6) I supplement as follows: *Yu* 與, the last character of this passage, is usually used to make a sentence a question. The reason Confucius put this character at the end of this sentence, even as the validity of the principle addressed here is unquestionable, is that he wanted to reprimand his contemporaries for their distrust of this teaching. Thus, this sentence seems to be satirical.

1.2.2 Arguments

1) He Yan argued, "*Ben* means a foundation." I would refute this as follows:

The root and ends are associated with one another like parts of a single body. However, a foundation is not necessarily associated with ends. This is why Master Zhu interpreted this word differently.

2) I question Master Zhu as follows:

Mencius says, "Humanity, rightness, ritual propriety, and wisdom are rooted in mind-heart" (*Mengzi jizhu*, 7A:21). In this respect, humanity, rightness, ritual propriety, and wisdom are analogous to flowers and fruits. Only do their roots reside in mind-heart. Thus, when mind-hearts of commiseration and shame arise inside, humanity and rightness are accomplished outside; when mind-hearts of deference and judgment arise inside, ritual propriety and wisdom are accomplished outside. Most Confucians today think that these four values of humanity, rightness, ritual propriety, and wisdom exist inside one's torso, like the five organs, and thus that the "four leads [四端]" stem from them. This understanding, however, is incorrect. Similarly, filial piety and respect for elders are the names of cultivated virtues. They are also accomplished outside. On what grounds could the two values of filial piety and respect for elders exist inside one's torso, like a liver or a lung?

The Master Cheng [程頤: 1033–1107] said, "How would filial piety and respect for elders exist in human inborn nature?" (*Lun yu jizhu*, 1:2a) What he meant by saying this is no more than that filial piety and respect for elders are accomplished outside. It does not necessarily imply, however, that in human inborn nature there are no principles that enable people to be filial to their parents and compliant with their elders. Nevertheless, Xiaoshan 蕭山 [毛奇齡] wanted to blindly oppose the neo-Confucian theories so that he turned filial piety and respect for elders to things existing inside. In this regard, his understanding is incorrect as well. Filial piety and respect for elders are equivalent to humanity, and humanity is equivalent to filial piety and respect for elders. The only difference is that humanity is a universal name. It embraces every humane deed, including acts of loyalty to kings, mercy to the people, compassion for orphans, and sympathy for widowers. In contrast, filial piety and respect for elders are particular terms, so only serving parents and giving respect for elders manifest these terms in reality. Therefore, Master You said that among all instantiations of humanity, filial piety and respect for elders were the root of humanity, and Master Cheng said that practices of humanity began with filial piety and respect for elders. They share the same kind of understanding. Master Cheng also said, however, "It is fine to say that filial piety and respect for elders are the root of practices of humanity, but it is disagreeable to say that they are the root of humanity itself" (1:2a). I do not believe that this saying is in harmony with what Master You said. It is unnecessary to strictly distinguish humanity from practices of humanity.

In conclusion, the sage kings in ancient times discerned what deeds to accomplish and which of these took priority over others so that they guided all under heaven with filial piety and respect for elders. Even though the values they honored were distinct from one another, the kings were identical in honoring the elderly. For this reason, in regard to serving the old in the Great Academy, even the Son of Heaven himself rolled his sleeves up to cut the sacrifice and carried sauces to offer the old. That was all for educating the children of the feudal lords.[27] Accordingly, the people at that time came to hardly ever defy their superiors, and rebellions and insurgencies never occurred. How wise this was! In contrast, later kings, as they did not discern what to do, attempted to prevent insurgencies from occurring only through producing hardened armors and sharp weapons and to stop people from defying their superiors only through authorizing complicated contractual agreements and severe punishments. This means that they had already lost the root. With what could they have led people to serve kings, devote themselves to the country, and eventually accomplish humanity?

For classical texts that support my argument here, see *Guanzi* 管子, which says, "Filial piety and respect for elders are the forefathers of humanity;"[28] "Ji yi," which says, "The fundamental teaching for all people is filial piety … [h]umanity is to love this; ritual propriety is to practice this; and rightness is to keep this right" (*Li ji zhushu*, 48:6b–7a); *Classic of Filial Piety*, which says, "In general, filial piety is the root of virtues and what teachings are derived from" (*Xiaojing zhushu* 孝經註疏, 1:3b);[29] *Lüshi Chunqiu*, which says, "Now, promoting filial piety and respect for elders were the foundational work of the three emperors and five lords" (*Lüshi Chunqiu* 呂氏春秋, 14:1b);[30] and "Yan Du zhuan 延篤傳," in *Hou Han shu*, which says, "One's merits are displayed on the outside, but they are rooted in one's mind-heart.… [A]lthough branches are lush, what makes them so is the root. In general, all humane people are filial. This is analogous with the fact that all limbs are associated with the mind and

---

[27] See "Ji yi 祭義" (*Li ji zhushu*, 39:20a).
[28] On this passage Fang Xuanling 房玄齡 (579–648) commented, "Humanity stems from filial piety and respect for elders. Thus they are the forefathers of humanity" (*Guanzi*, 10:3b).
[29] If teachings are put into practice, how can people not return to humanity? [This sentence should be regarded as Dasan's footnote, since it does not appear in *Classic of Filial Piety*.]
[30] This is what the sentence "The noble person works on the root" means.

abdomen. Therefore, Confucius [in *Classic of Filial Piety*] says, 'Filial piety is the pillar of Heaven, the rightness of Earth, and the due practice of people.' Master You says [in the *Analects*] 'Thus, are filial piety and respect for elders the root of humanity?'" (*Hou Han shu* 後漢書, 94:6b)[31]

3) Wang Yinglin 王應麟 (1223–1296) asked himself, "Why, among all Confucius's disciples, are only two, Master You and Master Zeng [曾子], called 'master'?" He answered, "Master Cheng [程子] said, '[It is because] this book [*The Analects*] was completed by students of Master You and Master Zeng.' Master Liu [柳宗元: 773–819] said, 'When Confucius passed away, all of his disciples placed Master You in the position of a teacher and revered him as such because he looked like Confucius. Later, they found that he could not properly respond to their inquiries, so they came to shun him, and demoted him. In other words, as the appellation of "teacher" had already been given to him, he was regarded eventually as a master.' I see that this theory is incorrect. This error derived from the work of Sima Qian 司馬遷 (145?–86 BCE), who collected all of the scandalous stories. Song Zijing 宋子京 (998–1062) and Su Ziyou 蘇子由 (1039–1112) already proved this point.

Mencius said, 'Zi Xia, Zi Zhang, and Zi You 子游 wished to serve Master You in the same way they had served Confucius because Master You resembled Our Master' (*Mengzi jizhu*, 3A:4). On this, Master Zhu explained, 'This remark concerns the similarity of their manners of speaking, acting, and behaving. For example, according to a record in "Tangong 檀弓," Zi You once said that You Ruo's remark was analogous with what Our Master said earlier' (*Mengzi jizhu*, 3:13a). How can this concern their physical resemblance? Mencius stated that Zai Wo 宰我, Zi Gong 子貢, and You Ruo were wise enough to understand the sage. Thus, he must have excelled in the discipline of language [among the four disciplines in Confucius's academy] alongside Zai Wo and Zi Gong. You Ruo's reply [to Duke Ai 哀], 'Why do you, sir, not simply tithe people' (*Lun yu jizhu*, 12:9), and his remark about sages standing out from people of the same kind and inspiring them (*Mengzi jizhu*, 2A:2) appear in the *Analects* and *Mencius*. Three chapters in the first book of the *Analects*—which respectively deal with filial piety, ritual propriety, and trustworthiness and respectfulness—contain You Ruo's remarks on the more essential and significant of his ideas. 'Tangong' includes his criticism of Master Yan's [晏子] ignorance of ritual propriety. *Xunzi* also says, 'Master You disliked falling asleep, so he often burnt his palm' (*Xunzi* 荀子, 15:11a), showing convincingly that he tried hard to study.

Master Zhu mentioned that Master You was earnest and gentle. When the state of Wu 吳 attacked the state of Lu, however, Wei Hu 微虎 wished to assault the barracks of the king of Wu, and Master You joined this assault (*Chunqiu*

---

[31] This passage discusses which one takes precedence between humanity and filial piety. It proves that a theory of giving priority to humanity existed even at that time.

Zuo zhuan zhushu 春秋左傳註疏 *Zuo zhuan zhushu* hereafter, 58:20b). This episode shows that he was courageous in acting in accordance with rightness. Then, he must have been more than merely earnest and gentle. *Jia yu* 家語 praised how he was 'diligent in learning and venerated the ancient Way' (*Kongzi Jia yu* 孔子家語, 9:4a). He was merely a little inferior to those who acquired the Way through dullness [曾子].

Someone asked, 'Are the remarks of Master You that are recorded in "Tangong" credible?' I answered that Wang Wujiu 王无咎 (1024–1069) already spoke about this. [According to "Tangong"] Master You confessed to Zi You that he wished to remove the rite of stamping one's feet in the mourning ritual. He also replied to Duke Ai that it was fine for him to set up a small crane when his son was dead [for the funeral]. These remarks are not acceptable. Only what is recorded in the *Analects* is acceptable" (*Kun xue ji wen* 困學紀聞, 7:9b–11a).

In my view, Master Cheng's explanation cannot be countered.

* * *

Dasan conveys here his simple and concrete views on "humanity"—the utmost virtue of Confucian ethics. Humanity, he believes, literally signifies two people being together because, as many scholars have demonstrated, the Chinese character *ren* 仁, which means humanity, can be broken into two characters, *ren* 人 and *er* 二, meaning "a person" and "two," respectively. Thus, humanity consists of nothing more, or less, than two people fulfilling their moral obligations to one another, thereby preventing any disturbances to their relationship. Just as we can only tell whether people fulfill their moral obligations from the actions they take, humanity does not exist a priori and cannot, strictly speaking, be regarded as an abstraction. Rather, like other virtues, it is realized through action. In contrast to other virtues, however, the name it is given is universal, applicable to all kinds of actual humane deeds. This simple understanding of humanity served a purpose. Through it, Dasan implied that he disfavored, if not abhorred, neo-Confucian efforts to internalize and abstract the virtue of humanity. Such efforts, and the resulting process of complicating the virtue, were liable to make people concerned more with theories than with practices.

This view must have been shared by those of his fellow scholars who had growing apprehensions of the impracticality of neo-Confucian metaphysics. In a retreat attended by thirteen scholars in 1795 to discuss the publication of *Garye jilseo* 家禮疾書 (*Hurriedly Made Essays on the Family Rituals*) of Yi Ik 李瀷 (1681–1763), Oh Guk-jin 吳國鎮 raised a question about the "recent trend" of understanding the four Confucian virtues as innate and intrinsic in human inborn nature: "Such feelings as commiseration and shame derive from the inside. Thus, only when they become expressed outside and applied to actual events can one call them either humanity or rightness" ("Seo-am ganghak gi 西巖講學記," 460a).

After the retreat, Dasan appears to have delved into this issue and eventually shared Oh's views. In a letter sent to the senior scholar in the retreat,

Yi Sam-hwan 李森煥 (1729–1813), Dasan made a similar inquiry: "Humanity, rightness, ritual propriety, and wisdom—these four virtues are accomplished only after they are related to events and things. In contrast, commiseration, and other sentiments in the four beginnings, derive from the inside. Regardless, people insist that the four virtues constitute the substance of human nature. If that were the case, the four beginnings would stem from the four virtues. I don't know how I could understand this" (460a).

Yi's response to this inquiry was somewhat disappointing to Dasan because it was aligned with the neo-Confucian explanation of the four virtues and four beginnings. Nevertheless, in the following passage, Dasan defines his own unique position by critiquing Yi's narrative explanation of the virtues: "In my view, if one realizes the mind-heart of commiseration, it becomes humanity; if one realizes the mind-heart of shame, it becomes rightness; if one realize the mind-heart of deference, it becomes ritual propriety; if one realizes the mind-heart of judgment, it becomes wisdom. Today's arguments that humanity, rightness, ritual propriety, and wisdom reside within the human mind-heart are doubtful" (460a).

Consistency between the foregoing argument, from 1795, and Dasan's commentary from 1813 on this chapter of the *Analects*, quoted earlier, is obvious. In other words, he held a firm stance on the issue of distinguishing the four virtues from the four beginnings throughout his entire scholarly life: the four virtues are accomplished through actions and practices, whereas the four beginnings are natural feelings endowed to human beings.

Gwon Cheol-sin 權哲身 (1736–1801) is also worth mentioning in this regard, given the epitaph Dasan wrote for him in 1801, in which he summarized Gwon's theory on the four beginnings as arguing that "humanity, rightness, ritual propriety, and wisdom are names of values achieved through taking action" ("Nok-am Gwon Cheol-sin myoji myeong 鹿庵權哲身墓誌銘," 334a). Dasan once linked his longer account, given from the same perspective, of the four virtues and four beginnings to "what [he] heard from one of [his] fellow scholars" (*Maengja yo-ui* 孟子要義, 107b). Thus, this understanding seems to have been shared by many liberal scholars in the school of Yi Ik, who are usually regarded as its left wing.

One interesting point in Dasan's discussion regarding this issue is the fact that he disagreed not only with Zhu Xi but also with Mao Qiling 毛奇齡 (1623–1716), who "wanted to blindly oppose the neo-Confucian theories." Rebutting Zhu Xi's theory on internalizing the virtue of humanity, Mao Qiling argued that humanity depended on filial piety and respect for elders and thus humanity could be accomplished only after fulfilling these moral obligations (See his *Lun yu jiqiu pian*, 1:7a–b). What Mao Qiling overlooked, in Dasan's view, was that in human inborn nature there are "principles that enable people to be filial to their parents and compliant with their elders." In other words, Dasan did not deny the existence of principles embedded in mind-heart. This fact may embarrass those readers who believe that Practical Learning solely rejected the Learning of Principle [理學]—that is, neo-Confucianism. To these readers' disappointment, Dasan never repudiated the concept of the existence of moral principles ingrained hereditarily in human nature. I will show, throughout, how profoundly Dasan relied on the notion of principle, when forming inferences, judgments, and conclusions. Indeed, what he rejected was the excessive neo-Confucian "focus" on the innate moral principles, not principle itself. Or, it would be more accurate to say that he refused the neo-Confucian excessiveness because striking a balance across various bifurcations in the Confucian tradition was his means of restoring genuine Confucian teaching.

The name of the great official of Lu—Wei Hu 微虎, in the Sinjo edition of *Noneo gogeum ju*—is given as Wei Hu 衛虎 in the *Established* edition, whereas in *Kun xue ji wen*, his name is spelled, correctly, the same way as it is in *Spring and Autumn*. It is intriguing that Wang Yinglin's long argument here, which Dasan extraordinarily quotes almost in full, is also recorded in *Shi yi lu*, which was written by Hu Kuang 胡燻 (fl. 1427) during the Ming dynasty (see *Shi yi lu* 拾遺錄, 1a–2b). It is also intriguing that Wei Hu's name is spelled in Wang Yinglin's argument the same way as it is in *Noneo gogeum ju*. This may imply that Dasan's direct reference, at least in this case, might have been *Shi yi lu*, not *Kun xue ji wen*, though the latter is one of the frequently cited sources.

1.3 The Master said, "It is rare for a man with artful words and charming countenance to be humane."[32]

子曰; 巧言令色, 鮮矣仁.

1.3.1 Grounds

1) Bao Xian commented, "Being well-spoken and embellishing one's facial expressions are aimed at pleasing people. Few people of this kind can be humane."

1.3.2 Arguments

1) I question Master Zhu as follows:

Having "artful words and a charming countenance" is not a crime. Confucius here notes "it is rare" because sages, in their observations of people, frequently encountered cases in which people with artful words and charming countenances turned out to be inhumane. In *Zuo's Commentary*, however, Shi Kuang 師曠 (572–532 BCE) is depicted as being good at remonstrating, so Shu Xiang 叔向 (d. c. 528 BCE) praised him by quoting a phrase from *Poetry*, "Artful words flow out smoothly like a current" (*Zuo zhuan zhushu*, 44:31b). "Da ya 大雅" also praised Shanfu's 山甫 virtue, singing "[he has] charming manners and a charming countenance" (*Mao Shi*

---

[32] In the Huang Kan edition, one more character, *you* 有, appears between *yi* 矣 and *ren* 仁.

zhushu, 25:79b). Thus, among those who have artful words and charming countenances are good people sometimes. The expression "it is rare" is really adequate. Had Confucius said that "there is no humane person among those people," it would have contradicted the reality.

In another passage Confucius said, "Artful words disrupt virtues" (*Lun yu jizhu*, 15:26). This is about the artfulness of evil words. In contrast, a sentence in "Biao ji 表記" reads: "When forming words, people want to be artful" (*Li ji zhushu*, 54:36b). This is about the artfulness of good words. If artful words can present either a good or an evil, a charming countenance must be more likely to do so. The whole passage under discussion just concerns how to understand one's personality. In this respect, Dazai Jun 太宰純 (1680–1747) proposed that we refer, when reading this passage, to another passage in the *Analects*: "Those who are upright, enduring, wooden, and inarticulate in speech are close to being humane" (*Lun yu jizhu*, 13:27). His proposal sounds excellent.

2) For classical texts that pertain to my argument here, see "Gao Yao mo 皋陶謨" (*Shang Shu zhushu* 尙書註疏, 3:25a, 4);[33] *Lun yu jizhu* 5:24;[34] and "Jiong ming 冏命" compiled by Mei Ze 梅賾 (*Shang Shu zhushu*, 18:21b, 1).

* * *

Here, Dasan again raises questions about Zhu Xi's interpretation. In respect to this passage, Zhu Xi commented, "Confucius just said that 'it is rare' merely because sages' words are usually not harsh. Thus, we know that there is no one humane among those people [with artful words and charming countenances]" (*Lun yu jizhu*, 1:2b). Zhu Xi, here, clearly exemplifies neo-Confucian rigorism, an attitude of repudiating any compromise between moral principles and reality. To Dasan, however, Zhu Xi's rigoristic conclusion itself contradicts reality in its extremity and lack of balance. In reality, Dasan thought artful words and charming countenances could convey morals to any degree. Moreover, in Dasan's eyes, sages were not harsh, as Zhu Xi also admitted. So Confucian scholars should learn from the mindset of the sages, to whom Zhu Xi's remark could not help but sound harsh. Although Dasan accepted that neo-Confucian rigorism played a positive role in purging Han-Tang Confucianism of impurities, he was simultaneously wary of its potential for fundamentalism. In the same manner as in the previous passage, Dasan here attempts to synthesize various lines of Confucian thought by maintaining a balance between ideals and reality, principles and applications, Han-Tang Confucianism and Song neo-Confucianism. Sages spoke and behaved

---

[33] A comment on this passage says, "Artful words means that one is able to address persuasively, but what he addresses is not feasible; charming countenance means that one keeps courteous appearances, but his arrogance has no limit" (*Shang Shu zhushu*, 3:25b).
[34] This saying appears in book 5, "Gongye Chang 公冶長."

in moderation: this was Dasan's understanding of the sages' teachings, which he wanted to restore.

The origin of this reading can be traced back even earlier to Huang Kan, who explained the reason Confucius said that "it is rare," rather than "there is no humane person," in a manner identical to Dasan's. Dasan points out the different wording of the main passage in the Huang Kan edition probably in hope of drawing attention to this fact.

To strengthen his argument, Dasan quotes Dazai Jun here. Dazai Jun's commentary on the *Analects, Rongo kokun gaiden* 論語古訓外傳 (*Outer Explanations of the Ancient Annotations of the* Analects), was Dasan's main, if not only, source for Japanese research on the *Analects*. The fact that Dazai introduces in *Rongo kokun gaiden* the commentaries of his predecessors, including Ogyu Nabematsu 荻生雙松 (1666–1728) and Ito Koreshada 伊藤維禎 (1627–1705), shows that Dasan was able to inquire into the intellectual inclinations of the school of Ancient Learning (古學派) in Tokugawa Japan. Scholars have investigated the relationship between Dasan's reading of the *Analects* and Dazai's commentary on it. They seem to agree that Dasan was excited to learn about the accomplishments of the Japanese scholars that he unexpectedly found in Dazai's *Rongo kokun gaiden*, insofar as Dasan sometimes extolled, approved, and borrowed from their interpretations, but he nevertheless intended to reveal the problems and shortcomings in their works, especially with regard to their "blind attack" on neo-Confucianism. Comparing Dasan's synthetic reading of the *Analects* with Dazai's critical revision of the normative neo-Confucian reading of it will remain one of this book's main points of discussion. The comparison is instrumental in clarifying the defining characteristics of the Joseon Practical Learning—or Joseon Confucianism, to speak more broadly—because Practical Learning and Ancient Learning both aspired to overcome neo-Confucian orthodoxy but in ways that were distinct. The distinction surfaces more clearly where Dasan criticizes Dazai's views on certain issues concerning the *Analects*. It is also worth noting that Dazai quoted, for his comments, the same passages from "Da ya," "Gao Yao mo," and "Jiong ming," that Dasan did.

1.4 Master Zeng said, "Every day I examine myself on three things. In serving others, have I not been wholehearted? In holding relationships with my friends, have I not been trustworthy? Have I not practiced what was transmitted to me?"[35]

曾子曰; 吾日三省吾身, 爲人謀而不忠乎? 與朋友交而不信乎? 傳不習乎?

---

[35] In the Huang Kan edition, the third sentence appears as "In holding relationships with my friends, have my words not been trustworthy?"

1.4.1 Grounds

1) Ma Rong 馬融 (79–166) commented, "Master Zeng refers to Confucius's disciple Zeng Shen 曾參."[36]

2) Master Zhu commented, "Master Zeng, with these three things, examined himself every day." He also explained, "*Chuan* 傳 ('what was transmitted to me') means what I have received from my teachers; *xi* 習 ('practiced') means to master what I have received from my teachers."

1.4.2 Arguments

1) Xing Bing argued, "This passage states that I examine myself three times a day."[37] I would refute this as follows:

   The basis for Xing Bing's reading of this passage is a line from *Record of Rites*: "King Wen 文 had an audience with Wang Ji 王季 three times a day" (*Li ji zhushu*, 20:1a). However, there are also cases in which it was used differently, as in: "The Master taught under four categories" (*Lun yu jizhu*, 7:24), or "[The parents of the people] accomplish the five upmost things and carry out three formless things."[38] Why can't the character *san*, located at the beginning of a sentence, signify 'kinds of things'?

2) He Yan argued, "This passage asks one to reflect on whether there wasn't anything, among things that one has transmitted, which was transmitted to others without having engaged in one's regular studies or practices."[39] Mao Qiling said, "*Chuan* means transmitting one's works. 'Rulin zhuan 儒林傳' in *Han shu* 漢書 records: 'The number of people who transmitted their works was growing' (*Qian Han shu* 前漢書, 88:34a); *Hou Han shu* also records: the family of Zhen Yu 甄宇 (fl. 25–56) 'transmitted their works' through three generations (*Hou Han shu*, 109-B:13a). *Shou* 受 ('to receive') means receiving another's works. *Hou Han shu* records: Bao Ziliang 包子良 [包咸] 'received lessons at Chang'an 長安' (109-B:2a); Du Fu 杜撫 (fl. 76–84) 'received lessons from Xue Han 薛漢 (fl. 70)' (109-B:5b). Therefore, *chuan* in the saying 'What should be prioritized to transmit [傳]' (*Lun yu jizhu*, 19:12) means to transmit to others. *Chuan* in the passage in 'Qu li

---

[36] According to *Shi ji*, "Zeng Shen, whose adult name was Zi Yu 子輿, was from Nanwu cheng 南武城 and [was] forty-six years younger than Confucius" (*Shi ji*, 67:17a).

[37] Ito Koreshada said, "In general, if the character *san* 三 ('three') appears at the beginning of a sentence [as in this passage], it means 'three times.' Here are a few examples: '[Nan Rong 南容] recited the poem Bai gui 白圭 three times a day' (*Lun yu jizhu*, 11:5); '[Tai Bo 泰伯] yielded all under heaven three times to his younger brother' (8:1). If the character appears at the end of a sentence, it signifies three things. Examples include: 'There are three things that the noble person cherishes in pursuing the Way' (8:4); 'There are three things that the noble person sees should be practiced in pursing the Way'" (14:30). Dazai Jun said, "Master Zhu ['Zhu Xi' in the Dazai's original writing], on seeing that what Master Zeng examined himself on came down arbitrarily to three things, eventually stated that Master Zeng, with these three things, examined himself every day."

[38] See "Kongzi xian ju 孔子閒居" (*Li ji zhushu*, 51:1a).

[39] Xing Bing also read this passage as saying, "Among things that one has transmitted to others, wasn't there anything that was recklessly transmitted to others without one's regular studies and practices?" He continued, "In regard to transmitting things to others, arbitrary distortion should be prevented, so Master Zeng elicited people's attention to it."

曲禮,' which reads: 'People at the age of seventy are called the old, and they transmitted their works to others [傳]' also means to transmit to others. In general, if the character *chuan* is used alone, it is equivalent to *shou* 授 (to give)" (*Sishu gai cuo* 四書改錯, 15:10a–b). I would refute this as follows:

The phrase "not practicing what was transmitted to me" suggests that one, while learning, does not practice what one has learned. The character *chuan* can be used broadly to mean both "receiving" and "giving." Regardless, Xiaoshan insisted that it is not proper to use *chuan* in cases in which one receives instructions from teachers. How shallow this understanding is! How could a person transmit things that he has not practiced to others? It is beyond principle to assume that one can transmit things without practicing them.

3) I question Master Zhu as follows:

Changes says, "All day long, a noble person ceaselessly endeavors. At night, he becomes pensive as if caught up in worries. Then, he is not at fault if mishaps occur" (*Zhou Yi zhushu*, 1:5a). The second sentence in this passage "At night, he becomes pensive as if caught up in worries" conveys the best method for sages to self-reflect. In contrast, Master Zhu said, "Examining oneself on three things is not the business of sages. When Master Zeng tried to refine his virtues in his later years, in no ways were those lagging vestiges still in his mind-heart" (*Lun yu jizhu daquan* 論語集注大全, 1:16b–17a). However, even King Tang 湯 remonstrated with himself with six things. Did Tang's remonstration occur because such vestiges remained in his mind-heart? Sages never stop reflecting on themselves.

* * *

In this passage, Dasan accepts Zhu Xi's interpretation of the characters *san* ("three things") and *chuan* ("to transmit"), while rejecting annotations by He Yan, Xing Bing, Ito Koreshada (1627–1705), and Mao Qiling, representative figures of the old commentaries on the *Analects*, the Ancient Learning of Tokugawa Japan, and the Qing Evidential Studies. Considering that he criticized Zhu Xi's interpretations in the previous chapters, this fact shows explicitly how Dasan, in deliberating on which interpretations to adopt as his own, was predisposed against nobody. As I will show, he delved into a vast range of sources with the sole purpose of garnering the most plausible readings of the given passages. They might originate from Zhu Xi, or from Mao Qiling, who "blindly opposed neo-Confucianism," as Dasan put it, or from the Japanese scholars, who could not grasp the quintessence of neo-Confucianism in Dasan's assessment, or even from Daoist theorists. This should not suggest, however, that Dasan lacked consistent criteria in endorsing certain views, since he allowed for such freedom of discretion only when they were amenable to his sense of reason. For example, when he concluded a discussion of the meaning of *chuan*, he made it clear that he did not accept another interpretation because it was "beyond principle [理]." Dasan relied heavily on *li* 理, a notion that most closely corresponds with the English terms "reason" or "principle," and makes reference to it throughout

Noneo gogeum ju in making selections, judgments, and conclusions. Though it is conventional to identify Dasan's philosophical and sociopolitical ideas with the Practical Learning, the frequency with which the neo-Confucian concept *li* appears in his writings invites a redefinition of his ideas in terms of the "Learning of Principle," one of the appellations of neo-Confucianism. Of course, his "Learning of Principle" distinguishes itself from neo-Confucianism, as it encompasses not only moral principles but also principles of nature, sciences, practical human relationships, and sociopolitical structures without assuming the sense of imbalance that is often observed in neo-Confucian discourses. Thus, in the introduction, I suggested that Dasan's philosophy be termed Learning of Practical Principle [實理學], a term that points to the synthesis of the Practical Learning [實學] and the Learning of Principle [理學]. *Noneo gogeum ju* offers many opportunities to return to this key point.

Dasan reveals his respect for Zhu Xi again by correcting Dazai Jun, after quoting him, for audaciously calling the Master by his personal name. Dasan must have felt that the Japanese scholar's attitude toward "Zhu Xi" and "Mr. Cheng" (disrespectful to the extent that Dazai ridiculed Zhu Xi's apparent ignorance of the ancient usage of the character *san*) was possibly blasphemous, at least to Joseon society.

Though Dasan accepted Zhu Xi's gloss on the Chinese characters under discussion, he also raised an important question about Zhu Xi's understanding of what constituted the nature of a Confucian sage. According to Zhu Xi, since sages are flawless, they have no need really to examine themselves. According to Dasan, sages become flawless by examining themselves every day. Dasan's view seems to me more compatible with the way Confucius depicted himself—as a man of learning, and not laureled as a man of humanity, unless it be as a sage. Indeed, it is Dasan's pervasive effort to restore genuine Confucianism by refusing any extremes and imbalances.

1.5 The Master said, "In guiding a state of one thousand chariots, be prudent in dealing with affairs so as to prove trustworthy; be moderate in expenditures and love men; call the people to work at the proper times."

子曰; 道千乘之國, 敬事而信, 節用而愛人, 使民以時.

1.5.1 Grounds

1) I supplement as follows: *Dao* 道 means to guide. Sage kings in ancient times shepherded all under heaven by guiding them to do good. Thus the act of ruling is rendered as guiding.[40]

2) Bao Xian commented, "A state of one thousand chariots is a state having an area of one hundred square *li*s. In the well-field system of ancient times, an

---

[40] The same use of this character is evident in the phrase "If one guides the people with virtues" (*Lun yu jizhu*, 2:3).

area of one square *li* constituted a well-unit of the system, and ten of these units together allowed for one chariot. So a state having an area of one hundred square *li*s could accommodate one thousand chariots."

3) I supplement as follows: *Jing shi* 敬事 ("being prudent in dealing with affairs") refers to setting the state's affairs in motion only after giving beginning and end due consideration and heeding potential evil consequences. This way, there would be no disturbances, and the people thereby would place full trust in the ruler.[41]

4) Dazai Jun commented, "*Jie* 節 ('be moderate') means to have limits, as in the way bamboos have nodes. They cannot be transgressed."

5) Yang Shi 楊時 (1053–1135) commented, "A passage in *Changes* reads: 'Be moderate with institutions and systems so as not to bring damage to resources and harm to the people' (*Zhou Yi zhushu*, 10:9a). In general, being extravagant in expenditures leads to bringing damage to resources, and bringing damage to resources must lead to harming the people. Therefore being moderate in expenditures is a prerequisite for loving men" (*Lun yu jizhu daquan*, 1:20a–b).

6) Bao Xian commented, "This passage teaches that when calling the people to work, one should not disrupt their farming."[42]

1.5.2 Arguments

1) Ma Rong argued, "*Dao* means to implement policies and education." Bao Xian also argued, "*Dao* means to rule." I would refute these claims.

2) Ma Rong argued, "According to *Sima fa* 司馬法 … [A] state of one thousand chariots has an area of more than 316 square *li*s, which only land enfeoffed to earls or viscounts can amount to. Even large states cannot secure a military asset larger than this." In this regard, He Yan argued, "Ma Rong made reference to *Zhou li* 周禮, and Bao Xian made reference to 'Wang zhi' and *Mencius*. As the meaning is not clear, I introduce both theories."

3) I question Master Zhu as follows:

Each of the three parts that make up the sentence in the main passage constitutes one affair. Early Confucians often assumed that this passage contains five affairs. I am afraid that it is not so.

* * *

---

[41] Consider an analogous passage from "Zi yi 緇衣," which says, "The noble person, when talking, should consider the consequences of his words and, when taking action, think of the interruptions his actions might cause. That way, the people will become responsible for their words" (*Li ji zhushu*, 55:7a).
[42] Xing Bing commented, "*Zuo's Commentary* says, 'In regard to public construction, when the Dragon Star appears [in February, according to the Zhou calendar], a plan should be announced, as the people's farm work comes to a close around that time; when the Great Fire Star appears at dawn [in November, according to the Zhou calendar], construction materials should be prepared; when Mercury appears high up in the sky at twilight [in December, according to the Zhou calendar], pillars should be erected; and at winter solstice [in January, according to the Zhou calendar] construction should be finished" (*Zuo zhuan zhushu*, 9:25a). "Wang zhi" also says, "The people's labor cannot be utilized for public construction for more than three days a year" (*Li ji zhushu*, 12:35b).

One of the lengthiest annotations in *Lun yu jijie* 論語集解 concerns the size and institution of the state of one thousand chariots, in which the editor, He Yan, introduces the theories of both Ma Rong and Bao Xian. Huang Kan and Xing Bing also devoted many lines in *Lun yu yishu* 論語義疏 and *Lun yu zhengyi* 論語正義, respectively, to discussions on this topic. According to Huang Kan, Ma's theories delineated the system of the Zhou dynasty and was based on *Sima fa* by Sima Rangju 司馬穰苴 (c. 548–490 BCE). In contrast, Bao Xian's theories stemmed from the Xia-Shang dynasties (Huang Kan) or the *Mencius* (Xing Bing). Zheng Xuan, a student of and successor to Ma Rong, implemented Ma's theories with more references to *Poetry* and *Spring and Autumn*. In short, this was an important subject among most of the renowned commentators of the *Analects* before the emergence of neo-Confucianism. Scholars of the Han Learning, as this academic trend was called, strove to extract precise meanings from key terms in the Confucian classics, believing that in doing so they would clarify the teachings of Confucius.

However, Zhu Xi scoffed, subtly, at this trend, saying, "In relation to this subject, it is sufficient to grasp a general outline of the ancient system. It is not necessary to delve into its details with great effort" (*Lun yu jizhu daquan*, 1:19a). To Zhu Xi, a meticulous investigation of the system appeared inessential, especially when compared with the right-minded endeavor to understand the moral principles embedded in the teachings of the Confucian classics. Dasan, in this matter, again proved a negotiator, in that he made use of Ma Rong's and Bao Xian's theories without belaboring all of the details.

Finally, his question about the number of affairs discussed in this chapter was primarily directed toward Zhu Xi and like all other questions was prefaced with the recurrent term *jil-ui* ("I question Master Zhu as follows"). However, since Huang Kan and Xing Bing understood this chapter in the same way Zhu Xi did, Dasan here lumps them together as "early Confucians."

1.6 The Master said, "A young person should be filial at home and show respect for elders in the community, be prudent and trustworthy, and care for the public in moderation but keep close to humane people. If he, after practicing these, is still capable of doing more, he should study literature."

子曰; 弟子入則孝, 出則弟, 謹而信, 汎愛衆, 而親仁, 行有餘力, 則以學文.

1.6.1 Grounds

1) Master Zhu commented, "*Qin* 謹 ('prudent') means having consistency in action; *xin* 信 ('trustworthy') means making one's speech substantial."

2) I supplement as follows: *Fan* 汎 ("in moderation") means not adhering to a specific thing;[43] *qin* 親 ("keep close to") means to cleave tightly to.

3) Ma Rong commented, "*Wen* 文 ('literature') refers to the literature transmitted from ancient times."[44]

1.6.2 Arguments

1) Dazai Jun argued, "*Qin* is related to one's diction, and *shen* 慎 (discretion) to one's mind-heart. The phrase 'be prudent and trustworthy' teaches that one should be cautious when talking." I would refute this as follows:

    Changes says, "Be prudent in your everyday behavior, and be trustworthy in your everyday speech" (*Zhou Yi zhushu*, 1:19a). Thus Master Zhu's comment should not be rejected.

2) Lu Deming 陸德明 (556–627) argued that *xing* 行 ("practicing") should be read as *hang* 行, meaning one's demeanor. I would refute this as follows:

    This passage recommends that one learn literature, when one is capable of doing more after practicing the five preceding items. *Xing* should be read in the level tone [平聲].

3) Mao Qiling argued, "According to Yao Lifang 姚立方 (1647–1715), '*Wen* does not refer to literary works on the six arts such as *Poetry* and *Documents*. It is simply related to efforts to encourage young people to study characters when they have leisure time.' *Shuo wen* says, '*Wen* is a combination of drawings.' Also *Zhou li* says, 'When the children of the royal family enter the lesser academy at the age of eight, the masters only teach them with the six categories of Chinese characters to master characters' " (*Si shu shengyan*, 1:18a). I would refute this as follows:

    The phrase "show respect for elders in the community" implies that one should serve one's seniors and superiors in the community. This is not the kind of business an eight-year-old child can undertake. The business of "[caring] for the public in moderation" is pretty much the same. How can such tasks be pertinent to the days when one is still learning characters? We should follow the old interpretation.

4) I question Master Zhu as follows:

    There are no grounds, in old commentaries, for rendering *fan* as "broadly" [as in *Lun yu jizhu*]. Also, broadly caring for the public is not something a young person can do. Confucius here teaches that one should care for the public in moderation; as for humane people, one should keep passionately[45]

---

[43] According to *Shou wen*, *fan* means being afloat (*Shuo wen jie zi*, 11-A:10a). It is to drift about at the mercy of the waves.

[44] Xing Bing commented, "It implies the six classics: *Poetry, Documents, Rites, Music, Changes*, and *Spring and Autumn*."

[45] Dazai Jun said, "Moderately caring for the public is a matter that concerns moral virtues in general. Keeping close to humane people is an effort to benefit from being guided by them."

close to them so that he does not stop at just broadly caring for them or protecting them in a broad sense.

5) In my view, although Confucius prioritizes practices over literature here, all five of the items mentioned in this chapter are lessons whose goal can be accomplished through diligent endeavor. One must have gathered energy to spare while practicing them. If one studies literature whenever one has energy to spare, his knowledge of literature cannot be exhausted. However, early Confucians, on the basis of this chapter, often excessively disdained literature and the arts. That was inconsistent with Confucius's original intentions. Therefore, Master Zhu deeply warned against doing so.

* * *

Rendering *fan* as "in moderation" had no precedent before Dasan. Though Dasan's questions regarding this allude to Zhu Xi's annotation, in this case Zhu Xi simply represents all of the commentators before Dasan. Dasan did not reveal the reason why he bothered to offer a new interpretation of this one word, but it would not be unreasonable to relate it to the Mohist concepts that the word connotes according to the traditional reading of this passage. In most English translations the phrase in question, "care for the public in moderation" in my translation, appears as "love all the multitude" or "love all people." Obviously, this reading evokes the Mohist concept of "universal love" or "love for all." If readers are cognizant of how fiercely Mencius tried to protect the Confucian manner of loving others—that is, "concentric love"—from the encroachment of this Mohist concept, they may wonder how this passage in the *Analects* can be reconciled with Mencius's ideas. With a new rendition of a key word in the passage, Dasan attempted to resolve a problem that commentators have not clearly addressed, probably due to the impediment that the specter of Confucius's authority posed to independent reasoning.

The fact that Dasan here is attentive to the value of learning literature cannot be overlooked, either, given that rigorist Joseon Confucians usually belittled the learning of literature and the arts in light of the significance of moral practices. Indeed, in the history of the Joseon dynasty, the court's administrative need to have officials talented in literature, who could help make administrative and diplomatic documents, was often ignored by those recalcitrant Confucians who wanted the calling for moral deeds to take precedence over the technical necessity. Accordingly, the dynasty experienced a recurring and hostile debate between prostate and proscholarship Confucians surrounding this issue. Dasan responded to this debate with a sense of moderation, on the one hand admitting that "Confucius prioritized practices over literature" and on the other hand criticizing how Confucians "often excessively disdained literatures and the arts." To make his argument more convincing, Dasan incorporated Zhu Xi's warning against inclining excessively toward moral practices over the learning of literature, which, in this regard, he implicitly compared to Wang Yangming's 王陽明 (1472–1529) focus on practices.

1.7 Zi Xia said, "A man who values worthies and thereby puts worthies in the place of beauties, who gives his very best in serving his parents, who offers his person in serving his lord, who is trustworthy in speech when holding relationships with his friends—even if he lacks formal learning, I would call him learned."

子夏曰; 賢賢易色, 事父母, 能竭其力, 事君, 能致其身, 與朋友交, 言而有信. 雖曰未學, 吾必謂之學矣.

1.7.1 Grounds

1) Kong Anguo 孔安國 (fl. 156–74 BCE) commented, "Zi Xia refers to Confucius's disciple Bu Shang 卜商."[46]

2) Kong Anguo commented, "This passage states that it is excellent for a man to cherish worthies in the same manner he cherished beauties."

3) I supplement as follows: *Zhi shen* 致身 ("offers his person") means devoting one's body to one's lord and thus not possessing it privately.

4) Master Zhu commented, "One's only possible pursuit in learning is to reach this stage. If there is anyone able to do as described above, he must have reached this stage through the utmost endeavor for learning, or otherwise through the beauty of endowed nature."

1.7.2 Arguments

1) In my view, this chapter should be read in connection with the chapter of "Learning extensively."[47]

2) For a classical text on the discussion here, see "Li Xun zhuan 李尋傳," in *Han shu*, which says, "In following the way of Heaven, sages valued worthies and thereby put worthies in the place of beauties" (*Qian Han shu*, 75:26a).[48] On this passage Yan Shigu 顏師古 (581–645) commented, "Revere and respect worthies, and attach little importance [易] to beauties."[49] I would refute this [Yan's comment] as follows:

   Yi se 易色 ("puts worthies in the place of beauties") simply means putting worthies in place of beauties.[50]

3) Huang Kan argued, "If you want to show your respect for worthies, you should change your mien and develop a demeanor of courtesy and reverence."[51] I would refute this as follows:

---

[46] According to *Shi ji*, Bu Shang was from the state of Wei 衛 and forty-four years younger than Confucius (*Shi ji*, 67:15a).

[47] See book 19, "Zi Zhang" (19.6).

[48] In a discussion on the heavenly images, it also says, "Shaowei 少微 [a star for scholars] is located in the foreground, and Nügung 女宮 [a star for court ladies] is located in the background. The teaching that one should value worthies and thereby put worthies in the place of beauties stems from this celestial image" (quoted in *Lun yu jiqiu pian*, 1:10a).

[49] Yan believed that *yi* 易 has the same meaning it has in *jianyi* 簡易.

[50] It would be redundant to read *yi se* instead as "replacing the mind-heart of cherishing beauties with the mind-heart of cherishing worthies." [This is a criticism of Dazai Jun's annotation.]

[51] Yichuan 伊川 also said, "On encountering worthies, one should change one's facial expressions" (*Lun yu jizhu daquan*, 1:24a).

Master Zhu said, "Confucius twice mentioned that he never saw a person who cherished the man of virtue in the same manner as he cherished beauties. *Constant Mean* also regards keeping away from beauties as one of the ways to support worthies. So, the meaning of *yi se* has already been clarified. And changing one's mien is quite an act of pretense, which is inferior to changing the mind-heart of cherishing beauties in showing one's sincerity" (*Lun yu jizhu daquan*, 1:24a).[52] Xu Fenpeng 徐奮鵬 (c. 1560–1642) also said, "Cherishing beauties belongs to human-mind [人心], whereas cherishing worthies to Dao-mind [道心]. Human-mind is presented all the time, but Dao-mind is usually met with languid responses. If one puts worthies in the place of beauties, it would be equal to transforming human-mind to something useful for Dao-mind" (Unknown source).

4) Xing Bing argued, "This passage discusses the affairs of those who have inborn knowledge and are innately able to do beautiful deeds." I would refute this as follows:

By and large, Zi Xia must have intended to say that the purpose of learning is no more than to reach this stage. How can one regard this passage as about sages with inborn knowledge? "Putting worthies in the place of beauties" implies being diligent in valuing worthies; "giving one's best" implies being diligent in loving parents; "offering one's person" implies being diligent in revering superiors; "being trustworthy in speech" implies being diligent in one's relationships with friends. These four things are all about diligence. Through learning, one can pursue nothing more than this.

5) Wu Yu 吳棫 (c. 1100–1154) argued, "Whenever Zi Xia addressed a concern, his way of placing stresses on words was quite excessive." I would refute this as follows:

Even Confucius said, "If Guan Zhong knew ritual propriety, who does not know it?" (*Lun yu jizhu*, 3:23) In one's speech, it is inevitable to place some stresses on words.

* * *

Dasan's suggestion that this passage should be read in connection with a passage on extensive learning in "Zi Zhang" appears twice in "Overview of the Original Meanings" (in the second and the 166th sections)—the only case of such repetition in "Overview." This appears indicative of the special attention Dasan paid to complementing each passage with the other, whose focuses are distinct but whose speaker is the same "sage," Zi Xia. As confirmed by Zhu Xi, the passage seen here in "To Learn" aims at demonstrating the priority of practices over learning. In contrast, the passage in "Zi Zhang" highlights the

---

[52] *Xushi bijing* argues, "*Se* refers to courteous demeanors. *Se* in another passage [*Lun yu jizhu*, 14:37], 'Those next in worth withdraw because of their courteous demeanors [*se*],' also relates that the courteous demeanors have diminished" (*Xushi bijing* 徐氏筆精, 2:12b). This understanding, however, is also incorrect.

need for learning and inquiry: "Learn extensively and retain your purposes firmly; inquire carefully and reflect on what is near—humanity lies in this" (*Lun yu jizhu*, 19:6).

Indeed, throughout the entire Confucian tradition of religious and philosophical discourse on universality, it has been a challenging question how to reconcile learning with practices (two reciprocally supplementary but hardly coexistent values) within a substantially limited scope of activities. In the history of Confucianism, most of the sages regarded as representing the orthodox side of Confucianism, such as Yan Yuan 顏淵 and Zeng Shen, are frequently linked to practices, but the necessity of learning, mainly proclaimed by Xunzi, has never been relegated to insignificance. Among the neo-Confucians, Zhu Xi is widely viewed as promoting learning over practices, whereas Wang Yangming undoubtedly conferred supreme authority on practices with his theory of the unity of practices and knowledge. Thus, Dasan's attempt to integrate the two passages from Zi Xia into a single lesson—whose substantial teaching is that "one who knows must practice, and one who practices must know"—exemplifies the synthetic aspect of his interpretation of the *Analects* and of his Confucian teachings, broadly speaking, as I will repeatedly point out.

With regard to Dasan's aforementioned endeavor, however, Dazai Jun's criticism of the neo-Confucian emphasis on learning or knowledge also deserves discussion. Partly privileged by changes in intellectual trends during the late Tokugawa period, Dazai unleashed excoriation on Cheng-Zhu neo-Confucian thought as in what follows: "Learning aims at practicing what one has learned. If one does not practice while learning, it is the same as not learning.... [W]u Yu's annotation on this passage can be called deranged.... [I]n the case of the Cheng brothers, they fancied themselves disciples of Confucius, but what they studied was the way of Buddha."

Part of Wu Yu's comment, rejected by Dazai here, was also quoted by Dasan, as seen here. Put briefly, Wu Yu considered Zi Xia's emphasis on practices quite excessive—a view taken by Zhu Xi as well—while Dazai and Dasan were on the same page in countering Wu Yu. Though Dasan definitely did not accept Dazai's disrespectful assault on Cheng-Zhu neo-Confucianism, he agreed somewhat with Dazai on the degree of stress to be laid on practices. Thus, Dasan's synthetic interpretation can be deemed a result of his efforts to balance not only Zhu Xi with Wang Yangming but also Zhu Xi's neo-Confucianism with anti-Zhu Xi intellectual challenges made in Tokugawa Japan. This is one of the more incisive characteristics of Dasan's thought.

It is also worth noting that Dasan here denies the association Xing Bing draws between this passage and sages who supposedly possess inborn knowledge, which is in line with Dasan's general attitude toward any kind of a priori virtue: he persistently claimed that all virtues, including that of having knowledge, could only be accomplished through moral deeds in one's community. He might agree that in order to understand the ancient sages' teachings, one has to read and learn. In this regard, readers can refer to Dasan's explanation of a passage in which Confucius himself rejects the notion that he is a sage with inborn knowledge (see 7.20). Dasan consistently proved himself a rationalist, notwithstanding what "rationality" meant to him. His "rational" and restrained understanding of the literal meaning of the Chinese characters under discussion enabled him to suggest a new translation of *yi se*—"to put worthies in the place of beauties."

Finally, Dasan introduces Xu Fenpeng's view of human-mind and Dao-mind, however out of context it may seem, because it epitomizes at least a part of Dasan's theory on the same topic. (For more explanations, see 2.4.)

1.8 The Master said, "A noble person who lacks gravity does not inspire awe, and even his learning will remain unstable. Take as your mainstay being wholehearted and trustworthy, and do not befriend those not as good as you. When you have faults, do not be reluctant to correct them."

子曰; 君子不重則不威, 學則不固. 主忠信, 無友不如己者, 過則勿憚改.

1.8.1 Grounds

1) He Yan commented, "If a person is incapable of being solemn and grave, he will naturally inspire no awe and dignity, and even his learning will not be solid and stable."

2) I supplement as follows: *Zhu* 主 ("take as your mainstay") is opposed to *bin* 賓 (guests), which should be read as appears in the saying "People's sons do not take the southwest corner as their main place to stay [*zhu*] at home."[53] This explains that when one grounds one's thinking and acts according to one's principles, one should take being wholehearted and trustworthy as the mainstay.

3) Master Zhu commented, "No benefits, but only harm could come out of befriending those not as good as you are."

4) Zheng Xuan commented, "*Dan* 憚 ('be reluctant') means 'to take on with difficulty.'"

1.8.2 Arguments

1) Kong Anguo [who read this chapter as saying, "A noble person who lacks gravity does not inspire awe, but if he learns he will not be benighted."] argued, "*Gu* 固 ('unstable') corresponds to *bi* 蔽 (benighted)."[54] I would refute this as follows:

In this passage, "[A noble person who] lacks gravity" cannot be paired with "learning."

---

[53] See "Qu li" (*Li ji zhushu*, 1:24b).

[54] Xing Bing argued, "This sentence asserts that if one extensively hears of teachings and tries hard to remember them, he will not [be] out of touch with the times and benighted."

2) Huang Kan argued, "According to Kong Anguo, *gu* corresponds to *bi*. And *bi* is synonymous with *dang* 當 (to fit). Thus this sentence explains that if one is incapable of being solemn and grave, one cannot meet the moral principles even when he learns." I would refute this as follows:

Huang translated *gu* as *bi*, and then *bi* as *dang*. Besides, he redundantly added the term "moral principles" to this sentence. How deeply devious!

3) Zheng Xuan argued, "*Zhu* means 'to keep close to.'"[55] I would refute this as follows:

When Confucius went to the state of Wei, he kept close to [*zhu*] Yan Chouyou 顏讐由 and Qu Boyu 蘧伯玉. When he went to the state of Chen, he kept close to the Citadel Overseer Zhenzi 貞子. These records must be what Zheng Xuan based his judgment on. In his discussion, however, he shifts abruptly to an examination of the behavior appropriate for a guest in the midst of discussing self-cultivation. I am afraid that this is not acceptable. *Zhu* here means "to abide by" or "to take something as the main principle."

4) I question Master Zhu as follows [because Zhu Xi rendered *dan* as "be afraid of"]:

According to *Shuo wen, dan* corresponds to *ji* 忌 (to shun) or *nan* 難 (to take on with difficult). When it is said that Ji An 汲黯 (d. 112 BCE) was shunned [*dan*] due to his strictness, *dan* also carries the meaning of "to shun" or "to take on with difficulty." It by no means implies that Emperor Wu 武 was afraid of seeing Ji An. Also on the matter of correcting one's faults, what should we be afraid of? If a person becomes reluctant to correct his faults, it means that there exists hesitance in his sentiment. Thus *Documents* says, "In correcting your faults, do not be hesitant" (*Shang Shu zhushu*, 7:11a).[56]

5) I question Master Zhu as follows:

Mao Qiling said, "In this passage, the first sentence ending with 'will remain unstable' actually constitutes one separate remark, and the rest constitute another remark. The second saying originally belonged to 'Zi Han 子罕' but was [mistakenly] recorded again here. Zhu Xi already commented that it appeared twice, but the comment appears in the book 'Zi Han,' not here. Consequently, he caused the two originally separate sayings to be concatenated with each other disproportionately and awkwardly" (*Lun yu jiqiu pian*, 1:10b–11a). In my view, Mao's argument is compatible with principle.[57]

* * *

---

[55] Xing Bing argued, "In general, the people I keep close to should be those who strive to do their best and to be trustworthy."

[56] Xu Xuanhu 徐玄扈 (1562–1633) also said, "The reason that one's faults grow every day is that there exists a slight feeling of reluctance" (Unknown source).

[57] Su Zixi 蘇紫溪 (1542–1599) said, "Having gravity is like securing farmland; doing one's best and being trustworthy are like planting seeds; having friends is like growing them; correcting one's faults is like a harvest" (Unknown source). He tried to link all of the sentences in this passage to form them into one passage as well.

Dasan attributed the first comment in "Grounds" to He Yan, who actually attributed it to an anonymous commentator with the opening "One says that [一曰]" when introducing the comment in his *Lun yu jijie*. It became somewhat conventional to attribute to He Yan all of the comments that follow that opening in *Lun yu jijie*, He Yan's compilation of ancient commentaries, since Xing Bing had explained, in his *Lun yu zhengyi*, that these comments primarily convey He Yan's interpretations of the ancient commentaries (see his annotation on this passage in *Lun yu zhengyi*). Of course, modern skeptics may not concur with this practice. If Xing Bing's view is correct, He Yan might have used the opening "One says that" when presenting his own interpretations, in order to show deference to the ancient commentators. Huang Kan, who preceded Xing Bing, was not likely aware of this implicit intention and formed a few tenuous judgments on the originality of the "anonymous comments." He conjectured, in relation to this passage, that the comment under discussion might have come from Kong Anguo, not He Yan. This reveals that Dasan did not accept Huang Kan's judgment on the originality of the comment and followed Xing Bing's general understanding of the opening in *Lun yu jijie*.

As a matter of fact, Dasan's disfavor toward Huang Kan's comments is quite perceptible in *Noneo gogeum ju*. They appear more frequently as targets of Dasan's philosophical and exegetical attacks than as bases for his investigation on the "original meanings." Even in this chapter, Dasan criticizes Huang Kan's comment, as is evident in the second argument. Ironically, however, Huang Kan's understanding of the first sentence is identical to that of Dasan. Although it is true that "Huang translated *gu* as *bi*, and then *bi* as *dang*," Huang Kan, in doing so, sought greater consistency between the two comments by Kong Anguo, which Huang thus filtered through his perspective when he introduced them in his *Lun yu yishu*. Dasan's open criticism of Huang's view here manifests his disfavor for Huang Kan and further suggests that the scholarship of the Liang dynasty (502–557), Huang's era, was not palatable to Dasan.

The place of Mao Qiling, a devoted attacker of Zhu Xi, in *Noneo gogeum ju* resembles that of Huang Kan. In short, Dasan did not fully respect them. This should not be seen, however, as revealing that Dasan intended to exclude their comments from the sphere of correct understanding of the *Analects*. As seen in the second question to Zhu Xi, Dasan agreed with Mao Qiling, implicitly denouncing Zhu Xi's scholarship because Mao's view, in this case, looked more "compatible with principle" to him. A recurrent pattern is discernable in Dasan's book in which he conclusively endorses a specific comment after weighing which one sounds more "compatible with principle" or "reasonable," sometimes providing no explanation for why it is so. One of my tasks in this book is to define what Dasan's principle, reasonability, or rationality, consisted of.

1.9 Master Zeng said, "Be careful about matters concerning parents' end and be present at your parents' departure, and people will incline toward richness in virtue."

曾子曰; 愼終追遠, 民德歸厚矣.

1.9.1 Grounds

1) I supplement as follows: *Zhong* 終 ("end") means one's parents' last moments; *yuan* 遠 ("departure") means one's parents' fading-out; *shen* 愼 ("be careful") means preventing errors from happening and pertains to mourning rituals; *zhui* 追 ("be present") means to act as though one reaches out to one's parents and thus pertains to sacrificial rituals. This passage states that if people are able to do these things, their virtues will attain richness.

1.9.2 Arguments

1) Kong Anguo argued, "*Shen zhong* 愼終 ('Be careful about matters concerning your parents' end') is to be in deep grief during mourning rituals; *zhui yuan* 追遠 ('be present at your parents' departure') is to hold a great respect at sacrifice rituals."[58] I would refute this as follows:

Zi Si 子思 said, "In mourning rituals, the dead is put in a coffin on the third day after death. At this moment, everything that is to be placed on the dead should be prepared with sincerity and earnestness, so that there shall be no regret later. In the third month after death, the dead is interred. At this moment, everything that is to be placed into the coffin should be prepared with sincerity and earnestness, so that there shall be no regret later."[59] This is what "Be careful about matters concerning your parents' end" means. Though expressing one's grief by wailing and weeping also belongs to the final matters of serving one's parents, it is not all about *shen zhong*. Because of this, Master Zhu replaced the character *ai* 哀 ("grief") in Kong's comment with *li* 禮 ("ritual propriety"). [With regard to these rituals] can a person not be careful when he cannot redo what he might regret later? Can a person not be present if his parents depart all of a sudden?

2) Kong Anguo argued, "If a lord carries out these two things, the people will be influenced by him and their virtues will attain richness." I would refute this as follows:

Min 民 ("people") is synonymous with *ren* 人 (human), as seen in the following remarks: "Only a few people [民] could practice it for a long time

---

[58] Master Zhu said, "*Shen zhong* means to fulfill ritual propriety at mourning rituals; *zhui yuan* means to possess a great sincerity at sacrifice rituals."
[59] See "Tangong" (*Li ji zhushu*, 6:11a–b).

[in Dasan's reading]" (*Zhong yong zhangju*, 3b). "No people [民] are not good" (*Mao Shi zhushu*, 19:61b). How can only the commoners and the ignoble be designated by *min*? The rituals of mourning and sacrifice encompass the upper and lower classes. Thus it is unnecessary to interpret this passage in light of the people's observation of rituals and the lord's influence.

3) Huang Kan argued, "*Poetry* says, 'There is nothing that has no beginning, but it is rare to have an [good] end' (*Mao Shi zhushu*, 25:2a). So one should be careful about matters concerning the end. Maintain a memory of past occasions that faded away long ago by recording them—this is what *zhui yuan* means." I would refute this as follows:

Record of Rites says, "The noble person, when talking, should be considerate of what effects his words may have and, when taking action, thoughtful of what his actions might interrupt, and the people will become attentive to their words and prudent in their actions" (*Li ji zhushu*, 55:7b–8a). Huang's argument about *shen zhong* has this ground. But how about *zhui yuan*?

4) Lu Jiashu 陸稼書 (1630–1692) argued, "*Shen zhong* is applied to one's parents while *zhui yuan* is applied to not only one's parents but also all ancestors" (*Sishu jiangyi kunmian lu*, 4:22b). I would refute this as follows:

When one's grandparents pass away, one should be careful about matters concerning their end. In addition, the great officials and low-ranking officials are not allowed to perform sacrifice rituals for their early ancestors. Lu's argument is distorted.

* * *

Though Dasan's reputation is built on his reformative sociopolitical insights, he might have defined himself, given the opportunity, as an expert on Confucian rites. Starting from 1801, the year he was exiled, he spent a dozen years conducting exhaustive research on the rites before working on other Confucian classics and thinking about the politics of Joseon society, which resulted in the completion of his voluminous *Sangrye sajeon* 喪禮四箋 (*Four Commentaries on the Mourning Rituals*, fifty rolls), *Sangrye oepyeon* 喪禮外篇 (*Outer Compilation of the Mourning Rituals*, twelve rolls), *Sang-ui jeolyo* 喪儀節要 (*Essential Summary of the Protocols of Mourning*, six rolls), *Sarye gasik* 四禮家式 (*Family Rules of the Four Rites*, nine rolls), and *Ye-ui mundap* 禮疑問答 (*Questions and Answers on the Questionable Issues of the Rites*, three rolls). Reflecting his strenuous efforts to disentangle the Confucian rites from a complex web of interpretations, he once confessed to his son: "Only those achievements of mine related to the *Rites* and *Changes* will be safe from decay" (*Ye-ui mundap*, 497d).

Of the many possible motivations for his studies on the Confucian rites, two deserve special note. First, he was placed in the category of criminals whom the Joseon court branded as heretics out of its adherence to the Catholic rejection of Confucian mourning rituals. With a sentence imposed on him and his brothers, Dasan was sent into an exile that nearly destroyed his family. It is apparent in many of his writings that he wanted to restore the family's honor by proving the falsity of the accusation, and he might have hoped to do so by displaying his expertise on the orthodox understanding of the rites. Second, though he urged the dynasty to implement a series of reformative measures that were considerably apposite to every corner of Joseon society, his suggestions on ideal Confucian statecraft revolved around a strict adherence to the Confucian rites. He never overlooked the significance in Confucian statecraft of following the rites but rather set following the rites at the core of his method for maintaining social relationships.

To those readers who are aware of the tension between the notions of Practical Learning and those of Ritual Studies (that is, *yehak* 禮學, widely deemed a signature element of conservative Joseon Confucianism), Dasan's views on the Confucian rites may seem to contradict his consistent progressiveness. This is because Dasan tended to support the reinforcement of social stratification by endorsing strict execution of hierarchal Confucian rites. Most noticeable is how he took into grave consideration the social status of each individual in determining the appropriate form of one's practice of Confucian rites. In this regard, he sternly distinguished the ruler from the ruled, senior officials from low-ranking officials, and all officials from commoners, as seen in the following:

> The rites for the Son of Heaven and all feudal lords are different from those for the great officials and low-ranking officials. ("Jeongche jeonjung byeon 正體傳重辨," in *Sangrye oepyeon*, 405a)

> Only the Son of Heaven can perform the seasonal sacrifices in each of the four seasons; feudal lords can perform the sacrificial ritual three times a year; the great officials, two times; low-ranking officials, once; commoners can offer fresh food to their ancestors but cannot perform the ritual. ("Jegi go 祭期考," in *Sang-ui jeolyo* 喪儀節要, 478d)

Dasan's stress on the necessary differentiation of social strata in the performance of the rituals is closely related to *Ye song* 禮訟, the Dispute of Rites, an imbroglio that surrounded applications of Confucian mourning rites to the Joseon royal family when King Hyojong 孝宗 (r. 1649–1659)—the second son in the family but the highest authority in the state—died and later when his wife died. In short, in this transgenerational dispute, the Southerners [南人], a faction Dasan was associated with, insisted that the rituals for the king should be distinguished from those for Yangban bureaucrats, whereas their opponents, the Westerners [西人], emphasized the universality of the children's moral duty to their parents. As a consequence of participating through his writing in this dispute, Dasan was aligned with the Southerners' stance, though he theoretically attempted to synthesize and overcome the two factions' approaches. Therefore, Dasan's contestation against Lu Jiashu [陸隴其] seen in "Arguments" here and his new interpretation of *shen zhong*, which is based on that contestation (despite the fact that Lu did not truly insist that *shen zhong* may only be applied to one's parents), are compatible with his basic views on the Confucian rites. The reason he tried to make clear that this passage is about the rituals and not descendants' attitudes, as suggested by Kong Anguo, was also related to his expertise on the Confucian rites.

Despite his gravitation toward hierarchy in this discussion, Dasan in this passage eventually returns to maintaining balance by confirming the universal necessity for following the rituals. In contrast to the conventional interpretation of this passage, according to which responsibility for the rituals is primarily held by the ruler, Dasan claims that the rituals should be observed by all. In doing so, Dasan altered the nature of this passage from political advice for establishing an orderly society to an affirmation of universal moral obligation. This interpretation was unheard-of before Dasan.

1.10 Zi Qin asked Zi Gong, "When the Master arrives in a state, he always learns about affairs of state. Does he seek out this information, or is it offered to him?" Zi Gong replied, "Our Master is temperate, benign, deferential, and frugal, so he obtains it by being humble. The way Our Master manages to obtain it is, surely, different from the way others seek it out."[60]

子禽問於子貢曰; 夫子至於是邦也, 必聞其政, 求之與? 抑與之與? 子貢曰; 夫子溫良恭儉, 讓以得之. 夫子之求之也, 其諸異乎人之求之與?

1.10.1 Grounds

1) Zheng Xuan commented, "Zi Qin was Confucius's disciple Chen Kang 陳亢;[61] Zi Gong was Confucius's disciple whose family name was Duanmu 端木. His personal name was Ci 賜."[62]

2) I supplement as follows: *Shi fang* 是邦 ("a state") refers to any state in which Confucius arrived; *yu zhi* 與之 ("is it offered to him") means that the state officials provided it to Confucius without his request; *wen* 溫 ("temperate") means being agreeable; *liang* 良 ("benign") means being good; *gong* 恭 ("respectful") is the opposite of being arrogant; *jian* 儉 ("frugal") is the opposite of being extravagant.

3) I supplement as follows: "He obtains it by being humble" means that although Confucius was passive and humble, he finally came to learn about it. *Qiu* 求 ("obtain") in the sentence "the way Our Master manages to

---

[60] In the stele edition of the *Analects*, *yiyu* 抑與 in this sentence appears as *yiyu* 意予.
[61] *Jia yu* says, "Chen Kang was from the state of Chen 陳 and forty years younger than Confucius" (*Kongzi jia yu*, 9:6b).
[62] *Shi ji* says, "Zi Gong was thirty-one years younger than Confucius" (*Shi ji*, 67:8b).

obtain it" should be read as appears in a line of a poem, "The noble person manages to obtain [求] great lucks."[63]

4) Master Zhu commented, "*Qizhu* 其諸 is a particle."[64]

1.10.2 Arguments

1) Zheng Xuan argued, "[The phrase 'or is it offered to him' should be understood as meaning that] or did the lord himself want Confucius to take part in his administration?" I would refute this as follows:

Changes says, "What the hexagrams Lin and Guan connote is that sometimes we offer [與, to give] it, and sometimes we obtain [求] it." *Yu* 與 is synonymous with *shou* 授 (to give).

2) Zheng Xuan argued, "This passage states that Confucius obtained the information through these five virtues." I would refute this as follows:

Rang 讓 ("humble") should be read as a part of the next clause. *Documents* extolled the ancient sage kings' virtues, saying King Yao 堯 was "deferential, brilliant, literate, and considerate" (*Shang Shu zhushu*, 1:4a), King Tang was "solemn, sagacious, magnanimous, and profound" (12:36b), and King Wen was "benign, temperate, honorable, and respectful" (15:18b). When *Zuo's Commentary* applauded the Eight Pedestals [八元, the eight sons of Gaoxin shi 高辛氏] and the Eight Gallants [八凱, the eight sons of Gaoyang shi 高陽氏], it grouped four virtues together. Why was it necessary to group five virtues together only when Zi Gong praised Confucius's virtues? Because Zi Qin suspected that the Master obtained the information by seeking it out, Zi Gong responded, "He obtains it by being humble," and thereby expected to eliminate the suspicion. It is unacceptable to read *rang* as a part of the previous clause.

3) For a classical text on the discussion here, see *Xin shu* by Jia Yi (*Xin shu*, 8:6a, 3–4).[65]

In my investigation, the governmental studies in the Western Han uniformly held that *rang* should be included in the previous clause. This view, however, is not necessarily followed. "Guanren 官人," in *Da Dai Li ji*, also says, "He was humble by being respectful and frugal" (*Da Dai Li ji*, 10:13b), a use of terms different from that by which "humble" is connected to other virtues.

4) I question Master Zhu as follows:

The assertion that Zi Qin was Confucius's disciple is not supported by the authentic histories. *Jia yu* [the source for this assertion] is a forged work, with which Wang Shu wanted to renounce Zheng Xuan by interpolating

---

[63] Although the noble person has never pursued great luck, he eventually obtains it by performing good deeds. Therefore it says, "The noble person manages to obtain great fortunes" (*Mao Shi zhushu*, 23:18a).

[64] The same use is found in the sentence "Alas! It worried the Duke Huan" in the sixth year of the reign of Duke Huan in *Gongyang's Commentary*.

[65] It is an excerpt from "Dao shu 道術."

his own material. As Master Zhu did not trust *Jia yu*, he suspected that Zi Qin was Zi Gong's disciple. On the whole, however, the early Confucians regarded all people who appeared in the *Analects* as students of Confucius's academy. Consequently, such figures as Shen Cheng 申根 have been enshrined and honored with memorial ceremony at the holy shrine. This is one of the evil conventions of This Literature [斯文]. But how can this perception be applied to Zi Qin only?

5) I explore the textual differences as follows:

In the stele edition, *yiyu* 抑與 in this sentence appears as *yiyu* 意予. In general, *yi* 意 is synonymous with *yi* 億, and *yi* 億 and *yi* 抑 are homophones. Also *yi* 抑 phonetically resembles *yi* 意. Therefore the poem "Yijie 抑戒" has been called "Yijie 懿戒." Meanwhile, *yi* 予 and *yu* 與 are originally the same character.

* * *

Dasan again introduces a new reading of this passage here by placing a pause between *qian* ("frugal") and *rang* ("humble"), which all previous commentators regarded as among Confucius's five virtues. Dasan makes reference to this argument in "Overview of the Original Meanings." He found the ground for this argument in the Confucian classic texts: on most occasions, the ancient sages were praised for four virtues. This evidence would not satisfactorily rebut all possible counter-arguments, of course, but it sufficiently shows that Dasan had a creative mind and that he made good use of his knowledge of the Confucian classics to generate a fresh reading out of the huge legacy of exegetical studies on the *Analects*. In this regard, it is worth noting that he completed *Noneo gogeum ju* in 1813, after he delved into the five Confucian classics—*Rites, Changes, Poetry, Spring and Autumn*, and *Documents*—resulting in a series of works published in this same order from 1807 to 1812. In other words, *Noneo gogeum ju* is a crystallization of his studies of the Confucian classics and was made possible through his wide reading in the Confucian canon.

Dasan's remarks on the difference between the standard edition and the stele edition here, although prompted possibly by his reading of Dazai Jun's comment on the same issue, also displays his expertise on the classical texts, as he complemented Dazai's gloss with additional evidence from *Poetry*. According to Wei Zhao's 韋昭 (204–273) annotation in *Guo yu*, "Yijie 懿戒" was another name for a poem in *Poetry*, "Yi 抑," which was sometimes called "Yijie 抑戒" (*Guo yu* 國語, 17:14a). On this basis, Dasan drew the conclusion that the two *yis* were interchangeable. As "Yijie" was allegedly composed by Duke Wu of Wei [衛武公, r. 812–759 BCE] at the age of ninety-five, this term was frequently used by Korean Confucian scholars when they encouraged the old kings to regard themselves as not too old to work hard, as well.

When critical research on the alleged forgery of the so-called "old script [古文]" texts, from which almost all extant Confucian classics have stemmed, was embarked on under the name Evidential Studies in the Qing dynasty, *Kongzi jia yu* by Wang Shu had to bear the brunt of their criticism because he had been most responsible for the eventual triumph of the "old script" texts over the "new script [今文]" ones. Scholars discovered that *Kongzi jia yu* was full of evidence of manipulations: he used terms that had definitely been unavailable in the historical period he was describing to dismiss the scholarship of Zheng Xuan, who tried to incorporate into his commentaries the insights of two antithetical academic traditions of Chinese textual studies. Though many tend to think that Qing scholars initiated the criticism of the "old script" texts, in fact, Zhu Xi was an earlier harbinger who raised questions about the authenticity of the ancient Chinese classics. In particular, he doubted, as did most of Qing's critical scholars later, that the work titled *Documents in the Old Script* [古文尚書] was forged. This version of *Documents*, which is the very same one that today's readers encounter, had borne an air of mystery ever since Mei Ze, from the Eastern Jin dynasty (265–420), claimed that he had discovered it and that it was Kong Anguo's ancient version of *Documents*. In comparison to his firm stance on the forgery of *Documents*, Zhu Xi showed an ambiguous attitude about the manipulations of *Kongzi jia yu* in his comment on this passage, in which he introduced both the account in the *Kongzi jia yu* about the identity of Zi Qin and an account that differed from it. Dasan's questions about this vagueness here stem from his conviction, asserted throughout *Noneo gogeum ju*, that *Kongzi jia yu* was forged. It is intriguing to see that Mao Qiling and Dazai Jun, the two main figures among his contemporaries to whom Dasan referred, completely accepted *Kongzi jia yu* as a trustworthy source, for they were persistent in attacking Zhu Xi's views. Thus Dasan's views on the issue of the forgery of ancient Chinese classics texts was much closer to those of the mainstream of the Qing Evidential Studies, represented by Yan Ruoqu 閻若璩 (1636–1704) and Yao Jiheng 姚際恒 (1647–1715).

1.11 The Master said, "When his father is alive, look at his will; when his father passes away, look at his conduct. Only if for three years he does not change the way of his father, can he be called filial."[66]

子曰; 父在觀其志, 父沒觀其行, 三年無改於父之道, 可謂孝矣.

1.11.1 Grounds

1) Kong Anguo commented, "When his father is alive, the son cannot be self-governing, so people should look at his will only."
2) I supplement as follows: *Dao* 道 ("way") here refers to political orders and administrations.

---

[66] The sentence starting with "Only if" is repeated in book 4, "Li ren 里仁" (4.20).

1.11.2 Arguments

1) Huang Kan argued "First, how can a son discern the right and wrong of politics when he is coping with deep grief and a feeling of loss? Therefore, after a lord meets his demise, the crown prince should follow the prime minister's decisions for three years. Second, for three years, as his mind is filled with sorrow and longing, he serves the dead as if they are still alive. Subsequently, he has no heart to change his father's way."[67] I would refute this as follows:

With reluctance over immediately having autonomy, the son experiences gradual development in his conduct. However, this passage should be compared with the passage where Master Zeng praises Meng Zhuangzi's 孟莊子 filiality (Lun yu jizhu, 19:18). In other words, this passage was primarily addressed to members of the class of the great officials. Thus following the prime minister's decisions for three years has nothing to do with its original meaning. The Son of Heaven and feudal lords—if they witness their late fathers' misgovernment, which could bring about the devastation of all under heaven and endanger the royal ancestral shrine, they should enact changes in due manner, as if extinguishing a fire or rescuing a person from drowning. How could they dare to follow it for the sake of filial piety and commemoration? Lü Huiqing 呂惠卿 (1032–1111), citing this passage, once perturbed Emperor Zhezong 哲宗 (r. 1085–1100) of the Song dynasty during the early period of his reign. This is what the students of the Way should discuss and clarify.[68]

2) For classical texts that support my argument here, see Lun yu jizhu 19:18;[69] "Fang ji 坊記" (Li ji zhushu, 51:23a, 3); Da Dai Li ji (Da Dai Li ji, 4:18a, 4–7).[70]

* * *

In this passage Dasan's ardent aspiration for social reforms for the declining Joseon society generates a new perception of the Confucian test of filiality. To observe the three-year mourning ritual was a universal duty for all Confucians, Dasan thought. In this passage, however, he discusses how society can suffer severe damage when the government malfunctions. As many people had previously asked, searchingly, what if the new ruler is stuck on a path of bad

---

[67] He also said, "One might ask, 'If the father's government went awry, how can a son not change the way?' I would reply, 'The prime minister deals with the politics by himself, and seneschal and local administrators deal with administrative tasks by themselves. So the surviving son does not need to be involved in these affairs.'"

[68] Zhen Xishan 眞西山 (1178–1235) said, "King Wu replaced King Wen's aspirations with his own, which he never changed in his entire life. King Xuan 宣 (r. 827–782 BCE) ascended the throne after the atrocity of King Li 厲 (r. 877–841 BCE), which he could not let linger for three years. In other cases, one should not change [the way of his father] for three years" (Lun yu jizhu daquan, 1:34b).

[69] See book 19, "Zi Zhang."

[70] See "Zengzi ben xiao 曾子本孝."

politics due to universal moral obligation? Unfortunately, Dasan, who never rejected Confucius's teaching, saw that Confucius clearly stated that the son should not change the way of his late father's government for three years. The intelligent solution Dasan came up with for this dilemma was to set a limit on the audience for this passage: Confucius's teaching in it is applicable only to the great officials. In this interpretation, the Joseon kings could not find an excuse to procrastinate on urgent reforms, and at the same time Dasan could preserve the veracity of Confucius's sayings.

Dasan was inclined toward thinking that could help liberate the Joseon kings from their bond to the universal Confucian norms when he thought an emphasis on universality might hinder them from immediately implementing various reforms. To this end, Dasan sometimes differentiated kings from all of their subjects, in this respect, and conceded to the kings a privilege of immunity from certain Confucian moral duties. This is tantamount to laying stress on the court's initiative over that of the Confucian bureaucrats, the so-called scholar-officials. This was Dasan's response to a subtle issue that was debated, throughout the Joseon dynasty, between the court and Confucian bureaucrats and between rival factions. Especially significant in this regard was Joseon's factional strife between the Westerners, who were prone to accentuate the universality of Confucian morals, and the Southerners, who were inclined to speak for the Joseon court.

1.12 Master You said, "In the application of ritual propriety, harmony is valuable. The Way of the former kings marked this as beautiful, and all people high and low followed it. However, there is something unacceptable. You know the value of harmony and keep pursuing it without regulating it with ritual propriety—this is also something unacceptable."[71]

有子曰; 禮之用, 和爲貴. 先王之道, 斯爲美, 小大由之. 有所不行, 知和而和, 不以禮節之, 亦不可行也.

1.12.1 Grounds

1) I supplement as follows: *Li zhi yong* 禮之用 ("the application of ritual propriety") means that one applies and practices ritual propriety. *Xiao da* 小大 ("all people high and low") here are equivalent to *shang xia* 上下 (high and low). They refer to the Son of Heaven, the feudal lords, the great officials, and low-ranking officials. *You zhi* 由之 ("followed it") means that all people followed the Way of the former kings.

2) I supplement as follows: The phrase "there is something unacceptable" is an expression used to lead to another topic to be remarked on; the phrase

---

[71] There is no *ke* 可 in the stele edition.

"this is also something unacceptable" is an expression used to conclude the topic making the remark. Ritual propriety usually takes rigidity as its mainstay, but in its application, you should value harmony. Similarly, music takes harmony as its mainstay, but in taking precautions against its side effects you should be wary of dissipation.

1.12.2 Arguments

1) Xing Bing argued, "In all things small and great, people practice ritual propriety. However, if they do not harmonize it with music, their administration will not work." I would refute this as follows:

   This interpretation is not found even in Ma Rong's annotation in *Lun yu jijie*, and is nothing but the commentator's misreading. It is also a major mistake that later Confucians, since they wanted persistently to state their objections to *Lun yu jizhu*, divided this passage into three different pieces, following Xing Bing's annotation in reverse. *Record of Rites* says, "If music solely prevailed, dissipation would arrive. If ritual propriety solely prevailed, apathy would arrive" (*Li ji zhushu*, 37:15a). It also says, "Music was created in accordance with Heaven; ritual propriety was established in accordance with Earth. When acts of establishment become excessive, disorder will emerge; when acts of the creation becomes excessive, violence will emerge" (37:21a). These remarks indeed convey the implications of the complementary use of ritual propriety and music. However, the so-called music made reference to in these quotations does not point to the actual music played on musical instruments such as bells, drums, plucked lutes, and zithers.

2) Dazai Jun argued, "A sentence in 'Ru xing 儒行,' 'Ritual propriety regards harmony as valuable' (*Li ji zhushu*, 59:11b), shares with this passage the same style of placing pauses in a sentence. Thus it is incorrect that [Zhu Xi] placed a pause after *yong* 用 ('in the application')." I would refute this as follows:

   "Li qi 禮器" also says, "Ritual propriety regards a multitude of things as valuable.... [R]itual propriety regards the paucity of things as valuable" (23:21b–22a). The way of separating phrases in "Li qi" is precisely the same as that in "Ru xing." How could this aspect of "Li qi" be used to negate the [Zhu Xi's] way of reading this passage? And though the theory of substance and application (*ti-yong*) stemmed from the Buddha, our school has never stopped discussing applications. For example, *Changes* says, "To what can this be applied? It can be applied to even two baskets of grains in sacrifice rituals" (*Zhou Yi zhushu*, 7:15b). "Hongfan" also says, "With regard to building respect, apply five affairs.... [W]ith regard to building cooperation, apply the five orders of time" (*Shang Shu zhushu*, 11:5b). So how is it misguided to address the issue of the application of ritual propriety? "Yan yi 燕義" says, "Harmony and peace attest to the application of ritual propriety" (*Li ji zhushu*, 62:24a). "Waiqi shi jia 外戚世家," in *Shi ji*, also says, "In the application of ritual propriety, one should be cautious about marriage affairs"

(*Shi ji*, 49:2a). Thus there is abundant evidence of instances of "the application of ritual propriety." How could you doubt it?

* * *

Many English translations follow Xing Bing's reading of this passage, separating the phrase "all people high and low followed it" from the preceding phrase. For example, in one translation the part under discussion reads: "However, if matters small and great all follow them, sometimes it will not work" (See Chichung Huang, 49). Dasan did not accept this reading. According to Dasan, Xing Bing also suggested that readers view *he* 和 ("harmony") as meaning "music." This interpretation actually derived from Huang Kan's: Xing Bing simply adopted it as his own. Dasan did not accept it either. In introducing the grounds for his disapproval, Dasan reveals the reason: "It is also a major mistake that later Confucians [made], since they wanted persistently to state their objections to *Lun yu jizhu*." "[L]ater Confucians" here refers to scholars of Evidential Studies in Qing China and of the Ancient Learning in Tokugawa Japan, such as Mao Qiling and Dazai Jun. In their attempts to criticize and overcome Zhu Xi's scholarship, they often resorted to the authority of earlier Confucian traditions, such as Han-Tang Confucianism, and presented their views as closer to the original teachings of Confucius. Some scholars have insisted, highlighting this commonality between Evidential Studies and the Ancient Learning, and in reference to Dasan's emphasis on the restoration of the genuine teachings of the ancient sages, that a "new" intellectual movement to revive the "old" ethical foundations was evident in East Asia beginning in the seventeenth century. Notwithstanding the plausibility of this claim, Dasan's stance, and more broadly Korean intellectual movements, should be distinguished from other parallel cases, because he decidedly stratified the Confucian scholarly traditions in favor of Zhu Xi's neo-Confucianism.

In this regard, it is noteworthy that Dasan tolerated the neo-Confucian adoption of *ti-yong* theory, a core neo-Confucian theoretical apparatus to make *li* 理 (principle) and *qi* 氣 (vital force) ontologically unseparable but at the same time perceptionally distinguishable, while admitting that it derived from the Buddha. This should not suggest that Dasan sought a compromise with Buddhism. He was a Confucian legitimist and thus intermittently joined efforts to remove the traces of Buddhist influence from the Confucian body. However, in Dasan's view, some Buddhist theories, such as *ti-yong* theory, could be incorporated into "our school" because Confucian philosophers were also concerned with the same topics, as the Confucian classic texts he quoted attest to. According to Dasan, it was legitimate to accept them, since Buddhist theory and, more important, the neo-Confucian theory influenced by it were interwoven with elements of Confucian ancient teachings. In other words, Dasan saw neo-Confucianism as partly representing the ancient teachings, whereas the other "later Confucians" deemed it powerfully devastating. Thus, Dasan synthesized neo-Confucian ideas with the ancient teachings he sought to restore; in the onslaught of other scholarly camps and their aggressive attempts at restoration, such ideas perished.

1.13 Master You said, "Trustworthiness is close to rightness, and one can keep one's words with it; respectfulness is close to ritual propriety, and one can keep shame and humiliation away with it. In addition, if a person does not lose his family's faith, he can be esteemed as a role model."

有子曰; 信近於義, 言可復也. 恭近於禮, 遠恥辱也. 因不失其親, 亦可宗也.

1.13.1 Grounds

1) He Yan commented, "*Fu* 復 ('keep') is synonymous with *fu* 覆 (to be covered). Being right does not necessarily entail being trustworthy, and thus trustworthiness is not the same as rightness. However, one can keep one's words with it, so it is said to be 'close to rightness.' If respectfulness is not in agreement with ritual propriety, it is not appropriate. However, one can keep shame and humiliation away with it, so it is said to be 'close to ritual propriety.'"[72]

2) I supplement as follows: The word *yin* 因 ("in addition") connects the previous sentence to the following one. Not to "lose his family's faith" means gaining the family's confidence.[73] *Zong* 宗 ("esteemed as a role model") means "to be respected." This passage states that if a person is trustworthy and respectful and, furthermore, does not lose his parents' and siblings' faith, he can be respected and taken as a role model, even when he does not reach the level of sages and worthies. "Tangong" says, "Who under heaven is able to esteem me as a role model [宗]?" (*Li ji zhushu*, 7:18a)

1.13.2 Arguments

1) I question Master Zhu as follows:
   It is true that respectfulness does not always accord with ritual propriety. The reason it is said to be "close to ritual propriety" is, however, that one can keep shame and humiliation at a distance with it. Trustworthiness does not always accord with rightness. The reason it is said to be "close to rightness" is, however, that one can keep one's words with it. On top of being

---

[72] Xing Bing said, "The death of Weisheng 尾生 [who appears in *Zhuangzi*], who was drowned while holding a bridge pillar [to keep his promise with a lady], exemplifies the maxim, 'trustworthiness is not the same as rightness.'" He also said, "Sitting under a table in humility is a case in which respectfulness is not in agreement with ritual propriety."
[73] *Constant Mean* says, "There is a way to gain the confidence of your superiors" (*Zhong yong zhangju*, 17b).

able to keep these two values, if a person is able not to lose harmony in his six relations, his personality can be honored as an exemplary standard and model. With regard to the first two sentences, the old commentary must remain unaltered.

2) Kong Anguo argued, "*Yin* is interchangeable with *qin* 親 (to favor). This passage states that, in respect of favoring someone over others, if a person does not fail to favor what he is supposed to favor, he can also be esteemed as a role model."[74] I would refute this as follows:

This interpretation is similar to the one in *Lun yu jizhu*. However, interpreting the phrase under discussion in this manner is extraneous and redundant, clouding the meaning of this passage. In general, as regards the way of understanding people, one should look into their behavior at their homes, even when their social conduct seems virtuous. The capacity to be trustworthy and respectful pertains to people's exterior performances in their relationships with others. If a person's exterior performances are already good and his interior behavior is also solid, he can be esteemed as a role model. *Constant Mean* says, "Is there a way to gain friends' trust? If a person is not compliant with his parents, he cannot gain his friends' trust" (*Zhong yong zhangju*, 17b). It was expected in ancient times for a person not to dare to socialize with others when his relatives were not pleased with it. Not to "lose his family's faith" is related to matters of filial piety, as well as compliance and harmonious relationships with relatives. Why would it be necessary to seek, in such a bizarre manner, the meaning of this phrase in social relationships? I am afraid that Yan Chouyou, Qu Boyu, and Citadel Overseer Zhenzi [all mentioned in *Lun yu jizhu*] have nothing to do with this passage.

3) For a classical text on the discussion here, see "Biao ji" (*Li ji zhushu*, 54:12a, 4–12b, 1).

In my view, this remark in "Biao ji" is indeed compatible with Master You's thought. The noble person looks down on unyielding trustworthiness, but it is still close to rightness. Being respectful without adhering to ritual propriety may entail problems of excessive industry,[75] but it is still close to ritual propriety. Confucius also said, "Be respectful so as to keep humiliation away" (*Li ji zhushu*, 54:3b) and "Be respectful, and you will not be humiliated" (*Lun yu jizhu*, 17:5). Respectfulness is inherently something by which one can keep shame and humiliation away, and trustworthiness is as well. Why should we add to them one more virtue in social relationships that would enable a man to keep his words and keep away shame and humiliation?

---

[74] Xing Bing argued, "What is implied in Kong's comment 'in respect of favoring someone over others, if a person does not fail to favor what he is supposed to favor' is that 'one should associate with the right people' (*Lun yu jizhu*, 4:10). If one is able to favor the humane person and associate with the right people, one should have brilliance at discerning people's qualities. Thus, one will earn their respect."
[75] Confucius also gave a lesson about this (see *Lun yu jizhu*, 8:2).

4) For a classical text on the discussion here, see "Wang Yuangui zhuan 王元規傳," in *Chen shu* (*Chen shu* 陳書, 33:19b, 6–20a, 2).[76] Ogyu argued, "The old form of the character *yin* here was interchangeable with those of *yin* 姻 (to marry) and *yin* 婣 (to marry)." [Ogyu interprets the last sentence in this passage as saying that "in marriage, if a person does not lose those to whom he is close, he can be esteemed as a role model."] I would refute this as follows:

King Yu 禹 chose his bride at Mount Tu 塗, and Duke Wen of Jin [晉文公, 636–618 BCE] took his bride from the Di 狄 tribe. Were they not esteemed as role models because of that? Should we take the village of Zhu-Chen 朱陳 [renowned for its endogamy] as a model in the future?

* * *

Zhu Xi rejected the old commentary that Dasan adopted here. Dasan usually invoked the old commentary whenever a revision by Zhu Xi was liable to confuse readers. In *Lun yu jizhu*, the first two sentences read, "When trustworthiness comes close to rightness, one can keep one's words; when respectfulness comes close to ritual propriety, one can keep shame and humiliation away." Indeed, Zhu Xi's reading must have seemed "bizarre" and incongruous, if not unacceptable, to Dasan because it created two conditional clauses for no good reason. Dasan was certain enough of his endorsement of the old commentary that he included it in "Overview of the Original Meanings," saying, "one should follow the old interpretations."

As for the meaning of *yin*, Dasan rejects both the old commentary by Kong Anguo and the new commentary by Zhu Xi, as well as Ogyu's interpretation. Rather, Dasan views *yin* as a word connecting two adjacent sentences. According to my research, Han Yu 韓愈 (768–824) initially proposed this view in *Lun yu bijie* 論語筆解, one of the earliest commentaries on the *Analects*, cowritten with Li Gao 李翱 (774–836). The two were among the most significant contributors to the restoration of the Confucian tradition in the late Tang dynasty. Dasan also referred to *Lun yu bijie* and quoted from its commentary when necessary. However, he here includes it in his supplementary explanation of the last sentence because Han Yu's understanding of the sentence differs greatly from Dasan's.

1.14 The Master said, "The noble person who seeks neither satiety in eating nor comfort in his dwelling, who is diligent in action but careful in speech, who presents himself to virtuous people to be rectified—such a man may truly be said to have a love of learning.

子曰; 君子食無求飽, 居無求安, 敏於事而慎於言, 就有道而正焉, 可謂好學也已.

---

[76] See "Rulin zhuan."

1.14.1 Grounds

1) Kong Anguo commented, "*You dao* 有道 ('virtuous people') refers to people with morals; *zheng* 正 ('to be rectified') means inquiring about right and wrong."

2) In my view, having appropriate ways of eating and dwelling is a means to cultivate the small body [physical body]. It has been addressed first here in order to clarify why the issue of "overcoming the [bodily] self" should be prioritized.

* * *

The distinction between the small body and the great body originated in *Mencius*: "Those who follow the great body will become the great person; those who follow the small body will become the petty person" (*Mengzi jizhu*, 6A: 15). Zhu Xi succinctly defined these concepts as follows: "What is humble and small is one's mouth and stomach; what is precious and great is one's mind-heart [心] and one's will" (*Mengzi jizhu daquan* 孟子集注大全, 11:47a). Whereas Dasan basically accepted Zhu Xi's definition of the terms, he tried to amend Zhu Xi's minor mistake: "Heart [心] is just one of the five organs, and one's will is what one's mind-heart is oriented toward. Thus they are insufficient to represent the great body" (*Maengja yo-ui*, 142a). Accordingly, Dasan suggests that the great body be more elaborately conceptualized as "the mysterious and bright body [靈明之體]" to emphasize its intangibility.

1.15 Zi Gong asked, "A man who is poor but does not flatter, or who is rich but is not arrogant—how good is he?" The Master replied, "Not bad, but not as good as a man who is poor but joyful, or who is rich but loves ritual propriety." Zi Gong said, "*Poetry* says, 'Like cutting, then filing; like breaking, then grinding.' This implies what you have just said, does it not?" The Master said, "Ci, I can discuss *Poetry* with him from now on. Informed about what has happened, he knows what is to come."[77]

子貢曰; 貧而無諂, 富而無驕, 何如? 子曰; 可也, 未若貧而樂, 富而好禮者也. 子貢曰; 詩云, 如切如磋, 如琢如磨, 其斯之謂與? 子曰; 賜也, 始可與言詩已矣, 告諸往而知來者.

1.15.1 Grounds

1) I supplement as follows: *Keye* 可也 ("not bad") is a phrase that conveys that Confucius accepted but did not deeply approve of the man; *qie* 切 ("cutting")

---

[77] In the stele edition, the expression "poor but joyful" appears as "poor but joyful of the Way."

means to chop; *zhuo* 琢 ("breaking") means to cleave. These constitute a process of rough trimming. *Quo* 磋 ("filing") and *mo* 磨 ("grinding") constitute a method of polishing, so the process is elaborate. Avoiding flattery and arrogance is to remove the evil, so the process is rough; being joyful and loving ritual propriety is to practice the good, so the process is elaborate.[78]

2) Master Zhu commented, "*Wang* 往 ('what has happened') refers to what has already been told; *lai* 來 ('what is to come') refers to what is yet to be addressed."

1.15.2 Arguments

1) Xing Bing argued, "The word for processing bones is *qie*, for processing ivory, *quo*, for jade, *zhuo*, and for stones, *mo*." I would refute this as follows:
   Xing Bing's interpretation comes from "Shi qi 釋器," in *Er ya* 爾雅.[79] However, bones should be filed as well, and ivory cannot avoid being cut. Unless it is ground, jade has no use even when broken; unless they are broken, nobody can grind stones even when he wants to. That each of the four processes were assigned exclusively to each of the four objects stemmed from an interpretative error whose origin is to be found in *Er ya*. The implications of elaborateness and roughness were first expounded on by Master Zhu, and his understanding of these surpassed all other ideas suggested generation after generation. Without the imagery of elaborateness and roughness, the dialogue in this passage might have been too plain to leave a distinctive taste, leading to eventual incomprehension of the meaning.

2) Kong Anguo argued, "*Wang* refers to Confucius's instruction of people 'poor but joyful of the Way,' and *lai* refers to Zi Gong's reply of 'Like cutting, then filing; like breaking, then grinding.'" I would refute this as follows:
   Wang is related to domains of what has already passed, whereas *lai* is related to affairs that are yet to happen. In other words, *wang* concerns what has already been revealed, whereas *lai* concerns what has not been materialized. Being joyful when poor, or loving ritual propriety when rich—examples of these attitudes are plainly visible. As for the elaborateness and roughness of the Learning of the Way, however, its principles are so subtle that only such a shrewd person can understand "that" on hearing about "this." This is what the sentence "Informed about what has happened, he knows what is to come" may mean.

3) I explore the textual differences as follows:
   Kong Anguo's commentary is quoted twice in *Lun yu jijie*, which reads, in both instances, "Poor but joyful of the Way." Giving consideration to this, I suspect that there was an additional character, *dao* 道, in the ancient editions.

---

[78] See "Qi ao 淇奧, Wei feng 衞風," in *Poetry*.
[79] Mao Chang 毛萇 (fl. 150 BCE) also quoted this source [in his annotation in *Poetry*].

4) I explore the textual differences as follows:

See "Fang ji" (*Li ji zhushu*, 51:12, 6), "Dizi liezhuan," in *Shi ji* (*Shi ji*, 67:9b, 3–4), and "Dongping Xianwang [Cang] zhuan 東平憲王傳," in *Hou Han shu* (*Hou Han shu*, 72:21a, 4–5). In my investigation, in its two quotations from Kong Anguo's annotation, *Lun yu jijie* uniformly states, "a man who is poor but enjoys the Way." Nevertheless, however, only the character *le* 樂 ("joyful") delivers a profound taste in this passage.

* * *

In his comment on this chapter, Dasan left an impressive remark: "As for the elaborateness and roughness of the Learning of the Way, however, its principles are so subtle." Learning of the Way [道學] is another name of neo-Confucianism because neo-Confucians have asserted that the Way can be learned, as seen in Zhou Dunyi's 周敦頤 (1017–1073) proclamation (*Zhou Yuangong ji* 周元公集, 1:27b). In the context of his comment, Dasan seems to think that a learner should grasp the elaborate aspect of the Learning of the Way, principles, because one's thorough understanding of the Way can possibly be demonstrated through one's comprehension of the subtlety ingrained in the learning. In comparison, in Dasan's view, the rough aspect of the Learning of the Way possibly refers to more practical issues, such as economy and politics. Given that his intellectual challenge came to be named the Practical Learning, this short remark may elicit curiosity as to how it can be integrated with the common understanding of the Practical Learning. With more reading of his philosophical ideas, readers may be assured that Dasan always intended to embrace the subtlety in a person's learning, which primarily concerns "principles." The reason for the frequent somewhat contemplative statements in Dasan's writing might be also found in this context, as in the following: "Among all things under heaven, something intangible [虛] is precious, and something practical [實] is humble; something with no form is precious, and something with form is humble. Morals, virtues, ritual decorums, and social teachings uniformly rule something practical by something intangible, and guide something with form by something with no form" (*Noneo gogeum ju*, 332c). Thus to adopt the term Practical Learning as a learning that is exclusive of principles is nonsensical.

1.16 The Master said, "Do not worry about whether others understand you. Worry about whether you understand others."

子曰; 不患人之不己知, 患不知人也.

1.16.1 Grounds

1) Xing Bing commented, "In people's common sentiments, it frequently happens that one becomes negligent about understanding others."

2) I supplement as follows: This passage states that one should worry about whether he understands other people's worthiness.

3) Wang Shu commented, "[Regardless of others' understanding of you,] you should only worry about whether you are incapable of understanding others."[80]

---

[80] This annotation is from the Huang Kan edition.

BOOK 2 | To Rule 爲政

2.1 The Master said, "Ruling with virtue may be compared to the North Constellation: when it keeps its right place, all stars move together with it." [In *Noneo gogeum ju* in traditional book binding, this chapter opens the second roll.][1]

子曰; 爲政以德, 譬如北辰居其所, 而衆星共之.

2.1.1 Grounds

1) I supplement as follows: *Zheng* 政 ("ruling") here is synonymous with *zheng* 正 (to rectify).[2] Thus it means that the ruler, by giving commands and issuing edicts, rectifies all government officials and thereby rectifies the myriad people.

2) I supplement as follows: *De* 德 ("virtue") means to align one's mind-heart with moral principle.[3] It suggests that one becomes filial to parents and respectful to elders before doing anything else and then leads all under heaven by means of humanity. The Master said, "If you lead the people with virtue ... they will have a sense of shame and be inspired" (*Lun yu jizhu*, 2:3).

3) I supplement as follows: *Beichen* 北辰 ("North Constellation") refers to the North Pole, which is aligned with the celestial pole. Since it has no fixed astral spots, it is called a "constellation." Though the South Pole is also aligned with the celestial pole, Our Master did not mention it because to him, born in China, the North Pole was visible above the horizon while the South Pole was not. The phrase "it keeps its right place" means that the North Pole, lying on the meridian, exists in a position of ruling the south and the north.

---

[1] This book contains twenty-four chapters. Xing Bing said, "According to *Zuo's Commentary*, 'one participates in ruling after learning' (*Zuo zhuan zhushu*, 40:31a). Thus this book follows the previous book."
[2] The character *zheng* 政 belongs to the category of phonosemantic compound characters [諧聲]—one of the six categories of Chinese characters.
[3] The meaning of the character is as above [because the character *de* can be broken up into to two characters: *zhi* 直 (to straighten out) and *xin* 心 (mind-heart)].

4) I supplement as follows: *Gong* 共 ("move together") is here interchangeable with *tong* 同 (together with). It means that when the North Constellation, revolving around the celestial pole, dwells in its right place all stars follow it, moving together with it. Therefore it is said, "[all stars] move together with it."[4]

5) I supplement as follows: Ruling is a means for the ruler to rectify the people. Only after he rectifies himself do things become rectified and the people follow his teachings and move together with him.[5]

2.1.2 Arguments

1) Bao Xian argued, "A man of virtue takes non-action. He is analogous to the North Star ["North Constellation" in Dasan's interpretation]: it does not move, but all the other stars revolve around it."[6] Xing Bing said, "[This passage states that] all the other stars pay homage to the North Star." I would refute this as follows:

The concept of preserving immaculacy and purity and taking non-action derives from the learning of Huang-Lao of Han Confucians and the discourses of Immaculacy and Emptiness in the Jin dynasty (265–420). This concept brought disorder to all under heaven and destroyed the myriad things; thus it is worse than all the other heretical and perverted strategies. Emperor Wen 文 (r. 180–157 BCE), by adopting this Way, fostered the Rebellion of the Seven States, and Emperor Hui 惠 (r. 195–188 BCE), by honoring this strategy, provoked the calamity of the five barbarian tribes. Is it acceptable to say that the great sages in this school [Confucianism] adopted "taking non-action" as their standard too?

In general, if the ruler takes non-action, there will be no action of ruling. Is it not amiss for Confucians to speak of "taking non-action" when Our Master here is clearly discussing how to rule? Confucius once said, "Shun 舜 was perhaps the one who achieved good rule by doing nothing! What did he do? He conducted himself respectfully, facing due south. That is it."[7] This remark, however, cannot be understood apart from the fact that Shun found twenty-two people he appointed to appropriate positions and thereby all under heaven became well ordered. At that time, Shun only conducted himself respectfully, facing due south. In other words, the remark was intended to emphasize that states need to acquire talented people. It conveys a feeling of admiration and adoration in its words and encourages people through its rhetoric.

---

[4] "Wang zhi" says, "Share it together [共之] with other people" (*Li ji zhushu*, 13:12a).
[5] The people move toward morals.
[6] Xing Bing said, "If the ruler preserves pure virtue without agitating it and leads people into an immaculate state of morality by doing nothing, politics will become moral. According to 'Tianwen zhi 天文志,' in *Han shu*, 'The constellation Middle Palace is also called the Heavenly Polestar. The Great One constantly dwells in its brightest spot. Its neighboring three stars are called the Three Ministers. . . . [T]he twelve stars that surround and protect them are called the Tutelary Subjects. These stars constitute the Purple Palace'" (*Qian Han shu*, 26:2a).
[7] See "Wei Linggong 衛靈公" (*Lun yu jizhu*, 15:5).

Later Confucians misread this passage and eventually said that when Yao and Shun ruled, they took "doing nothing" as their mainstay. With this understanding, the Confucians regarded the philosophy of Jia Yi 賈誼 (200–168 BCE) as delightful, Ji An as a man who knew the Way, and Wei Xiang 魏相 (d. 59 BCE) and Bing Ji 丙吉 (d. 55 BCE) as great ministers. As a result, the band of inept and incompetent men made their living dishonestly by indolently holding their offices and camouflaged their shortcomings by persistently clinging to the "greater body." They caused the myriad state affairs and a hundred regulations to fall into corruptions and iniquity so that they never gained their vigor again. These are the consequences of being hit by the poison. Alas! Isn't it sorrowful?

In my view, nobody excels Yao and Shun in passionately accomplishing merit in practical affairs. They took an inspection tour once every five years and received the feudal lords in audience every year, inquiring about issues and examining their speeches. In doing so, all under heaven became invigorated. On top of that, they dug out mountains to make waterways, arranged furrows and dredged field drains, established educational institutions and meted out punishments, created rituals and devised music, put villains to death and repelled swindlers. They also selected proper people to decide on uses for the whole range of plants, trees, birds, and wild animals and pressed these people toward achievement, based on their accomplishments. Their care and exertion were as constructive as this. Since Confucius himself finalized the canons and counsels in *Documents*, he must have been clearly aware of these attributes of Yao and Shun. Then how is it possible for Confucius to falsely distort them as taking "doing nothing" as the mainstay of their governments? In short, the idea of "ruling by doing noting" is unequivocally a vicious theory of heretics, not our Confucians' words.

In addition, the North Constellation has no fixed astral spots. Therefore, "Shi tian 釋天," in *Er ya*, says, "The North Pole refers to the North Constellation" (*Er ya zhushu*, 5:25b), and [on this point] Guo Pu 郭璞 (276–324) commented, "The North Pole conforms to the middle of heaven. It has been the foundation for making the four seasons accurate."[8] If it has no fixed astral spots, it is not even necessary to discuss whether it moves. If one should argue that the Great One dwelling in the constellation Middle Palace is *beichen* [it does not move], I would refute this argument too: no matter how small the sphere of the constellation, it moves around day and night, staying nowhere permanently. Then how can the Great One in it stay somewhere permanently?[9]

---

[8] Shao Kangjie 邵康節 (1011–1077) said, "An area on land that has no rocks is called 'earth;' an area in heaven that has no stars is called 'constellation [辰]'" (*Lun yu jizhu daquan*, 2:2b).

[9] Master Zhu said, "*Beichen* is the pivotal spot of heaven. Since it should be properly understood, people have chosen one small star beside it and named it the polestar. The polestar also moves around. Since it is close to the North Constellation, however, its movement is hardly observed. This can be compared to the disc for extracting sugar: the North Constellation corresponds to the stake at the

Han Confucians misunderstood this classic, in which the Great One dwelling in the constellation Middle Palace was eventually given the title the Great Lord of Heavenly Emperor. In addition, when they glossed various sacrificial rituals, such as the Jiao 郊 and the Chai 柴, they called the High Lord of Heaven the God of the Great One. It is superfluous to repeatedly mention their negligence and disruption. Furthermore, they installed a court in the empty blue sky with the Three Ministers, the Six Officials, the Nearby Wardens, and the Tutelary Subjects and said that all the other stars revolve around the North Star. In fact, the ground for this conception was a line from this classic: "all the other stars revolve around it ['all stars move together with it' in Dasan's interpretation]." How can it not be an error?

When sages teach people through metaphors, the metaphors are, without exception, elaborate. Therefore, if Confucius had said, "Comporting oneself with modesty by keeping one's hands folded and doing nothing can be compared to the North Constellation," their interpretation might be plausible. What is discussed in this passage, however, is "ruling with virtue," which obviously belongs to "doing something." How is it possible to compare this with the Great One, which stays still at its permanent place?

In conclusion, to rule is to rectify people. Since the essential ideas of sages are not complicated, even when they address them again and again, their remarks eventually interpenetrate. If people seek to understand the sages' final message, they will find that none of their statements is inconsistent with the others. When Duke Jing of Qi [齊景公, r. 549–490 BCE] asked Confucius about ruling, Confucius replied, "Let the ruler be a ruler; the subject, a subject; the father, a father; the son, a son" (*Lun yu jizhu*, 12:11). This concerns what is called "ruling with virtue." When Ji Kangzi 季康子 asked Confucius about ruling, Confucius replied, "To rule is to rectify people. If you, sir, take the lead by rectifying yourself, who would dare remain unrectified?" (12:17) This concerns the idea that "only after one rectifies oneself do other things become rectified." All the following excerpts also pertain to the passage under discussion:

The Master said, "If a man is correct in his person, things will work out without orders to do so. If a man is incorrect in his person, although orders are given, they will not be followed." (13:6)

The Master said, "If a man truly rectifies himself, what difficulties would he have in participating in government? If a man is not able to rectify himself, what can he do to rectify others?" (13:13)

---

center, and the polestar corresponds to what is close to the stake. Though it moves along the disc, its movement is hardly noticed because it is close to the stake. Shen Cunzhong 沈存中 (1031–1095) says, 'When one observes the polestar through a bamboo tube, it is not caught within the scope of the tube in the beginning. Later, however, the observer can see that the polestar moves around along the upper region of the tube'" (*Lun yu jizhu daquan*, 2:2b).

When Duke Ai asked Confucius about ruling, Confucius replied, "To rule is to rectify people. If the lord himself is correct himself, the people will follow his government. What the lord does is what the people follow. How can they follow what he does not do?" (*Li ji zhushu*, 50:11b–12a)

Mencius said, "Once the lord is rectified, the country will be firmly established." (*Mengzi jizhu*, 4A:20)

Master Dong [董仲舒: 179–104 BCE] said, "Rectify government officials at all levels by rectifying the mind of the lord; rectify the myriad people by rectifying government officials." (*Daxue yanyi* 大學衍義, 1:16a)

So how can the notion of an exceptional state of "not moving" or "doing nothing" serve as the norm for ruling, only in this passage?

The phrase "when it keeps its right place" means when the North Pole is aligned with the meridian. As the North Pole is aligned with the meridian, revolving around the celestial axis, all stars in the sky move together with it, leaving no stars awry or lagging behind. This is the meaning of the phrase "all stars move together with it." Likewise, when the lord of the people stays in the right place, ruling with virtue, government officials at all levels and the myriad people are without exception turned to the good under his influence. This truly accords with the reality of the North Constellation and all stars. The metaphor in this passage is intended to teach people this point, isn't it? What is the point of the interpretation "All the other stars surround and revere it as though they keep their hands folded?"

[Dasan's disciple] Goengbo 紘父 [李綱會, 1789–?] added, "When Zi Zhang asked about ruling, the Master said, 'Be tireless when you hold an office' (*Lun yu jizhu*, 12:14). This is truly opposite to staying still in a position and doing nothing. Is it possible that Our Master's discussion of ruling fluctuates like this? The conventional reading of this passage is invalid."

2) Xu Shicheng 許石城 (fl. Ming dynasty) said, "Interpreters adhered to the term 'non-action' in this passage, which eventually rendered the term 'ruling' meaningless. Isn't this close to the government proposed by Laozi or Zhuangzi?" (Unknown source) Su Zixi said, "Fostering virtues depends on the cultivation of one's person. If one's person is correct, all under heaven and states will be correct. Thus Confucius compared this to the relationship between the North Constellation, which stays in the right place, and all stars, which move together with it. Adding a notion of 'non-action' to this passage is needless and, moreover, dilutes it" (Unknown source). Fang Mengxuan 方孟旋 (1560–1628) said, "The metaphor of the North Constellation is intended to evoke the establishment of imperial standards. How is it related to the idea that the people will submit to the ruler when he rules through non-action?" (Unknown source) Zheng [鄭: *shao* 邵 in all editions of *Noneo gogeum ju*] Duanjian 鄭端簡 (1499–1566) said, "The addition of the term 'non-action' in the commentaries on this passage has

posed a great hindrance to men of letters and scholars" (Unknown source). Mao Dake 毛大可 [Qiling] said, "In my investigation of *Jin shu* 晉書, 'Geng ji zhao 耕籍詔,' composed by Emperor Wu 武 (r. 265–290), contains a passage that says, 'I consider my rule of the myriad states to consist of non-action.' This passage stemmed from the deterioration of Confucian theory brought on by Confucians of the time and it opened wide a gate for the ruinous rule of Emperor Hui 惠 (r. 290–301) and for the theory of preserving immaculacy while taking non-action. It was a sign of the gradual disruption of the holy state" (*Sishu gai cuo*, 17:4b).

In my investigation, some Ming Confucians already discussed the points above.

3) "Jitian fu 籍田賦," by Pan Yue 潘岳 (247–300), reads: "Crystal dew dries before the morning sunlight; all stars face [拱] the North Constellation" (*Wenxuan zhu* 文選注, 7:14a–b).[10] I would refute this as follows:

The original *gong* 共 cannot be changed to *gong* 拱. Moreover, *gong* 拱 refers to keeping hands folded.[11] "Yu zao 玉藻" contains the expression "keeping hands folded in a position below one's navel" (*Li ji zhushu*, 30:16a); "Tangong" contains the expression "keeping hands folded by placing the right hand on the left hand" (7: 17a); *Zuo's Commentary*, the expression "a piece of jade as big as the span of one's arms round" (*Zuo zhuan zhushu*, 38:43b); *Mencius*, the expression "a paulownia tree and Chinese catalpa tree as big as the span of one's arms round or half of it" (*Mengzi jizhu*, 6A:13). And Duke Mu of Qin [秦穆公, r. 659–621 BCE] said, "The timbers for your tomb are as big around as the span of one's arms."[12] All these expressions refer to keeping one's hands folded or holding one's hands together. Its rendering, as related to the notion "to surround and revere it," has never been heard among experts in the six categories of Chinese characters. If all the other stars were to surround and revere the North Constellation, what on earth could they do besides?[13]

* * *

This comment, one of the lengthiest in *Noneo gogeum ju*, is solely dedicated to disabusing followers of Confucius of the notion of "doing nothing" or "non-action." To achieve this goal, Dasan here proposes several new interpretations. First, he renders *beichen* as the North Constellation, which he argues is identical to the North Pole, rejecting the traditional understanding of it as the North Star. This new rendition might have been inevitable because to Dasan's

---

[10] The original *gong* 共 ("move together") is changed to *gong* 拱 (to keep hands folded) here.
[11] Xu Xuan 徐鉉 (916–991) commented, "[*Gong* means that] the thumbs of both hands prop each other" (*Yu ding Kangxi zidian* 御定康熙字典, 11:40a).
[12] See the thirty-second year of the reign of Duke Xi [魯僖公, r. 659–627 BCE] (*Zuo zhuan zhushu*, 16:17a).
[13] *Lun yu jizhu* also said, "*Gong* 共 means to face. It suggests that all the other stars gradually return to and face the North Star, twirling around the four sides" (*Lun yu jizhu*, 1:7b).

knowledge, the North Star does not move. Second, in his effort to maintain a consistency in his logic, he translates the expression *ju qi suo* 居其所 to "when it keeps its right place" in contrast with a conventional reading of it, "when it keeps its place." In the latter reading, "its place" refers to the permanent astral spot for the North Star, whereas in Dasan's reading "its place" is an abstract notion of one's morality. Third, he reads *gongzhi* 共之 as meaning "to move together with it," in an arduous rebuttal of the widely accepted interpretation according to which it was translated "to surround and revere it." The first two interpretations are designed to render this third and final one more plausible.

Dasan's intention in doing this seems obvious. He wanted to protect the legitimacy and superiority of Confucian teachings over other philosophies— especially, in this comment, that of Daoism, with its crucial emphasis on practicality or actions over the contemplation encouraged in other traditions. He argues that the heretical ideas has spoiled many secularized Confucians who are oblivious of the genuine spirit of Confucianism, causing dynasties throughout history to ruin their institutions and people's lives. Undoubtedly, this criticism can also be targeted at neo-Confucianism, along philosophical lines, and Joseon society, along historical ones. In this respect, the viewpoint entrenched in his comments and arguments here is in agreement with the ideas of the so-called Practical Learning of the Joseon dynasty. Indeed, this claim finds support in evidence, throughout his writings, of his detestation of excesses of abstraction that he thought provoked negligence of practical issues. If this claim alludes to the paucity of Dasan's interests in abstract notions, however, it should be clarified again that he attempted to create a synthetic structure of Confucianism, embracing neo-Confucianism as well as other Confucian legacies.

As Dasan notes, some Confucian scholars had already refused to incorporate the Daoist "non-action" notion into this passage and another passage in the *Analects* (15:5), which applauds King Shun's leadership using the term "non-action" (*wuwei*). Dasan presents a partial explanation of the passage, suggesting that it be read as a reminder of the significance of obtaining talented people for a successful government. As a matter of fact, this explanation was not Dasan's own creation but He Yan's. In other words, the explanation reflects a more traditional view of the passage prior to Zhu Xi's new understanding, according to which under the sage's rule, the people's moral enlightenment was accomplished without waiting to take some artful actions. Accordingly, theorists who hoped to restore the old tradition of Confucianism attacked this interpretation by Zhu Xi to show, like Dasan, that they agreed with He Yan. Some Confucian scholars, including Mao Qiling (whom Dasan quoted), were from the Ming and Qing dynasties, during which Zhu Xi's philosophy often met with challengers. Dazai Jun should be added to the list of these scholars as well.

What is more worthy of note in Dasan's comment here, perhaps, is his knowledge of astronomy, which raises the value of his new interpretation for Confucian theory, although it may appear too traditional to be considered advanced beyond the thinking of other nineteenth-century philosophers in Joseon. By displaying theoretical consistency along with a wide gamut of scientific knowledge, he succeeds in proving that he has various talents as not only a Confucian moralist but also a reader of science, philologist, expert in Confucian rituals, historian, and political reformer. From this passage, one can sense that he had a strong passion for validating his values, which were unavoidably abstract, and that with this passion he put forward an unprecedented understanding of a passage in the *Analects*, yet again. This new interpretation is listed in "Overview of the Original Meanings."

2.2 The Master said, "The three hundred poems in *Poetry* can be judged with one phrase: 'They have no evil thoughts.'"

子曰; 詩三百, 一言以蔽之, 曰思無邪.

2.2.1 Grounds

1) I supplement as follows: *Poetry* originally contained three hundred and eleven poems, of which six poems belonged to the poetry of the reed instrument [i.e., poetry that is believed to have been sung with the accompaniment of the reed instrument] and five to the songs of the Shang. The poetry of the reed instrument perished before *Poetry* was compiled, and the songs of the Shang were transmitted from the dynasty before the Zhou, so they do not count. Consequently, *Poetry* contains only three hundred poems.[14]

2) Han Yu commented, "*Bi* 蔽 ('to be judged') is here synonymous with *duan* 斷 (to judge)."[15]

3) Xing Bing commented, "The sentence 'They have no evil thoughts' comes from 'Lu Song 魯頌, Jiong 駉,' in *Poetry*."

4) I supplement as follows: The three hundred poems in *Poetry* were entirely composed by worthies. As their mindset is moral, their poems can be judged with the phrase "They have no evil thoughts."

2.2.2 Arguments

1) Bao Xian argued, "*Bi* is here synonymous with *dang* 當 (to correspond)." Zheng Xuan argued, "*Bi* is here synonymous with *sai* 塞 (to cover)."[16] I would refute this as follows:

A passage in the eighteenth year of the reign of Duke Ai in *Spring and Autumn* quotes [the lost] *Xia shu* 夏書 and says, "Only after the official of

---

[14] This is the master Seongho's 星湖 [李瀷] explanation.
[15] See *Lun yu bijie*.
[16] See *Jingdian shi wen* (*Jingdian shi wen* 經典釋文, 24:3a).

divination passes judgment [蔽] on the ruler's intention does he proceed toward the prime tortoise for the divination" (*Zuo zhuan zhushu*, 60:19a). On this passage Du Yu 杜預 (222–284) commented, "*Bi* is synonymous with *duan*."[17] Han Yu's gloss was based on this.

2) Bao Xian argued, "[The phrase 'They have no evil thoughts' means that] they have returned to goodness."[18] I would refute this as follows:

The phrase "They have no evil thoughts" means that the composers of the poems have no unfairness and malice when their mind-heart moves. If one focuses on the most consequential merits of *Poetry*, relating them to the phrase "They have no evil [無邪]," *si* 思 ("thoughts") cannot be rendered appropriately. Sima Qian said, "All three hundred of the pieces were composed by worthies and sages" (*Shi ji*, 130:15a). His remark must have some grounds. Due to this, Confucius edited and finalized the book, and in doing so it became a holy classic. Had the composers been initially immoral and unfair, how could it attain recognition as a holy classic? Bao's interpretation must not be right.

* * *

Dasan's general perspective on the Confucian classics, the "Six Classics and the Four Books" in his exegetical studies, is that they are errorless. In his view, they are a compilation of the sages' teachings on morals, rituals, history, and institutions, and to him the sages are those who have become impeccable a posteriori, both intellectually and morally, by virtue of their great endeavors. In accordance with this perspective, the primary method Dasan adopts to prove the validity of his interpretations is to secure their grounds in the classics: a certain theory is correct because it is compatible with the classic(s). Although this is not the only method he uses in his classical studies, his discussions of Confucian classics depending on this "primary" method are frequent.

In this regard, Dasan admits that two Confucian classical texts are not as immune as other classical texts to a potential criticism of the textual studies: Dasan believed that the extant edition of *Documents* was forged by Mei Ze, who arguably made use of Kong Anguo's reputation to legitimize his version, and that some chapters of *Record of Rites* were tainted by Han Confucians. This does not necessarily mean, however, that Dasan considered the main texts of the classics susceptible to skepticism. He assumed that when they were flawed it was because they had fallen in the wrong hands and were thereby damaged, even as it was impossible to determine what the passages originally in the classics had been. His

---

[17] Mei Ze also adopted this interpretation [for his "forged" *Documents in the Old Script*].

[18] Xing Bing said, "The essence of *Poetry* lies in discussing accomplishments, praising virtues, ending unfairness, and preventing malice. In general, it aims to return to goodness."

scholarly orientation is apparent in the contrast between the leniency he shows toward the main texts and his sometimes merciless attacks on the interpretations of their primary commentators, including Zheng Xuan and He Yan. It might be said that he was oriented toward a restoration of what he thought was original Confucianism. In light of the fact that the "original" Confucianism stands on the shoulders of the primary commentators, however, it would be more accurate to say that Dasan was following the traditional way of proposing a new thought—that is, via new annotations of the classical texts.

The reason Dasan wished to make clear that the number of poems initially recorded in *Poetry* was exactly three hundred, as stated in the passage from the *Analects*, is also closely related to his general approaches on the Confucian classics. Contrary to the old and new commentaries—that is, those of He Yan, Huang Kan, Xing Bing, and Zhu Xi, which uniformly assume that "three hundred" is a rough estimate—Dasan believed that it reflected the reality because the five Shang poems in the extant *Poetry*, with its 305 in total, should not count in a discussion of the original attributes of this classic. With this argument, Dasan hoped to enhance its immaculacy.

On the other hand this implies that Dasan thought that all but six of the poems in *Poetry* were composed during the Zhou dynasty. Since, in Dasan's thinking, the Zhou had the best polity ever to exist in history, this implication accords with his assumption of *Poetry*'s perfection. Hence the philosophical significance of Dasan's rejection of Bao Xian's comment, as is evident in his second argument here: all of the poems of *Poetry* were without exception composed by sages, portraying their immaculate personalities without signaling a return to goodness.

2.3 The Master said, "If you lead the people with laws and decrees and keep them orderly with punishments, they will try to evade them but have no sense of shame. If you lead the people with virtue and keep them orderly with ritual propriety, they will have a sense of shame and be inspired."

子曰; 道之以政, 齊之以刑, 民免而無恥. 道之以德, 齊之以禮, 有恥且格.

2.3.1 Grounds

1) I supplement as follows: *Dao* 道 ("lead") here is synonymous with *dao* 導 (to lead). The ancient sage kings led people to do the good and in doing so became the people's teacher. This is what the saying "Yao and Shun led all under heaven with humanity" (*Daxue zhangju* 大學章句, 9a) means. *Zheng* 政 ("laws and decrees") here refers to laws and institutions, which are the means to rectify the people.

2) I supplement as follows: *Qi* 齊 ("keep them orderly") means to even the tops of things out.[19] Punishments are a means of punishing the evil, and ritual propriety is a means of preventing wantonness. They are comparable to trimming things to make them even, when they grow out in a disorderly manner.

3) Master Zhu commented, "[The first sentence states that] the people will feel no embarrassment and humiliation even when they evade punishments in a pathetic manner. This means that, although they do not dare to do evil, their mind-heart for evil has not perished yet."

4) I supplement as follows: *De* 德 ("virtue") here refers to filial piety and respect for elders. *Documents* says, "Carefully set forth five teachings" (*Shang Shu zhushu*, 2:31b). This remark concerns the phrase "lead the people with virtue." Let the feudal lords practice the ritual propriety of feudal lords, let the great officials practice the ritual propriety of the great officials, let the low-ranking officials and common people do so as well—this concerns the phrase "keep them orderly with ritual propriety."

5) I supplement as follows: *Ge* 格 ("be inspired") is here synonymous with *ge* 假 (to be affected) and means being inspired. *Documents* says, "Yao inspired [格] Heaven and Earth" (*Shang Shu zhushu*, 1:4b), and "If they become inspired [格], they will be accepted and hired" (4:7b). *Poetry* says, "Inspiration [格] of the spirits cannot be measured" (*Mao Shi zhushu*, 25:21a). *Ge* in these quotations refers to being inspired.[20]

2.3.2 Arguments

1) Kong Anguo argued, "*Zheng* here refers to laws and inculcations." I would refute this as follows:

Inculcations rather pertain to the matter of leading the people with virtue.

2) Bao Xian argued, "*De* refers to the Way and virtue." I would refute this as follows:

What is the identity of the Way and virtue? Nowadays, people do not understand the concept *de* clearly, so whenever they come across it while reading the holy classics, they become helpless in their ignorance of its nature. As a result, the people whom they regard as close to virtue are merely kindhearted and ingenuous people, who nevertheless cannot discern the pure from the stained. They hope to rule conveniently all under heaven by virtue of this personality, envisioning that the myriad things automatically return to their roots and become inspired. When they take control in any given situation to handle its affairs, however, they do not know how to set to work. Isn't this silly? All under heaven is not renewed and experiences deterioration day after day because of this.

"Virtue" is a name given to one's adherence to human moral orders. It is no more than filial piety, respect for elders, and benevolence. *Record of*

---

[19] "According to *Shou wen, qi* means that the height of rice or barley, when it ripens, becomes even" (quoted in *Yu ding Kangxi zidian*, 1:30b).
[20] Ge Qizhan 葛屺瞻 (fl. Ming dynasty) commented, "*Ge* means to be touched" (Unknown source).

Rites says, "The ancients, who wanted to illustrate the illustrious virtues throughout all under heaven, first kept their states orderly" (*Li ji zhushu*, 16:1b). In addition, when it enters into a discussion of orderly governance of the state and making all under heaven peaceful, the classic regards filial piety, respect for elders, and benevolence as the foundation for the goals. So aren't filial piety, respect for elders, and benevolence illustrious virtues? "Yao dian 堯典" says, "By revealing his wonderful virtues, Yao brought harmony to the nine classes in his kindred" (*Shang Shu zhushu*, 1:6b). So doesn't the [phrase] wonderful virtues refer to filial piety and respect for elders? *Classic of Filial Piety* says, "The former kings preserved the utmost virtues and the vital Way and thereby disciplined all under heaven" (*Xiaojing zhushu*, 1:3a). So doesn't the utmost virtues refer to filial piety and respect for elders? In the Way of the former kings, they led all under heaven by practicing filial piety and respect for elders themselves before everyone else. This is what the phrase "lead the people with virtue" means. Virtue should not be an ambiguous or convoluted object.

When the ruler leads the people with virtue, however, punishments are also used. A passage in *Documents*, which reads according to Dasan's reading "After an announcement of the statutes, Bo Yi 伯夷 frustrated the disobedient people with punishments,"[21] hints that the former kings issued the five statutes first and then frustrated with punishments those who did not follow the teachings. According to "Da Si tu 大司徒," in *Rites of Zhou*, "The head minister over the masses [Da Si tu] oversees the myriad people with the eight local punishments" (*Zhou li zhushu*, 2:1a) for offenses related to filial piety, respect for elders, harmonious relationship with one's family, and harmonious relationship with one's in-laws. In addition, "Kang gao 康誥" regards unfiliality and antagonism between brothers as the prime evil and the worst kind of hatred, such that there [should] be no pardon in the meting out of justice. All these examples are related to the matter of "leading the people with virtue," not to a discussion of punishments and laws.

3) He Yan argued, "*Ge* is here synonymous with *zheng* 正 (to rectify)." I would refute this as follows:

It does not make sense to say, "They will have a sense of shame and be rectified."[22]

4) I question Master Zhu as follows:

Lun yu jizhu argued, "*Ge* is here synonymous with *zhi* 至 (to reach). [This comment suggests that] people feel ashamed for doing evil and often reach to goodness." In my investigation, the character *ge* first appears in "Yao dian." The relevant remark "Yao inspired [*ge*] Heaven and Earth" means that Yao inspired Heaven's mind above and the people's mind below. Mei Ze, in his annotation on this remark, rendered *ge* as *zhi* (to reach), but

---

[21] See "Lü xing 呂刑" (*Shang Shu zhushu*, 18:31b).
[22] This rendition of *ge*, which sees it as meaning "to rectify," derives from *Mengzi zhu* 孟子注 by Zhao Qi 趙岐 (108–201) (see *Mengzi zhushu* 孟子註疏, 7-B:14a).

his rendition is acceptable only when this remark is conjoined with the character *guang* 光 (bright), which appears in the previous sentence. If one attempts to understand the statement under discussion, while rendering *ge* as *zhi*, one should add two characters *yushan* 於善 (to goodness) to it to make the sentence grammatically correct. I am afraid that this interpretation may appear less self-evident than that which adopts the plain sense of *ge* as "being inspired." In general, the character *mian* 免 ("to evade them") refers to a superficial evasion in a pathetic manner, whereas *ge* ("be inspired") refers to a sincere inspiration within one's heart. If one infuses the phrase "have a sense of shame" with the notion of "being inspired" in order to render *ge* as *zhi*, the passage will be unbalanced because its first half becomes more important, contributing to the gradual diminishment of the vitality of the teaching. This must not be so.[23]

5) For a classical text on the discussion here, see "Zi yi," in *Record of Rites*, which says, "The Master said, 'As for the people, if the ruler teaches them with virtue and keeps them orderly with ritual propriety, they will have an inspired mind-heart [格心]; if the ruler teaches them with laws and decrees and keeps them orderly with punishments, they will have an evasive mind-heart [遯心]'" (*Li ji zhushu*, 55:3a).[24]

   In my view, the "inspired mind-heart" refers to the mind-heart as inspired and affected; the "evasive mind-heart" refers to the mind-heart that seeks to evade punishments.

6) For a classical text on the discussion here, see *Kong congzi* (*Kong congzi* 孔叢子, A:16a,4).

   In my view, *Kong congzi* is a forged book.

* * *

Dasan's argument that "virtue," a concept unquestionably essential in the Confucian tradition but ambiguous to many minds, in Confucian canons should be clearly understood in conjunction with three basic moral deeds—filial piety, respect for elders, and benevolence—is persistent in his writings beyond *Noneo gogeum ju*. For example, in his explanation of the concept "bright virtue [明德]" in *Great Learning*, he concludes: "The three characters—filial piety, respect for elders, and benevolence—sum up the five teachings. In the matters of teaching the offspring of the state in the Great Academy and of the offspring's studies on the people, what else will be required than these three characters?" (*Daehak gong-ui* 大學公義, 5d) Indeed, this is one of Dasan's signature theories and is one reason his philosophy stands out amid intellectual challenges to neo-Confucianism.

---

[23] Cai Chen 蔡沈 (1167–1230) placed an additional character, *gong* 功 (merits), before *ge* when he commented a passage in "Yue Ming 說命," which reads: "Their merits reached [格] toward the Great Heaven" (*Shujing jizhuan* 書經集傳, 3:36b).
[24] On this, Zheng Xuan commented, "*Ge* [假] here means to arrive."

Dasan appears to believe that with this terse definition of the terms of debate, society can eliminate unnecessary barriers often caused by pedantic and thus time-consuming discourses on abstract notions. If "virtue" is linked with measurable deeds, virtue itself will become a quantitative concept that will eventually prevent metaethical questions from delaying a reformative project for improving society's moral standards. Understandably, many contemporary scholars have included what they have called this "practical" definition of virtue by Dasan in their prefaces to their expositions of his thought.

Next to Dasan's representative theory, the fact that he advocated, to a certain degree, the use of legalist measures, laws and punishments, in his comments is also intriguing. Given that Confucius's intention in this passage is to attack legalist ideas, Dasan seems to walk a tight rope connecting Confucianism and Legalism in a dangerous manner. His tolerance of legalist ideas may help identify him at least as a realist, not a romanticist or idealist. This identification, however, should not prevent one from aligning him with the moralist camp, for as seen here, he views legalist measures as necessary only for the efficient improvement of morality.

As a matter of fact, it was usual for Joseon bureaucrats to bear dual silhouettes—as moralists advocating legalist actions—since they were in charge of real administrations. Distinct from the bureaucrats, a group of scholars (the mainsteam Joseon Confucian scholars whom contemporary experts consider in their retrospective evaluation of Joseon Confucianism), representing the values of the Sarim 士林 (a term meaning literally "assembly of scholars" but metaphorically "scholars in the forest"), without hesitation expressed despair over this hybridization. The different perspectives of these two groups are crucial for understanding the differences between schools, philosophies, ideals, and even individual choices; the bureaucrats' group represents the polar opposite of the Sarim, and together they constitute two comparable lineages of Joseon Confucianism: scholars-in-the-forest versus scholars-in-the-court. Although Dasan was in exile when he wrote *Noneo gogeum ju*, he basically is a member of the latter group, as is shown here (and will be shown more clearly later).

Dazai Jun would opt for the same group as Dasan. In fact, he was known as having a passion to participate in real politics. He had an affinity with Dasan in his rejection of the renditions of *ge* that He Yan and Zhu Xi proposed. Whereas he resorted to an ancient comment by Zheng Xuan in discovering the "ancient definition of the character," however, Dasan relied on the main passages of the Confucian classics. Likewise, Dasan, in his acceptance of the legalist measures, is different from Dazai because he is still a deontologist.

2.4 The Master said, "At fifteen I set my mind on learning; at thirty I stood firm; at forty I was free from confusion; at fifty I understood the decrees of Heaven; at sixty my ear became receptive; at seventy I did not overstep the standards even when I followed what my mind-heart desired."

子曰; 吾十有五而志于學, 三十而立, 四十而不惑, 五十而知天命, 六十而耳順, 七十而從心所欲, 不踰矩.

2.4.1 Grounds

1) I supplement as follows: *Zhi* 志 ("set my mind on") means to place an established orientation in the mind-heart; *li* 立 ("stood firm") means to keep one's person stable and calm;[25] *bu huo* 不惑 ("free from confusion") means that one discerns the principle clearly and thereby bears no confusion;[26] *zhi tianming* 知天命 ("understood the decrees of Heaven") means that one abides by the laws of the Lord [帝] and thereby has no doubts no matter whether prospering or stalling;[27] *er shun* 耳順 ("ear became receptive") means that people's words do not sound offensive to him.[28] This shows that as cordiality and friendliness have been accumulated in his mind-heart, even irrational words do not sound offensive to him.

2) I supplement as follows: When Dao-mind takes control and human-mind obeys its orders, following what one's mind-heart desires corresponds to following what Dao-mind desires. Thus one does not overstep the standards. Contrarily, following what the common people's mind-heart desires corresponds to following what their human-mind desires. Thus they fall into evil.[29] *Ju* 矩 ("standards") is a tool for setting up directions correctly.[30] "[Such a person as Confucius] takes an office when it is proper to take an office, retires from an office when it is proper to retire from an office, stays long when it is proper to stay long, leaves quickly when it is proper to leave quickly" (*Mengzi jizhu*, 2A:2). This is what the sentence "I did not overstep the standards even when I followed what my mind-heart desired" implies.

2.4.2 Arguments

1) Zheng Xuan argued, "[*Er shun* means that] on hearing people's words, Confucius came to understand their delicate meaning." I would refute this as follows:

Whose words did Zheng Xuan mean by "people's words?" This rendering could only be acceptable if a great person, sage and divine, existed who was worthier than Confucius. I am not so sure that such a person existed among Confucius's contemporaries. Alternatively, some may argue that [what Zheng Xuan meant was that] on hearing ordinary people's words, Confucius came to understand their delicate meaning. Ordinary people's speeches, however, lack delicacy and profundity. Why is it necessary to become sixty years of age to understand their meaning? Some may also argue that to the sage, all sounds become comprehensible in his

---

[25] "Xue ji 學記" says, "Standing firm and not falling back is called a great achievement" (*Li ji zhushu*, 36:4b).
[26] The *Analects*, in one of the following chapters, says, "A man of wisdom would not be confused" (*Lun yu jizhu*, 9:28).
[27] *Mencius* says, "Waiting for the end of life in the cultivation of one's person, having no doubts regardless of an early death or a long life, is the way to establish the decrees" (*Mengzi jizhu*, 7A:1).
[28] Usually, when people's words sound offensive, one becomes discontented with the words in one's mind.
[29] "Qu li" says, "One should not follow desires" (*Li ji zhushu*, 1:2b).
[30] It keeps the above and the below and the four directions orderly and correct.

mind-heart once they are heard, as in his ability to realize the meaning of self-origination on hearing the song of the water Cang Lang 滄浪.[31] [In this view] Zi Gong, who realized the meaning of the phrase "Like cutting, then filing; like breaking, then grinding" on hearing Confucius teaching "Be joyful even when you are poor, and love ritual propriety even when you are rich," can also be believed to have reached the state of *er shun*. Zi Gong, who was thirty years younger than Confucius, was a young man at that time. Is it persuasive to say that the young man Zi Gong could reach the state of *er shun*, whereas Confucius narrowly wished to reach it at the age of sixty? The phrase "understanding the decrees of Heaven" informs us that Confucius reached Heaven's virtue, and the level of this accomplishment is extremely high. The so-called *er shun* excels this level. How can it be a subject of people's casual conversation?

In our encounters with defamation, applause, glory, and humiliation, all words that sound offensive cannot help but make people discontented with them in their minds. If, by deeply understanding the decrees of Heaven, a person becomes tolerant and immaculately mature, defamation, applause, glory, and humiliation cannot agitate his mind-heart. When nothing can agitate his mind-heart, no words will sound offensive. This state is called *er shun*. In their discussion of sages, people in later generations uniformly exalt them to the extent that they see sages as miraculous and inexplicable, overlooking what made them sages. As a result, people tend to think that although sages are truly honorable and miraculous, they have nothing to do with me and that there is no point in admiring sages. This is the reason sages do not emerge today and the Way eventually becomes obscure. Alas!

2) Su Zixi argued, "*Ju* ('standards') in this passage refers to the Emperor of Yu 虞 [King Shun] holding onto the mean and King Wen following the laws of the Lord" (Unknown source).

* * *

Neo-Confucian scholars created many theoretical frames to capture the ontological origin of the concepts of immorality or morality, frames that were centered on relationships between the kernel concepts in their philosophy, including the principle (*li*), the vital force (*qi*), mind-heart, human inborn nature, sentiments, the supreme polarity (*taiji* 太極), nonpolarity (*wuji* 無極), and so on. The only neo-Confucian theory that Dasan was also engaged with was the theory of Dao-mind and human-mind. This theory assumed that the mind-heart could be aligned with either the Way or secular desires, which amounted to a bifurcation of morality: if your mind-heart was tuned with the Way, you would be good. If not, you would be endangered (in neo-Confucianism) or definitely not good (in Dasan's philosophy). Dasan's ontological explanation of

---

[31] See the comment of Chen Li 陳櫟 (1252–1334) (*Lun yu jizhu daquan*, 2:10a).

the origin of morality—different from neo-Confucian discourses, which do not come to an end with this theory—seems to go no further.

Dasan might have engaged with this theory because, differently from other neo-Confucian metaphysical theories that were often affected by "heretical" ideas, it derived from a passage in one of the classics that Dasan always showed respect for—in this case, *Documents*. In this regard, *Documents* says, "Human-mind is dangerous, and Dao-mind is subtle; sincerely hold on to the mean through a thorough examination and concentration" (*Shang Shu zhushu*, 3:12b). The problem is that this passage is only found in the so-called *Documents in the Old Script*, which Dasan openly criticized as forged by Mei Ze. As a matter of fact, when Yan Ruoqu divested the extant *Documents* of the mantle of holy classic with his revolutionary research on the possible interpolations of newer material into it, the authority of neo-Confucianism was damaged as much as the dignity of the classic itself, because this passage had formed a part of the foundations of Zhu Xi's metaphysics. Mao Qiling, who honored ancient knowledge more than the research of his contemporary Yan, attempted to counter Yan's argument in his *Guwen Shang Shu yuanci* 古文尙書冤詞 (*A Speech Full of Qualms Regarding* Documents in the Old Script), and on this issue Dasan sided with Yan to disprove Mao's counter-arguments by writing *Maessi Sangseo pyeong* 梅氏尙書平 (*Fair Discussions on* Documents of Mei Ze). In this work, Dasan stated that he accepted the passage under discussion as an essential teaching among ancient sage kings, such as Shun and Yu, because the crucial terms and ideas in the passage appeared in other classical sources: the phrase "holding on to the mean" was found in the *Analects* (*Lun yu jizhu*, 20:1) and *Shi ji* (*Shi ji*, 1:12a), and the expression "the dangerousness of human-mind and the subtlety of Dao-mind" was found in *Xunzi,* alongside the concepts "a thorough examination" and "concentration" (*Xunzi*, 15:9b). In other words, Dasan believed that the passage genuinely reflected the teaching of the sages, although Mei Ze had interpolated it into "Da Yu mo 大禹謨" when he forged it. Dasan later obtained Yan Ruoqu's *Shang Shu guwen shuzheng* 尙書古文疏證 from Hong Hyeon-ju 洪顯周 (1793–1865)—in 1827, ten years after he was released from exile and fifteen years after he finished *Noneo gogeum ju*. Due to his new understanding of Yan's views, Dasan revised his *Maessi Sangseo pyeong* sometime between 1827 and 1834.

Readers may wonder how Dasan answers a question that involves his theory of human-mind and Dao-mind: what is the ontology of Dao-mind and human-mind? In his contemplation on this issue, Dasan actively utilizes the concept of Heaven, which overlaps with the concept of the Lord or the High Lord in his philosophy, in the same way the ancient classics resort to it whenever they confront ontological questions. With regard to the paradigm of the psychological bifurcation that can be possibly in tune with either the Way or secular desires, Dasan admits the existence of human subjectivity, a power endowed by Heaven. As for the substantial quality of the Way, he relates it to the human inborn nature that is again related to Heaven. Due to his heavy reliance on the concept of Heaven or the Lord, some scholars have insisted that Dasan's philosophy evolved under the influence of Christianity, for which he had once had a passion. Despite plenty of evidence that Dasan regretted his early engagement with the "heretical" idea and that he eventually wanted to be identified as a sincere student of Confucius, it will not be easy for disputes on the role Christian ideas played in Dasan's philosophy to cool down, for as is evident in his remarks on Heaven in this passage, he was not reluctant to convey his unique, if not Christian, understanding of Heaven, even in the writings he completed in the last phase of his life. For example, in his comment here on the term *zhi tianming*, a foundational concept in all branches of Confucianism, he says, "[This] means that one abides by the laws of the Lord and thereby has no doubts no matter whether prospering or stalling."

Notwithstanding the profound implications of this comment, Dasan did not provide more explanation or list it in "Overview of the Original Meanings" (if it was arranged by him). Rather, his interpretation of *er shun*—that is, "people's words do not sound offensive to Confucius"—is listed there. Finally, his rejection of the line of thinking that links the Confucian sages to incipient notions about the apriorism of their knowledge is worth noting, because it is in harmony with his persistent emphasis on learning and is distinguishable from the stance of neo-Confucianism and his contemporary philosophers. I will discuss this later in detail.

2.5 Meng Yizi asked about filial piety. The Master said, "Never be disobedient." Fan Chi was driving, and the Master informed him of the conversation, saying, "Mengsun asked me about filial piety, and I replied, 'Never be disobedient.'" Fan Chi asked, "What did you mean by that?" The Master said, "When your parents are alive, serve them according to ritual propriety; when they are dead, bury them according to ritual propriety; offer sacrifices to them according to ritual propriety."

孟懿子問孝. 子曰; 無違. 樊遲御, 子告之曰; 孟孫問孝於我, 我對曰; 無違. 樊遲曰; 何謂也? 子曰; 生事之以禮, 死葬之以禮, 祭之以禮.

2.5.1 Grounds

1) Kong Anguo commented, "Yizi refers to Zhongsun Heji 仲孫何忌 (d. 481 BCE), the great official of the state of Lu.[32] 'Yi' in Yizi is his posthumous title."[33]
2) Xing Bing commented, "*Wu wei* 無違 ('Never be disobedient') means to be compliant with ritual propriety."

---

[32] See the sixth year of the reign of Duke Ding [魯定公, r. 509–495 BCE] (*Zuo zhuan zhushu*, 20:14b–15a).
[33] Xing Bing commented, "Those who were generous, mild, worthy, and moral are given the title 'Yi.'"

3) Zheng Xuan commented, "Fan Chi was Confucius's disciple Fan Xu 樊須."[34]

4) Xing Bing commented, "Fan Xu was driving a carriage for Confucius."

5) Master Zhu commented, "Mengsun refers to Zhongsun.[35] . . . [A]t that time, the three families violated ritual propriety, so the Master warned them with this teaching. As the meaning of his remarks is implicit, however, it seems to have not been addressed for the three families only."[36]

2.5.2 Arguments

1) Huang Kan argued, "This passage states that people who practice filial piety are obedient to their parents in every affair, never resistant or defiant to them." I would refute this as follows:

   With regard to serving one's parents, there is the concept of "remonstrating with parents gently" (*Lun yu jizhu*, 4:18). What is the basis for the concept of obeying parents in every affair and not resisting or defying them? Fan Chi asked about Confucius's intention, and Confucius answered Fan Chi's question. Although their question and answer are self-explanatory, awkward interpretations have continued to emerge. Is this not troublesome?

2) Qi Lüqian 齊履謙 (fl. 1321) argued, "In the twenty-fourth year of the reign of Duke Zhao [魯昭公, r. 541–510 BCE], when Meng Xizi 孟僖子 (d. 524 BCE) was about to die, he asked Confucius for the caregiving of Yue 說 [南宮敬叔] and Heji so that they could learn about ritual propriety from him. At that time, Confucius was thirty-four years of age. Fan Chi must have driven for Confucius after the state of Lu invited Confucius, at the age of seventy, with courteous gifts. By that time, many years had passed since Meng Xizi died. Nevertheless, Yizi asked about filial piety—which is worthy of note. If Yizi had not resisted his father's instructions, following Confucius's teaching, Xizi could have been comforted" (*Lun yu jizhu daquan*, 2:15a–b).[37] I would refute this as follows:

   The phrase "Never be disobedient" does not mean never to resist any of the instructions of one's father. Xizi ordered Heji to learn about ritual propriety from Confucius, but Heji did not follow his father's instructions [If this passage concerns that event] Confucius would have replied to Yizi's questions by saying, "Never be disobedient to your father's orders." In this context, Confucius would not have replied to Fan Chi's questions

---

[34] According to *Shi ji*, "Fan Xu, whose adult name was Zi Chi 子遲, was from the state of Qi and [was] thirty-six years younger than Confucius" (*Shi ji*, 67:22b).

[35] "According to *Gongzi pu* 公子譜, by Du Yu, since Zhong Qingfu committed regicide, the family changed their name to Meng" (*Lun yu jizhu daquan*, 2:14a).

[36] Jin [Jin Lüxiang 金履祥 (1232–1303), Xu 許, in all editions of *Noneo gogeum ju*] commented, "As regards the three families' violation of ritual propriety, such actions as observing the ritual of erecting pillars [in a burial process] and using ropes for carrying a coffin violated the burial rituals, and such actions as having eight rows of dancers or removing the ritual vessels with the accompaniment of the Yong 雍 song violated of sacrifice rituals" (*Lun yu jizhu kaozheng* 論語集注考證, 1:11a).

[37] Mao Qiling argued, "Xizi ordered Heji to learn ritual propriety. Not disobeying one's parents means to practice ritual propriety fully. The passage about 'gentle remonstration' also says, 'Be very respectful and never be disobedient' " (*Si shu shengyan*, 4:2b–3a).

with the notion of "serving them according to ritual propriety and burying them according to ritual propriety." Rather, he might have answered Fan Chi's question by saying that "Meng Xizi ordered Mengsun to learn about ritual propriety from me, but Mengsun did not follow his father's instructions. So, I advised him accordingly." The main passage does not support this rendition.

Confucius's teaching here implicitly discloses Heji's crime of disobeying his father's orders and at the same time explicitly reveals the principle of mandatory obedience to the orders by bringing up the notion of "serving them according to ritual propriety and burying them according to ritual propriety." Doesn't this passage contain a profound message? Yizi in the first place did not want to learn about ritual propriety from Confucius. This would mean that he himself rejected Confucius. Is it compatible with principle to assert that Yizi, thirty years after he rejected Confucius, all of sudden came to Confucius to ask about filial piety? Regarding the two characters, *wu wei* ("Never be disobedient"), Confucius talked about them and personally provided a comment. It is unnecessary to make conjectures based on distorted ideas, yielding nonsense and self-contradiction.

3) For a classical text on the discussion here, see *Lun heng* (*Lun heng* 論衡, 9:2b, 7–3a, 4).

On this, Dazai Jun argued, "When Our Master taught people, 'he does not clear the way for anyone who is not bothered; he does not enlighten anyone who is not saddened' (*Lun yu jizhu*, 7:8). 'Xue Ji' says, 'In their teachings, noble people lead but do not drag; they encourage but do not discourage; they open the way but do not accompany their followers to the end' (*Li ji zhushu*, 36:16a). It also says, 'If explanations are already given but they still do not have any knowledge, it would be fine to give them up' (36:22b)."

* * *

Huang Kan's view, which Dasan refutes here, might seem extreme since, according to it, Confucius encouraged people to resist none of their parents' orders. Dasan refuted this view of Huang Kan, and other commentators also clarified that Confucius's advice in this passage, "Never be disobedient," is primarily related to ritual propriety (Xing Bing) or the moral principle (Zhu Xi). However, Huang Kan's comment does not necessarily contradict Confucian ideas, given that in the tradition, Shun embodied filial piety with his complete submission to his parents—especially his father, who attempted to kill him. In this regard, Mencius once praised Shun, who just went to a field to cry out and weep when he felt that his father disliked him, without acting in defiance (see *Mengzi jizhu*, 5A:1). In contrast, in a teaching that derived from a different genealogical source, Confucius advised his students: "remonstrate with one's parents gently," when one's parents are obviously on the wrong track. Dasan accepts this teaching to refute Huang Kan's interpretation and furthermore makes it clear that it is not compatible with Confucian norms to blindly submit oneself to one's parents. This point is more evident in Dasan's translation of Confucius's teaching in book 4, "Li ren": "The Master said, 'When serving your parents, remonstrate with them, but gently. This is to show that you intend not to follow their orders'" (*Lun yu jizhu*, 4:18). This translation is quite interesting because in many commentators' readings, the passage is usually translated as "The Master said, 'When serving your parents, remonstrate with them, but gently. When they show their intention not to follow your advice.'"

In relation to the political or philosophical implications of Dasan's unique attitude toward the son's obligation to follow his parents, in the diverse factional disputes during the Joseon dynasty, absolutization of the son's submission to his parents was commonly upheld by the Westerners—the faction that confronted the Southerners (that is, Dasan's faction). Indeed, Dasan is persistent in his prioritization of public values over personal family relationships, regardless of many Confucians' claims that family relationships reflect public values. In this passage, ritual propriety represents public values, but other things (such as, the court, the state, and Confucian statecraft) can also represent them in Dasan's philosophy.

Although omitted in the translation here, in a discussion in "Wen Kong 問孔" (Questions to Confucius), Wang Chong 王充 (27–97) criticized Confucius for his convoluted method of teaching Meng Yizi; Confucius did not clearly convey his main point in this passage but just said, "Never be disobedient." Dasan quotes Dazai Jun here to advocate Confucius's method: even if a student fails to understand the implications of his teacher's instructions, it is not the teacher's fault.

2.6 Meng Wubo asked about filial piety. The Master said, "Let your parents worry about nothing other than your illness."

孟武伯問孝. 子曰; 父母唯其疾之憂.

2.6.1 Grounds

1) Ma Rong commented, "Wubo refers to Zhongsun Zhi 仲孫彘, Yizi's son.[38] 'Wu' is a posthumous title.[39] This passage states that filial sons make their parents worry about them only when they get ill because they do not dare do wrong."[40]

---

[38] See the seventeenth year of the reign of Duke Ai (*Zuo zhuan zhushu*, 59:28b).
[39] "According to *Shi fa* 諡法, those who were upright, unyielding, straightforward, and strict were given the title 'Wu'" (*Lun yu zhushu*, 2:4b).
[40] Xing Bing commented, "Besides becoming ill, they do not dare to commit misdeeds that would worry their parents."

2.6.2 Arguments

1) Wang Chong in *Lun heng* argued, "Wubo frequently worried about his parents. Thus, Confucius said, 'You should worry only about their illness.' "[41] I would refute this as follows:

    This kind of person is not a man of filiality.

2) I question Master Zhu as follows:

    Ma Rong's annotation here is truly acceptable. However, many people's sons often make no effort to behave themselves, sometimes giving themselves over to wine and women or sometimes ruining their health in wild circumstances. Consequently, they are attacked by illness and thereby make their parents worried. The new interpretation of Master Zhu, in that respect, is also plausible. Nevertheless, later Confucians criticized and excoriated it severely. What foolishness!

* * *

While accepting the old interpretation of this passage by Ma Rong, Zhu Xi suggested a new possible rendition of it: "Parents worry about nothing other than your illness." Mao Qiling and Dazai Jun rejected this new reading for various reasons, and Dasan rebutted their arguments while agreeing with Zhu Xi's. This is a recurrent pattern in *Noneo gogeum ju*.

2.7 Zi You asked about filial piety. The Master said, "Nowadays, filial piety refers to being able to attend one's parents. However, even dogs and horses attend people. Without reverence, what is there to distinguish them?"[42]

子游問孝. 子曰; 今之孝者, 是謂能養. 至於犬馬, 皆能有養, 不敬, 何以別乎?

2.7.1 Grounds

1) Kong Anguo commented, "Zi You is Confucius's disciple Yan Yan 言偃."[43]
2) I supplement as follows: *Yang* 養 ("to attend one's parents") means taking care of one's parents from nearby.[44]
3) Bao Xian commented, "Dogs stand guard and horses obviate the need for human labor. They also attend people."[45]

---

[41] In this interpretation, sons do not constantly need to worry about their parents when serving them. Only when their parents become ill should they worry.

[42] [According to Dazai Jun, but not to the extant edition] in *Yan tie lun*, *wei* 謂 ("refers to") in the first line appears as *wei* 爲 (to do) (See *Yan tie lun* 鹽鐵論, 6:27b).

[43] According to *Shi ji*, "Yan Yan was from the state of Wu 吳 and [was] forty-five years younger than Confucius" (*Shi ji*, 67:14b).

[44] This should not be taken to mean just feeding the parents.

[45] Xing Bing commented, "Although dogs and horses can attend people, they cannot have reverence because they lack intelligence."

4) I supplement as follows: If one attends his parents but does not revere them, he is not distinguished from dogs and horses.[46]

2.7.2 Arguments

1) Xing Bing argued, "*Neng yang* 能養 ('able to attend one's parents') means that one nourishes the parents with food." I would refute this as follows:

Mao Qiling explained, "According to 'Jixi li 既夕禮,' 'Those who take care of a sick person [養者] should purify themselves' (*Yi li zhushu* 儀禮註疏, 13:48a). According to 'Wenwang shizi 文王世子,' 'King Wen took care [養] of his ill father, dressed in dark-colored garments' (*Li ji zhushu*, 20:44a). These are related to how to take care of sick people. That said, people would never feast sick and fatigued people. 'Tangong' records: 'With regard to serving one's parents, one should approach them and take care of [就養] them from nearby' (6:3a). The annotation for this sentence explains that it means that one helps one's parents' bodies. Serving the ruler and teachers is also said to be 'approaching and taking care of them [就養].' That said, I have never heard of the ruler receiving food from his subjects or the teacher approaching his students to give them lessons in the same manner in which teachers are received and fed by students these days. Owing to these sources, I now understand that *yang* means to take care of someone, not to feed them. *Classic of Filial Piety* says, 'Affection for one's parents grows up under their knees, and one comes to attend [養] them' (*Xiaojing zhushu*, 5:6a). If *yang* means to feed one's parents, how can a newborn baby feed his parents?" (*Lun yu jiqiu pian*, 1:15a–b)

2) He Yan argued, "People can nourish [養] even dogs and horses. Without reverence, there is no way to distinguish this from that. *Mencius* says, 'Feeding someone without loving him is like breeding a pig; loving someone without respecting him is like breeding a domestic animal' (*Mengzi jizhu*, 7A:37)." I would refute this as follows:

Xu Zhongshan 徐仲山 (fl. Qing dynasty) explained, "Since dogs and horses manage [能] to serve people, it is said that they 'can.'[47] If people nourish dogs and horses, how can it be said that they 'can?'[48] How many times do we see people who cannot breed domestic animals?" (Quoted in *Lun yu jiqiu pian*, 1:16a) For a classical text that supports this explanation here, see "Fang ji," which says, "Even petty people can manage to attend their parents. If noble people do not revere them, how can they be distinguished from others?" (*Li ji zhushu*, 51:24a) In this passage, "petty people" refers to people of lower status, while "noble people" refers to men of nobility. The "petty people" can be compared with "dogs and horses" in the main

---

[46] "Ji yi" says, "Zengzi said, 'Filial piety has three different levels. The greatest one is revering the parents; not making the parents humiliated follows it; attending them is the lowest one" (*Li ji zhushu*, 48:6a).

[47] The character *neng* ("can") is here used because it leaves a strong impression.

[48] There is nothing special.

passage and the noble people with people's sons. The structure of the passage in "Fang ji" is thus identical to that of this classic. In conclusion, the character *neng* is generally adopted to show one's admiration.

3) For a classical text that supports my argument here, see "Ji yi" (*Li ji zhushu*, 48:6b, 6–7).

In my investigation, this passage originally comes from "Zengzi daxiao 曾子大孝."[49]

4) For classical texts that support my arguments here, see the memorial of Ma Zhou 馬周 (601–648) in *Xin Tang shu* (*Xin Tang shu* 新唐書, 98:10b, 2–3) and "Cimian qifu biao 辭免起復表," by Wang Fengfu 王豊甫 from the Song dynasty (quoted in *Lun yu jiqiu pian*, 1:16b, 7–8).

In my view, these two passages show that their authors accepted Bao Xian's interpretation.

* * *

Zhu Xi's interpretation is distinct from Dasan's in two respects: to him, *yang* means to feed someone, and with regard to the second sentence, the recipients of the action, *yang*, are dogs and horses—not, as in Dasan's comment, people. Dasan's repudiation of Zhu Xi's view is largely indebted to Mao Qiling's research. Dasan not only introduces Mao's argument here but also reproduces Mao's citations, including Ma Zhou's memorial and Wang Fengfu's writing, to reinforce his view. Interestingly, this interpretation, initially provided by Bao Xian and later revived by Mao Qiling, is listed in "Overview of the Original Meanings." In contrast, that list omits some of Dasan's more contentious and seemingly more significant arguments (e.g., his argument about the laws of the Lord in relation to "the decrees of Heaven [天命]" in 2.4.). So if Dasan is held to have truly arranged "Overview of the Original Meanings" to represent the gist of his arguments, this imbalance in "Overview" will definitely raise some questions that will not easily be resolved.

Dasan does not mention "Overview of the Original Meanings" in his voluminous writings. The only document that cites it and provides basic information about its nature is *Sa-am seonsaeng yeonbo* 俟菴先生年譜, the chronology of Dasan's life that was composed by Jeong Gyu-yeong 丁奎英 (1872–1927), Dasan's great-great-grandson, in 1921. Since it is difficult to find consistent criteria from the list, one might suspect that Jeong Gyu-yeong or someone other than Dasan himself made the list.

2.8 Zi Xia asked about filial piety. The Master said, "Managing one's facial expression is the difficulty. When there is work to be done, the young

---

[49] See *Da Dai Li ji* (*Da Dai Li ji*, 4:22a).

undertake the labor; when there is wine and food, they serve these to the seniors first: Is this enough to be considered filial piety?"

子夏問孝. 子曰; 色難. 有事, 弟子服其勞, 有酒食, 先生饌, 曾是以爲孝乎?

2.8.1 Grounds

1) I supplement as follows: *Se nan* 色難 ("Managing one's facial expression is the difficulty.") means that when serving one's parents, it is difficult to maintain a happy facial expression.[50]

2) I supplement as follows: *Dizi* 弟子 ("the young") is an appellation for the lower-standing and juniors; *xiansheng* 先生 ("the seniors") is an appellation for superiors and elders; *fu* 服 ("undertake") means that one takes on a responsibility, similar to an ox accepting a harness;[51] *zhuan* 饌 ("serve") means to produce an array of wine and food before the seniors. Principally, in a gathering of the young and the old, the lower-standing and juniors usually undertake the toil when there is work to be done, and when there are wine and food, what is to be offered to superiors and elders is usually set before them earlier. This is one of the constant rituals in villages. When sons serve their parents, they should maintain a smiling face and happy expression along with the constant rituals. If one stops at merely following the constant rituals between the old and the young, is it enough to be considered filial piety? *Ceng* 曾 ("enough") is here used to tone down the rhetoric of this passage.[52]

2.8.2 Arguments

1) Bao Xian argued, "*Se nan* means that it is difficult for one to behave in a manner that is responsive to the facial expressions of one's parents." I would refute this as follows:

   Chen Li explained, "Bao's interpretation is only acceptable when additional characters [父母承順] are inserted into the original passage" (*Lun yu jizhu daquan*, 2:18b).

2) Ma Rong argued, "*Xiansheng* refers to parents and older brothers." I would refute this as follows:

   In his teaching, Confucius obviously distinguished one's parents from *xiansheng* ("the seniors") and one's own children from *dizi* ("the young"), hoping to have a cordial countenance and a grateful demeanor in addition to the constant rituals between the old and the young. The early Confucians carelessly interpreted *xiansheng* as indicating one's parents and thus made

---

[50] Master Zhu recited a quotation: "Filial sons who have deep love for their parents must be cordial; those who are cordial must have happy facial expressions; those who have happy facial expressions must have smiles on their faces" (*Lun yu jizhu*, 1:10a). This is a quotation of a passage in "Ji yi."

[51] According to "Kao gong ji 考工記," a spot between two harnesses is called *heng ren* 衡任 (balancing responsibilities) (*Zhou li zhushu*, 40:4a).

[52] This is a definition of *ceng* in *Shuo wen* (*Shuo wen jie zi*, 2-A:2a).

Confucius's words extremely ambiguous. Who on earth calls his own parents *xiansheng* and his own children *dizi*?

3) Ma Rong argued, "*Zhuan* signifies food and drinks." I would refute this as follows:

"Shi guanli 士冠禮" says, "Make an array [饌] of the divining stalks at the western hall" (*Yi li zhushu*, 1:6a). Another saying in "Shi hunli 士昏禮" also reads: "Make an array [饌] of fish condiments and soy sauces at the center of the room" (2:13b). *Protocols and Rites*, in its many chapters, adopts the character *zhuan* to convey the meaning of making an array. Is the said translation of *zhuan* into food and drinks acceptable?

4) Wu Cheng 吳程 (?) argued, "In the past, *ceng* 曾 ('enough') was read as identical to *zeng* 增 (to add). However, *Lun yu jizhu* reads it as it is" (Unknown source). Cheng Fuxin 程復心 (1257–1340) argued, "*Ceng* is pronounced the same as *ceng* 層 (a layer), an example of which is found in a chapter of the *Analects*, 'Can it really [曾] be said that Mt. Tai ...?' (*Lun yu jizhu*, 3:6) According to *Shi wen* 釋文, it means 'already.' Or, it is a word used to refer to an unexpected situation or changes of tone" (Unknown source).[53]

In my investigation, a poem in "Da ya 大雅" that employs the character *ceng* four times says, "That you should have [曾] such violent and repressive people; that you should have [曾] such exploiting people; that you should have [曾] them in government offices; that you should have [曾] them in charge of affairs" (*Mao Shi zhushu*, 25:3a–b). It also contains a line: "However, you have not [曾] abided by them" (25:9b), which uses *ceng* once.[54] In addition, in *Mencius*, a sentence reads: "How dare [曾] you compare me to this person?" (*Mengzi jizhu*, 2A:1) *Ceng* in these sentences neither conveys the meaning of "already" nor registers the changes of tone. I would say that *Shuo wen*'s explanation of the character—that is, that it is used to shift the tone down— is nearly correct. And when this character is used to indicate a grandchild [曾孫], it is pronounced in the same way as *zeng* 增, whereas its meaning is the same as that of *ceng* 層. Thus I am afraid that it would be incorrect to pronounce the character as *ceng* only in the aforementioned passage in the *Analects*: "Can it really [曾] be said that Mt. Tai ... ?"

* * *

In respect to the interpretation of *se nan*, Dasan seems to follow Zhu Xi's view, which challenges the "old" view shared by Ma Rong and Xing Bing. It should be noted, however, that Zhu Xi's understanding of the term overlaps with that of Zheng Xuan, who left the oldest comment on it. He Yan, in his

---

[53] According to *Shi er bian* 示兒編, by Sun Yi 孫奕 (fl. 1190), "Nowadays, scholars pronounce the character *ceng* 曾 in the same way as *ceng* 層, except for cases in which it is used to indicate one's family name or a grandchild. In ancient classics and histories, however, no sentence supports this practice. Thus it should be read as identical to *zeng* 增" (quoted in *Yu ding Kangxi zidian*, 13:34a).

[54] "Da ya" also contains a line, "They did [曾] not tend us the people" (*Mao Shi zhushu*, 24:110a), which employs *ceng* once.

Lun yu jijie, introduced part of Zheng Xuan's comments on the *Analects*, but the one on this term is missing in *Lun yu jijie*, as it did not contain the entirety of the Zheng's comments. As a matter of fact, they are unavailable even now, although contemporary scholars have recently succeeded in restoring and compiling the comments that are available into a book, *Lun yu Zhengshi zhu* 論語鄭氏註 (the oldest title of which must have been *Lun yu Zheng Xuan zhu* 論語鄭玄註, according to *Jingdian shi wen*), thanks to archaeological discoveries made in Dunhuang and other places. Zhu Xi's understanding of *se nan*, as it is conveyed in *Lun yu Zhengshi zhu*, proves identical to that of Zheng Xuan. Dasan, however, was not a beneficiary of the modern excavations.

Dasan's arguments in this chapter mainly deal with the correct meaning of a character or term and thereby show affinity with the philological studies of the Han and Tang dynasties. Since Dasan is persistent in opposing the excessive inclination toward philological content in Han and Tang Confucianism, it could be conjectured that he gravitates toward the same topic in this chapter in order to show that he is qualified to participate in the complicated exegetical discourses surrounding this important classical text. As the reader will see, a large portion of his commentaries on the *Analects* served that purpose.

"Overview of the Original Meanings" lists a light dismissal by Dasan of Ma Rong's view on *xiansheng*. Since this dismissal does not accompany any statement of a philosophical stance, it was presumably placed in the list because Zhu Xi also followed Ma Rong's view. In consideration of the bluntness of Dasan's criticism on this issue, it is obvious that he was greatly displeased with this view and that, if he did create "Overview of the Original Meanings," he wanted to show his severe criticism, without directly targeting Zhu Xi, by including it in "Overview."

2.9 The Master said, "Once, I talked with Hui;[55] he did not raise an objection all day, as though he were stupid. When he withdrew, however, I observed his private relationships and found that he was so competent that he manifested what I taught. Hui is not stupid at all."

子曰; 吾與回言, 終日不違如愚. 退而省其私, 亦足以發, 回也不愚.

2.9.1 Grounds

1) Kong Anguo commented, "Hui refers to a disciple of Confucius whose family name was Yan 顏. His adult name was Zi Yuan 子淵."[56]

---

[55] This should be read with a pause here.
[56] According to *Shi ji*, he was a man of the state of Lu and thirty years younger than Confucius. At the age of twenty-nine, his hair turned entirely gray, and he died at an early age (*Shi ji*, 67:2b–3b).

2) Master Zhu commented, "*Bu wei* 不違 ('did not raise an objection') means that, as his opinions did not conflict with those of Confucius, Yan Hui 顏回 was quietly listening without raising a question."

3) I supplement as follows: *Tui er xing* 退而省 ("he withdrew, however, I observed") means that Yan Hui withdrew, and Confucius observed.

4) Dazai Jun commented, "*Si* 私 ('private relationships') is opposite to *gong* 公 (public). Confucius's disciples regarded having an audience with Confucius as a public affair and mingling with their friends as a private matter."

5) Kong Anguo commented, "Confucius observed Yan Hui when he withdrew and found that he manifested and illustrated the great body of Confucius's teachings while discussing moral principles with a couple of his colleagues."

6) I supplement as follows: *Fa* 發 ("manifested") refers to an act of flowering after sprouting buds. A line in *Changes* reads: "That which it keeps a beauty but should endure is for manifesting [發] it in due time" (*Zhou Yi zhushu*, 2:6b).[57]

2.9.2 Arguments

1) Jin Lüxiang argued, "A pause should be placed after *zhongri* 終日 ("all day"), making 'I talked with Hui all day' a whole sentence" (*Lun yu jizhu kaozheng*, 1:12b). I would refute this as follows:

Reading *zhongri* in conjunction with *yan* ("talked") hardly makes sense according to the writing principle. When a pause is placed after *yan*, making "Once I talked with Hui" and "he never raised an objection all day" two separate sentences, the reading of this passage becomes smoother.

2) I question Master Zhu as follows:

When Yan Hui stayed alone in his personal residence, he must have merely sat up straight without talking. So how could Confucius know whether he had the competence to manifest what was taught? *Si* should be taken to mean private discussions among friends. Zengzi also displayed a similar attitude. When Confucius said, "My Way is penetrated by one thing," Zengzi replied, "Yes." This shows that he never raised an objection. After Confucius left, he answered his colleagues' question about the meaning, saying, "Our Master's Way is wholeheartedness and the correlation of minds, nothing more" (*Lun yu jizhu*, 4:15). This shows that he had the competence to manifest what was taught.

* * *

Dasan names Jin Lüxiang only as a commentator who argued that a pause should be made after *zhongri*, but this reading appears to be universal among

---

[57] The succinctness of the Master's words can be likened to having buds; Master Yan's manifestation of the meaning of his teachings bears resemblance to flowering.

all interpreters who indicated how to treat the term, including Xing Bing and Zhu Xi. Accordingly, Dasan could not find grounds for his unique reading, so attempted to justify his reading with the term "principle"—an interesting and recurrent foundation for Dasan's arguments. This undefined "principle" may seem subjective, unless logical explanations about it are provided for skeptical minds. However, Dasan's reading is absolutely acceptable, if not the only correct one. In fact, given Dasan's creative suggestion, one may wonder why this persuasive reading was not proposed by commentators earlier. To some, it might prove more persuasive than the common reading because it would have been, practically speaking, difficult for Confucius to talk with his disciple(s) all day. When it is combined with the sentence "he never raised an objection," it can more easily be rendered as an idiomatic expression rather than as indicating a real passage of time. Surprisingly, however, this innovative reading is not listed in "Overview of the Original Meanings."

From the same perspective from which he considers the feasibility of exegetical theories, Dasan here questions Zhu Xi because Zhu Xi saw *si* as meaning the time Yan Hui stayed alone in his personal residence. If so, Dasan thought, "How could Confucius know whether he had the competence to manifest what was taught?" Even though Dasan did not utter this openly, he must have felt that Zhu Xi's interpretation was not compatible with "reasonability" or "principle."

2.10 The Master said, "Look how a man is motivated; observe how he proceeds; examine where he dwells content. How, then, can he hide himself? How can he hide himself?"

子曰; 視其所以, 觀其所由, 察其所安. 人焉廋哉? 人焉廋哉?

2.10.1 Grounds

1) I supplement as follows: *Shi* 視 ("look") is to see something often indifferently;[58] *guan* 觀 ("observe") is to see something with intentions;[59] *cha* 察 ("examine") is to see something in a more scrupulous manner.

2) I supplement as follows: *Yi* 以 ("motivated") means to arise from;[60] *you* 由 ("proceeds") means to pass through;[61] *an* 安 ("dwells content") means to stay without moving.[62] In understanding one's personality, whenever a man takes on a business, you should observe by what reason he has been

---

[58] A sentence in *Great Learning* reads: "If the mind is absent, we look but do not see" (*Daxue zhangju*, 0:7b).
[59] *Changes* says, "One observes out from a door" (*Zhou Yi zhushu*, 4:26b).
[60] A poem in "Bei feng 邶風" says, "Why does it take this long? There must be a reason [以]" (*Mao Shi zhushu*, 3:53a).
[61] He Yan commented, "This means to observe how one has traversed."
[62] *Mencius* says, "I dare to ask in which of these do you dwell content [安]" (*Mengzi jizhu*, 2A:2).

motivated, on what path he has traveled, and at what point he eventually arrives.[63] Then, no one can conceal the reality.

3) Kong Anguo commented, "*Sou* 廋 ('hide') means to conceal."

2.10.2 Arguments

1) For a classical text on the discussion here, see *Da Dai Li ji*, which says, "Inspect what a man does; observe how he proceeds; examine where he dwells content. In doing so, speculate on what is to come based on what has occurred, and speculate on what is implied based on what has been uncovered."[64]

In my view, Master Zhu based his rendering of *yi* 以 ("motivated"), which sees it as synonymous with *wei* 爲 (to do), on *Da Dai Li ji*. *Da Dai Li ji*, however, is composed of multifarious quotations, so it contains no exquisite meanings.[65]

* * *

According to Dasan, Confucius illustrated his method for understanding other people, or other people's personalities, in *Analects* 1.3, 1.13, 14.46, and in this chapter. This is a method to measure a person's inner virtue through an examination of his outer behavior. Confucians have tended to believe in the functional relationship between the two more firmly than have adherents of other religious traditions in East Asia, partly because of their emphasis on ritual propriety. Dasan also accepts this proclivity toward judgment in the tradition, as is seen here, but not blindly, as is seen in his comments on "artful words and charming countenance" in chapter 1.3.

In *Noneo gogeum ju*, Dasan quotes passages from *Da Dai Li ji* more than twenty times, rendering it one of the important classical sources he used for his arguments. As shown here, however, Dasan did not accede to the authenticity of *Da Dai Li ji*, so he quoted passages from it selectively. This selection is primarily indebted to his judgment on reasonability, not to his philological investigations of words and phrases. This aspect distinguishes Dasan's research from that of the school of Ancient Literature and Writings and from the work of Dazai Jun, which was inclined toward a discovery of the philologically original meanings of words and phrases.

2.11 The Master said, "He renews what he has learned and acquires new knowledge; it is worth being a teacher."

子曰; 溫故而知新, 可以爲師矣.

---

[63] Xing Bing commented, "Examine where he feels comfortable."
[64] See "Wenwang guanren 文王官人" (*Da Dai Li ji*, 10:8b).
[65] According to *Guliang's Commentary*, "*Shi* means to see ordinarily, while *guan* means to see in an unusual manner" (*Chunqiu Guliang zhuan zhushu* 春秋穀梁傳註疏, 2:5a).

2.11.1 Grounds

1) He Yan commented, "*Wen* 溫 ('renews') is here interchangeable with *xun* 尋 (to heat up, according to Dasan)."

2) Xing Bing commented, "'Zhong yong 中庸' [as a chapter of *Li ji* in this context] says, 'He renews what he has learned and acquires new knowledge.' On this saying, Zheng Xuan commented, '*Wen* here should be read as meaning to warm up as in *wen* in *xunwen* 燖溫 (to heat up and warm). In other words, *wen* here means that a person at times practices what he has learned after having mastered it" (*Li ji zhushu*, 53:12a).[66]

3) Master Zhu commented, "*Gu* 故 ('what he has learned') refers to what one has heard in the past; *xin* 新 ('new knowledge') refers to what one acquires today.

4) I supplement as follows: "It is worth being a teacher" means that the teacher's position is quite valuable. When a man loses interest in what he learned in the past, he could take the opportunity to renew it and acquire new knowledge through teaching. Isn't this a matter of improving ourselves? Therefore it is worth it for a person to be a teacher.

2.11.2 Arguments

1) He Yan argued, "He who investigates and draws inferences from [尋繹] things in the past and thereby acquires new knowledge is fit to be a teacher."[67] I would refute this as follows:

   In respect of said expression in "Yousi ce," "Warm up the ritual utensils for the surrogate body of the ancestor," Kong Anguo commented, "In ancient writings, *re* 爇 (to heat) always appears as *xun*" (*Yi li zhushu*, 17:3a).[68] *Record of Rites* often adopts *xun* 燖 (to boil) in place of *xun* 尋, and *Zuo's Commentary* also contains a sentence "If something can be heated up [尋], it can also be cooled down" (*Zuo zhuan zhushu*, 59:4b).[69] In conclusion, *xun* does not convey the meaning of drawing an inference.

2) Also in my view, the way of being a teacher ranges too widely for the only requirement for becoming a teacher to be that people "renew" ("investigate and infer about" in He Yan's reading) the past learning. By inserting a word, "then

---

[66] In the twelfth year of the reign of Duke Ai, *Zuo's Commentary* says, "Duke Ai had a meeting with the lord of Wu at Tuogao 橐皋. With a command from the lord, Pi 嚭, the prime minister of the state of Wu, asked Duke Ai to renew [尋] their alliance.... [Z]i Gong said, 'An alliance between countries can be either warmed up [尋] or cooled down'" (*Zuo zhuan zhushu*, 59:4a–b). On this record, Jia Kui 賈逵 (30–101) commented, "*Xun* is here interchangeable with *wen*" (59:4b). In addition, "Yousi ce 有司徹" says, "Warm up the ritual utensils for the surrogate body of the ancestor [尸]" (*Yi li zhushu*, 17:3a). These are the examples in which *xun* is interchangeable with *wen*.

[67] Xing Bing argued, "Investigate and draw inferences from things in the past and thereby acquire new knowledge—then you can be a teacher."

[68] This notion, expressed differently, appears in *Protocols and Rites*, which was discovered in Confucius's house.

[69] An annotation on the terms "raw meat [腥]" and "half-boiled meat [爛]" in "Jiao tesheng 郊特牲" clarifies this point: "*Xun* 尋 [爛 in all editions of *Noneo gogeumju*] is often replaced with *xun* 燖" (*Yi li zhushu*, 17:3a).

[則]," into his interpretation of this passage, Xing Bing distorted its meaning. Even when a man loses interest in the past learning, he can take the opportunity to renew it and acquire new knowledge every time he teaches. I believe that Confucius saw that it was advantageous to address this point in this passage.

* * *

Dasan's creative reading appears again in this chapter with regard to what is translated here as "it is worth being a teacher." All English translations and later commentators, without exception, follow He Yan's interpretation (or Kong Anguo's interpretation according to *Lun yu bijie*, by Han Yu), viewing the preceding sentence as stating qualifications for becoming a teacher. In contrast, Dasan sees it as one of the benefits of being a teacher, and his reading would again be plausible to readers who are not intimidated by long conventional practices. With new interpretations of this sort, Dasan accommodates a desire for new insightful readings of this old classic, an attempt that can only be made possible by an indomitable spirit. This view is listed in "Overview of the Original Meanings."

In line with Dasan's preference for certainty over ambiguity in understanding given expressions and sentences, he here renders *wen* as "to renew," a meaning that stems from the character's primary definition, "to heat up." He Yan, rendering it as "to investigate and infer about," did not clarify what should be inferred, thus allowing later thinkers to associate this passage with the investigation and inference of abstract notions, as seen in Zhu Xi's school.

2.12 The Master said, "The noble person does not limit himself to being a tool."

子曰; 君子不器.

2.12.1 Grounds

1) Master Zhu commented, "All tools suit their functions so that they cannot be intermixed."[70]

Xing Bing commented, "Boats and oars are the means of crossing rivers; carriages and carts the means of traveling over land. They do not work if switched around."

2.13. Zi Gong asked about the noble person. Confucius replied, "He puts his words into action first; he utters his words after the action."

子貢問君子. 子曰; 先行其言, 而後從之.

---

[70] Master Cheng commented, "Pursuing one talent or one art is to regard oneself as a tool" (*Lun yu jizhu daquan*, 2:25b–26a).

2.13.1 Grounds

1) Zhou Fuxian 周孚先 (fl. 1538) commented, "The noble person takes action before talking and talks after taking action" (*Lun yu jizhu daquan*, 2:26b).

2.13.2 Arguments

1) I question Master Zhu [who adopted Cheng Yi's and Fan Zuyu's comments in his *Lun yu jizhu*] as follows:

When Zi You asked about filial piety, Confucius taught him a notion of reverence. On this, Master Cheng commented, "Zi You was able to nourish his parents but sometimes lack an attitude of reverence" (*Lun yu jizhu*, 1:10b). When Zi Xia asked about filial piety, Confucius taught him a notion of managing facial expressions. On this, Master Cheng commented, "Zi Xia failed to have cordial facial expressions" (1:10b). When Zi Gong asked about the noble person, Confucius taught him notion of putting one's words into action first. On this, Fan Zuyu 范祖禹 (1041–1098) commented, "Zi Gong's problem lies in the fact that he uttered without deep consideration" (1:11a–b).

Though the words given in lessons for inspiration are purported to be effective for overcoming one's problems, when there is no clear evidence, it is difficult to inquire into the details. If the aforementioned comments are acceptable, Master Yan then proves a man incapable of overcoming his bodily desires because, when he asked about humanity, Confucius taught him a notion of overcoming one's bodily desires (*Lun yu jizhu*, 12:1). Also Yuan Xian 原憲 then appears to be a man who is willing to take a government office even in a disorderly state because, when he asked about shame, Confucius taught him a notion of [taking a government office in a state] lacking the Way (*Lun yu jizhu*, 14:1). Does this mean, in consideration of their realities, that it was excessive to compliment Master Yan for his swiftness in recovering the moral principles or Yuan Xian for his joy in the midst of poverty?

When Zi Lu 子路 asked about government, Confucius taught him a notion of not being negligent (*Lun yu jizhu*, 13:1). When he asked about serving the lord, Confucius also taught him a notion of presenting a bold remonstration (*Lun yu jizhu*, 14:23). In general, Zi Lu is believed to have excelled others in keeping courage. Thus, when he took on the responsibility of governing a state, people became worried about his potential excessiveness in dedication; when he came to serve his lord, people became worried about his potential excessiveness in presenting a bold remonstration. Notwithstanding his shortcomings, according to the comments under discussion, it can be assumed that in his teaching for Zi Lu, Our Master not only excused his problems but also encouraged him to do more to aggravate them. Is this assumption persuasive? Overall, I am afraid that topics of this sort are not necessarily discussed in detail.

2) Huang Kan commented, "The words of the noble person must inform the standard of things. Therefore by his every word, he helps later people follow and respect them." I would refute this.

* * *

In this chapter, Dasan refutes Cheng Yi's and Fan Zuyu's comments against the background of Confucius's teachings, which show that Confucius taught his disciples with specific concerns in order to help them overcome their shortcomings. In this discussion, a subtle but significant difference between Dasan and the two forerunners of Zhu Xi's neo-Confucianism in their perception of Confucius's disciples is revealed. In short, Dasan does not accept their views that the three disciples they mention—Zi You, Zi Xia, and Zi Gong—suffered from their chronic problems. Dasan addresses here the reason he did not accept this assumption: there is no evidence for these claims. More fundamentally, however, Dasan's refusal stems from his different understanding of Confucius's students.

As is well known to us, neo-Confucians intended to restore what they thought was the orthodoxy of Confucian tradition, and to that end they actively utilized the notion of the lineage of the Way. According to this notion, the Confucian truths had been transmitted chronologically from one master to another, despite the existence of certain "dark" periods. Among Confucius's students, who received lessons directly from him, Yan Yuan and Zeng Shen were honored as the carriers of Confucian legitimacy, and their "legitimate" ideas were believed to have been made manifest again by Zi Si and Mencius later, until the lineage temporarily vanished. Neo-Confucians see these four scholars as four sages, who were superior to other disciples. Neo-Confucians insist that other major disciples of Confucius, such as Zi You, Zi Xia, and Zi Gong, were not as exemplary as the four sages, because they could not perfectly overcome their problems.

This neo-Confucian perception seems incompatible with Confucius's evaluation of his own disciples, since Confucius named ten of his students as representatives of the four disciplines in his academy, including Yan Yuan in ethics, Zi You and Zi Xia in literature, and Zi Gong in language, without suggestion of a hierarchy among them. It is understandable that neo-Confucians wanted to stratify these ten prominent disciples, with a focus on ethics or morality. However, Dasan might have thought of this stance as neo-Confucian. Dasan's philosophy does not gravitate toward ethics as much as neo-Confucianism does, although morals still play an essential role in it. Dasan was always wary of excessiveness of morals, in the same way he worried about excessiveness of politics: he wanted to build a synthetic structure for Confucian philosophy. In adherence to this grand goal, Dasan entrusted the Confucian achievements to all ten of these ten disciples without discrimination: literature and language were as crucial as ethics in maintaining the Confucian tradition. Accordingly,

Dasan opposed any groundless attempt to defame the major disciples of Confucius and, furthermore, sometimes advocated his minor disciples, such as Fan Xu. In this context, Dasan often confronted neo-Confucian efforts to prioritize one of the disciplines in Confucius's academy, that is, ethics, ahead of other disciplines, including literature, language, and politics. In his comments on this chapter of the *Analects*, Dasan apparently tried to protect the honor of the three disciples whom neo-Confucians somewhat belittled. This endeavor was intentional. This point may enhance the argument that Dasan was aligned with the scholars-in-the-court in the philosophical and political tensions between them and the scholars-in-the-forest.

Uniquely in *Noneo gogeum ju*, Dasan here does not provide counterarguments to Huang Kan's comment, which leads to an interesting interpretation of this chapter by Huang Kan, although he says he refutes it. In Huang Kwan's interpretation, this chapter of the *Analects* would read as follows: "The noble person puts his words into action first so that people can follow his words later." In general, Dasan did not engage in unnecessary discussion when a comment had obvious errors in his view.

2.14 The Master said, "The noble person enters into relationships through virtue and not through power; the petty person enters into relationships through power and not through virtue."

子曰; 君子周而不比, 小人比而不周.

2.14.1 Grounds

1) I supplement as follows: *Zhou* 周 ("enters into relationships through virtue") here is synonymous with *mi* 密 (intimate);[71] *bi* 比 ("enters into relationships through power") is synonymous with *bing* 並 (together with).[72] All of these word denote intimacy in relationships. *Zhou* and *mi*, however, are related to one's mind-heart, whereas *bi* and *bing* are related to power. When the noble person encounters a man who is his equal in virtue, they without exception become intimate with each other, but they are never associated through their interest in power. The petty person, whenever he encounters a relationship of power and profit, without exception collaborates with others who share the same interests and forms a faction, but he never befriends others through his mind-heart and rightness. This is the difference.

---

[71] This is *Shou wen*'s definition of the character [according to *Kangxi zidian*]. [See *Yu ding Kangxi zidian*, 4:25b. In *Shou wen*, *bi*, not *zhou*, is defined as *mi*. See *Shuo wen jie zi*, 3:7a.]

[72] The ancient forms of the characters, *bing* and *bi*, bear a resemblance. Thus their definitions are similar to one another.

2.14.2 Arguments

1) Kong Anguo argued, "*Zhou* means to be wholehearted and trustworthy;[73] *bi* is tantamount to flattery." I would refute this as follows:

The quotation above is worth a note, but its meaning is unclear. This quotation from "Lu yu" can also be understood as stating that only a man of wholeheartedness and trustworthiness can become intimate with the lord. A passage in *Guanzi* that also contains the character *zhou* says, "The former kings valued reticence [周]. Reticence refers to an attitude of refraining from uttering words or from having emotional facial expressions" (*Guanzi*, 4:14a).[74] "Yao yue 堯曰" also contains a passage that says, "Although I have close relatives [周親], it would be better for me to have men of humanity" (*Lun yu jizhu*, 20:1). In this passage *zhou* means to be very close to.

On the other hand, a poem in *Poetry* reads: "Matched [比] are the four black steeds" (*Mao Shi zhushu*, 17:30a). Here *bi* means being matched in power.[75] "Da she yi 大射儀" also contains the sentence "Eventually, compare [比] the three pairs" (*Yi li zhushu*, 7:37b). In this context, *bi* means to compare their power.[76] *Bi* in a sentence in "Wang zhi," "He duly examined the bigger and smaller paralleled cases [比]" (*Li ji zhushu*, 13:12a), also conveys the same meaning. In addition, a remark in "Mu shi 牧誓," "Join [比] your shields" (*Shang Shu zhushu*, 10:23a), also means that things that have the same power should be joined together.

In my investigation, there is a record in the eighteenth year of the reign of Duke Wen [魯文公, r. 626–609 BCE] in *Zuo's Commentary*: "Emperor Hong 鴻 [the Yellow Emperor] had incompetent descendants. The wicked and antagonistic people mingled [比周][77] with each other." Thus *bi* and *zhou* consistently refer to an intimate relationship.[78] When a discussion touches on their difference, however, they are distinguished from each other in relation to the difference between the noble person and the petty person. For example, *Great Learning* adopts two characters, *jiao* 驕 (arrogant) and *tai* 泰 (pompous), to convey the meaning of arrogance or defiance. However, the *Lu Lun* 魯論 [literally, the *Analects from the state of Lu*, the extant edition of the *Analects*] distinguishes them from one another, saying, "The noble person is self-composed [泰] but not arrogant [驕]; the petty person is arrogant but not self-composed" (*Lun yu jizhu*, 13:26).

---

[73] Xing Bing explained, "This rendition derives from 'Lu yu 魯語'" (See *Guo yu*, 5:2b).

[74] On this passage, Fang Xuanling commented, "Being deeply implicit and unfathomable is called *zhou*" (*Guanzi*, 4:14a).

[75] This definition comes from Zheng Xuan's annotation on the song under discussion (*Mao Shi zhushu*, 17:30a).

[76] This is also Zheng Xuan's annotation.

[77] According to Du Yu, "*Zhou* means being intimate" (*Zuo zhuan zhushu*, 20:24a–b).

[78] A passage in "Jin yu 晉語" reads: "Viscount Xuan of Zhao [趙宣子, d. 601] says, 'I heard that those in the service of their lords assemble [比] but do not make a faction. Nominating the right person to an office out of intimacy [周] is assembling; nominating a person to an office out of a private relationship is making a faction'" (*Guo yu*, 11:3a).

2) Huang Kan argued, "*Zhou* is used to note the means of reaching out extensively. So it is said [in Kong Anguo's annotation], '*Zhou* means to be wholehearted and trustworthy.' *Bi* is used to note the means of making a close relationship of indulgence. So it is said [in Kong Anguo's annotation], '*Bi* means to flatter.'" Sun Chuo 孫綽 (320–377) also argued, "If a person, who preserves the principles, is harmonious; a person, who has no private interest, does not practice flattery" (*Lun yu jijie yishu*, 1:26b). I would refute these as follows:

   In this context, the expression "reaching out extensively" refers to loving others extensively. If so, does it mean that the noble person only adopts the means of extensively loving others, having no intimate relationships at all? If this is what the annotations intend to point out, isn't this close to the notion of holding no distinction in love [like the Mohist philosophy]? *Zhou* here is synonymous with *mi*; *bi* here is synonymous with *bing*.

3) For a classical text on the discussion here, see "Zi yi," which says, "The great ministers have no intimacy with the lord;[79] ministers close to the lord have a private relationship [比] with the lord" (*Li ji zhushu*, 55:12a).

   In my investigation, "Xiaguan 夏官, Xingfang shi 形方氏," in *Rites of Zhou*, says, "Let the greater states be acquainted [比] with the smaller states" (*Zhou li zhushu*, 33:31a). This passage suggests the teaching of a passage in *Changes*, "Be intimate with the feudal lords" (*Zhou Yi zhushu*, 3:7b). How could *bi* only refer to becoming intimate privately? *Bi* means to unite powers.

* * *

Dasan again proposes a new reading of this well-known passage, distinguishing *zhou* from *bi* only in terms of the different ways of being intimate with others. As Kong Anguo and Huang Kan made clear, commentators prior to Dasan believed that *zhou* referred to associating oneself fairly with others regardless of personal relationships, whereas *bi* referred to making a faction. Dasan refutes this interpretation, primarily on the basis that the noble person cannot help but have personal relationships. To him, efforts to form factions should not be subjected to harsh criticism because Confucianism pursues not universally equal relationships among people but a community led by a group of good people. As Dasan points out, this would be one of the crucial differences between Confucianism and Mohism, two philosophies that share the same interests in the community. To those who are mindful, perhaps to a fault, that Dasan's milieu is necessarily linked to the factional strife in Joseon society, he may seem to be voicing his support of this reality.

Dasan tried to enhance the plausibility of this argument with his textual and philological knowledge, as is evident in his scrupulous investigations of the key terms and vocabulary (although this passage is not listed in "Overview

---

[79] A pause should be placed here when reading this passage.

of the Original Meanings"). These textual and philological investigations of his were selective, in that they followed the questions that arose through his philosophical reasoning and rational reflection on the ideas and their contexts. Unless a conventional reading seemed unreasonable, he did not spend his time inquiring into related terms and vocabulary. Thus *Noneo gogeum ju* is not a result merely of his textual and philological researches, a value-neutral academic report, but is a proclamation of philosophical ideas that he hoped were validated through textual and philological studies. Even when he delved into Confucian rituals, historical events, and definitions of words out of a pure curiosity, his endeavors in these scholarly activities eventually fortified his philosophical stance, because in Joseon's academia, extensive knowledge on some topics often rendered a scholar immune to some criticism that readers otherwise raised.

As is also seen in his argument, he uses the term *Lu Lun* to refer to the extant edition of the *Analects*, which is often juxtaposed with *Gu Lun* 古論 (the ancient *Analects*) and *Qi Lun* 齊論 (the *Analects* from the state of Qi). This shows that Dasan agreed that the extant edition of the *Analects* was transmitted to us through the scholarship of the state of Lu.

2.15 The Master said, "If one studies but does not think, one will be easily deceived; if one thinks but does not study, one will be in danger."

子曰; 學而不思則罔, 思而不學則殆.

2.15.1 Grounds

1) I supplement as follows: *Xue* 學 ("study") means to verify one's understanding with records and books;[80] *si* 思 ("think") means to investigate a topic through one's mind-heart;[81] *wang* 罔 ("deceived") means to be presented with a deception;[82] *dai* 殆 ("in danger") means to be endangered. If a person hastily trusts ancient books without inquiring about the fundamental and the incidental, he is sometimes given over to a false accusation and deception.[83] If a person hastily becomes confident in his own mind-heart without inquiring about the fundamental and the incidental, his knowledge will meet with a danger.[84] Neither of these two values should be abandoned.

---

[80] A detailed definition will follow.
[81] This means that one explores and examines a topic.
[82] *Mencius* says, "The noble person can hardly be deceived [罔] with what is contrary to the Way" (*Mengzi jizhu*, 5A:2).
[83] Huang Kan commented, "[The person who does not think] comes to falsely accuse and betray the Way of the sages."
[84] In such case, it cannot be determined whether his knowledge is righteous or valid. Thus it becomes dangerous.

2.15.2 Arguments

1) Bao Xian argued, "If one does not actively reflect on the meaning of what one is learning, one will be lost [罔] and gain nothing from it."[85] I would refute this as follows:

Confucius said, "I once spent a whole day without eating and a whole night without sleeping in order to think, but to no avail. It would be better to study."[86] When Confucius found it fruitless just to think, he retired from it. Then where would Confucius want to move to for a study? A study is an action to verify the Way of the former kings through examinations of texts and books, not a simple reception of a teacher's lessons, drawn from books.[87] In their commentaries on the classics, the Han Confucians prioritized investigations on the ancients that fell short of insightful arguments. As a result, they risked absorbing perverted theories related to the incantational and apocryphal texts. This is an example of the evil effect caused by "studying but not thinking." In their discussions on the classics, later Confucians took an investigation of the principles as their mainstay. Therefore, their verifications were not solid and at times revealed inaccuracies regarding the institutions and the names of things. This is an example of errors caused by "thinking but not studying."

And in my view, the character wang 罔 is a combination of two characters, wang 网 (a net) and wang 亡 (to lose), deriving its meaning from wang 亡.[88] In order words, wang means to lose something abruptly. Then Bao Xian's comment, "he would be lost and gain nothing from it," may imply that a person would abruptly forget what he has learned if he were not to review the lessons he has received. However, this is relevant only to children's practices. How could the sage's admonition be centered on this?[89]

2) He Yan argued, "Thinking without studying would cause one's spirit to become exhausted and endangered." I would refute this as follows:

It is usual to see one's spirit become exhausted. However, what does it mean for one's spirit to become "exhausted and endangered?" If a person were not to explore the complete texts of the former kings, solely relying on his personal opinions, his understanding will go astray into the realm of heresy. This is the reason the sage saw it as dangerous.

---

[85] Xing Bing argued, "If one already began to study under a teacher, he should reflect on the connotations of the teaching. If not, he would be lost and gain nothing from it."

[86] See "Wei Linggong" (Lun yu jizhu, 15:31).

[87] Yi Goengbo added, "Constant Mean contains ideas of extensive learning and prudent deliberations. The extensive learning there should refer to extensive reading of a variety of books. If to study means to receive lessons from a teacher, the idea of 'extensive' learning does not make sense."

[88] This belongs to the phonosemantic compound characters in the six categories of Chinese characters.

[89] "Shao yi 少儀" says, "The case in which one does not know the names for one's clothes even when one is wearing them is called wang [罔]" (Li ji zhushu, 35:35b). In line with this passage, Wang Shiqian 王時潛 (fl. 1280) argued: "Wang in the passage in the Analects, 'If one studies but does not think, one will be easily lost [罔: This is a more traditional translation that Dasan did not accept]' must convey the same meaning as this wang" (Li ji daquan 禮記大全, 16:40a).

3) Xu Jing'an 許敬菴 (1535–1604) argued, "If one studies but does not think, one will behave stupidly; if one thinks but does not study, one will be given over to abstruse thoughts" (Unknown source).

In my view, the first sentence in this comment is truly apt for describing the problem of ancient learning; the second sentence is truly apt for describing the problem of today's learning.

* * *

What Dasan opposes here is the view that this chapter teaches the ideal way to increase one's knowledge. According to Bao Xian, whose interpretation later commentators have by and large accepted with regard to this chapter, it is essential to combine lessons from a teacher with self-reflection or a review of the subject in order to have a firm understanding of it because without this process, one's learning cannot fully develop into concrete knowledge. According to Dasan, however, this chapter discusses the ideal of scholarship, in which investigations on texts are balanced with contemplation of what is recorded in the texts. It is intriguing that he criticizes later Confucians, scholars in neo-Confucianism, for losing the balance to the same extent that Han Confucians failed to build a sense of balance. To him, Han Confucians were excellent in their investigations of the ancient institutions and the original meanings of key terms but poor in their efforts eventually to discover what their knowledge was all about. Similarly, neo-Confucianss were successful in achieving prominence with their profound discourses on the Confucian Way in the history of Confucianism but ineffective in persuading readers to adopt their philosophy because their theories were mostly groundless. In other words, Han Confucianism was excessively disciplined and particular; neo-Confucianism was excessively abstract and universal. Dasan diagnosed the serious problems that arose out of their imbalance as consisting of the vulnerability of Han Confucianism to heretical ideas and the the vulnerability of neo-Confucianism to practical criticism.

This short statement on the ideal scholarship manages succinctly to set the stage for the publication of *Noneo gogeum ju*. Indeed, it is not difficult to foresee what Dasan planned to do after addressing his criticism of both Han Confucianism and neo-Confucianism or to understand why he titled his book *Noneo gogeum ju, Old and New Commentaries on the* Analects. In that syncretism was the main methodology adopted by Korean thinkers who wanted to create a universal framework for people's lives and society, Dasan was a successor of such syncretists in tendency in Korea. To be recognized as such, like the other Korean thinkers, he had to dare to render neo-Confucianism equal to Han Confucianism during a period when the neo-Confucian ideology was deeply entrenched in the society.

2.16 The Master said, "To devote oneself to unorthodox learning is only harmful." [In *Noneo gogeum ju* in traditional book binding, this chapter opens the third roll.]

子曰; 攻乎異端, 斯害也已.

2.16.1 Grounds

1) Fan Zuyu commented, "*Gong* 攻 ('to devote oneself to') is to be exclusively specialized in a subject."[90]
2) I supplement as follows: *Duan* in *yiduan* 異端 ("unorthodox learning") refers to the end of a thread [緒].[91] Thus *yiduan* means whatever does not carry on at the point where the former kings left off.[92] All learnings that do not concentrate on the study of human inborn nature, the mandate of Heaven, and the teachings from the classic texts, including the multifarious studies of techniques, belong to unorthodox learning. Though some of them are helpful for people's everyday lives, if a noble person is exclusively specialized in a subject, it is detrimental to his learning.[93] *Yeyi* 也已 ("only") is a particle.

2.16.2 Arguments

1) Xing Bing argued, "*Yiduan* refers to the texts of the Many Masters and One Hundred Schools.[94] Those books often disrespect Yao and Shun and denounce humanity and rightness."[95] I would refute this as follows:

   At the time of Confucius, Laozi, Zhuangzi, Yangzi, and Mozi had not established their schools yet,[96] and thus the situation was different from that in the later period, when the three teachings existed, like the three legs of a tripod, disregarding the principles of others and revering their own. Therefore they were not what Confucius mentions here. If "unorthodox learning" refers to today's heretical ideas, people who are devoted to studying them are disruptive defilers. In that case, it is unacceptable to imagine

---

[90] "Kao gong ji" introduces artisans specializing [攻] in woodwork and artisans specializing in metalwork.

[91] *Fang yan* 方言, by Master Yang [揚雄], records: "In the southern part of the state of Chu 楚, people occasionally use *duan* 端 for *xu* 緒" (quoted in *Yu ding Kangxi zidian*, 21:105b).

[92] A poem in "Lu Song" says, "Carry on at the point where Taiwang 太王 [the founding father of the Zhou royal lineage] left off" (*Mao Shi zhushu*, 29:29b).

[93] In other words, *yiduan* does not refer to the ideas of Yangzi 楊子, Mozi 墨子, Buddha, or Laozi.

[94] Huang Kan argued, "*Yiduan* refers to miscellaneous books."

[95] He Yan argued, "The good Way has an axis. Thus even when we take different paths, we will return to the same destination. The heretic ideas, *yiduan*, do not return to the same destination."

[96] Zhen Xishan commented, "Lao Dan, Yang Zhu, and Mo Di were approximately contemporaries of Confucius. Their theories, however, could be vociferously heard merely because the teaching of Zhu Si 洙泗 [names of two rivers that are associated with the area where Confucius established his academy] was about to shine" (*Lun yu jizhu daquan*, 2:30b).

that Confucius just said that they were "only harmful." In addition, in this interpretation, those who condemned the heretical ideas would be the chief masters of Confucianism. If that is the case, they should not say that "unorthodox learning" is "only harmful." Both of these interpretations are not persuasive.

The expression "only harmful" is a light comment and a light criticism, not a blasting expression of strong disapproval. Then how could "unorthodox learning" indicate today's heretical ideas? When Fan Chi requested that he be taught farming, Confucius disparaged him as a petty person (*Lun yu jizhu*, 13:4). When Duke Ling of Wei [衛靈公, r. 534–492] asked Confucius about military formations, Confucius replied, "I have never studied military affairs" (*Lun yu jizhu*, 15:1). In general, the study of military affairs and agriculture is for the practical end of state administration, and the noble person should have some knowledge of them. If a scholar specializes in these subjects, however, it will eventually bring harm to the study of the body, mind-heart, human inborn nature, and the mandate of Heaven. Due to this, Confucius lightly pointed out the problem—on the one hand encouraging people to become familiar with these subjects only occasionally and on the other dissuading them from specializing in them.

Regarding this, Lu Xiangshan 陸象山 (1139–1192) argued, "At the time of Confucius, Buddhism was not introduced to China and, although he already existed, Laozi's theory had not become visible yet. How can *yiduan* here refer to the ideas of Buddha and Laozi? Someone asked me about *yiduan*, and I replied, 'What you have already known of constitutes one end. All things different from it are *yiduan*'" (*Xiangshan yulu* 象山語錄, 2:20b).

2) I question Master Zhu as follows:

The interpretation of *gong* as exclusively devoted to something has had a firm ground in "Kao gong ji" from the beginning. Moreover, the sins and evil deeds that Yang Zhu and Mo Di committed, who disregarded their parents and the rulers, and by Buddhists, who defied Heaven and insulted the sages, are grave and extreme, so both spirits and human beings resent them. How could harms appear only after people became specialists? It is evident that *yiduan* does not refer to today's heretical ideas. In this regard, Yuan Liaofan 袁了凡 (1533–1606) commented, "Cai Xuzhai 蔡虛齋 (1453–1508) contended that *yiduan* does not refer to the ideas of Yang Zhu, Mo Di, Buddha, and Laozi because at the time of Confucius Yang Zhu and Mo Di did not exist. This view is truly correct" (Unknown source).

3) For classical texts on the discussion here, see *Han Shi waizhuan* (*Han Shi waizhuan* 韓詩外傳, 6:3a, 8); "Bian zheng 辨政," in *Kongzi jia yu* (*Kongzi jia yu*, 3:15a, 6–15b, 9);[97] "Du Yu zhuan 杜預傳," in *Jin shu* (*Jin shu*, 34:18a; 4–6);

---

[97] In the edition of *Jia yu* with commentary by Wu Jiamo 吳嘉謨 (fl. 1589), from the Ming dynasty, the last sentence in this passage appears differently.

the Preface of *Zuo's Commentary on Spring and Autumn*, by Du Yu (*Zuo zhuan zhushu*, 0:27b, 2–3); the Preface of *Guliang's Commentary*, by Fan Ning 范甯 (c. 339–401) (*Chunqiu Guliang zhuan zhushu*, 0:13b, 5); the Preface of *Wangjian ji* 王儉集, by Ren Fan 任昉 (460–508) (*Han Wei Liuzhao baisan jia ji* 漢魏六朝百三家集, 91:54b, 2–3); the Preface of *Wen xin diao long*, by Liu Xie 劉勰 (fl. fifth century) (*Wenxin diaolong* 文心雕龍, 10:12a, 4).

In my view, these passages are examples of writings that show that the early Confucians of the Han and Jin dynasties did not render *yiduan* as the ideas of Yang Zhu, Mo Di, Buddha, and Laozi.

4) I explore the textual differences as follows:

In "Da Wang Shangshu shu 答王尚書書," Master Zhu records: "The noble person merely returns to the classics. If the classics are treated rightly, no wicked and distorted theories will prevail. Now, if you confront and attack [攻] the evil and wicked ideas out of hatred, it will rather lead to your fall, in self-devastation" (*Zhuzi yu lei*, 24:35a). In my investigation, Master Zhu translated *gong* as "being specialized in" in his *Lun yu jizhu*. In this writing, however, he translated it as "attack." The two interpretations are contradictory.[98]

5) The First Emperor of Ming said, "If the heretical ideas are attacked [攻] and eradicated, their harm will stop spreading [止] here" (*Ming Taizu wenji* 明太祖文集, 15:50a).[99]

* * *

Dasan's definition of "unorthodox learning" upsets any expectation of radical tolerance on his part of science and technology. According to his definition, modern reformers are distinguishable from neo-Confucian scholars on the ground that the former are the chief constituents of unorthodox learning. In this chapter, Dasan affirms that they "will eventually bring harm to the study of the body, mind-heart, human inborn nature, and the mandate of Heaven." This understanding of the "unorthodox learnings" seems historical.

Most historians today would agree with Dasan's opinion that Confucius did not know about the "heretical" ideas, such as Buddhism and Daoism. In all likelihood, Zhu Xi might have known that the term *yiduan* in the ancient texts did not refer to the heretical ideas because there is much evidence that argues against such a claim, as Dasan partly introduces in his comment. However, Zhu Xi's era required Confucian scholars to protect the Confucian orthodoxy from fierce intimidation from adherents of other religious and philosophical

---

[98] Mao Qiling commented, "Originally, the *gong* under consideration conveys the meaning of *gong* in *gongji* 攻擊 (attack). I do not understand why Master Zhu, in his commentary on the *Analects*, glossed it as meaning 'being specialized in'" (*Si shu shengyan*, 1:13b). In *Shi er bian*, Sun Yi also said, "*Gong* is synonymous with *gong* in the phrase, 'Attack [*gong*] others' wrongdoings'" (*Shi er bian*, 4:15a).
[99] *Yi* 已 ("only") in the main passage is interchangeable with *zhi* 止 (to stop).

ideas. Zhu Xi aspired to respond to the mission given to his contemporary Confucians and interpreted *yiduan* in the way stated in his *Lun yu jizhu*, regardless of evidence to the contrary. This means that Dasan's awareness of the imperilment of the heretical ideas was not as intense as that of Zhu Xi, although at the time of Dasan the Joseon Confucians usually considered Catholic theology a very dangerous heretical idea.

At this point, let us reconsider whether Dasan truly vilified the "unorthodox learnings"—the learning of science and technology. It is undeniable that in those thoughts of his that are addressed in this chapter, the study of human inborn nature and the mandate of Heaven takes precedence over the unorthodox learnings. This does not necessarily mean, however, that he denied the necessity of learning these subjects. He made it clear that they were "for the practical end of state administration, and the noble person should have some knowledge of them." He also found quite a lot of space to argue that this chapter delivers Confucius's "light" criticism of the type of person who is devoted "solely" to such subjects and ignores the demand to study about the moral mandates given to all humans. In Dasan's view, it is essential for a person to cultivate himself morally to be a noble person, but it would be disappointing if his study were interrupted by his satisfaction with his moral advancement. In a more comprehensive reading of Dasan's works, one would easily learn that he never stopped offering suggestions of a sociopolitical nature to reform Joseon society. In his view, it was ideal for a person to become capable of handling the practical subjects after he had cultivated a solid morality. What if a person were to become magnificent in dealing with practical subjects at the expense of his cultivation of morality? Confucius would criticize him, Dasan feels, but only lightly. Dasan's unique definition of *yiduan* is listed in "Overview of the Original Meanings."

2.17 The Master said, "You, shall I teach you what it means to know? When you know, say you know; when you do not know, say you do not know. This is knowledge."

子曰; 由! 誨女知之乎? 知之爲知之, 不知爲不知, 是知也.

2.17.1 Grounds

1) Kong Anguo commented, "You refers to Confucius's disciple Zhong You 仲由. Zi Lu is his adult name."[100]
2) Xing Bing commented, "Zi Lu had a strong temper and, because of that, often pretended to know when he did not know. Thus Confucius discourages him here." For a classical text related to this comment, see "Zi dao 子道," in *Xunzi*

---

[100] According to *Shi ji*, "Zi Lu was a man of Bian 卞 and nine years younger than Confucius" (*Shi ji*, 67:5a–b).

(*Xunzi*, 20:10b, 5–8).[101] *Han Shi waizhuan* contains the same record as the one in "Zi dao" (*Han Shi waizhuan*, 3:18b). For another classical text related to this comment, see "San shu 三恕," in *Jia yu* (*Kongzi jia yu*, 2:13b–14a).

* * *

Although Dasan does not refute the conventional evaluation of Zi Lu's quick temper here, his understanding of Zi Lu was greatly distinct from that of the majority Confucian scholars. This point is eloquently addressed later in one of Dasan's arguments, related to a chapter (5.6) in which Confucius's remark pleases Zi Lu to a certain degree. In short, to Dasan, it was a great mistake to regard Zi Lu as an unintelligent and incompetent person. He says, "In the writings of the early Confucian scholars, Zi Lu appears a stupid person who does not understand things. This directly leads readers to ridicule and mock him as though they were dealing with a madman. This is a great disturbance" (*Noneo gogeum ju*, 195b).

Nevertheless, Dasan could not deny that Confucius tries to teach Zi Lu here the right attitude toward knowledge probably because of his concerns about Zi Lu's personality. Since Dasan already criticized Cheng Yi's view that Confucius often taught his disciples with specific concerns about their shortcomings in mind (see Dasan's question in chapter 2.13), Dasan's comment here seems to lack consistency. However, Cheng Yi's view was speculative, while Zi Lu's quick temper was documented in this classic in a number of places. This seeming inconsistency can be explained in terms of Dasan's persistence in resting on the records of the classical texts for his arguments.

2.18 Zi Zhang was learning about gaining an official salary. The Master said, "Listen to much, leave out what is doubtful, be careful when speaking about the rest, and you will make few errors. Look at much, leave out what is dangerous, be careful when acting on the rest, and you will have few regrets. If you make few errors in speech and have few regrets in action, an official salary lies in this."[102]

子張學干祿. 子曰; 多聞闕疑, 愼言其餘, 則寡尤. 多見闕殆. 愼行其餘, 則寡悔. 言寡尤, 行寡悔, 祿在其中矣.

2.18.1 Grounds

1) Zheng Xuan commented, "Zi Zhang refers to Confucius's disciple Zhuansun Shi 顓孫師."[103]

---

[101] See passages preceding this passage, too (*Xunzi*, 20:10a–b).
[102] In *Shi ji*, *xue* 學 ("learning") appears to be *wen* 問 (to ask) (*Shi ji*, 67:16a).
[103] According to *Shi ji*, "Zhuansun Shi was a man of Chen and forty-eight years younger than Confucius" (*Shi ji*, 67:16a).

2) Zheng Xuan commented, "*Gan* 干 ('gaining') means to look for."

3) Master Zhu commented, "*Lu* 祿 ('an official salary') refers to a salary for a person who occupies a government office."

4) I supplement as follows: To "listen" is a means to acquire knowledge through teachers and colleagues; to "look" is a means to acquire knowledge through books and texts.

5) Lü Dalin 呂大臨 (1044–1091) commented, "*Yi* 疑 ('what is doubtful') refers to what I cannot trust; *dai* 殆 ('what is dangerous') refers to what I do not feel comfortable with" (*Lun yu jizhu*, 1:12a).

6) I supplement as follows: There must be something dangerous among the things you hear and something doubtful among things you see. Some people take action on listening, and some people speak on looking. Thus the first two sentences in this chapter are complementary. *Que* 闕 ("leave out") is to empty out.[104]

7) Bao Xian commented, "If one leaves out what is doubtful, the rest would elicit no doubt. Even after this action, if one becomes careful when speaking, there should be few errors."

8) Master Cheng commented, "Errors arrive from the outside; regrets spring from the inside." I supplement as follows: When a person speaks, someone must listen. Hence errors come from outside. One's actions, however, are sometimes not known to others. Hence regrets spring from inside.

9) Zheng Xuan commented, "If one follows this teaching on speech and action, one will be regarded as having mastered the way of gaining an official salary even when one has not actually gained it."

2.18.2 Arguments

1) I question Master Zhu as follows:

The noble person never gives up hope to take an office. The difference lies in the fact that he pursues it only through the Way. This is what is uttered in the chapter, "The way Our Master manages to obtain it is, surely, different from how others seek it out" (*Lun yu jizhu*, 1:10). Confucius also said [in Dasan's unique interpretation], "People learn because an official salary lies therein; people farm because hunger lies therein" (*Lun yu jizhu*, 15:32). With regard to this topic, Dazai Jun commented, "Master Cheng ['Mr. Cheng' in Dazai's original comment] argued that people such as Yan Hui and Min Zi Qian 閔子騫 might have never had a question of this sort. This reveals that he did not understand that Yan Hui and Min Zi Qian never abandoned their hope to take offices and that they just did not want to receive an improper salary. Although Zi Zhang made an inquiry

---

[104] If a door structure has the frame but not the door, allowing the door space to be used as part of a path, it becomes a *que*.

on this topic, how could he be viewed as a person pleasantly receiving an improper salary?"

* * *

As a former government official, and as a Confucian scholar who never gave up hope to help the Joseon court run the state in an ideal way, Dasan in this chapter firmly advocates the general desire among Confucians to join the government. This stance forms a clear contrast with the perspective of Cheng-Zhu neo-Confucianism, in which even a discussion of gaining a salary was deemed impure. Thus his definition of "scholars" in the following passage may provoke some recalcitrant neo-Confucians:

> In my view, there are four categories of people: scholars, peasants, artisans, and merchants. The meaning of the character *shi* 士 (scholar) is to take government offices; the meaning of *xue* 學 (to learn) [in the main passage of the *Analects*] is to learn how to serve in those offices. (*Noneo gogeum ju*, 367d)

> Xing Bing said, " 'Scholar' is the name given to a person of virtue." I refute it. The four people referred to are scholars, peasants, artisans, and merchants. The meaning of "scholars" is to take government offices, and those who take government offices are those who govern people. Therefore, those who learn how to govern people are also called scholars. (287c)

> Learning the Way is for taking government posts in the future. (289d)

> Those who are devoted to the Way are to take government offices in the future. Therefore, although they hold no government office at the moment, they can be called scholars. (190a)

In this regard, readers will confirm through Dasan's *Analects* that he consistently supported King Wu, Guan Zhong 管仲 (725–645 BCE), and other rulers who were the subjects of neo-Confucian deontological criticism, emphasizing their social merits. As a matter of fact, King Wu's revolution had traditionally been regarded in Confucianism as a polemical issue. King Wu actually founded the Zhou dynasty, in which the most archetypal elements of Confucian culture and rituals were created, but he did that by "revolution," becoming disloyal to his lord, King Zhou 紂 (r. 1075–1046 BCE) of the Shang. In terms of merits, he outstripped many Confucian sages, but in terms of following moral principle, he was not exemplary. He was a brilliant leader to the utilitarians, who emphasized an ethics of consequences, but to the deontologists he violated ethical codes, which they interpreted in terms of duties and rights. Dasan apparently favored King Wu and should thus be considered a utilitarian in this matter.

2.19 Duke Ai asked, "What should be done to make the people cheerfully obedient?" Confucius replied, "Raise up the honest and place them over the crooked, and the people shall become cheerfully obedient. Raise up the crooked and place them over the honest, and the people shall become disobedient."

哀公問曰; 何爲則民服? 孔子對曰; 擧直錯諸枉, 則民服, 擧枉錯諸直, 則民不服.

2.19.1 Grounds

1) Bao Xian commented, "Duke Ai is the posthumous title for a lord of Lu."[105]
2) I supplement as follows: *Fu* 服 ("cheerfully obedient") means to obey wholeheartedly.
3) Master Zhu commented, "The adoption of the expression 'Confucius replied' is intended to show respect for the lord."
4) I supplement as follows: *Ju* 擧 ("raise up") means to hold something up;[106] *cuo* 錯 ("place") means to place something down stably;[107] *zhi* 直 ("the honest") refers to the right people; *wang* 枉 ("the crooked") refers to the unworthy people; *zhu* 諸 is a particle. Allowing the worthies to occupy higher positions and the unworthy people to sit in lower positions pertains to the sentence "raise up the honest and place them over the crooked"; allowing the unworthy people to occupy higher positions and the worthies to endure lower positions pertains to the sentence "raise up the crooked and place them over the honest." This situation can be compared to a scene in which a man tries to straighten things out using a carpenter's square. When the square is straight and things are crooked, he surely can straighten them out. However, if the square is crooked and things are straight, he cannot straighten them out.

2.19.2 Arguments

1) Bao Xian argued, "[The beginning part of Confucius's reply means that one ought to] raise up and hire the right and the honest [擧直] and abandon the many wicked and crooked people [錯諸枉]."[108] I would refute this as follows:

   Cuo 錯 originally meant to place the ritual vessels down on the ground. So it is fine to render it as "to place." However, are there any grounds for Bao's rendition, according to which *cuo* means to abandon? Also in this chapter, *zhu* 諸 is a particle. *Changes* contains a line that says, "One places a mat of

---

[105] According to "Lu shi jia 魯世家," in *Shi ji*, Duke Ai's personal name is Jiang 蔣, and he is a son of Duke Ding (See *Shi ji*, 33:24a). According to *Shi fa*, "those lords who are polite and benign but perish early are given the title 'Ai'" (*Shi fa*, 3:17b).
[106] This means raising something up high.
[107] Originally, *cuo* means to place the ritual vessels down on the ground. *Protocols and Rites* contains a sentence that says, "Place the *dou* 豆 vessel down; place the *zu* 俎 vessel down" (*Yi li zhushu*, 12:45b).
[108] Xing Bing argued, "If the lord abandons the wicked and crooked, the people shall become cheerfully obedient; if the lord abandons the right and honest, the people shall become disobedient."

white *mao* 茅 grass" (*Zhou Yi zhushu*, 5:27a). On this Confucius commented, "It would be fine to place them down on the ground [錯諸地], too" (11:28a). This phrase, "place them down on the ground," bears grammatical affinity here with the phrase "place them over the crooked" in the main text. Given this fact [that *zhu* is here obviously a particle], would it be fine to render *zhu* as referring to "many"? Wang Yinglin, in his examination of the differences among editions of the *Analects*, explained: "Sun Jihe 孫季和 (1154–1206) said, 'If the lord raises up the honest to place them above the crooked, the people will eventually obey him, since the crooked and stubborn people will submit themselves to the honest; if the lord raises up the crooked and places them on the honest, the people will not obey him, since the honest people cannot be subdued by the crooked and stubborn people'" (*Kun xue ji wen*, 7:12a–b).[109]

2) For classical texts that support my argument here, see "Yan Yuan" in the *Analects* (*Lunyu jizhu*, 12:22); "Xi ci zhuan 繫辭傳" (*Zhou Yi zhushu*, 11:46b, 2); "Yue ji 樂記" (*Li ji zhushu*, 39:25a, 3).

In my view, *cuo* usually means to lay down what has been raised. Many commentators' interpretations in which *ju* and *cuo* are regarded as a pair of contrasting words are incorrect.

* * *

It was typical, prior to Wang Yinglin, to accept Bao Xian's interpretation of the phrase under discussion, according to which *ju* and *cuo* consisted of a pair of contrasting words, respectively meaning "to raise up" and "to abandon." If one follows the old interpretation, Confucius's reply to Duke Ai's question begins: "Raise up the honest and abandon the crooked, and the people shall become cheerfully obedient." Although Dasan directly criticized only Bao Xian and Xing Bing, Zhu Xi also followed Bao's comment. In addition, although Dasan did not clarify this point, the commentator who read *zhu* as meaning "many" was Zhu Xi. Thus Dasan's argument in this chapter substantially targets Zhu Xi. The reason Dasan did not take Zhu Xi as an open target here must be related to his respect for Zhu Xi's scholarship or his wish to avoid needless dispute with the rigid Joseon Confucians loyal to Zhu Xi. Since his argument disapproves of the major commentators' views, old and new, it is listed in "Overview of the Original Meanings."

2.20 Ji Kangzi asked, "What drives people to be reverent, loyal, and mutually encouraging?" The Master said, "If you demonstrate gravity when dealing with them, they will be reverent; if you become filial and benevolent,

---

[109] If the early commentators' view were correct, why was the character *zhu* used twice in the main text? Sun Jihe's remark here also appears in *Langya daizui bian* 琅琊代醉編 [according to *Rongo kogun gaiden*].

they will be loyal; if you raise up the able to instruct those who are not, they will be mutually encouraging."

季康子問; 使民敬忠以勸, 如之何? 子曰; 臨之以莊則敬, 孝慈則忠, 舉善而教不能則勸.

2.20.1 Grounds

1) Kong Anguo commented, "Ji Kangzi was the minister of Lu, Jisun Fei 季孫肥 (d. 468 BCE). Kang is his posthumous title."[110]
2) I supplement as follows: *Quan* 勸 ("mutually encouraging") means that the people move forward in the arts of virtue with self-motivation.
3) Bao Xian commented, "*Zhuang* 莊 ('gravity') is here synonymous with *yan* 嚴 (rigid)." I supplement as follows: *Zhuang* refers to showing no negligence in executing policies and laws.
4) Bao Xian commented, "If the lord is able to be filial to his parents and benevolent to the people, they will be loyal."
5) I supplement as follows: *Shan* 善 ("the able") refers to the worthies and the talented.

2.20.2 Arguments

1) I question Master Zhu as follows:

   Zhuang was interchangeable with *yan* in ancient times. Due to this, Bao Xian rendered *zhuang* as "gravity." Of course, gravity should be distinguished from a rigidity that is combined with an intimidating manner. Reflecting this difference, *Lun yu jizhu* has changed the meaning of *zhuang* to a manner in which one "has a well-kept countenance." However, that manner often amounts to a display of facial grandeur. A person displays facial grandeur but tends to compromise inner matters—this is what the noble person should be wary of. I am afraid that Master Zhu's interpretation may be imbalanced.

2) Bao Xian argued, "*Ju shan* 舉善 ('if you raise up the able') means to hire the good people." Ogyu also argued, "*Shan* ('the able') here is contrasted with *bu neng* 不能 ('those who are not'), which is synonymous with *neng* 能 (to be able to)."[111] I would refute Bao's comment as follows:

   Bao Xian's annotation is truly invalid, and Dazai Jun's also evades the point. Having those who are able to commit virtuous deeds instruct others who are not able to follow the virtues of filiality and respect for elders is, indeed, without exception an action of raising up the able. Dazai, in his explanation, only focuses on techniques and arts, so he also evades the point. Ogyu's theory, however, has no problem.

* * *

---

[110] According to *Shi fa*, "those lords who care for the people so that they live in comfort and joy are given the title 'Kang'" (quoted in *Lun yu zhushu*, 2:10b).
[111] Dazai Jun argued, "*Shan* here is equal to *shan* in such senses as being good [善] at archery, being good at driving, being good at calligraphy, and being good at drawing."

Even though Dasan always laid stress on the need for rulers to possess the virtue of benevolence, he maintained a conservative approach to the issue of overcoming class distinctions. As shown here, he saw it as ideal for the rulers to display gravity when dealing with the people probably because he thought the rulers should be distinguished from the ruled. In the historical context of Joseon society, this stance may have been linked to the Southerners' political proclivity to protect the authority of the monarchs from the incessant intimidation of the powerful group of Confucian subjects, the Patriarchs, who tended to define the moral duties imposed on kings as universal and indistinguishable from those imposed on all people. This point is more clearly addressed in chapter 12.12.

Bao Xian read *shan* as "the good people," whereas Dasan interpreted it as "the able." Dasan's refutation was motivated by the fact that *shan* here is contrasted with *bu neng*, which means "not to be able." In other words, Dasan here scrutinized the meaning of key terms, and in this regard his research was in harmony with that of the school of Ancient Literature and Writing, which attempted to discover the accurate meaning of such terms. However, Dasan also refuted Dazai's argument in which *shan* is solely associated with one's techniques and arts. Instead, Dasan imbued this vocabulary with moral connotations by arguing that "the able" referred to those who were able to be moral. In this regard, his view was in harmony with Zhu Xi's view. This is a simple example, but it shows well where Dasan stood.

2.21 Someone said to Confucius, "Sir, why do you not take charge of governing?" The Master replied, "*Documents* says: 'Be filial, only be filial, and be friendly to your brothers. You can extend this to the administration of your office.' This is also taking charge of governing. Why must I take charge of governing otherwise?"[112]

或謂孔子曰; 子奚不爲政? 子曰; 書云, 孝乎惟孝, 友于兄弟, 施於有政. 是亦爲政, 奚其爲爲政?

2.21.1 Grounds

1) I supplement as follows: *Wei zheng* 爲政 ("take charge of governing") refers to taking control of a state's government;[113] *you zheng* 有政 ("the administration of your office") refers to the administrative responsibilities assigned to each of the government officials.

2) I supplement as follows: *Documents* here is the lost part of *Documents*.[114]

---

[112] In the stele edition, *xiaohu* 孝乎 ("Be filial") appears as *xiaoyu* 孝于.

[113] For more details, see the following explanation.

[114] In other words, the edition excavated from the wall of Confucius does not contain the text under consideration.

3) Bao Xian commented, "'Be filial, only be filial' is an expression that praises the great filial piety."

4) I supplement as follows: *Yi* 施 ("extend") means to reach forth.[115]

2.21.2 Arguments

1) Bao Xian argued, "Someone suggested that holding a government position is *wei zheng*."[116] I would refute this as follows:

Wei zheng means that one holds the reins of government in one's hand. *Commentaries on Spring and Autumn* frequently adopts this expression, as is evident in the following examples: "Viscount Xuan of Zhao took control of the government [爲政];"[117] "When I die, you must be in charge of the government [爲政]."[118] As a matter of fact, despite the existence of many ministers, only the chief minister can take charge of the government. Based on this, we could further infer that all actions pertaining to supervising given affairs can be deemed *wei zheng*. For example, *Zuo's Commentary* says, "You were in charge of [爲政] serving the soldiers with lamb yesterday. I will be in charge of [爲政] military maneuver today."[119] If all of the officials of a state were permitted to take charge of governing, it would eventually lead the state to disorder.[120]

In fact, all of the government officials assume responsibility for the administration of their offices. Therefore *Documents* says, "You can extend this to the administration of your office" (*Shang Shu zhushu*, 17:15b). In general, *wei zheng* ("take charge of governing") and *you zheng* ("the administration of your office") are worlds apart. Accordingly, Confucius here acknowledged that he managed his business and made it parallel with "taking charge of governing." If *wei zheng* meant to occupy an office, the individual referred to in the main passage would not have asked about Confucius's *wei zheng*, because Confucius also took responsibility for a government post. Actually, *you zheng* would be equivalent to the administration of a position [有位] or the administration of a piece of land [有土], as mentioned in *Documents*. It is evident that *you zheng* means to hold a government post with given responsibilities. Thus I am afraid that the interpretation in *Lun yu jizhu*, which regards *you zheng* as meaning to govern a house, is incorrect.

2) For classical texts on the discussion here, see *Baihu tong* 白虎通 (*Baihu tongyi* 白虎通義, B:48a, 1–2); "Xian ju fu 閒居賦," by Pan Yue 潘岳

---

[115] This character, in this context, is pronounced *yi*. A line in "Da ya" reads: "It was extended [施] to his descendants" (*Mao Shi zhushu*, 23:90b).

[116] He also argued, "If one's practices incorporate the way of governing, they can be regarded as *wei zheng*."

[117] See the first year of the reign of Duke Xuan 宣 (*Zuo zhuan zhushu*, 21:7b).

[118] See the twentieth year of the reign of Duke Zhao (*Zuo zhuan zhushu*, 49:28a). This remark is related to Zi Chan 子産 (d. 522 BCE) of Zheng 鄭.

[119] See the second year of the reign of Duke Xuan (*Zuo zhuan zhushu*, 21:10a).

[120] The argument introduced up to this point is Dazai Jun's.

(247–300) (*Wenxuan zhu*, 16:4a, 7); "Kundi gao 昆弟誥," by Xiahou Zhan 夏侯湛 (243–291) (quoted in *Lun yu jiqiu pian*, 1:18a);[121] "Youzhou shi Futu song 幽州石浮圖頌," by Wang Lizhen 王利貞 (fl. Tang dynasty) (1:19a); "Zengzi zan 曾子贊" by Zhang Qixian 張齊賢 (943–1014) (1:19a).[122] In this regard, Mao Qiling argued, "*Lun yu jizhu* mistakenly separated the phrase 'be filial' [which Zhu Xi thought was Confucius's words] from 'only be filial [which Zhu Xi thought came from the lost *Documents*].' No such case as this has existed thus far, in which [Confucius's] colloquial words are inserted between the phrase '*Documents* says' and the beginning of the main text of the classic."[123]

In my view, as seen in the classical texts introduced above, the phrases "be filial" and "only be filial" always appeared combined in the writings of the Han, Wei, Tang, and Song. Owing to this finding, the fact that Mei Ze's *Documents* [which only contains the phrase "only be filial"] was a forged text becomes clearer. This is the real problem, although Xiaoshan did not realize it. How could Mei Ze's problem be limited to something like inserting Confucius's words?[124]

3) Yuan Liaofan argued, "Duke Zhao is the elder brother, and Duke Ding is his younger brother. Since Jisun felt no regret when he ousted the elder brother to help the younger brother seize power, the way of filial piety and respect for elders ebbed away. The Master thus addressed this issue in the main passage" (Unknown source).

✳ ✳ ✳

It is unique to interpret the meaning of *wei zheng* as distinct from that of *you zheng* as Dasan does here. Before Dasan, Dazai Jun refuted Zhu Xi's interpretation of *wei zheng*, as Dasan's quote shows, and Dasan added his rendition of *you zheng* to it to finalize his own argument. Dasan and Dazai agreed not only in their interpretation of *wei zheng* but also in the idea that those people who stand at the pinnacle of the social hierarchy, such as the prime minister, are exclusively qualified to govern the state. Dasan's firm stance on protecting the Joseon social hierarchy can be confirmed here again.

---

[121] The remark "Be filial, only be filial" also appears in "Qing dafu xiaozhuan zan 卿大夫孝傳贊," by Tao Yuanming 陶淵明 (c. 365–427), and "Huaiyang jun Huangshi Youyu chuan ming 淮陽郡黃氏友于川銘," by Zhang Lei 張耒 (1054–1114) (quoted in *Lun yu jiqiu pian*, 1:18a–b).
[122] A quotation of the *Analects* in *Taiping yulan* 太平御覽 also regards the two phrases "Be filial" and "only be filial," as combined [according to *Lun yu jiqiu pian*].
[123] When someone suspected that the phrase "Be filial, only be filial" was undecipherable, Yan Qianqiu 閻潛丘 [閻若璩] replied, "This phrase conveys the same grammatical structure apparent in the following remarks: 'Ritual propriety, oh, ritual propriety!' in *Record of Rites*; 'How presumptuous, how truly presumptuous!' in *Han shu*; 'What a literary purity, oh, what a literary purity!' in Han Yu's writing. By taking the same grammatical structure, the phrase here praises the utmost filial piety. So Bao Xian said, 'it is an expression that praises the great filial piety'" (quoted in *Lun yu jiqiu pian*, 1:19b).
[124] In "Jun Chen 君陳," in Mei Ze's *Documents*, the phrase under discussion, "Be filial," does not exist.

Whereas Xing Bing and Zhu Xi held that the quotation from *Documents* in the main passage came from "Zhou shu 周書," a part of the extant *Documents*, Dasan contended that it came from the lost *Documents*. This difference stems from Dasan's persistent belief that the extant *Documents* were partially modified by Mei Ze. Since Zhu Xi accepted the authenticity of "Jun Chen" in the extant *Documents*, where part of quotation appears without the phrase "be filial," he speculated that the phrase "be filial" must have been Confucius's words, which were inserted into the quotation at some moment. Dasan disagreed, because he discovered a corpus of classical texts that served as proof that the remark "be filial, only be filial" had been widely used in many dynasties by many writers. He was not bothered by the fact that the extant *Documents* did not contain the phrase "be filial" because he did not trust the version known as *"Documents of Mei Ze."* Rather, he argued, it stood as one piece of evidence that Mei Ze modified the *Documents* and interpolated many passages into it. Furthermore, Dasan chastised Mao Qiling because, although he correctly pointed out the problem with Zhu Xi's interpretation, he was not aware that the extant *Documents* was tainted by Mei Ze's hands. As mentioned earlier, Mao Qiling valued the extant *Documents* and wished to guard it against Yan Ruoqu's incisive philological and textual attacks on its authenticity. Dasan also knew what Mao's stance was regarding the extant *Documents*. Thus, despite the fact that his criticism targets Mao Qiling here, it is substantially a criticism of Zhu Xi as well, because he based his textual speculation on the extant *Documents*.

2.22 The Master said, "If a person is not trustworthy, I do not know how he can get on. A big cart without a clamp, or a small cart without a collar-bar—how can it be made to go?"

子曰; 人而無信, 不知其可也. 大車無輗, 小車無軏, 其何以行之哉?

2.22.1 Grounds

1) Bao Xian commented, "A big cart refers to an ox-cart;[125] a small cart refers to a cart drawn by a team of four horses;[126] *ni* 輗 ("clamp") is a horizontal wooden crosspiece attached to the ends of a yoke to fasten it;[127] *yue* 軏 ('collar-bar') is a vertical hook-shaped piece attached to the ends of a yoke."[128]

2) I supplement as follows: A cart and an ox are initially separate things. Their bodies are distinctive, having no direct relations. Only after people tie them together, using clamps and collar-bars, do they form in one body. When an ox moves, the cart also moves along. Confucius here compares this to

---

[125] Master Zhu commented, "It is a freight wagon moving along a level road."
[126] Master Zhu commented, "This kind includes field carts, military carriages, and passenger carriages."
[127] Xing Bing commented, "It is used to put a yoke on the neck of an ox."
[128] Xing Bing commented, "It is a tool that joins together two horses' necks for a yoke."

the value of trustworthiness. I am initially a different person from others. Unless we are tied together through trustworthiness, there is no way for us to move together.[129]

* * *

Like other commentators, Dasan here understands that the clamp and the collar-bar are a metaphor for trustworthiness, one of the five constant virtues in Confucianism. However, in his explanation of the teaching of this chapter, he suggests an interesting interpretation. Whereas trustworthiness is required simply for self-cultivation in many interpretations, Dasan regards it as indispensable for associating with others. Like the clamp and the collar-bar that link two different things together, Dasan thinks trustworthiness allows two different individuals to get along. This is one of the examples that display Dasan's concrete and thereby persuasive interpretations. It is listed in "Overview of the Original Meanings."

2.23 Zi Zhang asked, "Can we know what ten ages hence will be like?" The Master said, "The Yin followed the rituals of the Xia, and what has been removed and added is known to us. The Zhou followed the rituals of the Yin, and what has been removed and added is known to us. Should there be, by any chance, any state that succeeds the Zhou, even a hundred ages hence can be foreknown."[130]

子張問; 十世可知也? 子曰; 殷因於夏禮, 所損益可知也, 周因於殷禮, 所損益可知也. 其或繼周者, 雖百世可知也.

2.23.1 Grounds

1) Master Zhu commented, "The point at which a kingly ruler receives the mandate of Heaven after changing the ruling lineage marks the start of an age [世].[131] Zi Zhang here asks if the affairs of ten future ages are predictable."
2) I supplement as follows: Yin 因 ("followed") here is interchangeable with reng 仍 (to succeed) and xi 襲 (to inherit).[132] This means that a dynasty inherits the principal rituals of the former dynasties[133] while slightly

---

[129] Xu Dongyang 許東洋 (?) commented, "Clamps and collar-bars form the points at which carts and oxen or horses are joined. Trustworthiness is the point at which I am joined with others. The metaphor in the main passage is exquisite." (Unknown source)

[130] Lu Deming says, "In some editions, ya 也 (a particle) appears as hu 乎 (a particle)" (Lun yu jizhu, 1:13b). This regards the first ya in this chapter.

[131] Chen Li commented, "This age is different from one generation of thirty years" (Lun yu jizhu daquan, 2:39b).

[132] Mencius says, "To build a thing high, one must follow [因] mounds and hills" (Mengzi jizhu, 4A:1).

[133] This means that a dynasty inherits the backbone structure of rituals.

modifying the protocols of culture.[134] What has been removed and added is all documented in texts and books,[135] and thus one is able to know of it through an investigation. "Rituals," in this context, refers to the institutions, decrees, laws, and regulations of a king.

3) I supplement as follows: The rituals of the Xia were not immaculate, so the Yin, although it followed the rituals of the Xia, removed something from and added something to them; the rituals of the Yin were not immaculate, so the Zhou, although it followed the rituals of the Yin, removed something from and added something to them. On the establishment of the Zhou, its institutions, decrees, laws, and regulations became immaculate and spotlessly beautiful. As a result, no part of them deserved to be removed or added to. Should there be a king who takes the throne, he must inherit the rituals of the Zhou without making changes for one hundred ages. Therefore it says, "Should there be, by any chance, any state that succeeds the Zhou, even a hundred ages hence can be foreknown." If no king emerges, however, it would entail a disorderly rise of the impure and the turbulent, presenting no agreed-to norms for society. Then the changes will be unpredictable. Because of that, Confucius said, "By any chance [huo 或]." *Huo* is a word intended to show that things are yet undetermined.

2.23.2 Arguments

1) Kong Anguo argued, "This passage discusses the dynasties' choices that range between the value of natural substance [質] and that of refined expressions [文], as well as changes of rituals." Ma Rong also argued, "What they followed was the three principles and five constants [三綱五常]; what they removed or added concerns natural substance and refined expressions as well as the three axes [三統]."[136] I would refute these as follows:

The perception that "the Xia prioritized the value of wholeheartedness; the Yin, the value of natural substance; and the Zhou, the value of refined expressions" originated in *Chunqiu fanlu* 春秋繁露, by Dong Zhongshu 董仲舒 (179–104 BCE).[137] And the theory of choices between natural substance and refined expressions was already formulated in *Shang Shu daquan* by Fu Sheng 伏生 (fl. 213 BCE).[138] Han Confucians, in their discussion of the three

---

[134] This refers to the minor codes of rituals.

[135] At the time of Confucius, the rituals of the Xia and the Yin had not entirely perished yet.

[136] Xing Bing argued, "According to the *Shang Shu daquan*, 'That which has alternated, by virtue of the king's will, between natural substance and refined expressions emulates the way of Heaven and Earth'" (*Shang Shu daquan* 尚書大傳, 1:21b).

[137] "Du Xin zhuan 杜欽傳," in *Han shu*, says, "The Yin followed the Xia but prioritized natural substance; the Zhou followed the Yin but prioritized refined expressions." It continues, "As the Han has succeeded the Zhou and the Qin, which had such defects, it should suppress refined expressions and prioritize natural substance" (*Qian Han shu*, 60:14b).

[138] *Baihu tong* says, "With what ground is it said that for the kings' practices to have alternated between natural substance and refined expressions emulates Heaven and Earth and complies with *yin* and *yang*? When *yang* reaches its vertex, *yin* rises; when *yin* reaches its vertex, *yang* rises. This apparently shows that two of *yang* or two of *yin* cannot stay execution consecutively" (*Baihu tongyi*, B: 26b–27a).

dynasties, uniformly took these conceptions as a core topic. Nevertheless, unfortunately, they could not meticulously revisit the mutual contradictions embedded in the theories. In general, "wholeheartedness" is a term that refers to an all-embracing and unswerving sincerity.[139] Nothing pertains more to natural substance than that. So why did the Yin not move toward refined expressions but succeed the Xia with a focus on natural substance? With this problem, the theory of alternation between natural substance and refined expressions has already turned out to be groundless.

When the sage kings acquire all under heaven, they must seek out the utmost moral principle that could possibly endure for a long time without revealing flaws. Without considering their own advantages and disadvantages, they must have hoped only to make use of it to establish the standards. In contrast, the theory of alternation between natural substance and refined expressions is a conservative adherence to prefixed options, like the alternation between day and night that allows no room to bring about changes. Does there exist such a principle as this?

Indeed, not only the sage kings but also common people can understand well the idea implied in the following passage: "When natural substance overwhelms refined expressions, one will be like a rustic; when refined expressions overwhelms natural substance, one will be like a scribe" (*Lun yu jizhu*, 6:16). Is it acceptable to say that only King Tang and King Wu were so unable to understand it that they, when establishing a dynasty and creating standards, sometimes prioritized natural substance and sometimes prioritized refined expressions? Isn't it the same to say that they did not realize the fact that Qu Dao's 屈到 preference for water caltrop and Zeng Zhe's 曾晳 preference for jujube [which are recorded in the fifteenth year of the reign of Duke Xiang 襄 in *Zuo's Commentary* and 7B:37 in *Mencius,* respectively] simply derived from their biased desires?

Han Confucians asserted that refined expressions prevailed in the way Zhou ruled and that their defects should be amended with natural substance. Subsequently, they ruined the rituals and discarded music, uniformly following the Qin's legacies, to make it impossible for the rules of Yao, Shun, and the three kings to be revived in this world. This was because the theory of refined expressions and natural substance led them astray. Confucius said, "The Zhou reflected on the previous two dynasties. How replete are its refined expressions! I follow the Zhou."[140] As seen here, Confucius did not regard refined expressions as a malady and averred that he followed the Zhou. Why did only Han Confucians vilify them?

The rituals of the Zhou arose after deliberation on the part of the previous two dynasties and a process of removal, addition, amendment, and

---

[139] This is Master Zhu's definition (see *Lun yu jizhu daquan*, 2:39b).
[140] See "Ba yi 八佾" (*Lun yu jizhu* 3:14).

embellishment that came to reveal no flaws even after they were transmitted one hundred ages hence. Therefore when Confucius discussed the kingly way, he said, "I follow the Zhou"; when he discussed future ages, he said, "Should there be, by any chance, a state that succeeds the Zhou, even a hundred ages hence, it can be foreknown." If one were to interpret the main passage as saying that a newly emerging dynasty in place of the Zhou could possibly rule the state only after a project of removal, addition, and changes is completed, I would disagree. In fact, the affairs of even one age are hardly predictable. How can we know what it will be like one hundred ages hence? "Tangong" says, "In the Yin, people condoled with the chief mourner right after a burial mound was finished; in the Zhou, people condoled with the chief mourner when he returned home from the burial site to do the ritual weeping. Confucius said, 'The rituals of the Yin are too undecorated. I follow the Zhou" (*Li ji zhushu*, 9:22b). *Constant Mean* says [in Dasan's creative reading], "I [Confucius] may talk about the rituals of the Xia, but they cannot be sufficiently verified in the affairs of Qi; I have learned the rituals of the Yin, and some of them are preserved in Song; I have learned the rituals of the Zhou, and they are still in practice. I follow the Zhou" (*Zhong yong zhangju*, 24b). Confucius repeatedly made clear that he followed the Zhou because the practices of its rituals would not demonstrate any flaws for one hundred ages. Why do people want to alter them tumultuously for no reason? This is a gigantic problem that has appeared in our literature for two thousand years.

In my view, the three principles and the five constants are moral laws, not a state's rituals. Is it not a fallacy that Ma Rong designated them as rituals? It would be possible to subject the process of removal and addition to the values of refined expressions and natural substance because some could remove natural substance by adding refined expressions while others could remove refined expressions by adding natural substance. The theory of the so-called three axes, however, only contains ideas of changes, not successions. How can this theory be applied to the process of removal and addition?

2) For a classical text on the discussion here, see "Dazhuan 大傳" (*Li ji zhushu*, 34:5a, 8–5b, 6).

In my view, a number of commentators based their interpretations on this writing. However, the phrase under discussion in the main passage says, "What has been removed and added is known to us." In contrast, in the writing in "Dazhuan," we are able to know only what is safe from removal and addition, so what has been removed and added will still remain unknown to us. Does the writing from "Dazhuan" provide a ground strong enough to be adopted for an interpretation of this passage?

3) I question Master Zhu as follows:

Lun yu jizhu commented, "The Five Constants refer to humanity, rightness, ritual propriety, wisdom, and trustworthiness" (*Lun yu jizhu*, 1:13b). In respect of this, Yuan Liaofan says, "A discussion of rituals does not pertain to the three Principles and the five Constants. The relationships between the lord and the subject, between the father and the son, and between the husband and the wife constitute the great moral order for living people. In contrast, humanity, rightness, ritual propriety, wisdom, and trustworthiness are human inborn nature. How can these values be said to become rituals? What has been removed and added is not relevant to the theory of the three axes as well. The three distinctive ways of establishing their calendars in the three dynasties [three axes]—that is, the Xia's way of setting it up at *yin* 寅 [one of the twelve celestial directions], the Yin's way of setting it up at *chou* 丑 [the same as above], and the Zhou's way of setting it up at *zi* 子 [the same as above]—are related to a prefixed heavenly time. How can these ways be said to pertain to the process of removal and addition? It would be more plausible simply to apply the theory to the values of refined expressions and natural substance" (Unknown source).[141]

In my view, Yuan's explanation is clear and solid. He seemed, however, not to have realized the meaning of the main passage when he noted that it was plausible to apply the process of removal and addition to the values of refined expressions and natural substance.

4) Wu Wuzhang 吳無障 (?) argued, "At that time, Confucius wanted to reduce the refined expressions of the Zhou by adding the wholeheartedness of the Xia and the natural substance of the Shang. This is the great meaning of the main passage" (Unknown source).[142] I would refute this as follows:

Confucius said, "The Zhou reflected on the previous two dynasties. How replete are its refined expressions! I follow the Zhou." Confucius made it clear that he followed the Zhou, outspokenly glorifying it. Still, someone distorts his view and says, "Confucius wanted to reduce the refined expressions of the Zhou." Isn't this a willful opinion? Those who understand the beauty of the Zhou's rituals must bring no removal and addition to them even after a long period during which one hundred kings will have emerged and faded away. Because of this, Confucius became confident that he would know what one hundred ages hence would be like. If removal, addition, alterations, and changes occur as though clouds and rainbows

---

[141] Dazai Jun argued, "In my investigation, the term 'five constants' first appeared in a sentence in 'Taishi 泰誓,' in *Documents*: 'They disrespected the five constants' (*Shang Shu zhushu*, 10:16b). On this, Kong Anguo commented, 'This means that they treated the teaching of the five constants negligently. So, they disrespected it and did not put it into practice.' 'Shundian 舜典' also contains the remark 'Shun carefully illuminated the five cardinal codes [五典].' On this, Kong Anguo commented, 'The five cardinal codes refer to the teaching of the five constants—that is, rightness of the father, benevolence of the mother, brotherhood of the older brother, politeness of the younger brother, and filial piety of the son.' Given these remarks, it is evident that the five constants are equivalent to the five cardinal codes. Since Ban Gu 班固 (32–92) mentioned that humanity, rightness, ritual propriety, wisdom, and trustworthiness constitute the five constants, the commentaries of Xing Bing and Zhu Xi uniformly adopted Ban Gu's theory. However, it is not the ancient meaning of the term."

[142] Guo Qingluo 郭青螺 (1543–1618) gave his consent to this opinion.

keep appearing and disappearing, we cannot know even tomorrow's happenings, let alone one hundred ages hence.

5) For classical texts on the discussion here, see "Li qi," which says, "The rituals of the three dynasties were uniform. Thus all the people commonly observed them. Regarding colors, however, one dynasty valued white more while another valued green more. As for certain forms of ritual decorum, the Xia created them, and the Yin inherited them" *(Li ji zhushu*, 23:32b), and the contention of Shusun Tong 叔孫通 (d. c. 188) in *Shi ji* says, "Confucius's remark, which says that he could know what was removed and added to the rituals of the Xia, the Yin, and the Zhou, pertains to the fact that the dynasties did not inherit the rituals from previous dynasties" (*Shi ji*, 99:8a–b).

In my view, if the dynasties did not inherit the rituals from previous dynasties, there is no way for us to know them. How could Confucius say that we can know what it will be like one hundred ages hence?

* * *

One of the differences between Dasan and the majority of Confucian scholars, including Han-Tang Confucians, neo-Confucians, and Qing Confucians, lay in their perceptions of the three dynasties. The majority of Confucians believed that each of the three dynasties enjoyed its cultural efflorescence under the rule of the sage kings (such as King Yu in the Xia, King Tang in the Yin, and King Wen and King Wu in the Zhou). But all of them uniformly confronted the same fate of decline when they came to have dishonorable leaders. In contrast, Dasan observed a lineal development through the establishments of new dynasties because, in his view, the later dynasty—led by certain brilliant leaders, especially in its inceptive period—must have attempted to improve its system by an examination of the merits and demerits that the preceding dynasty displayed in its historical experiences. Consequently, to Dasan, the Zhou was the best among the three dynasties and, furthermore, the best among all dynasties that existed historically because after the Zhou there were no more sage kings. Dasan's idealization of the Zhou system led him to affirm the immaculateness of the Zhou's rituals, as shown in his comment here. As "rituals" here refers to decrees and regulations, according to Dasan, his praise of the Zhou's rituals implies that he considered the entire Zhou system ideal.

In line with this, Dasan did not accept the theory that the three dynasties each opted for and prioritized one of the three values: wholeheartedness, natural substance, and refined expression (in chronological order). Dasan refuted it because, above all, the theory lacks reasonability: there is no rational ground to link each of the values to each of the dynasties; moreover, it is not persuasive to insist that a dynasty that prized wholeheartedness (that is, the Xia) was succeeded by another dynasty (that is, the Yin) that emphasized natural substance— a value parallel to wholeheartedness. However, Dasan's acknowledgement of the perfection of the Zhou system remains in the background of his rebuttal of the theory, since the theory renders the Zhou as unbalanced as other dynasties. This argument is listed in "Overview of the Original Meanings."

Dasan also did not agree with Ma Rong and Zhu Xi, who argued that the three dynasties shared the same essential moral values, such as the three principles and the five constants, whereas they employed their own ritual protocols in accordance with their circumstances. This point should not be taken to imply that Dasan did not accept the everlasting nature of the values. The values are permanent and supertemporal to Dasan as well, although he was aligned with Dazai Jun, not with Zhu Xi, in the specific designation of the five constants: Zhu Xi listed the five virtues—humanity, rightness, ritual propriety, wisdom, and trustworthiness—as the components of the five constants, unlike Dazai Jun, who drew his definition of the term from the earlier classical text. Dasan might have favored Dazai's identification of the five constants because it was less abstract than Zhu Xi's. The reason Dasan did not agree with Ma Rong and Zhu Xi in this regard, despite his identical understanding of the transcendental nature of the core values of human morals, was that it was improper to discourse on these moral values in this chapter, in which Confucius simply discussed the rituals. Dasan's rational efforts to discover a more accurate and concrete interpretation of each passage are manifest here again.

It is also intriguing to read his remark that even Confucius could not confidently assert that he could predict what it would be like one hundred ages hence unless the Zhou's rituals are preserved intact throughout the ages. This terse but unswerving rationalist's attitude permeates every corner of his writing—as, for example, in the following quotation: "If removal, addition, alterations, and changes occur as though clouds and rainbows keep appearing and disappearing, we cannot know even tomorrow's happenings, let alone one hundred ages hence." This argument is listed in "Overview of the Original Meanings" as well; Dasan's comment on this chapter is the only one that registers two "original meanings" in the list.

2.24 The Master said, "To sacrifice to spirits that do not belong to you is flattery. Failing to take action when you see what is right is want of courage."

子曰; 非其鬼而祭之, 諂也. 見義不爲, 無勇也.

2.24.1 Grounds

1) Master Zhu commented, "*Fei qi gui* 非其鬼 (spirits that do not belong to you) refers to spirits other than those one ought to sacrifice to.[143] *Chan* 諂 (flattery) is to conduct sycophancy."

---

[143] Master Zhu also commented, "This chapter pertains to the practices in which the Son of Heaven sacrifices to Heaven and Earth, the feudal lords sacrifice to mountains and rivers, the great officials sacrifice to the five [places for] sacrificial rituals [五祀], and common people sacrifice to their ancestors.

1) Zheng Xuan argued, "Spiritual beings that were once humans are called *gui* ('spirits').[144] To sacrifice to spirits other than one's own ancestors is to seek out good luck through flattery." Mao Qiling also argued as seen in the following:

> A passage in *Zuo's Commentary* reads: "Gods do not receive sacrifices offered by people with different lineages; people do not sacrifice to spirits in different tribes" (*Zuo zhuan zhushu*, 12:23a).[145] This passage duly concerns human spirits.[146] Therefore, when Duke Cheng of Wei [衛成公, r. 634–632, 632–600 BCE] wanted to sacrifice to Xiang 相 of the Xia[147] after he moved the capital to Diqiu 帝丘, Ningwuzi 甯武子 (fl. 632 BCE) dissuaded him, saying, "Impossible! To whom shall the states of Qi 杞 and Ceng 鄫 [states enfeoffed to the descendants of the Xia] sacrifice, then?"[148] Also in the other case, the earl of Zheng 鄭 requested that he discontinue the sacrifices to Mount Tai in order to sacrifice to the Duke of Zhou.[149] These are evidence that people wanted to sacrifice to spirits other than their own. "Ji fa 祭法" clarifies that "spirits [鬼] refer to dead humans" (*Li ji zhushu*, 46:9b). Officials of ritual services regard the kings and the founders of a state as spirits; common people regard their dead fathers as spirits. If one [Zhu Xi] believes that *fei gui* pertains to the sacrifices to Heaven and Earth or mountains and rivers, as seen in the performance by the head of the Ji family of the Lü 旅 sacrifice to Mount Tai, I would say that I have never heard of people calling heavenly gods the *gui* of heaven and the god of Mount Tai the *gui* of Mount Tai" (*Lun yu jiqiu pian*, 1:19b–20a).

I would refute these as follows:

Though the names of heavenly gods, earth-souls, and human spirits are different from each other, three characters [神, 示, 鬼] used for the names are interchangeable. Due to this, the character *shen* 神 has the *qi* 示 radical in it. When *Constant Mean* praises the virtue of *gui* and *shen*, it is obviously related to the Jiao sacrifice [to heavenly gods]. It implies that the heavenly gods were sometimes called *gui*. The five sacrificial rituals in *Rites of Zhou* apparently belong to the earth-souls. Nevertheless, in the royal scribe Yin's 囂 (fl. 720 BCE) remark recorded in "Jin yu," Rushou 蓐收 is called "heavenly god" (see *Guo yu*, 8:7a).[150] Meanwhile, "Jiu ge 九歌," in *Chu ci* 楚辭,

---

People can observe a sacrificial ritual lower in level than those they are allowed to, but they cannot observe a ritual higher in level than those they are allowed to" (*Lun yu jizhu daquan*, 2:42a).

[144] Xing Bing argued, "The head minister [大宗伯] oversees the rituals of heavenly gods [天神], earth-souls [地示], and human spirits [人鬼]."

[145] This is a remark by Hutu 狐突 [a great official of Jin, ?–637 BCE].

[146] For example, Han sacrificed to Duke Luan [欒公]; the state of Wu sacrificed to Marquis Jiang [蔣歆]; the state of Shu 蜀 sacrificed to King Guan [關羽].

[147] Xiang is a descendent of Qi 啓 [the legendary second king of the Xia].

[148] See the thirty-first year of the reign of Duke Xi (*Zuo zhuan zhushu*, 16:14a).

[149] See the seventh year of the reign of Duke Yin 隱 (*Zuo zhuan zhushu*, 3:13b).

[150] Viscount Xian of Wei [魏獻子, d. 509 BCE] viewed Rushou as an earth-soul that is linked to the five sacrificial rituals.

contains the term "mountain-spirits" [山鬼], and *Guanyinzi* 關尹子 contains the term "earth-spirits" [土鬼]. *Chi* 魑, *Mei* 魅, *Wang* 魍, and *Liang* 魎 were originally monsters living in mountain forests, but these characters all have the *gui* radical. One of Confucius's sayings, "Show respect for spirits and gods but keep them at a distance" (*Lun yu jizhu*, 6:22), should not be understood as teaching that we should keep our ancestors at a distance. Sir Zheng [Zheng Xuan] unfairly relied on just one passage in "Da Zongbo 大宗伯" to interpret the main passage in this classic, and thus his interpretation was distorted from the beginning. Nevertheless, Xiaoshan accepted it and, furthermore, attempted to verify it. How can this not be an error?

Indeed, Ningwuzi and Hutu mentioned that gods do not receive sacrifices from people unrelated by lineage. However, Zhan Qin 展禽 (720–621 BCE) of Lu declared, "Great Yu [King Shun] performed the Jiao sacrifice to Yao";[151] "Ji fa" says, "Great Yu performed the Jiao sacrifice to Ku 嚳 [Lord Ku] and revered Yao as the chief ancestor" (*Li ji zhushu*, 46:1a); in *Rites of Zhou*, people sacrifice to all Five Lords.[152] In addition, prior to King Tang of the Yin, people sacrificed to Zhu 柱 as the grain god, whereas after him, they sacrificed to Qi 棄 as the grain god. This practice has not changed over the generations, and it is preserved even now. Why should only one's own ancestors be presented in the ritual codes?

Zhong 重, Gai 該, Xiu 修, and Xi 熙 are the four uncles of Shaohao 少皞 [one of the Five Lords in some records], and Li 黎 and Julong 句龍 are the sons of Zhuanxu 顓頊 [the same as above] and Gonggong 共工 [the same as above]. However, they were uniformly offered sacrifices in the five sacrificial rituals, a practice that persisted throughout the three dynasties.[153] If it is true that one cannot dare to offer sacrifices to spirits other than one's own, it would mean that all the sage kings in the three dynasties committed flattery. The speeches of Ningwuzi and Hutu should be construed as saying that those who lack merits and virtue should not be presented in the codes of sacrificial rituals, nor should those who cannot achieve spiritual communication with people with whom they bear no affiliation by way of lineage or tribe. How can their remarks be construed as claiming that one cannot offer sacrifices to spirits other than one's own, in accordance with Sir Zheng's interpretation? In conclusion, kings, princes, and great officials all have their own codes for sacrificial rituals. All recipients of rituals that have been incorporated into the codes become their spirits; all recipients of rituals that are difficult for the codes to incorporate become the "spirits that do not belong to you." Can the interpretation of *Lun yu jizhu* be altered?

2) For a classical text on the discussion here, see "Qu li," which says, "A sacrificial ritual in which people sacrifice to what they should not sacrifice

---

[151] See "Lu yu" (*Guo yu*, 40:2a).
[152] Lord Ku was not the ancestor of Yu 虞 people; the Five Lords are not the ancestors of Zhou people.
[153] See the speech of Viscount Xian of Wei in the twenty-ninth year of the reign of Duke Zhao (*Zuo zhuan zhushu*, 53:14ab).

to is called a licentious sacrifice. A licentious sacrifice brings no blessing" (*Li ji zhushu*, 5:26ab).

In my view, what is discussed in "Qu li" does not exclusively concern human spirits.

* * *

The main passage in this chapter consists of two sentences. Since the sentences have no direct relationship with each other, commentators have suspected that they were consolidated into a single passage by later hands. The first sentence discusses ritual propriety; the second sentence teaches people with an ethical attitude that is consistent with many teachings of Confucianism, such that questions hardly arise. Dasan's quite lengthy comment in this chapter is solely engaged with the first sentence because, first, it is where a dispute lies, and second, a clarification of details of ritual performances always attracts Dasan's interest. In this chapter, as in many other chapters, he emerges as a specialist in Confucian rituals more than a sociopolitical reformer or a philosopher.

His argument in this chapter is intended to advocate Zhu Xi's view on the meaning of the term "spirits that do not belong to you." Unlike Zheng Xuan, who represented the old commentary in this regard, Zhu Xi and Dasan held that the term referred to all recipients of illegitimate sacrificial rituals and should not be reductively understood as meaning human spirits. Dasan, through his attack on a comment of Mao Qiling that showed that he accepted the old commentary, intends to strengthen Zhu Xi's logic by finding as many classical sources as possible in which the Chinese character *gui* ("spirits") might mean a vast range of recipients of Confucian rituals. Whether contentions of Zhu Xi and Dasan are persuasive remains unanswered, because in the main passage Confucius says that people's performances of a dishonest ritual of this kind are regarded as flattery—an action designed to please someone by complimentary speeches or offers. In contrast, illegitimate sacrifices, of which Zhu Xi provided some examples, such as a sacrifice in which a feudal lord sacrifices to Heaven, are usually performed out of arrogance or a desire to display the performer's majesty. Thus Zhu Xi's motive to reject the old commentary and to apply this teaching to a broader spectrum of people's ritual activities becomes comprehensible: he wanted to fortify the social hierarchy by reminding people of what they were not allowed to do in accordance with their social status. This goal matches Dasan's efforts to sustain Joseon's social hierarchy.

In Joseon society, it was a politically sensitive issue whether the dynasty was entitled to sacrifice to Heaven. Especially in early Joseon, when Joseon's loyalty to Ming China was not fortified yet, some scholars insisted that Joseon deserved to sacrifice to Heaven because the country originated from historical developments that were distinct from Chinese history, and the state of Lu, a feudal state that worshiped Heaven, had already set a precedent. Although this "nationalist" voice was eventually suppressed by the Joseon legitimists, it haunted the Joseon academy from time to time when it was accused of dependency. Dasan was not able to speak for Joseon's independence in its relationship with China in a more radical way because by his time Joseon was too deeply Sinicized to venture into a realm of national sovereignty and he saw it as necessary to sustain the social hierarchy, internationally and domestically, in order to bring order and reform simultaneously to Joseon society. His criticism of the state of Lu's traditional practices of performing the sacrifice to Heaven, which he saw as a violation of ritual propriety, is further discussed in the first few chapters of book 3.

BOOK 3 | Eight Rows of Dancers 八佾

3.1 Confucius said of the Ji family, "They had eight rows of dancers dance in their courtyard. If they could bear to do this, what can they not bear to do?" [In *Noneo gogeum ju* in traditional book binding, this chapter opens the fourth roll.][1]

子謂季氏, 八佾舞於庭, 是可忍也, 孰不可忍也?

3.1.1 Grounds

1) I supplement as follows: The Ji family refers to the descendants of Ji You 季友 (d. 644), the duke's prince [公子].[2]
2) Master Zhu commented, "*Yi* 佾 ('rows') refers to a row of dancers."
3) Ma Rong commented, "The son of Heaven is entitled to have eight rows; the feudal lords are entitled to have six rows; the ministers and great officials, four rows; the low-ranking officials, two rows.[3] Eight dancers make up a row, so the eight rows consist of sixty-four dancers."
4) Master Zhu commented, "[This passage states that] if they can bear to handle even this affair, what affairs can they not bear to handle?"

3.1.2 Arguments

1) Ma Rong argued, "The state of Lu was allowed to use the rituals and music for kings owing to its relation to the Duke of Zhou [whose descendants were the rulers of the state of Lu], so it conventionally had the practice of having eight rows of dancers. [At the time] Ji Huanzi 季桓子 (d. 492 BCE), the head of the Ji family, had the performance in the courtyard of his family shrine in violation of ritual propriety [僭]." Mao Qiling also argued as seen in the following:

> I was able to eventually understand this passage when I wrote *Daxiaozong tong-shi* 大小宗通釋. All things considered, the state of Lu became the state of chief

---

[1] This book contains twenty-six chapters.
[2] Duke Huan [魯桓公, r. 711–694 BCE] had three sons besides his successor. The eldest was Zhong Qingfu 仲慶父 (d. 660 BCE); the next was Shu Ya 叔牙 (d. 662 BCE), who was followed by Ji You.
[3] This was originally a passage from the fifth year of the reign of Duke Yin in *Zuo's Commentary* (*Zuo zhuan zhushu*, 2:38a).

descendant [宗國] because the Duke of Zhou, King Wu's brother, became one of the chief descendants of King Wen [alongside King Wu] after he was given the title Another Son [別子]. According to *Record of the Rites*, "Another Son establishes a chief-descendant's lineage and should offer sacrifices to those from whom he was born."[4] Subsequently, the Duke of Zhou erected the shrine for King Wen in the state of Lu.[5] Since this shrine commemorated the origin of the Duke of Zhou, it was named the Shrine of the Origin King.[6] Was it possible for the state of Lu not to use the rituals and music for the Son of Heaven, when they offered sacrifices to King Wen? The state of Lu used the rituals and music for the Son of Heaven [in this shrine] because they were dedicated to the Origin King [King Wen]. And the state of Lu offered sacrifices to the Origin King because it was the chief descendant [state] of King Wen. All three of the Huan [三桓] were princes of Duke Huan of Lu. Since Ji You was the only legitimate son, however, he became the chief minister and was thereby allowed to offer sacrifices to his family's original ancestors. Thus he erected the shrine for Duke Huan. Han Confucians did not understand this, so someone [Zheng Xuan] even said that a state shrine [the shrine for Duke Huan] was established in a private house [of the Ji family].[7] This shrine commemorated the origin of the three Huan. Since they all originated from Duke Huan, it was called the hall of the three families; since the Ji family was the major chief descendant, the main passage singled out the Ji family. All in all, owing to its relationship with Duke Huan, the Ji family used the rituals and music for the Son of Heaven; Duke Huan could use them because they were initially adopted for King Wen; and finally, all dukes of Lu and their descendants came to use them conventionally one after another. (*Si shu shengyan*, 2:16a–b)

I would refute these as follows:

Mao's theory is half correct and half incorrect. His argument that the violation of ritual propriety of the three houses stemmed from the practice of offering sacrifices to Duke Huan is fine. His insistence that the violation of ritual propriety by all the dukes of Lu stemmed from their practice of offering sacrifices to King Wen, however, is not necessarily true. Xiaoshan boasted that he shed light on what had remained unexplained by his predecessors in the study of the major and minor chief descendants. In my research on the classical texts, however, his theories often turn out to have errors, frequently showing disharmony with the texts. For example, Mao argued as follows: Qingfu and Shu Ya were sons of a concubine; therefore, though they were older than Ji You, none could be designated the major chief descendant; in contrast, Ji You could be designated the major chief descendant because he was a legitimate son,

---

[4] See "Dazhuan" (quoted in *Si shu shengyan*, 2:16a).
[5] See *Shi ji* (*Shi ji*, 32:8b).
[6] See *Zuo's Commentary* (*Zuo zhuan zhushu*, 31:35b).
[7] See "Jiao tesheng 郊特牲" (*Li ji zhushu*, 25:21a).

though he was the youngest; as a result, he was respected as the chief descendant by all three houses.

This argument seems to be valid but is actually not. "Dazhuan" says, "In some cases, people cannot respect others as chief descendants, even when they have no chief descendant. Princes of the dukes fall under this category" (*Li ji zhushu*, 34:16b). This reveals that princes of the dukes, despite their large number, were supposed to become the chief descendants themselves and could not be commingled with other lineages. Thus they chose a man among their sons or grandsons who could continue their lineage and anointed him as the chief descendant. As for the princes themselves, however, they could not become chief descendants, because their royal status could not be degraded. Therefore it is said, "In some cases, people cannot respect others as chief descendants, even when they have no chief descendant. Princes of the dukes fall under this category." This meaning has not been clearly noted thus far primarily because people have relied on Zheng Xuan's incorrect annotations of "Dazhuan."[8]

As a matter of fact, if one examines the given issue according to the principle of human relationships, Mao's theory can be immediately disproved even without a reference to the classical texts. What does this mean? Suppose that there are three princes—one legitimate son and two illegitimate sons, as in the case of the three Huan—and that the legitimate son is accepted as the major chief descendant, as Xiaoshan argues. This theory is still supposedly fine. If all three princes were illegitimate sons, however, who would become the major chief descendant? If you recommend that the eldest son be taken as the major chief descendant, it means that the major chief descendant could be even among the illegitimate sons. According to *Protocols and Rituals*, someone who continues a lineage "will become the major chief descendant in the next generation" (*Yi li zhushu*, 11:42a).

Early Confucians usually said that the lineage of the minor chief descendant should be discontinued when there are no more descendants. If this is true, the lineages of the Mengsun 孟孫 [Zhong Qingfu's lineage] and the Shusun 叔孫 [Shu Ya's lineage] should have been discontinued, because they failed to beget their own descendants. However, Zhong Yingqi 仲嬰齊 [of the Mengsun family, d. 576 BCE] and Shusun Bao 叔孫豹 [of the Shusun family, d. 538 BCE] were busy [when they became the head of their families] implementing a plan to determine who could continue their lineages. How could they do so? It was because there was a major chief descendant even among the illegitimate sons. Then how can sons of the Son of Heaven not establish a major chief descendant? Each of them was enfeoffed with land to build a state and allowed to establish a major chief descendant to manage his lineage with a sense of autonomy. Therefore, in general, the feudal lords came to have

---

[8] A more detailed discussion appears in my commentaries on the Confucian rituals (see *Sangrye sajeon*, 241d–244d).

many minor chief descendants. Then is it acceptable in light of principle to say that the lords of states [of Lu] cannot become major chief descendants?

There is another unacceptable point in Mao's theory. It is now clear that the Zhou allowed the Duke of Zhou to become the major chief descendant because he was one of the legitimate sons. When it reached the era of Duke Yin, however, a son of a concubine [Duke Yin] succeeded the royal power of Lu. Then could such states as Cai 蔡, Wei, Cao 曹, and Teng 滕 [the brother states of Lu] truly respect the state of Lu as their major chief descendant? In the same manner, suppose that the state of Lu had allowed Ji You to become the major chief descendant because he was a legitimate son. When it reached the era of Ji Daozi 季悼子 (fl. 550 BCE),[9] however, a son of a concubine [Ji Daozi] carried on the family line. Then could the families of Mengsun and Shusun truly respect him as the major chief descendant? If the tradition of holding legitimate sons in high regard over illegitimate sons was already deeply rooted to that extent, it would not make sense in principle to assume that when an illegitimate son succeeded a legitimate son to the throne, others would continue to respect him as the chief descendant.

Indeed, the lord of Teng once made mention of "The former lords of the state of Lu, our chief descendant's state" (*Mengzi jizhu*, 3A:2). Based on this remark, Mao Qiling argued that all states that stemmed from the Ji 姬 family [the royal family of the Zhou] respected the state of Lu as their chief descendant. At the time, however, those states that stemmed from the same family mutually called the other the state of the chief descendant. Due to this practice, when the states of Teng and Xue 薛 vied for the position of seniority, Duke Yin of Lu commissioned Yufu 羽父 (fl. 719–709 BCE) to ask a favor for the Teng [to the marquis of Xue], saying, "In the alliance of the chief descendants of the Zhou, states stemming from different families are inferior."[10] If one is allowed to call the alliance of members of the same family the "alliance of the chief descendants," there is no reason to disallow calling states of the same family "the chief descendant's states" [as seen in Teng's case].[11]

As for the Shrine of the Origin King, it existed in every state. For example, when Duke Zhuang of Wei [衛莊公, r. 757–735 BCE] recited a written prayer to the ancestors, he said, "I dare to report precisely to the imperial progenitor King Wen."[12] This suggests that the state of Wei also established the shrine for King Wen. The state of Zheng offered sacrifices to King Li 厲; the state of Kui 夔 sacrificed to Yuxiong 鬻熊;[13] the state of Zeng offered sacrifices to Xiang of the Xia.[14] How could all these states stem from legitimate

---

[9] This refers to Jisun He 季孫紇, the illegitimate son of Jisun Shu 季孫宿 (d. 535 BCE) [季孫叔 in all editions of *Noneo gogeumju*].

[10] See the eleventh year of the reign of Duke Yin in *Zuo's Commentary* (*Zuo zhuan zhushu*, 3:30b).

[11] "Jin yu" records: "Zhouzhi Qiao 舟之嬌 [a great official in the state of Guo 虢, fl. 651 BCE] took the state of Wu 虞 as the chief descendant's state" (*Guo yu*, 8:7b).

[12] See "Jin yu" (*Guo yu*, 15:7b).

[13] See the twenty-sixth year of the reign of Duke Xi in *Zuo's Commentary* (*Zuo zhuan zhushu*, 15:11a).

[14] See the thirty-first year of the reign of Duke Xi in *Zuo's Commentary* (*Zuo zhuan zhushu*, 16:14a).

sons without exception? In general, sons of the Son of Heaven offered sacrifices to their origin king even when they had not been enfeoffed with land but given an appanage. Therefore, *Rites of Zhou* mentions that the official who supervises the rituals of the chief descendants [都宗人] offers sacrifices to their progenitorial king and helps [the king of] the state partake of sacrificial food and drink (*Zhou li zhushu*, 27:31a). On this record Zheng Xuan commented, "The descendants of the king [of Zhou] established a shrine for their progenitor king" (27:31a). Here the "progenitor king" is identical to the origin king. How can it be justified to say that only legitimate sons could establish the Shrine of the Origin King? Actually, even in the Han dynasty this tradition remained in practice. According to the laws of Han, feudal lords established the origin emperor's shrine in their states.[15] In line with this, even those lords who descended from illegitimate sons were not prohibited from keeping this practice.

The states of Cai, Wei, Cao, and Teng already respected the Great Zhou as their chief descendant. Had they respected the state of Lu as their chief descendant when they withdrew from the Zhou court, it would mean that they had two Sons of Heaven. Similarly, the families of Mengsun and Shusun already respected the royal house of Lu as their chief descendant. Had they respected the family of Jisun as their chief descendant, it would mean that they had two lords. Would this practice not have disturbed all under heaven?

Each of the families of three Huan had a shrine for Duke Huan, and they uniformly used the Yong ode while removing the ritual vessels. Thus the *Analects* says, "The three families used the Yong ode while removing the ritual vessels" (*Lun yu jizhu* 3:2). Had the Ji family exclusively performed the sacrificial ritual for Duke Huan, no one would have recorded it as it appears in the passage "The three families used the Yong ode while removing the ritual vessels." There is no such a principle. The Ji family's violation of ritual propriety was merely the most grave among violations committed by the three families because they performed the Yong ode while removing the ritual vessels and again had eight rows of dancers. As a result, Confucius first excoriated them for what was their fault alone [in this passage] and later castigated all three families for what they shared [in the next passage]. If someone now were to confuse the Ji family with all three families and confuse the three families with the Ji family without distinguishing them from one another, would it be acceptable?

Furthermore, the so-called eight rows of dancers and the Yong ode not only were used for the sacrificial rituals for Duke Huan but also were adopted in the rituals for Zhong Qing[fu], Shu Ya, and Ji You. Confucius's words are therefore imbued with his feelings of devastation to the extent seen in the main passage. If the three families had adopted the protocols for the Son of Heaven only in the sacrificial rituals for Duke Huan, their sin would not have surpassed that of the lords of Lu. From the beginning,

---

[15] See *Han shu* (*Qian Han shu*, 22:16a).

Confucius intended to convey to the state of Lu the remark "If they can bear to do this, what could they not bear to do," while not directly exposing the state's evil tradition. Indeed, King Cheng 成 [of Zhou, r. 1042–1021 BCE] ordered the state of Lu to offer sacrifices to the Duke of Zhou with the protocols for the Son of Heaven, and because of that, the lord of Lu, in violation of ritual propriety, came to have eight rows of dancers in the shrines for all the dukes of Lu; they disturbingly had eight rows of dancers in the shrines of all the dukes of Lu in violation of ritual propriety, and because of that, the Ji family had eight rows of dancers in the shrine for Duke Huan. They eventually came to have eight rows of dancers dance in the courtyard of the Ji family. Then was it wrong when I said that Xiaoshan's theory was half correct and half incorrect? When it argues that the three families' violation of ritual propriety stemmed from the practice of offering sacrifices to the origin duke [Duke Huan], it is still fine. When it insists that the violation of ritual propriety of the state of Lu stemmed from their practice of offering sacrifices to King Wen, however, it is invalid.

2) Xing Bing argued, "Although the main passage simply mentions 'the Ji family,' Ma Rong knew that it was Ji Huanzi because he was a contemporary of Confucius." I would refute this as follows:

Ji Huanzi did not initiate the Ji family's violation of ritual propriety. A record in the twenty-fifth year of the reign of Duke Zhao in *Zuo's Commentary* says, "In autumn, the Di 禘 sacrifice for Duke Xiang [魯襄公, r. 572–542 BCE] occurred. There were two dancers.[16] Most dancers danced in the house of the Ji family" (*Zuo zhuan zhushu*, 51:24a).[17] Zijia Ju's 子家駒 (fl. 516 BCE) dispute about the eight rows of dancers also occurred in the same year. Duke Zhao's banishment to the state of Qi 齊 also happened in that year.[18] The head of the Ji family in that year was Ji Pingzi 季平子 (d. 505 BCE).[19] It is obvious that Confucius's lamentation [seen in the main passage] was expressed in that year. Is it possible to link it to Ji Huanzi?[20]

3) Xing Bing argued, "Dukes adopt the number six, having six rows of six dancers; great officials adopt the number four, having four rows of four dancers; low-ranking officials adopt the number two, having two rows of two dancers.[21] In the understanding of Fu Qian 服虔 (fl. 168), an adoption of the number six leads to having six rows of eight dancers; the number four to four rows of eight dancers, in the case of great officials; and the number two to two rows of eight dancers, in the case of low-ranking officials. Today, dancers must be set in a square formation. If the number of rows is reduced, the number of dancers in each row should also be reduced.

---

[16] This means that there were only two dancers for the duke.
[17] This means that most dancers went to the house of the Ji family.
[18] Confucius also went to the state of Qi in that year.
[19] His name was Jisun Yiru 季孫意如.
[20] Ji Huanzi is Jisun Si 季孫斯, Ji Pingzi's son.
[21] Du Yu and He Xiu accepted this understanding.

Therefore I concur with He Xiu and Du Yu's theory." I would refute this as follows:

Zhongzhong 眾仲 (fl. 717 BCE) of the state of Lu once said, "Dances are a means of putting the eight sounds in harmony and allowing [the folks of] the eight directions to practice."[22] Thus, unless we have eight dancers per row, their dances would not be in harmony with the eight sounds. Accordingly, an adoption of the number six means having six rows of eight dancers; the number four [means] having four rows of eight dancers; and the number two [means] having two rows of eight dancers. In line with this, the lord of Zheng once bribed the viscount of the state of Jin, using two bands of eight female musicians [the eleventh year of the reign of Duke Xiang in *Zuo's Commentary*]. Isn't this evidence for my argument? "Zhaohun fu 招魂賦," in *Chu ci*, says melodiously, "Two bands of eight female entertainers wait, on call, through the night; when dishes are repeated, they are replaced anew" (*Chu ci zhangju* 楚辭章句, 9:6b). It also says, "Two bands of eight female musicians are featured in unity; they rise to dance to the music of the state of Zheng" (9:9b). If low-ranking officials have two bands of two dancers, how could a dance be performed?

4) Xing Bing argued, "All people's violations of ritual propriety should be punished without exoneration. The Ji family, as vavasors, used the rituals for the Son of Heaven in violation of ritual propriety, which was the hardest thing to tolerate. Thus it says, 'If they can be tolerated, who cannot be tolerated?'" I would refute this as follows:

At the beginning of the main passage, it says, "Confucius said of the Ji family." This makes it clear that Confucius was blaming the psychological attitude of the Ji family for their deeds, revealing that what they did was not something a human can dare to do. If Xing Bing's interpretation is correct, the beginning of the passage should be "Confucius said."

5) For a classical text on the discussion here, see *Gongyang's Commentary* (*Chunqiu Gongyang zhuan zhushu*, 24:10a, 5–11b, 5).[23]

In this record, in my view, the state of Lu is criticized for violating the rituals for the Son of Heaven because it had eight rows of dancers in the shrines for all the lords of Lu. One might infer from this fact that the Ji family enjoyed a performance of eight rows of dancers in the courtyard of Ji You as well. How could it be confined to the shrine for Duke Huan?

6) For a classical text on the discussion here, see "Ji tong 祭統" (*Li ji zhushu*, 49:30a, 7–30b, 4).

In my view, Han Confucians forged the record in "Ji tong." Had King Cheng granted the state of Lu the privilege of adopting the rituals for the

---

[22] See the fifth year of the reign of Duke Yin in *Zuo's Commentary* (*Zuo zhuan zhushu*, 2:38b).
[23] See the twenty-fifth year of the reign of Duke Zhao.

Son of Heaven, why would Zijia Ju have condemned the royal house of Lu? This is unacceptable.[24]

7) For classical texts on the discussion here, see *Jin shu* (*Jin shu*, 73:10b, 2; 8:23a, 2); *Sui shu* (*Sui shu* 隋書, 4:2b, 2); and *Ming shi* 明史 (quoted in *Lun yu jiqiu pian*, 1:21a, 1–2).

In my view, the modified uses of part of the main passage ["If they can bear to do this, what may they not bear to do?"] have long been transmitted through the relationship between masters and disciples. However, they were misused.

* * *

As is summarized in "Overview of the Original Meanings," Dasan argues in his lengthy discussion of the major and minor chief descendants in this chapter that the Jisun family was not the chief descendant of the families of the three Huan. According to him, every son of a feudal lord, not to mention sons of the Son of Heaven, was entitled to establish the chief descendant to distinguish his lineage from others'. In this line of thinking, it is fine for the three families or for all the feudal lords to pay homage to their origin duke or origin king through certain rituals that are reserved for the chief descendants. Mao Qiling, Dasan's main target in this dispute, did not understand this point and thus falsely criticized their practice of assuming the chief descendant's position in their rituals. It was problematic, however, that the state of Lu and the three families adopted rituals and music for the Son of Heaven in their observation of the rituals, because it was a violation of ritual propriety.

In the Confucian heritage, the state of Lu holds a position that is distinct from those of other feudal states in the Zhou system due to the Duke of Zhou's huge contributions to its foundation, and correspondingly the majority of Confucian scholars overlooked the state of Lu's appropriation of the kingly rituals in its state shrine. Given this fact, Dasan's accusations against the state of Lu's conventional practices seem to further his cause of protecting the Confucian social hierarchy. On the other hand Dasan recognized the privilege of all princes to establish their own separate family traditions, a view that is also unique among the interpretations that appear in various commentaries. In the sense that Dasan's endorsement would lend support to an unnecessary abundance of strong families, it contradicts his advocacy for the maintenance of social hierarchy.

An understanding of Dasan's ardent loyalty to his lord, King Jeongjo 正祖 (r. 1776–1800), might resolve questions that stem from this seeming contradiction. At the time, a powerful Confucian faction, the Patriarchs, closely observed the king's policies and deeds to check if his rule went astray from the Confucian

---

[24] Had King Cheng granted the state of Lu the privilege, there would be no reason for King Kang to grant it again to Lu. "Ji tong" says, however: "King Cheng and King Kang bestowed it to Lu" (see *Li ji zhushu*, 49:30a). It reveals that the record in "Ji tong" has no firm grounds.

orthodoxy. Although Jeongjo's goal in his administration—to restore the ideal Confucian statecraft—did not differ from that of the Patriarchs, he might have felt intimidated by the presence of the recalcitrant Confucian ministers in his court. Dasan always had concerns about his lord's susceptibility to that faction and tried to help him handle state affairs without experiencing severe interruptions. In this sense, Dasan's advocacy for social hierarchy in this monarchical state must have been intended to enhance the monarch's power.

Jeongjo, however, was one of the princes in the Chinese imperial system and thus was supposed to adhere to the imperial order. As a matter of fact, the Patriarchs often reminded Jeongjo that he was not truly autonomous in administering the country because the country was grounded on the imperial structure. This concept, known as "We the Small China," played the role of deterrent to many actions Jeongjo wanted to implement. This situation might have impelled Dasan to assert that all princes in the imperial system were allowed to have some level of autonomy, even according to Confucian principles. In view of the family-centric values of Confucianism, the prerogative of princes to create their own family traditions symbolically supported Jeongjo's autonomy.

Those who regard this explanation as needlessly affected by reflections on Joseon politics are advised to read this chapter in connection with the next one. In the next chapter, Confucius notes that all three of the families used the Yong ode when they removed the ritual vessels, whereas in this chapter he criticizes only the Jisun family. In contrast to the majority of commentators, who believed that the ultimate import of Confucius's remark in this chapter was connotative, Dasan viewed it as descriptive and thus demonstrating actual occurrences. As for the question that inevitably arose of how all three families could adopt rituals and music for the Zhou kings in their shrines, Dasan explained that each of the three families allegedly had a shrine of their own for their origin duke.

3.2 The three families used the Yong ode while removing the ritual vessels. Confucius said, "'Assisting are royal princes; the Son of Heaven stands majestic.' How could this song be used in the halls of the three families?"

三家者以雍徹. 子曰; 相維辟公, 天子穆穆, 奚取於三家之堂?

3.2.1 Grounds

1) Ma Rong commented, "The 'three families' refers to the families of Zhongsun, Shusun, and Jisun."
2) Master Zhu commented, "Yong is the name of a poem in 'Zhou song 周訟' of *Poetry*."
3) I supplement as follows: *Che* 徹 ("removing the ritual vessels") refers to removal of the ritual vessels at the conclusion of sacrificial rituals. *Rites of*

Zhou says, "At the end of the Son of Heaven's meal, officials remove the ritual vessels [徹] while music is being played."[25]

4) Master Zhu commented, "When the Son of Heaven has sacrificial rituals at the royal shrine, the ritual vessels are cleared away while the Yong ode is sung. At that time, the three families used it in violation of ritual propriety. *Xiang* 相 ('assisting') means to give assistance to. *Bigong* 辟公 ('royal princes') refers to the feudal lords."

5) Bao Xian commented, "*Mumu* 穆穆 ('stands majestic') refers to the Son of Heaven's countenance. This song is performed because the feudal lords and the descendants of the two kings [the first rulers of the states of Song and Qi 杞] come to give assistance for the rituals. Now, the three families are merely vassals of the state of Lu. How could they dare to make use of this implication?"[26]

3.2.2 Arguments

1) Mao Qiling argued, "The Ji family was the chief minister [of the three ministers of Lu]. They erected a shrine for Duke Huan in order to demonstrate where the major chief descendant [the Ji family] had stemmed from, naming it the Shrine of the Origin Duke. They eventually also had this ode sung when they offered sacrifices to Duke Huan. They were only aware that they should offer sacrifices to the figure they traced their origins to but did not understand that the nobles from the progenitor were not the same" (*Si shu shengyan*, 3:7a).[27] I would refute this as follows:

If the three families shared one shrine to offer sacrifices to Duke Huan, it still would be fine to call the shrine the hall of the three families [三家之堂] [in Dasan's view, this term refers to the three shrines dedicated to each of the progenitors of the three families—that is, Ji You of the Jisun family, Zhong Qingfu of the Zhongsun family, and Shu Ya of the Shusun family, respectively. When the term is translated as the hall or shrine of the three families, as is the case in almost all translations in various languages, it should be taken to mean the shrine for Duke Huan, the origin duke of the three families.] However, it would be inappropriate for the conventional practice of classical writing to introduce an event related to the hall by saying,

---

[25] See "Tianguan 天官, Shanfu 膳夫" (*Zhou li zhushu*, 4:5a).

[26] Xing Bing commented, "According to 'Yue shi 樂師,' in *Rites of Zhou*, 'During the removal of the ritual vessels, the teachers of music lead princelings to perform the Che' (*Zhou li zhushu*, 32:7a). On this passage Zheng Xuan commented, 'The Che refers to the singing of the Yong ode' (32:7b). According to 'Xiao shi 小師,' 'On the removal of the ritual vessels, they sing' (23:26b). On this passage Zheng Xuan commented, 'When the staff of the ritual administration [有司] remove the ritual vessels, they sing the Yong ode' (23:26b). In light of these sources, it is apparent that, when the Son of Heaven has the sacrificial rituals in the royal shrine, they conclude the ritual with the singing of the Yong ode."

[27] He continued, "Qingfu [of the Zhongsun family] and Shu Ya [of the Shusun family] were either poisoned or strangled to death by Ji You. Between Ji Wenzi 季文子 (d. 568) and Ji Wuzi 季武子 [季孫宿, Ji Wenzi's son], who would be pleased to have Ji You, Qingfu, and Shu Ya in the same shrine in an imitation of the case of the three Sons of Heaven? There should be no such case" (*Xihe ji* 西河集, 18:13a).

"The three families used the Yong ode while removing the ritual vessels." Furthermore, the two events—having eight rows of dancers and removing the ritual vessels with the Yong ode in background—are alike in nature. Would it have been compatible with the principles of writing for Confucius, in dealing with these similar events, to have solely criticized the Ji family for having eight rows of dancers while addressing all three families for using the Yong ode? Should it be deemed an arbitrary modification? Mao's theory would betray any attempt to understand it.

Nevertheless, Mao continued to hold onto a warped theory as though he did not know how to stop, repeating and reiterating the same words. He initially argued that sons of a concubine [such as Qingfu and Shu Ya] were not allowed to erect a shrine for the origin duke. Later, however, he changed his view, probably because he grew worried that his first theory was not very persuasive, to argue that since Qingfu and Shu Ya were either poisoned or strangled to death, they could not establish their own shrines.[28] Unfortunately, his second theory was also inflexible and pale in comparison with the fruits of profound learning.

According to *Zuo's Commentary*, Cheng Ji 成季 [Ji You] had Zhenji 鍼季 [a great official of Lu, fl. 661 BCE] poison Shu Ya. Zhenji said, "Drink this. If you do so, you will have your descendants in the state of Lu; if you refuse it, you will die and have no descendants" (*Zuo zhuan zhushu*, 9:35b). In the end, Shu Ya drank the poison made out of the *dan* 酖 bird and made his way back home. He died when he arrived at Kuiquan 逵泉, and Ji You established the Shusun family.[29] [In relation to Qingfu] Duke Min [閔公, r. 661–660] had already been assassinated [by Qingfu], and Gongzhong 共仲 [Qingfu] had already been strangled to death. However, Ji You, out of recognition of the grace of his parents, wanted to be with the family of Shu Ya and allowed the Mengsun clan to stay safe. To reduce the gravity of Ji You's crime, *Spring and Autumn* did not record that Ji You murdered them. Consequently, the descendants of Qingfu formed the Mengsun family.[30] Owing to that, Gongsun Ao 公孫敖 [Qingfu's son, fl. 625 BCE] could take the position as heir and become a transgenerational minister [世卿].[31] On Gongsun Ao's death, the lord of Lu put Wenbo 文伯[32] (d. 613 BCE) in the position of the family's head, whose power was transmitted to Huishu 惠叔[33] (fl. 612 BCE) and finally to Zhongsun Mie 仲孫蔑 (d. 554 BCE).[34]

The fact that the descendants of the two families [of Mengsun and Shusun] maintained their aristocratic rank and were honored with government titles over several generations without discontinuity is well recorded

---

[28] See Mao's other argument (*Xihe ji*, 18:13a).

[29] See the last year of the reign of Duke Zhuang (*Zuo zhuan zhushu*, 9:35b).

[30] See Kong Yingda's 孔穎達 (574–648) scholium on a record in the second year of the reign of Duke Min (*Zuo zhuan zhushu*, 10:11a).

[31] With an honored title, he was called [Meng] Mubo 穆伯.

[32] This refers to Gu 穀, Gongsun Ao's son.

[33] This refers to Nan 難, Wenbo's younger brother.

[34] See the fourteenth year of the reign of Duke Wen (*Zuo zhuan zhushu*, 19:25a–26b).

in historical documents and books. The descendants of the Mengsun and Shusun families were entitled to become transgenerational ministers only after Qingfu and Shu Ya had their own shrines and families. Then is it acceptable to say that since Qingfu and Shu Ya were either poisoned or strangled to death, they could not establish their own shrines? It is true that the state of Lu did not allow the Mengsun family to adopt the rituals for ministers when Gongsun Ao's corpse was returned to Lu and interred [as argued by Mao]. However, why would it have been necessary to receive permission from the lord of Lu when the Mengsun family wanted to use the Yong ode while removing the ritual vessels?[35] Mao's theory is adulterated, lacks reasonability, and deserves no further discussion. If they had temporarily used the Yong ode only for the sacrificial rituals for Duke Huan, not daring to use it for the rituals for Qingfu, Shu Ya, and Ji You, Confucius's chastisement might not have been as severe as it was in the main passage, although the use of the ode is still incompatible with and violates ritual propriety.

2) For a classical text on the discussion here, see "Jiao tesheng" (*Li ji zhushu*, 25:21a, 3–4).

In my view, the three Huan did not appropriate the practice of offering sacrifices to the origin dukes in the families of noblemen. Kong Kui 孔悝 [a great official of Wei, fl. 480 BCE] set up a tabernacle for his origin duke;[36] Ziqi [a son of King Ping of Chu] had the sacrificial rituals for King Ping.[37] That is the common way people behave. Is it acceptable to refute the claim that each of the three families had a shrine for Duke Huan, when the state of Lu had a shrine for Zhou? The writing in "Jiao tesheng" is not reliable.

3) I question Master Zhu as follows:

Indeed, King Cheng [of Zhou] ordered the state of Lu to offer sacrifices, following the ritual protocols for the Son of Heaven, to the Duke of Zhou. However, he did not grant the country, the state of Lu, the privilege of using the rituals for the Son of Heaven.[38] Yang Shengan 楊升菴 (1488–1559) wrote "Lu zhi Jiao Di bian 魯之郊禘辯," and his explanation is so clear and acute that it should not be altered.[39] Also in my view, the expression "insane creation out of ignorance" [as seen in Zhu Xi's annotation] is only applicable to uneducated people. Is it acceptable to address the sin of the three families as "insane creation out of ignorance"? Confucius's wording sufficiently

---

[35] Mao argued, "The lord of Lu did not allow them to conduct the interment ritual for ministers. How could he have possibly allowed them to instate the sacrificial rituals for the Son of Heaven?" (*Xihe ji*, 18:15a)

[36] See [the sixteenth year of the reign of Duke Ai in] *Zuo's Commentary* (*Zuo zhuan zhushu*, 60:4a).

[37] This means that he offered sacrifices to his origin king. See "Chu yu 楚語" (*Guo yu*, 18:4a).

[38] According to *Lüshi Chunqiu*, "Duke Hui of Lu [魯惠公, r. 768–723 BCE] commissioned Zairang 宰讓 [a great official of Lu] to ask the Zhou king to allow the state of Lu to use the ritual protocols and music for the sacrificial rituals for Heaven [郊] and royal ancestors [廟]. King Ping of Zhou [周平王, r. 770–720 BCE] sent the royal scribe Jiao 角 to the state of Lu and allowed them to" (*Lüshi Chunqiu*, 2:12a).

[39] See my discussions on *Spring and Autumn* (*Chunchu gojing* 春秋考徵, 296a).

displays his feelings of devastation and his strictness, and in doing so, it becomes clear that their sin cannot be exonerated.

4) For a classical text on the discussion here, see "Kongzi yan ju 孔子燕居," which says, "When two lords hold a meeting . . . [and] when the guest goes out, they sing the Yong; when the things are taken away, they sing the Zhen yu 振羽" (*Li ji zhushu*, 50:26a–b).[40]

In my view, when ancient people utilized music, poems dedicated to the Son of Heaven were sometimes used for the feudal lords. This is the reason why the three families committed violations of ritual propriety.

* * *

Dasan's commentary in this chapter builds off of his argument in the previous chapter. In brief, Dasan suggests that each of the three Huan had their own shrine for the origin duke and violated ritual propriety when they offered sacrifices to him. Dasan's insistence is supported by the fact that all three Huan prospered with their distinctive family traditions, which could not possibly have been created if they did not have their own family shrine.

What may attract readers' attention in Dasan's comments on these first two chapters of "Ba yi" is that he denies two records from the *Record of Rites*: in the previous chapter, he denies the record of "Ji tong"; in this one, that of "Jiao tesheng." The relevant record in "Ji tong" reads:

> In ancient times, the Duke of Zhou made efforts and contributions for all under heaven. When he passed away, King Cheng and King Kang wished to respect the state of Lu through their commemoration of the duke. Therefore, they bestowed sacrificial rituals with solemnity on the Lu. . . . [T]hey allowed the state of Lu to perform the Tai Wu 大武 dance with the accompaniment of vermilion shields and jade halberds and the Tai Xia 大夏 dance with eight rows of dancers. These are music for the Son of Heaven, but King Kang bestowed it on the Lu out of his admiration for the Duke of Zhou. (*Li ji zhushu*, 49:30a–30b)

This record provides the most crucial textual ground for the claim that the state of Lu's appropriation of rituals and music for the Son of Heaven was endorsed by the Zhou kings. Dasan did not accept this claim and insisted that Han Confucians fabricated this record. The record in "Jiao tesheng" is also crucial for the claims Dasan opposed, such as Mao Qiling's claim. It reads: "The feudal lords are not entitled to offer sacrifices to the Son of Heaven as their ancestor; the great officials are not entitled to offer sacrifices to the feudal lords as their ancestors; and it is inappropriate to establish a state shrine in

---

[40] On this passage Kong Yingda commented, "When the guest retires from the room the Yong ode is sung; when the ritual vessels are removed, the Zhenlu 振鷺 [振羽] ode is sung" (*Li ji zhushu*, 50:27a).

a private house: All these practices were initiated by the three Huan" (*Li ji zhushu*, 25:21a). Dasan accused Han Confucians of interpolating this record in the Confucian classic as well.

Today's scholars may agree that Han Confucians compiled *Record of Rites* out of several layers of ancient records from different times, including the one from the Han. In Chinese textual studies today, this conclusion has been drawn from investigations on the periods of formation of worldviews, initial uses of certain terms, names of historical figures, and historical events. Dasan's view in this respect corresponds to that held by today's scholars, but he did not prove his rejection of these records in the same way they do. Dasan, of course, also discovered a crucial textual ground for his argument—the record in "Daquan," in this case. "Daquan," however, is also a chapter in *Record of Rites*. It would be a challenge to find more legitimacy in "Daquan" than in the other two chapters of the same classical text. It is obvious that the "interpolated" records, according to Dasan, contradict his interpretations in these chapters, and those who want to counter Dasan's understanding may regard them as instrumental to a discussion of the chapters. Although he offered a textual ground for his argument, he encouraged people to explore the complicated issues in the ancient rituals by relying on "the principle of human relationships" (事理)—a principle that probably appears subjective to modern skeptics. He seems to urge people to weigh in on the issues, with the assistance of human reason or rationality, when he says, "Then is it acceptable in light of principle to say that the lords of states [of Lu] cannot become major chief descendants" or "It would not make sense in principle to assume that, when an illegitimate son succeeded a legitimate son to the throne, others continued to respect him as the chief descendant."

This argument would not have been acceptable to some of his contemporaries from the Qing Evidential Studies or Japanese Ancient Learning schools, not to mention scholars in today's textual studies, because it represents a typical use of neo-Confucian inferences. For intellectuals who have taken issue with neo-Confucianism, neither individual contemplation nor subjective judgments can be validated by a claim that they are closer to a universal principle. Dasan was aware of the strength of the new studies of verification and evidence that sought textual grounds. Nonetheless, he tends to discuss any issue at hand while mindful of the universal principle. This shows, again, the syncretic aspect of Dasan's philosophy.

3.3 The Master said, "If a man is not humane, what can he do to ritual propriety? If a man is not humane, what can he do to music?" [In *Noneo gogeum ju* in traditional book binding, this chapter opens the fifth roll.]

子曰; 人而不仁, 如禮何? 人而不仁, 如樂何?

3.3.1 Grounds

1) I supplement as follows: Humanity [仁] is the accomplished virtue of the human moral order. It is the foundation, and ritual propriety and music derive from it.[41] Thus if a man loses humanity, the foundation will be uprooted.[42] Then what can a man do to ritual propriety and music?
2) Xing Bing commented, "*Ru* 如 ('how') is here interchangeable with *nai* 奈 (how)."
3) Bao Xian commented, "This passage states that if a man is not humane, he must not be able to practice ritual propriety and music."[43]

3.3.2 Arguments

1) In my view, humanity is the name applied to wholeheartedness and filial piety when they are fulfilled. Ritual propriety derives from the practice of humanity; music derives from one's enjoying humanity. Humanity is the natural substance; ritual propriety and music are the refined expressions.[44] The Ji family, who committed inhumane deeds at will, wanted to accomplish refined expressions through the practice of ritual propriety and performance of music. Could it be accomplished?[45] The idiomatic expression *ru ci he* 如此何 [that is adopted in the main passage] is convertible to *mo ru zhi he* 末如之何. It implies that inhumane people can do nothing to ritual propriety and music, even when they want to be presented with performances of ritual propriety and music and put them in practice.[46]

* * *

Dasan's reading of this passage may seem to follow a reading shared by many commentators but is actually unique. The uniqueness lies in the fact that he interpreted the idiomatic expression *ru ci he*, which is translated as "what does one want to do with this," as interchangeable with *mo ru ci he*, which means "one has no way to handle this." Taken literally, Dasan's reading suggests that rituals and music do not exist unless one realizes humanity; his reading can

---

[41] "Ru xing 儒行" says, "The codes of ritual propriety make up the appearance of humanity; performance of music represents the harmony of humanity" (*Li ji zhushu*, 59:17b).
[42] Mencius regarded filial piety and respect for elders as equivalent to humanity and rightness and said, "The substance of ritual propriety is to regulate these two things culturally; the substance of music is to enjoy these two things" (*Mengzi jizhu*, 4A:27).
[43] Xing Bing commented, "Ritual propriety and music are practiced through their reliance on humanity."
[44] Master Zeng said, "Humanity is to love this [filial piety]; ritual propriety is to practice this; music derives from one's compliance with this; punishments arise from one's defiance against this" (*Li ji zhushu*, 48:7a).
[45] This remark pertains to their performances of the Lü 旅 ritual at Mount Tai, the eight rows of dancers, and the singing of the Yong ode.
[46] The same use of this expression is found in a passage beginning "What can Huan Tui 桓魋 (fl. 500–481 BCE) do to me?" (*Lun yu jizhu*, 7:22)

alternatively be construed as suggesting that rituals and music exist but have no point unless they are associated with one's practice of humanity. Rituals and music exist in reality no matter what, of course, so this interpretation implies that Dasan could not put more emphasis on the necessary cohesion between rituals and music on the one hand and human morals on the other. Given that in Confucianism, a continuum tends to be preserved between morality and other disciplines, Dasan's reading further exemplifies the quite rigid way he sometimes represented Confucian orthodoxy.

Dasan's ascribing to humanity the status of foundation or substance and, as naturally follows, to rituals and music the status of derivative or refined expression also resonates with the pervasive Confucian theory of the relationship between roots and branches. Confucians usually utilize this theory to invoke the idea that roots take precedence over branches. And if one were to infuse the "roots" with metaphysical qualities, it would help to constitute a neo-Confucian discourse. Dasan, however, gives here again his "practical" definition of humanity, stating that it is merely "the name applied to wholeheartedness and filial piety when they are fulfilled"—a repetition of his argument that one should not consider humanity a virtue that exists a priori, probably because he was also wary of this far-fetched attempt.

If rituals and music can exist even while dissociated from humanity, they can be subjected to critique from Confucian minimalists, who tend narrowly to concentrate on inner virtues and thus diminish the importance of rituals and music because they are not truly conducive to the realization of humanity. However, in Dasan's reading, rituals and music are immune to a total negation of them because they are ingrained in humanity. In this reading, Confucian minimalists' accusations against rituals and music always turn false because what they disapprove of is not a genuine form of rituals and music. My claim that Dasan consistently pursued harmony between natural substance and refined expressions, rejecting any prioritization of one of them, is substantiated in this chapter, as well as in his comments in the next chapter.

3.4 Lin Fang asked about the prime principle of ritual propriety. The Master replied, "A great question indeed! As regards ritual propriety, it is better to be frugal than lavish; as regards mourning, it is better to be in deep sorrow than at rest.

林放問禮之本. 子曰; 大哉問! 禮, 與其奢也寧儉, 喪, 與其易也寧戚.

3.4.1 Grounds

1) Zheng Xuan commented, "Lin Fang is a man of the state of Lu."
2) I supplement as follows: *Ben* 本 ("the prime principle") refers to the primary intention of creation [of ritual propriety]; *li* 禮 ("ritual propriety")

here encompasses the rituals of both good fortune and misfortune; *sang* 喪 ("mourning") refers solely to the rituals of misfortune.

3) Bao Xian commented, "*Yi* 易 ('at rest') is here interchangeable with *he* 和 (calm)."

4) I supplement as follows: With what primary intention was ritual propriety created? People are so invested with desires at birth that, unless they are regulated by ritual propriety, lavishness would grow without limit. Ritual propriety was thus created in view of the mean between lavishness and frugality. Wicked and immoral people are liable to forget, when evening comes, that one of their parents passed away in the morning. Mourning rituals were thus created in view of the mean between being at rest and being in sorrow.[47] Although displays of excessive frugality or sorrow hamper one's keeping to a mean, the primary intention of those who designed the rituals lay not in that [lavishness or rest] but in this [frugality or sorrow]. Therefore, Confucius taught that it is better, if a man cannot attain the mean, to be frugal or in deep sorrow than to be lavish or at rest, although attainment of the mean is best.

5) In my view, Lin Fang's question about ritual propriety was triggered by the three families' violation of it. Both having eight rows of dancers and using the Yong ode on the removal of the ritual vessels are germane to ritual propriety. The three families merely knew how to pay homage to their ancestors by means of adopting grand rituals but did not understand the primary intention of the creation of the rituals. This is the reason that Lin Fang inquired about it. Their performances with eight rows of dancers and use of the Yong ode undoubtedly stemmed from their failure to keep the lavishness under control. This is the reason that Confucius replied to him with this teaching. His supplementary address of the mourning rituals purports to give an example—a metaphor that should not be regarded in tandem with the teaching of ritual propriety.

3.4.2 Arguments

1) I question Master Zhu as follows:

Being lavish or at rest does not necessarily pertain to refined expressions. Similarly, being frugal or in deep sorrow does not necessarily pertain to natural substance either. In their primary intention, the creators of the rituals were concerned with lavishness and resting, not with frugality and having deep sorrow. Our Master, accordingly, has clarified that point. In addition, Lin Fang asked about the prime principle of ritual propriety, not its natural substance. Moreover, [in the times of Confucius] the Zhou was on the verge of eclipse, entailing debacles of rituals and music, and in due course people worried about the extinction of refined expressions, not

---

[47] In doing so, they hoped that those unfilial people would be mindful of the rituals and eventually gain familiarity with them.

about their prevalence. If Confucius had wanted to suppress the refined expressions, accelerating this trend, they would have completely vanished. How could this be the sage's idea?

2) For a classical text on the discussion here, see *Changes* (*Zhou Yi zhushu*, 10:18a, 8–18b, 1).

In my view, both excessive sorrow and excessive frugality are errors that come from losing balance. Thus the words "better … than" are used in the main passage. This expression aims to show that the lesser of the two errors is preferred.

3) For a classical text on the discussion here, see "Tangong" (*Li ji zhushu*, 7:26a, 6–7).

In my view, Zi Lu's remark introduced in "Tangong" has something to do with another teaching. It is unnecessary to refer to it in respect to understanding this classic. [In *Lun yu jizhu*] Fan Zuyu mistakenly quoted it.[48]

* * *

Dasan in this chapter again warns neo-Confucian scholars about their proclivity to prioritize natural substance over refined expressions. A misunderstanding of this chapter would contribute to this proclivity, when one mistakenly uses a hyphen to conjoin "being lavish" or "being at rest" with "refined expression," since in this chapter Confucius seems to teach that "being frugal" or "being sorrowful" is better than "being lavish" or "being at rest." Dasan also admits in this chapter that "being lavish" in rituals seems a more serious misdemeanor than "being frugal" is. However, that is precisely because this chapter discusses "the grand principle" of ritual propriety: ritual propriety was created in order to control people's natural desire for lavishness. In his general discussion of ritual propriety, Dasan notes that it makes perfect sense to juxtapose "being frugal" with "being lavish" because both of them lead to a loss of balance; it also makes perfect sense to juxtapose being excessively sorrowful in mourning rituals with being at rest for the same reason. Moreover, "being lavish" or "being at rest" has nothing to do with refined expressions, in Dasan's eyes. On what grounds, Dasan might have asked, can a prioritization of frugality over lavishness be justified?

As a matter of fact, Zhu Xi also believed that "being frugal" in rituals was as defective as "being lavish" in terms of perpetuation of ritual propriety. In this regard, he differed from Fan Zuyu, who appeared to permit frugality while revealing his disdain for lavishness. In Dasan's view, however, Zhu Xi still made a mistake by associating frugality with natural substance and lavishness with refined expressions. To him, refined expressions are a display of humanity, not

---

[48] Yang Shi's quotation of the remark [which is again quoted by Zhu Xi in *Lun yu jizhu*], "[In the past] people would use a puddle as a jar and cup their hands to drink water," was also irrelevant to the true meaning of this classic (*Lun yu jizhu daquan*, 3:9a).

an exhibition of lavishness. Although Fan's viewpoint is supported by a passage from *Record of Rites*, Dasan simply denies its relevance to this chapter. Given that Joseon neo-Confucians adhered to the same values Fan Zuyu presented and that refined expressions were often instrumental for displaying the majesty of the Joseon court, Dasan's recurrent insistence on the balance between natural substance and refined expressions marks his advocacy of the Joseon court, whose authority the neo-Confucian fundamentalists often undermined.

3.5 The Master said, "Having rulers in a barbaric state is not as good as losing rulers for All the Xia."

子曰; 夷狄之有君, 不如諸夏之亡也.

3.5.1 Grounds

1) Bao Xian commented, "*Zhu Xia* 諸夏 ('All the Xia') refers to China.[49] *Wu* 亡 ('losing rulers') is here interchangeable with *wu* 無 (to lack)."
2) I supplement as follows: *Yi Di* 夷狄 ("a barbaric state") refers to one's adoption of the way of the Yi and Di barbarians. *Zhu Xia* refers to one's adoption of the laws of All the Xia. If the ruler does not act like a ruler and the subject does not act like a subject, they are no more than barbarians as well. Keeping the ruler's position in a poor manner, not bothered by the ways of barbarians, is inferior to losing the position in order to follow the laws of the former kings and cultivate the ritual propriety of the beautiful Xia. In the twentieth year of the reign of Duke Zhao, when the state of Lu offered sacrifices to Duke Xiang, the dancers were not well prepared,[50] because most dancers went to the house of the Ji family to perform the Tai Wu dance.[51] Duke Zhao became enraged and tried to kill the head of the Ji family [Ji Pingzi].[52] When his plan ended in failure, however, he fled to the state of Qi.[53] At the time, Confucius also went to Qi.[54] Consequently, the post for the duke of Lu fell vacant, and the people of Lu blamed Duke Zhao for this. In this regard, here in the main passage Confucius made clear that their blame could not be justified, as if by saying, "Keeping the ruler's position in a poor manner, not bothered by the ways of barbarians by which the ruler does not act like a ruler and the subject does not act like a subject, is not as good as losing the position through an attempt to eradicate the instigators of disorder and rebellion to cultivate the laws of the beautiful

---

[49] [Dasan's student] Gongmok 公牧 [尹峒] added, "China was called 'All the Xia' in the same manner in which outer barbarians were called all the barbarians."
[50] There were only two dancers.
[51] A large band of dancers danced for the Ji family.
[52] He discussed this matter with Zijia Ju.
[53] See *Zuo's Commentary* (*Zuo zhuan zhushu*, 51:24a–27b).
[54] See *Shi ji* (*Shi ji*, 47:6a).

Xia." [In doing so, he also taught that] for the Lu people, it would be better not to have a ruler in return for illuminating this rightness than to keep the ruler at the cost of accepting the rebel [the head of the Ji family].

3) Goengbo added, "In this book, 'Ba yi,' all the chapters from the first to this one and the next record Confucius's discussion of the sin of the Ji family when he stayed in the state of Qi."

3.5.2 Arguments

1) Xing Bing argued, "Although barbarians also have rulers, their cultures are devoid of ritual propriety and rightness. In comparison, although China sometimes lacks rulers, as in the period when Duke Ding of Zhou [周定公] and Duke Mu of Shao [召穆公] coruled the country [841–828 BCE], ritual propriety and rightness have never perished. Therefore it is said, 'The Yi and Di barbarians with rulers are not as good as Chinese states without them [in a widely adopted translation of the main passage].'" I would refute this as follows:

    Confucius wished to live among the nine tribes of the Yi, so the Yi and Di barbarians do not deserve to be humiliated. Furthermore, would it be decent for one to state, "Your country with rulers is inferior to my country without them," recklessly defaming it without consideration of the sins and errors it obviously committed? Joint reigns such as that of Duke Ding of Zhou and Duke Mu of Shao occur only once every few thousand or few hundred years. Is it compatible with principle for one to argue that Confucius was boastful about his country based on this rare case?

2) I question Master Zhu [who introduced Master Cheng's view in his comment] as follows:

    Master Cheng argued, "This passage states that even the Yi and Di barbarians have regard for their sovereigns, unlike All the Xia, which instead do not distinguish between superiors and inferiors in terms of the violation and disorder [of ritual propriety]." In my investigation, *Shi ji* contains the passage "Those who embroider beautiful patterns are not as good as [不如] those who put their shoulders on the gates of a market" (*Shi ji*, 129:18a). As seen in this example, *bu ru* 不如 is a phrase that expresses that the beauty of this is held back out of envy that stems from the ugliness of that. Ancient people used to say, "Wealth and honor from immorality are not as good as poverty and humility in the preservation of the Way." The structure of writing in the main passage is duly identical to that of this quotation. Had Confucius wanted to stress that the beauty of the Yi and Di barbarians was superior to the ugliness of All the Xia, he would not have used *bu ru* for his remark.

3) *Lun heng* by Wang Chong says, "The main passage means that barbaric states are inherited along with difficulties in ruling the country, whereas All the Xia may feel it easy to rule the country" (*Lun heng*, 9:12b). I would refute Wang Chong's comment as follows:

    I do not know what Wang Chong's comment means.

4) *Huang Ming dazheng ji* says, "The first emperor said, 'Barbarians are beasts. They lack the way of humanity, rightness, ritual propriety, and wisdom. Thus Confucius mentioned that although China had no rulers and leaders, each person in China is able to understand ritual propriety and rightness. It is better than a barbaric state that has rulers and leaders. Song Confucians often argued that [this passage means that] the people of China are inferior to barbarians, but it is an error" (*Huang Ming dazheng ji* 皇明大政記, unknown place). Lu Jugang 陸聚岡 (?) also argued, "That a barbaric state may be said to have rulers refers to the fact that its towns have some regulations and orders. Thus it is unnecessary to beautify their situation excessively. That All the Xia may be said to lack rulers merely means that subjects existed who ignored their superiors. In this context, saying that China lacks rulers is identical to saying that rulers exist but they seem not to exist" (Unknown source). I would refute this as follows:

These arguments are invalid.

* * *

In this chapter, Dasan censures a widely accepted Sino-centric rendering of this passage: even in the worst historical circumstances, China is superior to the barbarian states. These barbarian states undoubtedly included Korea, which was considered to be among the Yi tribes. In arguing for his views, Dasan insisted that this passage should be understood symbolically, not literally. In his reading, "barbarians" refers to states that are run in a barbarian manner, whereas "All the Xia" refers to states that follow the Chinese ideal statecraft—in other words, Confucian statecraft. It is possible in this reading for a historically "barbarian" state to excel China when it abides by Confucian standards. Readers may sense Dasan's strong disagreement with the Sino-centric interpretation from the fact that he even dismisses the warning of the founding emperor of the Ming to his successors about the alleged belligerence of non-Chinese states.

Dasan's rebuttal of the more common interpretation presumably discloses his "nationalistic" stance because it denies the inherited superiority of the Chinese polity, especially over that of Korea. As seen in his question to Master Zhu, however, he tends to think that the Chinese civilization inherently eclipses other civilizations. Although it is natural that he, as a Confucian scholar, should praise the Chinese civilization when it is regarded as Confucian civilization, his voice should not be blindly connected to Korean "nationalism," let alone Korean "centrism." He may have refuted the Sino-centric view simply because, as he put, it is not reasonable to think that the sage lost his decency and disrespected other states in a derogatory tone.

More interesting in Dasan's interpretation is his speculation, on the basis of Confucian classical studies, that this remark might have reflected an actual historical situation. According to Dasan, this passage was Confucius's response to the Lu people's condemnation of Duke Zhao: Confucius here shows his approval of the duke's unsuccessful attempt to eliminate the Ji family—a failure that compelled him to leave the state of Lu immediately. Even though this incomplete attempt to restore the ruler's authority resulted in the duke's personal misery, it was worthwhile in Dasan's eyes, because such a social hierarchy should be averted. This line of reasoning led Dasan to accept the contention of his student Yi Ganghoe (whose adult name was Goengbo) that this chapter alludes to Confucius's excoriation of the violation of ritual propriety by the three Huan in the previous chapters.

3.6 The head of the Ji family performed the Lü sacrifice at Mount Tai. The Master said to Ran You, "Could you not save him from this?" Ran You replied, "No, I could not." The Master said, "Alas! Did he say that Mount Tai is inferior to Lin Fang?"

季氏旅於泰山. 子謂冉有曰; 女不能救與? 對曰; 不能. 子曰; 嗚呼! 曾謂泰山不如林放乎?

3.6.1 Grounds

1) Ma Rong commented, "Lü is the name of a sacrificial ritual."[55]
2) I supplement as follows: Lü 旅 means to report something with an array of sacrifices. It is similar to today's sacrifices of reporting motives.[56]
3) Ma Rong commented, "In ritual propriety, the feudal lords offer sacrifices to mountains and rivers located on their enfeoffed lands. Now, a vassal [陪臣] offers sacrifices at Mount Tai. It is unacceptable according to ritual propriety.[57] Ran You refers to Confucius's disciple Ran Qiu 冉求.[58] At the time, he was an official for the Ji family."
4) Master Zhu commented, "Jiu 救 ('save') means to save the head of the Ji family from falling into the sin of appropriating the rituals in violation of ritual propriety."
5) Bao Xian commented, "Spirits do not receive sacrifices that are made in violation of ritual propriety. Lin Fang was already able to ask about ritual

---

[55] Xing Bing commented, "*Rites of Zhou* says, 'On encountering an important occurrence of the state, the Son of Heaven performs the Lü sacrifice to the High Lord and the mountains and rivers in the four cardinal directions' (*Zhou li zhushu*, 18:45a). On this record, Zheng Xuan commented, 'The occurrence here refers to ominous disasters. Lü, whose literal meaning is to set up, means to set up sacrifices to offer up a prayer. Its ritual is not as organized as other sacrificial rituals are'" (18:45b).

[56] *Documents* says, "[King Wu] performed the Lü sacrifice at Mount Cai 蔡 and Mount Meng 蒙 after leveling a road" (*Shang Shu zhushu*, 5:26a). It also says, "[King Wu] performed the Lü sacrifice after the timbers of the nine mountains were removed" (5:40b).

[57] Xing Bing commented, "*Pei* in *peichen* 陪臣 means to double [which implies that *peichen* is a subject of a subject]."

[58] According to *Shi ji*, "Ran Qiu, whose adult name was Zi You 子有, was twenty-nine years younger than Confucius." Zheng Xuan commented, "He was a man of Lu."

propriety. Then are the spirits of Mount Tai rather inferior to Lin Fang? The head of the Ji family wanted to deceive the spirits to offer sacrifices."

6) I supplement as follows: The last sentence in the main passage, "Did he say that Mount Tai is inferior to Lin Fang," implies that the Ji family strongly looked down on Mount Tai.[59]

7) In my view, a performance of the Lü sacrifice is one of the rituals. The fact that they performed it on encountering an important occurrence may indicate that they wished to put ritual propriety into place. However, they did it by means of violating their lord's rituals. How can this action be harmonious with the primary intention of the creation of the rituals? In dealing with ritual propriety, Lin Fang rather sought out its prime principle. Then are the spirits of Mount Tai not as good as he is? "Da Zongbo," in *Rites of Zhou*, records: "On encountering an important occurrence of the state, the Son of Heaven performs the Lü sacrifice to the High Lord and the mountains and rivers in the four cardinal directions" (*Zhou li zhushu*, 18:45a). At the time, the state of Lu did not experience any important events,[60] except taking down Fei 費 and expelling Buniu 不狃 from it, an important event only for the Ji family. Was that sufficient cause to offer sacrifices to the mountains? It was a great violation of ritual propriety.

3.6.2 Arguments

1) Ogyu argued, "[At the time] the state of Lu encountered an important event, so the Lü sacrifice should have been performed at Mount Tai. Since the lord of Lu felt sick or something, however, he could not oversee the ritual by himself. Consequently, he commissioned the Jisun family to supervise the ritual as his substitute. Thereupon the Jisun family made necessary preparations for the ritual in a lavish way. Due to this, Confucius here criticized their lavishness." I would refute this as follows:

   Whether the necessary preparations for the ritual were excessive or insufficient should be examined according to the standards of the categorized rituals such as *si* 緦 [the standard for three-month-long rituals] or *xiaogong* 小功 [the standard for five-month-long rituals]. However, the Ji family, as a vassal, offered sacrifices to mountains and rivers to report their private cause. Isn't this lavish? Had they done that as the substitute for the ruler, it would not have constituted lavishness.

2) According to *Fang yan* by Master Yang, "*Zeng* 曾 ('did') is interchangeable with *he* 何 (how). People in the fountainhead areas of the Xiang 湘 and Tan 潭 rivers as well as the southern tip of Jing 荊 use *zeng* in place of *he*" (*Fang yan* 方言, 10:1b).

---

[59] Dazai Jun commented, "*Wei* 謂 ('say') means that the head of the Ji family did say that."

[60] Master Ran [Ran You] began to serve the Ji family after the tenth year of the reign of Duke Ding.

In my view, *zeng* here is a word that streamlines the sentence and can convey a meaning or no meaning. The information in *Fang yan* is not in accord with the definition of the word in this classic.

* * *

Dazai Jun praised his teacher Ogyu Nabematsu for innovatively revealing the true meaning of this passage by linking Confucius's criticism of the Jisun family in this chapter with his teaching of the prime principle of ritual propriety. Confucius addressed this teaching to Lin Fang when he asked about it (see 3.4). Since Confucius compares Lin Fang to Mount Tai here and stresses frugality in his teaching of the prime principle, according to Ogyu, this passage should be understood in the same context: "As regards ritual propriety, it is better to be frugal than lavish." The Jisun family, conjectured Ogyu, must have provoked Confucius with their lavishness, not with their violation of ritual propriety, and the lavishness must have been evident in their preparations for the ritual.

It is true that prior to Ogyu, no commentator had raised questions about Ma Rong's views. Given that Dasan spares some space to discuss Ogyu's opinion here, he seems to have been impressed with Ogyu's inventive interpretation. However, Dasan still followed Ma Rong's interpretation because performing a ritual beyond the authorized level was another form of lavishness to him. While lavishness concretely meant, to Ogyu, an excessive consumption of resources, to Dasan it referred to psychological arrogance or pomposity.

This difference matters in understanding Dasan's views because Dasan pointed out that if the Jisun family were to serve in the ritual as a substitute for the lord of Lu, they would be immune to the criticism of excessive consumption of resources: consuming resources is unavoidable when materializing the ruler's power. This stance should be related to his consistent advocacy of the king's authority and refined expression of Confucian rituals.

Dasan's acceptance of Ma Rong's views also stemmed from his solid knowledge of the history of Lu. Ran You, whom Confucius thought was responsible for stopping the Jisun family, began to serve them as late as 501 BCE. After that year, Lu did not experience events that required its lord to report to Mount Tai. Thus, conjectured Dasan, the Jisun family performed the Lü ritual with motives of their own.

3.7 The Master said, "Noble people never contend for a victory except in archery. They bow and yield the way to each other as they ascend to the hall. When losing, they drink. Even in competition, they are decent."

子曰; 君子無所爭也, 必也射乎! 揖讓而升, 下而飲, 其爭也君子.

3.7.1 Grounds

1) Master Zhu commented, "The sentence 'They bow and yield the way to each other as they ascend to the hall' pertains to a ritual in 'Da she 大射' wherein they proceed as pairs and ascend to the hall after three bows."[61]

2) I supplement as follows: *Xia* 下 ("when losing") here means not winning. Generally, in all military affairs, gaining a victory is termed "dropping it" [下之].[62] In the rituals of archery, those who lose drink. This is what the sentence "When losing, they drink" means. Competition is opposite to yielding. In the competition, however, they yield the stairs to each other when ascending, and the winner yields cups to the loser when drinking. This is the competition of noble people.[63]

3.7.2 Arguments

1) Wang Shu argued, "They shoot at the archery hall. Every time they ascend to and descend from it, they bow to each other, make way for each other, and drink together."[64] Huang Kan argued, "According to 'She yi 射儀,' at the beginning of the ritual, the host bows to the guest and proceeds. Then they ascend to the hall, yielding the way to each other. When they finish shooting and the game is decided, they descend from the hall but still show that they are not negligent about ritual propriety by bowing and yielding to each other." I would refute these as follows:

   If the two sentences ("They bow and yield the way to each other as they ascend to the hall" and "When losing, they drink") are combined into one sentence, as in Wang Shu's interpretation, it is not compatible with the writing principles.[65] On top of that, in my view, in the archery ritual people drink when ascending but do not drink when descending. Thus the expression *xia er yin* 下而飲 ("When losing, they drink") does not mean that they drink when descending. It also does not make sense in principle to assume that Confucius changed *jiang* to *xia*.

2) I question Master Zhu as follows:

   Someone asked, "*Xia er yin*, does this mean that they drink when descending?" Master Cheng replied, "In ancient times, the drinking of the penalty cups always occurred at the foot of the hall." Someone asked again, "Do they descend from the hall and drink, only when they lose?" Master

---

[61] Xing Bing commented, "According to 'Da she,' they proceed together in a pair; in front of the stairs they bow; after going up the stairs they bow; after ascending the hall they bow."

[62] "Yue Yi zhuan 樂毅傳" says, "Yue Yi dropped seventy fortresses of the state of Qi except for Ju 莒 and Jimo 即墨" (*Shi ji*, 80:3a). In addition, "Xiang Yu benji 項羽本紀" says, "Waihunag 外黃 has not been dropped" (7:8b).

[63] Ma Rong commented, "The contender with more points allows his opponent to drink. This is what noble people compete for."

[64] Xing Bing argued, "Every time they drink, they ascend to and descend from the hall, bowing and making way for each other."

[65] In addition, there is no written example in which people use *sheng xia* 升下 in place of *sheng jiang* 升降 for "ascending and descending."

Cheng replied, "I suspect that both contenders descend from the hall together. However, the winner has the loser drink."[66] In my view, the practice whereby the winner has the loser drink in archery rituals and pitch-pot rituals fundamentally aims to provide nourishment, not punishment. Thus the drinking person, holding up the wine vessel, is expected to say, "I appreciate your pouring." The winner, kneeling down, encourages the loser to drink by saying, "I respectfully wish for your nourishment." In intention, the saying seems to express: "I was afraid that you could not hit the mark because you might have caught some illness. So, I wish for you to nourish yourself with this wine." *Poetry* says, "I shall hit the mark with my arrow and pray that you drink from this cup."[67] This poem bears connotations of the same meaning. When the winner is busy praying for nourishment for the loser, does he have time to punish the loser? According to "Chunguan 春官," in *Rites of Zhou*, Xiao xu 小胥 is in charge of delivering orders of punishment and forces those disrespectful people to drink. This relates precisely to giving penalty cups.

Meanwhile, *Poetry* contains the phrase "the curved rhino-cups."[68] On this, Zheng Xuan in his commentary explained that they were the penalty cups. Indeed, when the ancient kings held banquets with their subjects, they usually set up the curved rhino-cups to alarm the disrespectful. However, people never drank from the penalty cups at the foot of the hall. For this reason, when Duke Ping of Jin [晉平公, r. 557–532 BCE] was drinking, Du Kuai 杜蕢 entered the king's residence hall and, having ascended the steps, poured out a cup, saying, "Kuang 曠 [師曠], drink this." He poured out a cup again and said, "Diao 調 [李調], drink this." He then poured out a cup and, kneeling down on the hall with his face to the north, drank it himself. And he descended from the hall and went out hurriedly.[69] The scene of drinking from penalty cups must have been similar to this. Zheng Xuan commented on a passage in "Xiang she li 鄉射禮" that includes the expression "finishing the cups and receiving the cups" and related them to "penalty cups." However, this is a huge mistake. How can it be taken as the ground [for the interpretation in *Lun yu jizhu*]?

* * *

Dasan here rejects Wang Shu's reading, which represents the old commentary on this passage, for the following reasons: first, it is not compatible with the writing principles; second, it does not make sense in principle to assume that Confucius arbitrarily used the character *xia* to convey the meaning of *jiang*; third, in ancient archery rituals, people drank only when

---

[66] See *Er Cheng quanshu* (*Er Cheng yushu* 二程遺書, 22-B: 1b–2a).
[67] See the poem "Pin yan 賓筵" (*Mao Shi zhushu*, 21:55a).
[68] See "Zhou song 周訟, Cai yi 綵衣" (*Mao Shi zhushu*, 21:38a).
[69] See "Tangong" (*Li ji zhushu*, 9:42a–b).

ascending to the archery hall and not when descending from it; finally, in classical texts there was no written example of the usage of *sheng xia* to mean "ascending and descending." He concluded that a pause should be placed between *sheng* ("ascend") and *xia* ("losing"), assigning the two characters to two different sentences. On these points, Dasan's and Zhu Xi's views were in agreement.

Dasan did not agree with Zhu Xi in this chapter, however, as regards the meaning of *xia*. Dasan and Zhu Xi rendered it as "losing" and "descending," respectively. Dasan based his rendering on his investigation of the ancient archery rituals in which he thought only losers drank. Indeed, Zhu Xi also admitted that only losers drank. However, in his reading this information is not clearly conveyed. In addition, Zhu Xi thought that the loser drank from the penalty cup at the foot of the archery hall after descending, whereas Dasan insisted that this event occurred before the contenders' descending.

He might have been provoked to disprove the interpretation of *Lun yu jizhu* because he could not accept Cheng Yi's thoughts on the nature of drinking: Cheng Yi saw it as an act of punishment, whereas Dasan regarded it as an act of encouragement. In Dasan's view, it would be inappropriate to infuse a sense of violence or force into this beautiful competition among noble people. He derived this interpretation from a passage in *Poetry*. He repudiated the relationship Zheng Xuan drew between another passage in the same classic and Cheng Yi's interpretation of the nature of drinking. Therefore, he also criticizes Zheng Xuan in his comment in this chapter. All in all, in this chapter he rejects Wang Shu, Zhu Xi, Cheng Yi, and Zheng Xuan in order to unravel the true meaning of this passage, whose crucial part is introduced in "Overview of Original Meanings." In consideration of Joseon's severe censorship of heretical teachings, Dasan's contentious attitude (evident not only in this chapter but all throughout *Noneo gogeum ju* as well) may be symptomatic of the generic critical mindset of scholars of the Practical Learning or of the growing liberal academism of his society in general—or it may stem from a unique individual spirit of independence from and defiance of the standing academic authority.

3.8 Zi Xia asked, "'Pretty are her charming smiles! Limpid are her beautiful eyes! Make the ground white to add colors!' What does this mean?" The Master replied, "Painting comes after the white ground." Zi Xia said, "So, the rituals come after?" The Master said, "It is Shang who can elate me! I can begin to discuss *Poetry* with him now."

子夏問曰; 巧笑倩兮, 美目盼兮, 素以爲絢兮, 何謂也? 子曰; 繪事後素. 曰; 禮後乎? 子曰; 起予者商也! 始可與言詩已矣.

3.8.1 Grounds

1) Master Zhu commented, "This is a lost poem."[70]
2) I supplement as follows: *Qian* 倩 ("pretty") means pretty and good-looking;[71] *pan* 盼 ("limpid") refers to having well-defined pupils and sclera;[72]
3) Master Zhu commented, "*Su* 素 is whitened ground, the foundation of the painting; *xuan* 絢 is various colors, the decoration of the painting."[73]
4) I supplement as follows: Because her figure is substantially beautiful, her charming smiles and beautiful eyes become richly effulgent, as though painting comes after the white ground is made.
5) Master Zhu commented, "The work of laying colors on a painting follows the preparation of the white ground. According to 'Kao gong ji,' 'The work of laying colors on a painting follows the work of making the ground white' " (*Zhou li zhushu*, 40:38a).
6) Master Zhu commented, "Ritual propriety should take wholeheartedness and trustworthiness as its real substance. This is similar to the fact that one should first whiten the ground before laying colors on a painting."
7) Yang Shi commented, "Sweetness is integral to harmony in taste; white is integral to variety in color. The person who values wholeheartedness and trustworthiness can learn the rituals.[74] Without real substance, the rituals cannot be groundlessly practiced. This is what the theory of 'Painting comes after the white ground' speaks of" (*Lun yu jizhu daquan*, 3:14b).
8) I supplement as follows: *Qi* 起 ("elate") is here the same as *xing* 興 (to raise). This implies that Zi Xia's words were enough to elate Confucius.

3.8.2 Arguments

1) Ma Rong argued, "The first two lines [of the quoted poem] are found in 'Wei feng, Shi ren.' The last line is lost." Someone argued, "The last line was edited out by Confucius." On this, Master Zhu explained, "The last line carries the most profound meanings. How could it be edited out? In addition, the four poems in 'Shi ren' uniformly have seven lines; this poem should not exclusively have one more line. [The first two lines in the quoted poem here are correspondent to the sixth and seventh lines of the second poem in 'Shi ren.' If the last line was originally from the poem in 'Shi ren,' it comes to have eight lines.] There must have been a separate poem that was lost."

---

[70] This means that the quoted poem is not the one in "Wei feng, Shi ren 碩人."
[71] According to *Shou wen*, it resembles the grass and trees as being lush and luxuriant (quoted in *Yu ding Kangxi zidian*, 2:41a).
[72] This definition comes from *Yupian* (quoted in *Yu ding Kangxi zidian*, 20:75b).
[73] Ma Rong commented, "*Xuan* refers to refined expression."
[74] This is a saying in "Li qi" (*Li ji zhushu*, 23:24a).

In my investigation, *Poetry* has many lines that are repeated here and there like the following lines: "She put a single-layer garment on the silk robe" (*Mao Shi zhushu*, 5:8b). "Do not approach my dam" (19:68a).

2) Zheng Xuan argued, "*Hui* 繪 ('painting') refers to painting patterns. In general, when painting patterns people apply various colors first and then apply white between them to finish the patterns. This is like a beautiful lady who should perfect her beauty with ritual propriety even when she has pretty and beautiful substance." I would refute this as follows:

This is essentially Zheng's misunderstanding. He already distorted "Kao gong ji" and thereby distorted this classic again. Master Zhu attempted to rectify his errors, but his misunderstanding has not been thoroughly rebutted. Today poor learners and lesser Confucians still esteem Zheng's annotation of "Kao gong ji" as a classic and base their attacks on Master Zhu's theories on it. Isn't this absurd?

3) For a classical text on the discussion here, see "Kao gong ji" (*Zhou li zhushu*, 40:36a–38a). On this, Zheng Xuan commented, "*Su* is the color white. It is applied later because it is easily tainted" (40:38a). Zheng Sinong 鄭司農 (d. 83) also glossed the same passage in "Kao gong ji" in light of the following sentence from the *Analects*: "In painting patterns, application of the color white comes later [which is translated in accordance with Zheng Xuan's annotation]" (40:38a).

In my view, *su gong* 素工 [in "Kao gong ji"] is equivalent to today's work of whitening the ground. Whenever they are going to apply beautiful colors, such as green and red, painters without exception make the ground spotless first. And they start using pigmented materials for green and red. This process should not be different from that in the past. In "Kao gong ji" the color white is termed *bai* 白, whereas the work of making the ground white is called *su gong*. When these characters appear in "Kao gong ji," they are clearly distinguished without confusion. Zheng Xuan, however, confused the work with the color white. Isn't this a misunderstanding? Painters usually handle the colors green and red very carefully, out of concern for potential damage to the painting. This is because the more conspicuous a color is, the more regretful they will be [when the painting is damaged]. Assume that a master is teaching young painters the business of laying colors on a painting. If he were to say, "Apply the colors green and red first and then whiten the ground," everyone would throw away their jugs and brushes and be gone. Is Zheng's annotation reliable?

4) For a classical text that supports my argument here, see "Li qi" (*Li ji zhushu*, 23:2b, 6–7).

* * *

Dasan continues to criticize the old commentaries by Ma Rong and Zheng Xuan here. His straightforward introduction of the textual debate between Ma

Rong and Zhu Xi demands no further explanation, but the dispute over the meaning of *su* 素 ("make the ground white" in Dasan's translation) is convoluted. In this regard, the old and new commentaries share a view that having substantial morality is a prerequisite for the accomplishment of ritual propriety: ritual propriety is an expression of substantial morality. However, they disagree on what the character *su* symbolizes: for Zheng Xuan it symbolizes the application of the color white to delineate already-painted patterns, which is the last task in "drawing patterns"; for Zhu Xi it refers to whitening the ground, the first task in "drawing pictures." Thus, whereas Zheng Xuan related it to the performance of ritual propriety, Zhu Xi associated it with the cultivation of wholeheartedness and trustworthiness. In Zhu Xi's interpretation, it is more important to have a pure ground than to apply various colors when attempting to draw a beautiful picture, so his interpretation prioritizes natural substance [質] over refined expression [文], reflecting a persistent point of view in neo-Confucianism. In contrast, in Zheng Xuan's understanding, the application of the color white to various patterns, which is analogous to learning ritual propriety, is more crucial because beautiful patterns are produced through this final touch.

On noticing Zhu Xi's intention, Dazai Jun rejected Zhu Xi's comment and sided with the old commentary. In his view, Zhu Xi misunderstood the meaning of *su* and thereby misguided readers in focusing on natural substance, while the main passage just concerns the significance of ritual propriety. To Dasan, however, Dazai Jun's attack on Zhu Xi was another example of his reckless criticism of neo-Confucian interpretations of the Confucian classics. Dasan said that it was absurd for "today's poor learners and lesser Confucians" still to esteem Zheng's annotation and criticize Master Zhu's theories.

Although Dasan agreed with Zhu Xi as regards the meaning of *su*, he did not accept Zhu Xi's point of view, implicit in Zhu Xi's reading of this passage, on the matter of natural substance and refined expressions: to the same extent that Zhu Xi persistently prioritized natural substance over refined expressions, Dasan consistently advocated balance between the two. When he addressed how "Master Zhu attempted to rectify his [Zheng Xuan's] errors, but his misunderstanding has not been thoroughly rebutted," he must have been alluding to the shortcomings of Zhu Xi's views. In contrast to Zhu Xi, Dasan clearly regarded *su* as the result of human effort, not natural substance. This view corresponds with Dasan's philosophy, in which such virtues as wholeheartedness and trustworthiness are not endowed a priori but achieved through practice. Neo-Confucians tend to see them as ingrained in human nature.

3.9 The Master said, "I can talk about the rituals of the Xia, but they cannot sufficiently be corroborated by the affairs of Qi; I can talk about the rituals of the Yin, but it cannot sufficiently be corroborated by the affairs of Song.

This is because they do not have sufficient literature and worthies. Were they sufficient, I could verify them."

子曰; 夏禮吾能言之, 杞不足徵也, 殷禮吾能言之, 宋不足徵也. 文獻不足故也. 足則吾能徵之矣.

3.9.1 Grounds

1) Master Zhu commented, "Qi is the descendant state of the Xia;[75] Song is the descendant state of the Yin.[76] *Zheng* 徵 ('corroborated,' 'verified') here is interchangeable with *zheng* 證 (to prove); *wen* 文 ('literature') refers to books and texts; *xian* 獻 ('worthies') is here synonymous with *xian* 賢 (worthies)."[77]
2) I supplement as follows: The phrase "I can talk about" makes it clear that no one could explain the rituals at the time. As Confucius learned extensively, he could talk about them. Without verification, however, one would find it difficult to trust what has been told. Had the states of Qi and Song had literature and worthies, what they attested to would have corresponded to Confucius's explanations. Therefore, he said, "I could verify them." This is an expression of confidence.

3.9.2 Arguments

1) Bao Xian argued, "*Zheng* is here interchangeable with *cheng* 成 (to accomplish)." Zheng Xuan also argued, "[This passage states that] the reason Confucius could not accomplish the rituals [in the states of Qi and Song] was that the lords of the two states lacked refined laws and worthies."[78] I would refute these.
2) Ito Koreshada 伊藤維禎 (1627–1705) argued, "The two *zhis* 之 [that are placed before the names of the two states] in this passage should be read as combined with the succeeding sentences [making it a verb]" (quoted in *Rongo kokun gaiden*). I would refute this as follows:
   Ito's reading is based on "Li yun 禮運," but it is incorrect.
3) For classical texts that support my argument here, see *Constant Mean* (*Zhong yong zhangju*, 24b, 1–2) and "Li yun" (*Li ji zhushu*, 21:10b, 5–11a, 2).

* * *

With regard to Ito's translation, "Li yun" records, "Confucius says, 'I wished to know the way of Xia and for that reason went [之] to the state of Qi. However, the state lacked sources for its verification. Instead, I have obtained the book *Xia*

---

[75] Duke Donglou 東樓 was a descendant of King Yu, so King Wu enfeoffed him with the land of Qi.
[76] Weizi 微子 was an older illegitimate brother of King Zhou. [Weizi was born when his mother, the same mother as King Zhou's, was a concubine. Thus he was recognized as an illegitimate son, whereas King Zhou was regarded as a legitimate son.]
[77] A use of this kind appears in the phrase "All worthies in the myriad states" in "Yu shu 虞書" (*Shang Shu zhushu*, 4:14b).
[78] Xing Bing argued, "Since the lords of Qi and Song were obscure and weak, Confucius was not able to accomplish the rituals."

shi 夏時. I wished to know the way of Yin and for that reason went to the state of Song. However, the state lacked sources for its verification. Instead I have obtained the book *Qian kun* 乾坤." Ito believed that this chapter describes the same event as the one that is recorded in "Li yun." Although creative, this interpretation contradicts the fact that, according to more reliable sources, Confucius never traveled to the states of Qi and Song. The reliability of the record from "Li yun" can be further questioned due to the appearance of the titles of two apocryphal texts *Xia shi* and *Qian kun*. Considering that Qin Han academics produced a wide range of apocryphal texts and no historical documents exist to vouch for their authenticity, the aforementioned record of "Li yun" must have been interpolated by Qin Han scholars. As a matter of fact, in modern textual studies of the Chinese classical texts, "Li yun" is regarded as a product of Han scholarship, though partly composed of more ancient documents.

Dasan did not clarify the reason he rejected Ito's view. However, in another work, he states his overall assessment of "Li yun": "In my investigation of the chapter 'Li yun,' I have found that many of its records are incompatible with principle.. I suspect that this was written by secularized Confucians in the final days of the Qin dynasty" (*Jungyong gang-ui bo*, 85d). Although Dasan also referred to "Li yun" when necessary, he had strong reservations about its authenticity. It must have seemed unreasonable to him that Confucius could have obtained the two apocryphal texts during his visit to the two states.

According to Dasan, this chapter discloses one of the reasons Confucius wished to follow the rituals of Zhou. Confucius says, "I can talk about" the rituals of Xia and Yin; to Dasan, this phrase seemed to imply that Confucius had solid knowledge of the rituals of Xia and Yin. Dasan says that when Confucius's knowledge could not be verified with firm evidence, however, he must have been unable to act according to it, because "This Way [Confucianism] is always accompanied with verification." Dasan believed that Confucius's first concern in this chapter was not to discuss ancient rituals but rather to teach his students the importance of verifying one's knowledge (see *Jungyong jajam*, 59d).

3.10 At the Di sacrifice, after the first libation, I do not wish to look on.

子曰; 禘自既灌而往者, 吾不欲觀之矣.

3.10.1 Grounds

1) I supplement as follows: Di is the name of a seasonal sacrifice held at the royal shrine.[79] Essentially, this is a ritual for kings,[80] but the state of Lu

---

[79] According to "Ji yi," "They perform the Di sacrifice in the spring and the Chang 嘗 sacrifice in the fall" (*Li ji zhushu*, 47:1a).

[80] See the following discussion for details.

used it in violation of ritual propriety. *Guan* 灌 ("the first libation") is here interchangeable with *guan* 祼 (libation).[81] It is a ritual procedure to pour the Yuchang 鬱鬯 wine on the ground when the sacrificial offering is about to be received during the ritual, to invoke spirits.

2) I supplement as follows: In the ritual of the Di sacrifice, after the first libation, the performers, having stepped up to the ritual site, sing the Qingmiao 清廟 ode [in *Poetry*] and dance the Tai Wu dance with the scarlet-red shield and jade broadax.[82] These are the song and the dance dedicated to the Son of Heaven. Following the first libation, their violation of ritual propriety becomes more conspicuous. So Confucius did not wish to look on.

3.10.2 Arguments

1) Kong Anguo argued, "The Di sacrifice is the Xia 祫 sacrifice, and it aims to bring order to the Zhao Mu 昭穆 columns of the founder king's shrine. Thus, the spiritual tablet of the former king, whose shrine is to be removed, and those of all other former kings are merged into the founder king's shrine.[83] After the first libation, it is usual for an arrangement of the spiritual tablets of all the former kings to be made according to seniority, and for the order of the Zhao and the Mu columns to be finalized.[84] However, the state of Lu violated the sacrificial ritual by placing the tablet of Duke Xi before that of Duke Min [the predecessor of Duke Xi], which consequently disrupted the Zhao Mu columns. For this reason Confucius did not wish to observe it."[85] I would refute this as follows:

The Di sacrifice is a sacrifice for the emperors,[86] and it is next to the Jiao sacrifice in importance. Thus King Ding of the Zhou [周定王, r. 606–586 BCE] once mentioned, "In the rituals of the Jiao and the Di sacrifices, an offering of a whole-steamed sacrifice is performed."[87] Guan Yefu 觀射父 (fl. 516 BCE) also said, "For the sacrificial offerings for the Jiao and the Di sacrifices, a calf is exclusively taken."[88] He continued, "For the Di and the

---

[81] In the six categories of Chinese characters, this character belongs to the phonosemantic compound characters.

[82] See "Mingtang wei 明堂位" and "Ji tong" (*Li ji zhushu*, 31:8a; 49:30b).

[83] Xing Bing argued, "According to Zheng Xuan, 'In the rituals of the state of Lu, when the three-year mourning period is terminated, the spiritual tablet of the recently deceased king is merged with the shrine of the founder king. And, in the next spring, the Di sacrifice is performed at the shrine for all the ancestors.'"

[84] Xing Bing argued, "Following the spirits' descent, the wooden spiritual tablets begin to be arranged by seniority. In this arrangement, the tablet of the founder king is placed facing east; the tablets in the Zhao column are placed facing south; the tablets in the Mu column are placed facing north."

[85] Xing Bing argued, "According to 'Lu yu,' when they were going to place the tablet of Duke Xi before that of Duke Min, a staff member of ritual administration from the office of Zongbo said, 'This is not in accordance with the order of the Zhao Mu columns.' At that point [Xiafu 夏父] Fuji 弗忌 (fl. 627 BCE) intervened, saying, 'I am the head official of the office of Zongbo, and I want to place more brilliant kings in the Zhao column and the others in the Mu column. Is there any constant principle in this regard?'" (*Guo yu*, 4:13a–b).

[86] Thus the character *di* 禘 contains the *di* 帝 radical in it.

[87] See "Zhou yu" (*Guo yu*, 2:10b).

[88] See "Chu yu" (*Guo yu*, 18:4a).

Jiao sacrifices, the chief mourner himself shoots the sacrifice."[89] With these sources, it becomes evident that the sacrifice was extremely copious.

In the six volumes of *Rites of Zhou*, however, the name Di does not appear even once. Only the sacrifices to the five emperors are introduced passim in its record of the six offices. "Xiao Zongbo 小宗伯" says, "[The assistant ministers are responsible for] establishing the shrines for the spiritual tablets of the state and building the sanctums [兆] for the five emperors at the four suburbs" (*Zhou li zhushu*, 35:13b).[90] When the sacrificial ritual for the five emperors is performed, the prime minister of the offices of Heaven [天官冢宰] is in charge of releasing written warnings to the hundreds of officials; when the sacrificial ritual for the five emperors is performed, the officials for overseeing the temporal residence [掌次] for the king set up a large temporal residence and a small temporal residence; when the sacrificial ritual for the five emperors is performed, the head minister of the offices of Earth [地官大司徒] offers the sacrificial offering of an ox and lays the other precut sacrifices on the altar; when the sacrificial ritual for the Great High Lord is performed, the officials in the the offices of Spring who maintain garments [春官司服] help the king put on the great fur garment and the *mian* 冕 crown, and they do the same thing for the sacrificial rituals for the five emperors; when the sacrificial ritual for the five emperors is performed, the head minister of the laws and regulations [大司寇] accompanies the prime minister in the procedure of releasing written warnings to the hundreds of officials; when the sacrificial ritual for the five emperors is performed, the assistant ministers of the laws and regulations [小司寇] are in charge of filling a cauldron with water to purify the sacrifices.

Zheng Xuan viewed the five emperors as the heavenly gods of the five directions, such as Lingweiyang 靈威仰 and Chibiaonu 赤熛怒. However, this view stemmed merely from reckless misinformation and nonsense. As a matter of fact, in the sacrificial ritual for the five emperors, the surrogate bodies of the spirits [尸] are adopted. In accordance with this, "Xiao Si kou 小司寇" records: "When the sacrificial ritual for the five emperors is performed, the surrogate bodies should be washed" (*Zhou li zhushu*, 34:34b). Since the heavenly gods, such as Lingweiyang and Chibiaonu, are not human spirits, however, in principle there should be no surrogate bodies for them. Thus, the fact should remove any doubt that the five emperors refer to the legendary rulers, such as Fuxi 伏羲, Shengnong 神農, Xuanyuan 軒轅, and Di Ku 帝嚳. King Ding of the Zhou and Guan Yefu always paired the Di and the Jiao sacrifices when they mentioned them. And in the *Rites of the Zhou*, only the sacrificial ritual for the five emperors is comparable to the Jiao sacrifice in terms of the protocols and necessities. Therefore, it can be inferred that the sacrificial ritual of the five emperors is surely what the former kings called the Di sacrifice. Unfortunately, for the

---

[89] See "Chu yu" (*Guo yu*, 18:6b).
[90] *Zhao* 兆 here refers to the ritual platform area.

past two thousand years, there has been no one who recognized the ritual as the Di sacrifice. Anyway, for this reason, all sacrificial rituals for the emperors came to be called the Di sacrifice, and accordingly the sacrificial rituals for the kings designed to pay homage to their roots also came to be called the Di sacrifice.

In this regard "Daquan" says, "Only kings can have the Di sacrifice. The king, offering the Di sacrifice to the progenitor in his ancestry, enshrines their ancestors alongside the progenitor" (*Li ji zhushu*, 34:1a).[91] Zhan Qin of Lu said, "The kings of the Yu and the Xia offered the Di sacrifice to Huangdi 黃帝; the kings of the Yin and the Zhou offered the Di sacrifice to Di Ku."[92] These remarks are related to the Di sacrifice in their reference to the homage paid to the kings' roots. The Di sacrifice for the emperors might have been offered at the ritual platform for the Jiao sacrifice, whereas the Di sacrifice for paying homage to one's roots might have been offered at the royal ancestral shrine. This would be the difference.

From the time of Duke Xi, the state of Lu began to offer the Jiao sacrifice to Heaven and the Di sacrifice to Ku. In the thirty-first year of the reign of Duke Xi, *Spring and Autumn* records: "Summer, the fourth month: They had four divinations for [setting up the date for] the Jiao sacrifice. They eventually did not follow it" (*Zuo zhuan zhushu*, 16:10b). This record regards the beginning of the Jiao sacrifice in the Lu. A poem in "Lu Song" reads: "The son of Duke Zhuang 莊 [that is, Duke Xi] attends, with dragon-emblazoned banner, the sacrificial ritual. To the great sovereign emperor and his great ancestor Hou Ji 后稷, he offers the sacrificial offering of an ox, red and perfect. They enjoy, and they approve" (*Mao Shi zhushu*, 29:32a). This poem concerns the beginning of the Di sacrifice in the Lu.[93] As a sacrificial ritual, the Di is composed of the most opulent protocols and procedures. The state of Lu had already offered this sacrifice to Ku, as seen above and, furthermore, dared to apply this ritual to the Duke of Zhou. In relation to this, "Mingtang wei" says, "Late summer, the sixth month: They offered a sacrifice in the Great Shrine [the shrine for the Duke of Zhou], using the ritual of the Di sacrifice, to the Duke of Zhou" (*Li ji zhushu*, 31:8a). In the eighth year of the reign of Duke Xi, *Spring and Autumn* records: "They offered the Di sacrifice at the Great Shrine and placed the spiritual tablet of the lady of Duke Zhuang [哀姜] in it."[94] In the eighth year of the reign of Duke Xuan, *Spring and Autumn* also records: "There was a sacrificial ritual in the Great Shrine. As dancers for the Wan 萬 dance entered, the Yue 籥 dance was halted."[95] These records are related to the Di sacrifice for the Duke of Zhou.

---

[91] "Sangfu xiaoji" also contain the same record (*Li ji zhushu*, 32:16b).

[92] "Ji fa" also contains the same record (*Li ji zhushu*, 46:1a).

[93] For details see my discussions on *Poetry* and *Spring and Autumn* (*Sigyeong gang-ui*, 460b; *Chunchu gojing*, 320c).

[94] See the record of the fall, the seventh month (*Zuo zhuan zhushu*, 12:8b).

[95] Music was played only for the Di sacrifice. So this record is about the Di sacrifice. See the record of the summer, the sixth month (*Zuo zhuan zhushu*, 22:9b).

As seen above, the state of Lu had already offered the Di sacrifice to the Duke of Zhou and, furthermore, dared to apply this ritual to the various dukes of the state. Consequently, in the fifteenth year of the reign of Duke Zhao, they offered it at the shrine for Duke Wu 武;[96] in the twenty-fifth year of the reign of Duke Zhao they offered it to Duke Xiang;[97] in the eighth year of Duke Ding they offered it to Duke Xi.[98] These records are related to the Di sacrifice to various dukes. Accustomed to all these rituals, the state of Lu changed the name of the standard seasonal sacrificial ritual from Ci 祠 to Di. As a result, "Jiao tesheng" says, "In the spring, the Di sacrifice is offered; in autumn, the Chang sacrifice is offered" (Li ji zhushu, 25:11a);[99] "Wang zhi" says, "The sacrificial ritual offered in the spring is called Yue 礿; the one in the summer is called Di" (12:22b).[100] It also says, "When the feudal lords offer the Yue sacrifice, they do not offer the Di sacrifice; when they offer the Di sacrifice, they do not offer the Chang sacrifice" (12:26a). This is a brief history of the Di sacrifice.

To continue the discussion, there are two versions of the Di sacrifice offered at the royal ancestral shrine: the Joint Di sacrifice [袷禘] and the Separate Di sacrifice [殖禘]. The Joint Di sacrifice is offered at the Great Shrine before all the spiritual tablets of the dukes; the Separate Di sacrifice is offered at the individual shrine to just one duke. The laws of the Di sacrifice are as introduced above.

Nevertheless, the Confucians of the two Han capitals rose in discord to exchange vociferous arguments: sometimes one person would separate the Joint Di sacrifice into two different sacrificial rituals, while another would regard the clarification of the order of the Zhao and Mu columns as the primary meaning of the Di sacrifice. Someone also stated [who is quoted by Zheng Xuan from an apocryphal text of Record of Rites], "The Di sacrifice is performed once every five years" (Li ji zhushu, 12:27a), as though there existed a predetermined schedule of this sort.[101] Likewise, another person [Zheng Xuan] argued that at the termination of the three-year mourning period, the king should immediately clarify the meaning of the Zhao and Mu columns. Especially those who wove the so-called "immediate clarification of the order of the Zhao and Mu columns" into their theory made an error by taking as evidence the following two sentences: In the second year of the reign of Duke Min, "the auspicious Di sacrifice was offered to Duke Zhuang."[102] In the sixteenth year of the reign of Duke Xiang, the lord of Jin could not offer the Di sacrifice (Zuo zhuan zhushu, 33:6b). If the auspicious Di sacrifice was offered at the shrine for

---

[96] See the record for the spring, the second month (Zuo zhuan zhushu, 47:9a).
[97] See the record for the fall in Zuo's Commentary (Zuo zhuan zhushu, 51:24a).
[98] See the record for the winter, the eleventh month (Zuo zhuan zhushu, 55:24a).
[99] "Ji yi" contains the same record (Li ji zhushu, 47:1a).
[100] "Ji tong" contains the same record (Li ji zhushu, 49:25b).
[101] See my discussions on Spring and Autumn (Chunchu gojing, 320c).
[102] See the record for the summer, the fifth month (Zuo zhuan zhushu, 10:7a).

Duke Zhuang, the theory of "the clarification of the order of the Zhao and Mu columns" would automatically turn nonsensical.[103] In addition, at the time the lord of Jin had not even held the sacrificial ritual for the first anniversary of his father's death. Thus the Di sacrifice that the record said he offered must not have been an auspicious one.[104] Then how can Kong Anguo's explanation avoid a criticism of its groundlessness?

When it comes to the discussion of placing the spiritual tablet of Duke Xi before that of Duke Min, it should be noted that since he traveled widely, Confucius was sometimes not in the state of Lu. He was appointed to the office of laws and regulations for the first time in the eighth year of the reign of Duke Ding, and for several years after, he could stay in a powerful position. Thus the period in which he could have had an opportunity to visit the shrine for Heaven and the royal ancestral shrine might have coincided with this time of serving the state. By the eighth year of the reign of Duke Ding, however, the locations of the spiritual tablets of Duke Min and Duke Xi had already been determined.[105] A situation like the one in which a son enjoys the sacrificial offerings before his father does [as in the case of Duke Min and Duke Xi, who was the older brother of Duke Min but succeeded his younger brother] is predetermined by their inherited relationship. When the surrogate bodies were being received in the ritual after the first libation, Duke Min preceded Duke Xi. However, how could this cause Confucius not to wish to watch the ritual? Kong Anguo's theory was incorrect.

Why did Confucius not wish to watch the ritual then? In the Di sacrifice, a reception of the sacrificial offering of an ox follows the first libation. In relation to this, the fact that the prepared offering was a calf might have yielded the first reason.[106] The fact that when they served up the sacrificial offering using the tripod vessel they adopted the practice of having the offering steamed intact might have yielded the second reason.[107] The fact that the performers ascended to the hall to sing the Qingmiao ode,[108] which reads "Great is the number of officials; they grasped the virtue of King Wen" (*Mao Shi zhushu*, 26:3b), might have yielded the third reason.[109] The fact that they also danced the Tai Wu dance with the scarlet-red shield and jade broadax[110] might have yielded the fourth reason.[111] Currently the rest of the protocols and procedures adopted in the Di sacrifice cannot be delved into further.

---

[103] This is because the sacrifice was not offered at the Great Shrine.
[104] In other words, it was not one of the auspicious sacrificial rituals one can have at the termination of the mourning period.
[105] Yang Hu 陽虎 (fl. 502 BCE) played a decisive role in this.
[106] This is a violation of ritual propriety.
[107] This is a violation of ritual propriety.
[108] See "Ji tong" (*Li ji zhushu*, 31:8a).
[109] This is a violation of ritual propriety.
[110] See "Ji tong" (*Li ji zhushu*, 31:8a).
[111] This is a violation of ritual propriety. In the tenth year of the reign of Duke Xiang, *Spring and Autumn* records: "The state of Lu has utilized the music for the Di sacrifice and adopted it for the rituals of diplomatic greeting and sacrificial rituals" (*Zuo zhuan zhushu*, 31:8b).

In conclusion, since only the kings can have the Di sacrifice, the state of Lu's violation of ritual propriety was well manifested. Then in what way was the distorted sacrifice of Duke Xi and Duke Min related to this issue?

2) Goengbo added, "Confucius said, 'The Jiao sacrifice and the Di sacrifice in the state of Lu do not conform to ritual propriety. The Way of the Duke of Zhou has diminished.'[112] This remark addressed the Di sacrifice to Ku. The ritual violation of the Di sacrifice to Ku was self-evident without the experience of the first libation. Thus what the *Analects* discusses may pertain to the various Di sacrifices offered in the spring and the autumn,[113] not the other Di sacrifices."

3) Zhao Boxun 趙伯循 (fl. 766–779) argued, "In the Di sacrifice held at the shrine for the Duke of Zhou, King Wen is regarded as the progenitor and the Duke of Zhou is enshrined alongside him" (*Lun yu jizhu daquan*, 3:17a).

Although this view sounds great, no ground is found in the classics. Details are in my *Chunchu gojing* (*Chunchu gojing*, 325d), and a redundant explanation is unnecessary here.

4) I question Master Zhu as follows:

In the Di sacrifice, the first libation occurs before the reception of the surrogate bodies, and accordingly it is germane to the beginning part of the ritual. Although the lord and the subjects of Lu indeed lacked sincerity at the time, it would not be persuasive to say that they became lax immediately after the first libation. And those sloppy people always remain negligent. Their negligence would not become more serious after the first libation in the Di sacrifice. I am afraid that the reason Confucius did not wish to watch the ritual might not have been found in this point.

* * *

It is amazing that Dasan does not rely on any other commentator's opinions to define the meaning of the Di sacrifice here. He refers to various classical texts and tries to explain what the Di sacrifice was in order to integrate divergent passages that contain the vocabulary into his creative interpretation of this ritual. As he makes clear in his "Theory of the Di Sacrifice," in *Chunchu gojing*, the research he conducted in order to understand this complicated ritual began with the realization that *Rites of Zhou* does not introduce this seemingly crucial Confucian ritual: "The character *di* does not appear even once in the six volumes of *Rites of Zhou*, as though it is permissible for a great ritual to be missing in the classic. Is this compatible with principle?" (*Chunchu gojing*, 318b) In *Chunchu gojing*, his research resulted in twelve separate articles on various aspects of the Di sacrifice, constituting one of the most voluminous theoretical arguments on Confucian rituals during the Joseon dynasty. He was

---

[112] See "Li yun" (*Li ji zhushu*, 21:25b).
[113] This refers to the Di sacrifice offered at the Great Shrine to all former dukes.

not being boastful when he said, "Details are in my *Chunchu gojing*; a redundant explanation is unnecessary." He seems to have been satisfied with his findings, and he did not forget to display his confidence in his theory by saying, "Unfortunately, for the past two thousand years, there has been no one who recognized the ritual as the Di sacrifice." It is true that Dasan's theory, which is listed in "Overview of Original Meanings," is inventive.

In conclusion, according to Dasan's theory, the Di sacrifice has three different meanings. First, it refers to the sacrificial ritual for the five emperors. *Rites of Zhou* contains many descriptions of it, which is comparable in its grandiosity to the Jiao sacrifice, a sacrificial ritual for Heaven. Given that in other classical texts, such as *Guo yu*, the Jiao sacrifice is usually coupled with the Di sacrifice and that the offerings for the Jiao sacrifice and the Di sacrifice were identified as such, Dasan inferred that the ritual for the five emperors was actually the Di sacrifice; thus, *Rites of Zhou* contained substantial records of it despite the absence of any reference to it by name. Second, the Di sacrifice came to refer to rituals for honoring the primogenitors of kings as well (amounting to an expansion of the significance of the ritual). This development naturally occurred because the five emperors consisted of the legendary kings—the founding kings of ancient dynasties—not the heavenly gods. Dasan insisted that the Di sacrifice for the five emperors must have taken place on the ritual platform for the Jiao sacrifice, whereas the one for the founding kings must have been observed at the royal ancestral shrine. In the late Zhou dynasty, no feudal states were allowed to perform this ritual at their ancestral shrines because it was a king's ritual. The state of Lu, however, violated ritual propriety by performing the Di sacrifice at its ancestral shrine, first for the origin king of Zhou, then for the Duke of Zhou, and eventually for all the dukes of Lu. Due to this violation, Confucius could attend the Di sacrifice at the ancestral shrine of Lu, and many records from classical texts came to describe the ritual that occurred in the state of Lu. Third, the state of Lu further changed the name of the Ci ritual, the seasonal sacrificial ritual, to the Di, so that the Di sacrifice eventually referred to seasonal sacrificial rituals, as well.

Dasan's theory may not completely resolve the dispute concerning the Di sacrifice. His view on the reason Confucius did not wish to watch the ritual after the first libation, which is quite plausible in comparison with Zhu Xi's ambiguous explanation, may not satisfy everyone's curiosity either. By providing a sophisticated theory on ancient Confucian rituals, however, he was successful in proving himself independent and innovative enough to attempt to establish a new integral understanding of Confucian teaching.

3.11 Someone asked about the meaning of the Di sacrifice. The Master said, "I do not know. He who knows about it must deal with all under heaven as if he sees it here." And he pointed at his palm.

或問禘之說. 子曰; 不知也. 知其說者之於天下也, 其如示諸斯乎! 指其掌.

3.11.1 Grounds

1) I supplement as follows: The Di sacrifice is a sacrificial ritual for [five] emperors.[114] With the first change, it became the Di sacrifice held at the Great Shrine; with the second change, it became the Di sacrifice offered to all dukes of Lu. Eventually, it became the name of the regular seasonal sacrificial rituals. The violation of ritual propriety committed by the state of Lu thereby became more serious, so that Our Master could not endure the pain of speaking of it. Therefore Confucius replied, "I do not know."

2) Bao Xian commented, "This passage states that he who knows about the meaning of the Di sacrificial ritual would deal with the affairs of all under heaven as if he were pointing to things on his palm. This implies that it would be as easy as such."[115]

3) Master Zhu commented, "*Shi* 示 ('sees') is here interchangeable with *shi* 視 (to see)."

4) I supplement as follows: The five emperors cultivated the holy and magnificent virtue and thereby were well coupled with the High Lord. For this reason, the Di sacrifice for them was offered at the platform for the Jiao sacrifice.[116] As Ku [the progenitor of Lu] was coupled with Heaven as well, the Di sacrifice to him was offered at the Great Shrine.[117] *Changes* says, "The sages laid down instructions about the ways of mysterious beings, and all under heaven yielded to them."[118] Anyone who knows about the meaning of the Di sacrifice would be able to lay down instructions about the ways of mysterious beings. Thus for them, all under heaven would be easy to rule.

3.11.2 Arguments

1) Kong Anguo argued, "Confucius replied that he did not know because he wanted to avoid mentioning the faults of the state of Lu."[119] I would refute this as follows:

   My perspective on this issue was already introduced earlier.

2) For classical texts that contain a similar passage to this chapter, see *Constant Mean* (*Zhong yong zhangju*, 13b, 4–6) and "Zhong Ni yan ju 仲尼燕居" (*Li ji zhushu*, 50:22b, 1 and 6–7)

* * *

---

[114] Details about this were introduced earlier.

[115] Xing Bing commented, "At the time, Confucius raised an arm and turned his hand to point it with another hand in display for someone, saying, 'as if he sees it here.'"

[116] According to *Rites of Zhou*, they offered it to the five emperors.

[117] According to "Daquan," "The king offered the Di sacrifice to the progenitor in his ancestry" (*Li ji zhushu*, 32:9b).

[118] See the *duan* judgment of "Guan 觀" (*Zhou Yi zhushu*, 4:25a).

[119] Xing Bing argued, "Lu's placement of the spiritual tablet of Duke Xi before that of Duke Min brought disorder to the Zhao and Mu columns. If Confucius had spoken of it, it would have been deemed highlighting the evils of the state."

Dasan here seems to reject Kong Anguo's views on the reason Confucius said he did not know the meaning of the Di sacrifice. However, it was Xing Bing's explanation that Dasan, in fact, disagreed with, which he only loosely associated with Kong. Like Kong, Dasan believed that Confucius did not want to divulge his country's faults by engaging in a discussion of the Di sacrifice. Whereas Xing Bing thought that the state of Lu's fault lay in its disordering of the Zhao and Mu columns, Dasan related it to the state of Lu's rampant violation of ritual propriety concerning the Di sacrifice.

3.12 Confucius sacrificed to his ancestors as if they were present; he sacrificed to the spirits as if the spirits were present. The Master said, "If I were not to give assistance in a sacrifice, it would be as if I did not sacrifice."

祭如在, 祭神如神在. 子曰; 吾不與祭, 如不祭.

3.12.1 Grounds

1) Kong Anguo commented, "The sentence 'Confucius sacrificed to his ancestors as if they were present' means that he served the dead in the same manner as he served the living.[120] The sentence 'he sacrificed to the spirits' means that he sacrificed to the hundreds of spirits."[121]

2) I supplement as follows: Yu 與 ("give assistance to") is here interchangeable with zhu 助 (help). This refers to giving assistance at a sacrifice at the family shrine.[122] Confucius was not the eldest son, so he could not supervise the ritual. Therefore he spoke of giving assistance at it.

3) I supplement as follows: Only after giving assistance at a sacrifice can one offer one's devotion; only after offering his devotion can he sacrifice to ancestors as if they were present; only after sacrificing to ancestors as if they were present can it be said that he performed the sacrifice. If any of these conditions is not met, it is the same as not sacrificing.

3.12.2 Arguments

1) In my investigation, this passage was designated as one chapter in Lun yu jijie. In Lun yu jizhu, however, it is separated into two chapters.

2) Bao Xian argued, "When Confucius could not sacrifice in person due to his absence in the state or illness, he had a substitute do it. When this happened, he felt as if he did not sacrifice because he could not show his solemnity and respect." I would refute this as follows:

---

[120] Master Cheng explained, "This regards a sacrifice to the ancestors" (Lun yu jizhu, 2:4b).
[121] Master Cheng explained, "This regards a sacrifice to the spirits beyond one's lineage" (Lun yu jizhu, 2:4b).
[122] For details, see the following discussion.

Confucius's adult name is Zhong Ni 仲尼, so it is clear that he was not the eldest son. In ancient times, giving assistance at a sacrifice was termed *yu ji* 與祭. In correspondence to this, *Record of Rites* says, "Those who hit the mark in the archery ritual can give assistance [與] at the sacrificial ritual; those who do not cannot give assistance."[123] When Master Zeng asked whether a chief mourner in the five-month-long mourning ritual [小功] could give assistance [與] at the sacrificial rituals of others, Confucius replied, "In the mourning rituals of the Son of Heaven and the feudal lords, those who do not wear the mourning apparel of *zhan cui* 斬衰 [unhemmed sackcloth] cannot give assistance [與] at the rituals; in the mourning rituals of the great officials, those who wear the mourning apparel of *qi cui* 齊衰 [hemmed sackcloth with even edges] only can give assistance [與] at the rituals" (*Li ji zhushu*, 18:17b).

In another dialogue, in which Master Zeng asked whether people who are observing the mourning period can give assistance [與] at the sacrificial rituals of others, Confucius replied, "Those who are observing even the three-month-long mourning period do not participate in the sacrificial rituals. How can they give assistance [與] at the rituals of others?" (*Li ji zhushu*, 18:17b) As seen here, when a man supervises a sacrificial ritual it is termed "managing the ritual [主祭]"; when a man gives assistance at a sacrificial ritual it is termed "helping the ritual [與祭]." The expressions are distinctive in this way. Thus the comment that says "When Confucius could not sacrifice in person, he had a substitute do it" is unacceptable.

3) Ogyu argued, "The first half of this passage was excerpted from an ancient classical text, and Confucius's remark in the second half was introduced here to validate its teaching. The same case is found in the passage that begins 'Startled, the bird rose up'" (*Lun yu jizhu*, 10:18). I would refute this.

* * *

Dasan thought that *yu ji* 與祭 ("to give assistance in a sacrifice") was an idiomatic expression adopted frequently in classical texts. This understanding does not greatly conflict with translations other than his own, especially with the one a majority of commentators accepted: "to participate in a sacrifice." Although Dasan's interpretation was fresh and otherwise rigorous, he overlooked the fact that it was not until primogeniture was strictly applied to Confucian households under neo-Confucianism that the eldest son's privilege to perform the ancestral sacrifice became universal. Most researchers agree, that in Korea, it was not until the late Joseon dynasty that the society exclusively entitled the eldest son to perform the ritual.

---

[123] See "She yi" (*Li ji zhushu*, 62:15b).

Dasan does not provide the reason he refutes Ogyu's views here. Ogyu argued that this passage contains three different layers of ancient sayings: the first sentence, drawn from an unknown ancient classical text of Confucian rituals, constitutes one layer, which Ogyu translates as "When performing sacrifices, one has to act as if [the spirits] were present"; another consists of a comment on the first sentence, which can be translated as "[This means] when performing sacrifices for spirits, one has to act as if the spirits were present"; the last consists of Confucius's remark, which is intended to supplement the first two. As he always did, Dazai Jun praised his master's discovery and impugned the other comments, especially those by Zhu Xi. Since Dasan considered the entire passage in this chapter germane to Confucius's personal experiences, he could not agree with Ogyu.

In line with Dasan's callous disproval of Ogyu's view, Dazai aggressively criticized neo-Confucians for emphasizing internal attitudes over external expressions in their philosophies: "In this chapter, Zhu Xi's comment solely focuses on sincerity [誠], but it is a serious mistake. In general, those who supervise the sacrifices take reverence [敬] as their mainstay, not sincerity. The actualization of the value of reverence hinges on how thoroughly one follows ritual decorum in the form it is given.... [T]hat according to which one adheres to the value of sincerity without tending to matters of ritual propriety is the way of Buddhism. Fan Zuyu argued that sincerity was substantial while ritual propriety was unsubstantial. This is a falsehood.... [T]he learning of Song Confucians, which concentrated on the mind-heart, has distorted the Way of former kings to this extent." Dasan would have considered Dazai's views another example of losing balance, although they were, more or less, to the point.

3.13 Wangsun Jia asked, "'It is better to comply with the kitchen god than to comply with the inner room god.' What does this mean?" The Master replied, "Not so. He who sins against Heaven will have nowhere to pray to."

王孫賈問曰; 與其媚於奧, 寧媚於竈, 何謂也? 子曰; 不然. 獲罪於天, 無所禱也.

3.13.1 Grounds

1) Kong Anguo commented, "Wangsun Jia is a great official of Wei."[124] I supplement as follows: He was a hegemonic official and in charge of administering military affairs.
2) Master Zhu commented, "*Mei* 媚 ('to comply with') means to be intimate and compliant with."

---

[124] According to Luan Zhao 欒肇 (fl. 266–285), he originally came from the Zhou [as introduced in *Rongo kogun gaiden*].

3) I supplement as follows: *Ao* 奧 ("inner room god") refers to the southwest corner of a room,[125] where the housewife usually stays.[126] *Zao* 竈 ("the kitchen god") refers to the kitchen furnace,[127] where the kitchen maid usually stays. It also refers to a sacrificial ritual offered by old women.[128] A sacrificial ritual held in an early summer month is also called *zao*.[129] A proverb goes, "It is better to comply with the kitchen god than to comply with the inner room god." With borrowed names of sacrifices to gods, the proverb metaphorically relates the fact that the actual authority over food lies not in the housewife but in the kitchen maid, so one's chances to have a meal are greater when compliant with people of lower status.

4) Master Zhu commented, "The proverb metaphorically suggests that it would be better to flatter the hegemonic official than to be personally associated with the lord. [Wangsun] Jia was the hegemonic official of Wei, so he derided Confucius with this proverb."

5) I supplement as follows: *Tian* 天 ("Heaven") is the High Lord. Seeking out an intimate relationship by skewing the Way is a sinful action against Heaven. Heaven's fury cannot be replaced by luck from various gods. Thus, there is "nowhere to pray to."

3.13.2 Arguments

1) Kong Anguo argued, "*Ao* refers to the interior and symbolizes a subject close to the lord.[130] *Zao* symbolizes the authority of government."[131] I would refute this as follows:

When Confucius rejected Wangsun Jia, he said, "He who sins against Heaven will have nowhere to pray to." It clearly suggests that the expressions "to comply with the kitchen god" and "to comply with the inner room god" are related to the notion of praying to gods. Would it be adequate to decipher this passage only in terms of the place for people of higher status or the practical source of food and meals? Furthermore, if the southwest corner of a room is where people of higher status stay, it should symbolize

---

[125] This is a definition from *Er ya* (*Er ya zhushu*, 4:2b).

[126] According to "Qu li," "People's sons do not take the southwest corner as their main place to stay at home" (*Li ji zhushu*, 1:24b).

[127] This is a definition from *Shuo wen* (*Shuo wen jie zi*, 3-B:21b).

[128] See "Li qi" (*Li ji zhushu*, 23:28a). Zheng Xuan rendered it as interchangeable with *cuan* 爨, but he was wrong.

[129] See "Yue ling" (*Li ji zhushu*, 15:25a).

[130] Xing Bing argued, "Since the southwest corner of a room is calm and secure, people of higher status usually stay there. Though the place is more prestigious, however, people spend time at leisure there without dealing with practical affairs. Thus it metaphorically suggests that, although subjects close to the lord have more prestige, they do not give real benefits to people since they do not have the authority of awards and punishments."

[131] Xing Bing argued, "*Zao* (kitchen) is where food is made. Although the place of *zao* is humble and unclean, it provides a family with necessary resources. Thus it metaphorically suggests that those who are in charge of administering political matters, in practice, hold authority over awards and punishments and can give real benefits to people, although their status is relatively lower [than that of the royal family members]."

the lord of the state. However, in Kong's annotation, "it symbolizes a subject close to the lord." Is this acceptable? And the subjects close to the lord must exercise their authority. How is it possible that they would relegate themselves to a position of merely administering political issues? In addition, in the past the court eunuchs were usually considered subjects close to the lord. Then is it appropriate to compare them to people of higher status? Kong's explanation was incorrect.

2) I question Master Zhu as follows:

The five sacrificial rituals [五祀] refer to those for the gods of the five phases. *Zuo's Commentary* records an address by Cai Mo 蔡墨 (fl. 513 BCE) that says, "The officials of the five phases were ennobled as the top dukes [上公] and were offered sacrifices as illustrious gods. They were respected and revered through rituals of the gods of the five phases alongside rituals of the land god and the grain god. The head of Wood was called Goumang 句芒, and Zhong 重 assumed that position; the head of Fire was called Zhurong 祝融, and Li 黎 assumed that position; the head of Metal was called Rushou 蓐收, and Gai 該 assumed that position; the head of Water was called Xuanming 玄冥, and Xiu 修 and Xi 熙 together assumed that position; the head of Earth was called Hou Tu 后土, and Goulong 句龍 assumed that position."[132]

In the ancient institution, the five sacrificial rituals did not include the names of sacrifices to gates, the kitchen, or apartments. I do not know what the grounds for the records [which are cited by Zhu Xi] in "Ji fa" and "Yue ling" are. "Da Zongbo," in *Rites of Zhou,* regarded the land god, the grain god, and the gods of the five phases as spirits of the Earth. Thus even the Son of Heaven could offer sacrifices to these five gods. The five sacrificial rituals seen in "Qu li" involved no discrimination from the beginning in their application from the Son of Heaven to the great officials, and even low-ranking officials could follow them. In harmony with this, "Shi sangli 士喪禮" records: "Offer a prayer to the gods of the five phases."[133] In addition, the sacrifices to the gods of the five phases should be dedicated to all of them, without omitting any of them selectively. Contrary to this, "Ji fa" proposes a gradation, saying, "Kings arrange seven sacrificial rituals [to various posts of their residence]; feudal lords arrange five sacrificial rituals; great officials arrange three rituals; chief descendants in the families of low-ranking officials arrange two rituals; and the commoners arrange one ritual" (*Li ji zhushu,* 46:11a–b). This is obviously a record of the secularized Confucians in the final days of the Qin, and in conclusion, the kitchen god did not initially belong to the gods of the five sacrificial rituals.

According to the plebeian folklore of towns and villages, people sometimes offer a sacrifice to the kitchen god, so at the time of Confucius, a proverb like this was circulated. However, it does not make sense in principle to

---

[132] See the twenty-ninth year of the reign of Duke Zhao (*Zuo zhuan zhushu,* 53:8b).
[133] See "Jixi li" (*Yi li zhushu,* 13:49b). ["Shi sangli" might have been an error.]

assume [like Zhu Xi] that people offer a sacrifice to the kitchen god in the southwest corner. Even when they sacrifice to it in the southwest corner, the recipient of the ritual is still the kitchen god. Thus the use of this metaphor in the proverb might be inappropriate. I am afraid that the original meaning was not so.

3) Mao Qiling argued, "In my view, the annotation on a record in *Record of Rites* regarding the five sacrificial rituals quotes from a lost text on the ritual of the apartments. In the very beginning it says, 'The five sacrificial rituals are offered at the shrine and go with reciprocally distinctive procedures.' In general, when they sacrifice for the doors, the spiritual tablet is placed in the area west of the door of the shrine; when they sacrifice for the apartments, it is placed under the window of the shrine; when they sacrifice for the kitchen, it is placed in the area east of the gate outside; when they sacrifice for the gate, it is placed around the left hinge of the gate outside; when they sacrifice for the hall, it is placed in the area west of the shrine's gate outside. It should be noted that the sacrifices do not take place at the actual places relevant to the gods" (*Si shu shengyan bu* 四書賸言補, 1:5a–b). He also mentioned: "The southwest corner of a room in the house is where males and females sleep together on a mattress to have an impure relationship. How is it possible to offer a sacrifice to the kitchen god there?" (1:4b) I would refute this as follows:

Xiaoshan respected the kitchen god in an extreme way and came to think it inappropriate to sacrifice to the god in the southwest corner of a room, talking nonsense endlessly. However, he did not know that the kitchen god was not initially among the gods of the five sacrificial rituals that came to give such ambiguous explanations. What he quoted about the protocols of the five sacrificial rituals was without exception the unworthy theories of the apocryphal texts that Zheng Xuan had quoted. How can a knowledgeable person go this far?

4) Gu Yanwu 顧炎武 (1613–1682) argued, "What kind of god is *ao*? For the sacrifice to the kitchen god, people receive the surrogate body and offer sacrifices in the southwest corner of a room [奧]. However, the recipient is still the god of the kitchen.[134] In consideration of this, the contemporaries of Confucius often said, 'To have a good relationship with the lord, it is better to serve him at his leisure at home than to be loyal to him in the court.' Not knowing this, Zhu Xi commented that the inner room god symbolized the lord, while the kitchen god symbolized the hegemonic subject. Consequently, he separated them into two gods, though they are

---

[134] Gu also argued, "An annotation on a poem of *Poetry*, 'She sets forth the offering under the window in the ancestral shrine,' renders 'under the window' as indicating the southwest corner of a room, the so-called *ao*. In this regard, 'Qu li' says, 'People's sons do not take the southwest corner as their main place to stay at home.' In addition, in 'Zhong Ni yan ju,' the characters *ao* and *zao* 阼 [竈] appear to be interchangeable with one another. In conclusion, *ao* is primarily a place for people to stay, but in sacrifices people worship the spirits there" (*Re zhi lu* 日知錄, 7:2a–b).

the same god, ending up out of harmony with the meaning of this passage" (*Re zhi lu*, 7:2a–b). I would refute this as follows:

The royal ancestral spirits are enshrined in the royal shrine, whereas living people reside in a bedroom. However, the shrine and the bedroom are identical in terms of having doors, windows, the south corner, and the southwest corner in their designs. The southwest corner mentioned in the annotation on a poem of *Poetry*, "She sets forth the offering under the window in the ancestral shrine," absolutely refers to that of the royal ancestral shrine, not that of the bedroom. The bedroom is a place where males and females mingle with each other and toddlers urinate. Is it imaginable that people offer sacrifices to spirits there? In addition, the southwest corner of the shrine is an improper place to sacrifice to the kitchen god [so that *ao* and *zao* should be distinguished]. Tinglin's 亭林 [Gu Yanwu] theory sprouted from an end of a tree that cannot be adopted.

5) Huang Kan argued, "Luan Zhao commented, 'The southwest corner is a prestigious place but has nothing to do with substantial issues; the kitchen is a humble place, but something people look for is to be found there. At the time the Zhou court was declining, and the feudal lords held sway. [Following the trend of his time] Jia, a man of the Zhou, came to serve the state of Wei. So he tried to explain himself before Confucius, using the common saying.'" I would refute this as follows:

Luan Zhao speculated, by paying attention to the literal meaning of Wangsun [a descendant of the king], that Jia might have come from the Zhou and eventually fabricated this theory. It is not worthy of discussion.

* * *

In this chapter, Dasan refutes several theories that were proposed by major commentators of the *Analects*, such as Zheng Xuan, Kong Anguo, Luan Zhao (as quoted by Huang Kan), Xing Bing, Zhu Xi, Gu Yanwu, and Mao Qiling. This does not mean that he refutes all of their annotations. He was selective when dealing with each of them. He criticizes Kong Anguo primarily because Kong did not relate *ao* and *zao* to certain rituals, but follows Kong's views on the overall meaning of this passage; he refutes Zhu Xi's theory primarily because Zhu Xi regarded *zao* as one of the five sacrificial rituals (basing his claim on "Yue ling" and "Ji fa" from *Record of Rites*), but agrees with Zhu Xi that *ao* symbolizes the lord and *zao* connotes the powerful subject, Wangsun Jia. Dasan believed that the five sacrificial rituals had nothing to do with this passage because they were rituals for the gods of five phases—a point of view he refers to in "Overview of Original Meanings"; he censures Mao Qiling primarily because he relied on an apocryphal text from Han scholarship to define the *zao* ritual but accepts Mao's opinion that all of the rituals did not actually occur at the five places of a house but in the ancestral shrine; he rejects Gu Yanwu's comment primarily because Gu regarded the recipients of the *ao* and *zao* rituals as identical, uniformly symbolizing the lord, but he treats Gu's citations from *Poetry* and *Record of Rites* with reverence when he interprets the main passage. All of this exemplifies the methods Dasan uses to synthesize various exegetical traditions and establish a new integral understanding of the *Analects*. As a consequence of his synthesis, he concluded that *ao* and *zao*, thanks to an expanded sense of these notions, came to refer to rituals for the inner room god and kitchen god, respectively, which were popular among laypeople at the time of Confucius. Due to the actual benefits people could receive from the kitchen god, they circulated the proverb the main text introduces. Wangsun Jia, comparing himself to the kitchen god, tried to ridicule Confucius, who sought the audience of the lord of Wei without winning his favor.

Since the concept of Heaven obviously invites various speculations on its accurate meaning, commentators tried to discover the context in which Confucius adopted this notion: to Kong Anguo, it symbolized the lord of the state of Wei; to Zhu Xi, it meant *li*, the universal moral principle; and to Dasan, it meant the High Lord. Dasan's remark seems to have been intended to show his disagreement with the neo-Confucian understanding of the concept. Although he sometimes combined the two notions, Heaven and principle, into the notion of *tianli* 天理 (meaning "heavenly principle" or "principle of Heaven"), he posits that Heaven is more fundamental because it is the source of all being—the source, even, of the principle itself. "Principle derives from Heaven" (See "Ohak ron," 241a.). This view is clearly contrasted with the neo-Confucian claim that "Heaven is no more than principle."

3.14 The Master said, "The Zhou reflected on the previous two dynasties. How exquisite are its refined expressions! I follow the Zhou."

子曰; 周監於二代, 郁郁乎文哉! 吾從周.

3.14.1 Grounds

1) I supplement as follows: *Jian* 監 ("reflected") is here interchangeable with *jian* 鑒 (mirror), meaning that a man knows beauty and ugliness through taking a bright look at something.[135]
2) Master Zhu commented, "The previous two dynasties refer to the Xia and the Shang. *Yuyu* 郁郁 ('replete') is a term that portrays the efflorescence of refined expressions."
3) I supplement as follows: Confucius's remark "I follow the Zhou" implies that he chose and followed the best among all three dynasties.

---

[135] "Jiu gao 酒誥" says, "Rather than reflecting [監] on the water mirror, a man should reflect [監] on other people" (*Shang Shu zhushu*, 13:31a).

3.14.2 Arguments

1) Kong Anguo argued, "*Jian* is here synonymous with *shi* 視 (to compare)."[136]
I would refute this as follows:

The phrase *zhou jian yu* 周監於 ("The Zhou reflected on") may mean that the Duke of Zhou, when he established the rituals, reflected on the previous two dynasties. So he could remove their defects and supplement what was missing to make the rituals splendid and greatly prepared. Xing Bing's interpretation [attached to Kong's comment], however, implies that scholars are comparing the rituals of the Zhou with those of the previous two dynasties, a far-fetched understanding.

In general, things come to have refined expressions only after they are endowed with natural substances. The black-and-white pattern, *fu* 黼, can be completed only after the white ground is adorned with black emblems. How can the color black alone produce a pattern? Thus the refined expressions of the Zhou were surely a result of harmony between expressions and substance to create the replete beauty. Nevertheless, today's scholars, whenever they have a chance to speak, always say that in the Zhou dynasty the refined expressions prevailed: they seem to condemn the Duke of Zhou for bringing damage to the artless and honest cultural atmosphere of the Xia and the Shang by manipulations and deformations so that putrid expressions and unessential protocols gained ascendancy and generated countless evil effects. If they were correct, the Duke of Zhou would have been a man who distorted transgenerational education by ruining people's customs, causing their behavior to deteriorate, undermining humanity, and jeopardizing rightness. Does this even make sense? Confucius believed that the rituals of the Zhou were a genuine standard undeniable for one hundred ages. For this reason, to Zi Zhang's question, he replied, "Should there be, by any chance, any state that succeeds the Zhou, even a hundred ages hence can be foreknown" (*Lun yu jizhu*, 2:23). This shows that Confucius thought that the rituals of the Zhou would generate no evils even after they were transmitted over one hundred ages.

In this passage, Confucius clearly declared, "I follow the Zhou of all the three dynasties." This passage seems to leave no feeling of reservation. Then how can the prevalence of the refined expressions be viewed as a malady? Following the Qin and the Han, the refined expressions were destroyed as well as the natural substance that had already vanished. Since the refined expressions were already destroyed, it became harder to restore the natural substance. This situation of experiencing a long night has lasted for two thousand years without the break of day. Yet people now warn against

---

[136] Xing Bing argued, "This passage states that the ritual procedures and refined institutions of the Zhou, in comparison with those of the Xia and the Shang, lead one to exclaim, 'How replete they are! They have an elegant beauty in them.'"

the prevalence of the refined expressions. Isn't this an error?[137] For a classical text that supports my argument here, see *Constant Mean* (*Zhong yong zhangju*, 24b, 1–2).

2) "Tangong" says, "In the Yin, people condoled with the chief mourner right after a burial mound was finished; in the Zhou, people condoled with the chief mourner when he returned home from the burial site to do the ritual weeping again. Confucius said, 'The rituals of the Yin are too much austere. I follow the Zhou'" (*Li ji zhushu*, 9:22b).

In my view, Confucius's frequent remark "I follow the Zhou" may show that he deeply cherished what the Duke of Zhou created.

* * *

Who were those scholars—referred to here as "today's scholars"—who, according to Dasan, always claimed that the refined expressions prevailed in the Zhou dynasty? Chen Li, one of the major neo-Confucian commentators of the *Analects*, was one of them: on this passage he commented, "Confucius wished to adopt the refined expressions of the Zhou's heyday in which both refined expressions and natural substances found their appropriate places, not the refined expressions of the last days of the Zhou, when they prevailed over natural substances" (*Lun yu jizhu daquan*, 3:26b). However, the more influential thinker with whom Dasan disagreed on this issue was Cheng Yi, who once asserted, "In the last days of the Zhou, refined expressions prevailed over natural substances. Therefore, people back then often made such remarks [that the men of latter times are more decent in the practice of rituals and music] and did not know that the Zhou culture was excessively in favor of refined expressions" (*Lun yu jizhu*, 6:1a).

Dasan disapproved of this neo-Confucian perspective out of his unremitting insistence on the balance between natural substances and refined expressions: "Refined expressions are dependent on natural substances for their completion of cultural beauty; natural substances are dependent on refined expressions for their preservation of the moral foundation" (*Noneo gogeum ju*, 253d). Despite this underlying principle, he actually gave more weight to refined expressions, because he thought that in his time people suffered for lack of them—a failure that could be traced to the state's institutional systems: "What are the natural substances? They are filial piety, respect for elders, wholeheartedness, and trustworthiness. Today, however, the three bonds have dissolved and the nine laws have lapsed. Then how can the natural substances be preserved alone? Today's urgent business is to repair the refined expressions. Only after they are repaired may the natural substances be restored" (253d). Urgently advocating propriety for Joseon society, Dasan always showed

---

[137] Our Master once associated the four dynasties with one another when he answered Yan Yuan's question. However, he did not intend to remove the refined expressions of the Zhou. For more details, see my interpretation of the relevant passage (*Lun yu jizhu*, 15:10).

perfect respect for the Duke of Zhou and gave the Duke credit for his achievements in the practice of the Zhou's rituals and music, as seen in his comment in this chapter.

In line with this, it would be acceptable to say that Dasan hoped to follow in the footsteps of the Duke of Zhou rather than those of Confucius. It is beyond question that Dasan so greatly revered both of them that he never mentioned any of their flaws, but to him, the Duke of Zhou was "the one who acquired a position and thereby put the Way into practice," whereas Confucius was "the one who could not acquire a position, so he had no means to practice the Way" (*Jungyong gang-ui bo*, 90b). His writing abounds with evidence of his wish to serve the king and the country as a meritorious minister rather than a wise teacher—including the writing he did during his eighteen-year exile.

3.15 When the Master entered the Great Shrine, he asked about everything. Someone said, "Who says the son of the man of Zou knows the rituals? When he entered the Great Shrine, he asked about everything." On hearing this, the Master said, "This is the ritual."

子入大廟, 每事問. 或曰; 孰謂鄹人之子知禮乎? 入大廟, 每事問. 子聞之. 曰; 是禮也.

3.15.1 Grounds

1) Biao Xian commented, "The Great Shrine is the shrine for the Duke of Zhou.[138] This event occurred when Confucius, as an official of the state of Lu, helped offer a sacrifice [to the Duke of Zhou]."[139]
2) Master Zhu commented, "Zou is the name of a county in Lu. Shuliang He 叔梁紇, Confucius's father, was the great official of the town."
3) I supplement as follows: All ritual protocols adopted for the shrine of the Duke of Zhou were the rituals for the Son of Heaven. If Confucius had put them in practice without asking about them, it would have implied that Confucius took for granted the state of Lu's adoption of them. Thus he took action only after asking the chief litanist about everything.

3.15.2 Arguments

1) Kong Anguo argued, "Making an inquiry again even when one already knows about the ritual is the most careful attitude." I would refute this as follows:

---

[138] In the thirteenth year of the reign of Duke Wen, *Gongyang's Commentary* says, "The shrine for the Duke of Zhou is called the Great Shrine; the one for the dukes of Lu is called the Ancestral Chamber [世室]; the one for the feudal lords of other states is called the Hall [宮]" (*Chunqiu Gongyang zhuan zhushu*, 14:9a).

[139] Xing Bing commented, "Duke Ding appointed Confucius to the office of judicial administrator of the town Zhongdou 中都, then to the office of construction, and finally to the head office of laws and regulations."

Chunqiu fanlu records: "When Confucius entered the Great Shrine, he asked about everything. This shows his utmost carefulness."[140] This is the Han Confucians' understanding of the meaning of the main passage. The sage's learning during his entire life, however, did not depart from topics of rituals and music. In spite of this, if he had needed to ask about everything once he entered the royal shrine, what would have been the use of his learning? He would have asked about everything because he thought to himself: "In the shrines dedicated to the feudal lords, people should adopt the rituals for them. What I know [regarding the Great Shrine] is all about the rituals for the feudal lords, and I am supposed to not know about the rituals for the Son of Heaven [for the Great Shrine]. How can I stop asking the chief litanist about them to take action?" Thus on hearing someone's derision, Confucius responded, "It is the ritual." Were this not the real reason, what questions would Confucius have had, when the affairs of an ancestral chamber were self-evident in the chamber and when the affairs of an ancestral hall were self-evident in the hall? Confucius replied to Duke Ling of Wei, "In the matter of setting forth the ritual vessels, I have heard about it" (*Lun yu jizhu*, 15:1).[141]

2) I question Master Zhu as follows:

In his earliest career in administrative positions, Confucius became an accountant and then a supervisor of a stock farm. He went to the state of Qi at the age of thirty-five and was eventually appointed to the office of judicial administrator of the town Zhongdou, then to the office of construction, and finally to the head office of laws and regulations when he was over fifty. Thus he must have entered the Great Shrine when he was over the age of fifty. The way someone referred to him as "the son of the man of Zou" might not have been prompted by Confucius's age, when he was young enough to be belittled. *Changes* says, "The son of the Yan 顏 family had nearly attained the Way" (*Zhou Yi zhushu*, 12:20b). *Mencius* also says, "How could the son of the Zang 臧 family cause me not to meet the ruler who understands me?" (*Mengzi jizhu* 1B:23) At the time, people often used expressions of this sort to show their belittlement and derision.

* * *

Zhu Xi adopted Kong Anguo's view on the reason Confucius asked about everything when he entered the Great Shrine: in other words, the old and new commentaries agree on the point that Confucius pretended not to know the ritual protocols in order to show the inner virtue of carefulness. Dasan also agreed that Confucius purposefully asked about everything. To him, however, such inquiry is necessary for following ritual propriety because when a feudal

---

[140] See "Jiaoshi dui 郊事對" (*Chunqiu fanlu*, 15:10b).
[141] When Confucius was involved with other shrines, he did not have any questions. Thus it should be noted that this dialogue concerns the Great Shrine.

state attempts to use the rituals for the Son of Heaven in violation of ritual propriety, it is ritual propriety for ceremonial assistants to ask about everything out of feigned ignorance. This understanding is referred to in "Overview of Original Meanings." Thus, in Dasan's interpretation, Confucius's inquiry is only indirectly related to his inner virtue. In contrast, Zhu Xi and his students supplemented their comments by saying that the accomplishment of ritual propriety depends on one's cultivation of the virtue of carefulness. Dasan was always wary of an excessive internalization of Confucian morals. His comment here "The sage's learning during his entire life did not depart from topics of rituals and music" may also conflict with neo-Confucian moral rigorism because, according to the latter, rituals and music constitute a mere expression of inner virtues.

3.16 The Master said, "In ritual archery, hitting the mark is not emphasized because people's powers are not equal. This is the way of the ancients."[142] [This chapter opens the sixth roll of *Noneo gogeum ju* in traditional book binding and the second volume of it in the Sinjo edition, which corresponds to the eighth volume of the collection of classics in *Yeoyudang jeonseo*.]

子曰; 射不主皮, 爲力不同科, 古之道也.

3.16.1 Grounds

1) I supplement as follows: *She* 射 ("ritual archery") here refers to ritual archery such as the archery for greeting guests from other states or the archery for official banquets;[143] *pi* 皮 ("the mark") is the mark of a target; *zhu pi* 主皮 ("hitting the mark is [not] emphasized") means that in ritual archery stress is not laid on hitting the mark. According to a record regarding the carpenter's job in "Kao gong ji," there were three different types of targets for archery. The first one is the hide target, as seen in "Si qiu 司裘," in *Rites of Zhou*, which says, "In the king's great archery, the officials from the office of making clothes of fur and leather procure the tiger target, the bear target, and the leopard target" (*Zhou li zhushu*, 30:28b).[144] The second one is the colored target, as mentioned in Zheng Xuan's annotation, which says, "With the five colors in turn, they draw rising clouds" (6:8a).[145] The third one is the animal target, as seen in the memorandum attached to "Xiang she li," which says, "The Son of Heaven uses the target of the bear; the feudal lords use the target of the elk;[146] the great officials use the target of the tiger and leopard; the low-ranking

---

[142] *Wei* 爲 ("because") in the main passage should be read in the departing tone [去聲].
[143] See Zheng Xuan's annotation in "Xiang she li" (*Yi li zhushu*, 26:24a).
[144] The side of each target was decorated with the relevant hide.
[145] This means that people draw the pattern.
[146] All of these animals are drawn.

officials use the target of the deer and boar"[147] (*Yi li zhushu*, 5:76b). As for the utility of the targets, the hide target is used for accomplishing merits [through a competition];[148] the colored target is used for offering rituals to guests from other states;[149] the animal target is used for offering relaxation and holding a banquet.[150] These are the differences among them.

Of the three targets, only the hide target is furnished with the mark, while the others are not. Thus "Kao gong ji" says, "Arrange the hide target and furnish it with the mark. This is for accomplishing merit in the spring" (*Zhou li zhushu*, 41:27a).[151] "Si qiu" also says, "In the king's great archery, the officials procure the tiger target, the bear target, and the leopard target and furnish them with the mark."[152] With these records, it becomes evident that they furnished the hide target with the mark. In doing so, they placed the mark at the center of the target after they decorated the sides of the target with the relevant hide.[153] The mark occupied one-third of the target.[154] In the archery for accomplishing merit, hitting the mark is emphasized because [in the competition] they value one's hitting of the mark. In the archery for banquets, hitting the mark is not emphasized, so they do not furnish the target with the mark.

2) I supplement as follows: *Li* 力 ("powers") refers to talents and abilities; *ke* 科 in *bu tong ke* 不同科 ("not equal") refers to a specific quantity or level.[155] *Record of Rites* says, "When pulling a heavy tripod, they do not take into consideration [程] their power."[156] *Bu tong ke* means that everyone has his own limited powers.

3) I supplement as follows: At the time of Our Master, hitting the mark was often emphasized, even in ritual archery. Thus Confucius recited a line of an ancient classic and lamented, "This is the way of the ancients."

3.16.2 Arguments

1) For a classical text on the discussion here, see "Xiang dafu 鄉大夫," in *Rites of Zhou*, which says, "The great official of villages checked with all people

---

[147] Zheng Xuan commented, "For the targets of the rulers, they draw one animal, whereas for the targets of the subjects they draw two animals. This pertains to the numeric regularity of *yin* and *yang*" (*Yi li zhushu*, 5:77a).
[148] "Kao gong ji" says, "[This target is made] in the spring to accomplish merit" (*Zhou li zhushu*, 41:27a).
[149] "Kao gong ji" says, "[This target is made] to deal with the remote states" (*Zhou li zhushu*, 41:27b).
[150] Zheng Xuan commented, "[This target is made] to give relaxation to the old people and comfort the envoys from other states, as in the case in which the ruler and the subjects drink together and have an archery performance" (*Zhou li zhushu*, 41:28b).
[151] See the record of the carpenter's [梓人] job.
[152] "In the feudal lords' archery, the officials procure the bear target and leopard target. In the ministers and the great officials' archery, they procure the elk target. For all these targets, they furnish all of these targets with the mark" (*Zhou li zhushu*, 7:9b).
[153] See the scholium by Jia Gongyan 賈公彥 (fl. 650–655) in "Si qiu" (*Zhou li zhushu*, 7:11a).
[154] See "Kao gong ji" (*Zhou li zhushu*, 41:24a).
[155] The character *ke* displays the form of rice [禾] within a bushel [斗]. This implies that its capacity is limited.
[156] See "Ru xing" (*Li ji zhushu*, 59:6a).

about the five items relevant to the ritual of village archery: the first item was harmony; the second was countenance; the third was hitting the mark; the fourth was harmony and countenance; the fifth was how to dance" (*Zhou li zhushu*, 11:32b).

In my view, "harmony" concerns whether the deportment of participants was harmonious with the music; "countenance" concerns whether their appearance was harmonious with the ritual;[157] "harmony and countenance" is a combination of the previous two items. These three items were applied to the archery for greeting guests from other states or that for official banquets. The third item, "hitting the mark," informs us that hitting the mark was emphasized in archery. So it was applied to the archery for accomplishing merits.[158] Zheng Xuan's annotation on this record was incorrect and failed to convey the meaning of the classic. The great official of villages encouraged villagers to participate in the archery and asked about all of the five things. In this respect, the difference between this record and that of "Xiang she li," in *Protocols and Rituals*, is that this record includes "hitting the mark."

2) For a classical text on the discussion here, see "Xiang she li," which says, "In ritual archery, hitting the mark is not emphasized. In the archery aiming to hit the mark, the winner continues to shoot, whereas the loser descends from the hall" (*Yi li zhushu*, 5:83b). On this record, Zheng Xuan argued, "Ritual archery includes the great archery, the archery for greeting guests from other states, and the archery for official banquets. What is meant by 'hitting the mark is not emphasized' is that in this archery people value the harmony between the participants' appearance and the ritual and that between their deportment and music. In contrast, hitting the target is not regarded as the purpose of this archery. When hitting the mark is emphasized, no formal target is adopted. Rather, they set up the animal's hide and try to hit it since this archery trains them to capture animals eventually" (5:83b–84a).

According to my investigations, in the great archery people adopted the hide target and furnished it with the mark. In contradiction to this, Zheng Xuan argued that hitting the mark was not emphasized, even in the great archery. This was his first error. In the archeries for greeting guests and for official banquets, hitting the target was also valued. In these practices, people merely did not furnish the target with the mark. So the archery performance was halted when someone hit the target. In contradiction to this, Zheng Xuan argued that hitting the target was not the purpose of those archeries. This was his second error. In all under heaven, there has never been such archery in which people shoot arrows at the animal's hide only. In contradiction to this, Zheng Xuan argued that they set up the animal's hide and tried to hit it. This was his third error.[159]

---

[157] "She yi" should be taken as a reference for this meaning.

[158] The implication of the fifth item, "how to dance," is unclear.

[159] Master Zhu commented, "The sentence 'in the ritual archery, hitting the mark is not emphasized' is an excerpt from 'Xiang she li'; the sentence 'people's powers are not equal' is Confucius's interpretation of the ritual" (*Lun yu jizhu*, 2:5b).

3) Ma Rong argued, "The Son of Heaven uses three targets made of the bear hide, the tiger hide, and the leopard hide. The main passage states that in archeries not only is hitting the hide regarded as valuable but showing harmonious deportment is also considered necessary." I would refute this as follows:

If hitting the hide were not to be regarded as valuable when the target is made of the hide, it would mean that people do not value hitting the target. Is there any archery in which hitting the target is not highly valued? In "Xiang dafu," "hitting the mark" is apparently related to the responsibilities of the great official of villages. Regardless, Ma Rong seems to argue that in all kinds of archery in all under heaven, hitting the mark is not emphasized. Is this acceptable? *She* in the main passage refers to ritual archery; *zhu pi* refers to hitting the mark.

4) Ma Rong argued, "*Wei li* 爲力 ('because people's powers') refers to the projects of mobilized labor. They constitute three different levels: upper, middle, and lower. Thus it is said [in Ma Rong's understanding of *bu tong ke*], '[For the projects of the mobilized labor] their levels should vary.'"[160] I would refute this as follows:

"Diguan 地官, Junren 均人" says, "Based on the estimated crop yield, the policies of the mobilized labor are divided in two: the upper and the lower. In the rich year, the people are mobilized for three days on average for public affairs; in the median year [中年: 凶年 in all editions of *Noneo gogeum ju*], they are mobilized for two days on average for the public affairs; in the bad year, they are mobilized for one day on average for the public affairs" (*Zhou li zhushu*, 13:24a). Ma Rong's interpretation derived from this article. However, the two characters, *wei li*, cannot make up a full sentence. Note that Master Zhu commented, "*Wei* should be read in the departing tone."

5) I question Master Zhu as follows:

The phrase in "Yue ji," "shooting arrows to penetrate the hardened leather [革]" (*Li ji zhushu*, 39:19b), concerns penetration of one's armor [not the mark]. In ancient times, armor was made of hardened rhino leather so that penetrating the armor was equivalent to penetrating the hardened leather. In addition, the animal target and the colored target were not furnished with the mark from the beginning. Only the hide target was furnished with the mark. Even in this case, however, the mark was made by weaving in animal hairs, not with the hardened leather. Thus it is not acceptable to call the penetration of the mark "penetration of the hardened leather." Moreover, landing arrows on the mark as well as penetrating the mark should be considered hitting the mark. In general, powerful people are good at archery, and if a man is good at archery he usually hits the mark. How could he be regarded as powerful only after he penetrates the target?

---

[160] Wang Yinglin commented, "Wufeng 五峰 (Hu Hong 胡宏: 1105–1161) accepted this interpretation" (*Kun xue ji wen*, 7:21b).

Mencius thought that [not only muscle power but also] powers of vision and hearing were powerful in other respects.

* * *

In this chapter Dasan again proves his expertise on ancient Confucian rituals, on which all of his refutations of interpretations by his predecessors of the archery practice are based. In "Overview of Original Meanings," Dasan summarizes his long argument in the form of a single creative interpretation of the passage; he asserts that the archery discussed in the main passage only pertains to archery for greeting guests from other states and archery for official banquets—two of the three types of ancient ritual archery. As in most of the other cases in which he suggests an inventive interpretation, he attempts to propose a new understanding of the passage here precisely because he is dissatisfied with the influential comments of his predecessors. In this chapter, the reader may notice his dissatisfaction with existing interpretations—especially in his remark "Is there any archery in which hitting the target is not highly valued?" To him, it was unacceptable to argue, as Ma Rong did, that "in all kinds of archery in all under heaven, hitting the mark is not emphasized," because it contradicted the nature of archery: according to common sense, archery consists of the act of hitting the target by shooting arrows. Dasan must have felt that the interpretations of Han scholars were incorrect. So what could the "original meaning" be? And how might a new interpretation be validated? Dasan must have started to read the classical texts in light of this discussion and found a fresh way to read this passage. This was the usual process by which Dasan created new interpretations (numbering in the hundreds) of the *Analects*.

In other words, Dasan, I believe, did not find problems in previous interpretations of the *Analects* on the basis of his reading of the Confucian classics. Rather, he did that through his rational thinking and then tried to look for evidence in the Confucian classical texts to support his conclusions. Due to this hypothetical method in his research, the reader may notice recurring expressions in his comments like "it is not compatible with principle," "it does not make sense in principle," "it goes against principle," "in light of principle," "in accordance with principle," and many other analogous expressions. All of these expressions contain the character *li*, or *i* in Korean, which may lead the reader to reevaluate the role of the concept *li* in Dasan's philosophy.

As a matter of fact, Zhu Xi also felt that the interpretations of Han scholars, who argued that hitting the mark was not emphasized in all archery rituals, were unacceptable. Zhu Xi's solution was distinct from Dasan's, however, in that he translated the expression *zhu pi* ("hitting the mark") as "penetrating the hardened leather [of the mark]." In Zhu Xi's reading, hitting the mark was still valued, which is in harmony with the nature of archery, but penetrating the mark made of hardened leather was not valued. Dasan did not follow Zhu Xi's reading for the same reason: it does not make sense. As noted in his question to Zhu Xi, Zhu Xi's new interpretation conflicts not only with what is recorded in the classical texts but, more important, with reasonable thought, because archery, in general, must aim at hitting the mark, which can be achieved by landing arrows on the mark—not by penetrating it. So his solution for disentangling the strands of this complex discussion was to apply the teaching of the main passage only to ritual archery, after a thorough investigation on the topic.

More intriguing is that the old commentaries by He Yan, Huang Kan, and Xing Bing uniformly read this passage in a way drastically different from Zhu Xi's reading—something contemporary scholars have not noted. According to the old commentaries, this passage mainly concerns the state's mobilization of labor and not archery rituals. In this interpretation, this passage reads: "In archery, hitting the mark is not emphasized. [Like this] it is the way of ancients to differentiate the levels of labor mobilization [according to the physical conditions of the people who are to be mobilized.]" According to this interpretation of the old commentaries, Confucius criticizes in this chapter the reckless administration of labor mobilization during the last days of the Zhou dynasty and mentions the practice of archery just to give a decent example in which consideration of disparities in people's power belongs to a beautiful tradition. Thus it was Zhu Xi who drastically changed the topic of this passage: in his interpretation, this passage mainly concerned the archery rituals. Dasan followed Zhu Xi in this regard, which reflects how he generally respected Zhu Xi more than he did other commentators. He simply refutes Ma Rong's view on the expression *wei li*, saying that one could not form a full sentence out of these two characters, though Ma did not try to do so.

3.17 Zi Gong wanted to dispense with the sheep for serving the Son of Heaven's envoy for the announcement of the first day. The Master said, "Ci! Do you care for the sheep? I care for the ritual."

子貢欲去告朔之餼羊. 子曰; 賜也! 爾愛其羊? 我愛其禮.

3.17.1 Grounds

1) I supplement as follows: *Gao shou* 告朔 ("the announcement of the first day") refers to the visits of the Son of Heaven's envoy to announce the first day of the year. *Rites of Zhou* records: "The Great Scribe announces the

first day to the enfeoffed states."[161] *Xiyang* 餼羊 ("the sheep for serving the Son of Heaven's envoy") refers to the sheep for serving guests.[162] Since the Zhou was waning at the time, the Great Scribe never visited the states again. Nevertheless, the staff of ritual administration continued to feed the sheep. So Zi Gong wanted to dispense with it.

2) Master Zhu commented, "*Ai* 愛 ('care for') is synonymous with *xi* 惜 (to save)."

3) Bao Xian commented, "If the sheep still exist, the ritual will remain recognizable. If the sheep are removed, however, the ritual will eventually perish."[163]

3.17.2 Arguments

1) Zheng Xuan argued, "Raw sacrifices are called *xi* 餼. It is ritual propriety that the lords of people report on the first days of each month to the royal ancestral shrine. At the time, they hold a sacrificial ritual and call for the court's reception at the ancestral shrine.[164] From the time of Duke Wen, the state of Lu stopped following the ritual of observing the first day. Since Zi Gong realized that the ritual had been discontinued for a long time, he wished to dispense with the sheep." I would refute this as follows:

In my view, the interpretation of *gao shou* and *xiyang* has been an issue upsetting people throughout the ages. For 240 years, the entire duration of the Spring and Autumn period, only one ruler, Duke Wen of Lu, could not follow the ritual of observing the first day four times, due to his illness. Yet people have brought accusations forward of the greatest evil under heaven against all the lords and the subjects of a state [Lu] by saying that the lords of Lu, from Duke Xuan (r. 608–591 BCE) and Duke Cheng (r. 590–573 BCE) onward, never followed the ritual.[165] If this is untrue, is it not an issue that they have provoked the greatest resentment throughout the ages? In my calculation, from the sixteenth year of the reign of Duke Wen (611 BCE) to the time of the people's capture of a giraffe, 130 years passed. If the historians, singling out Duke Wen, recorded that "Duke Wen did not follow the ritual four times," while none of the lords followed the ritual for 130 years, Duke Wen would have felt severe resentment. In contrast to this, one could insist that the lords' observation of the ritual occurred intermittently, without consistency. Then how could Zi Gong encourage the lord to do evil by hastily dispensing with the sheep?

Basically, the ritual of observing the first day consists of three phases. The first phase is the announcement of the first day, in which the lord

---

[161] See "Chunguan" (*Zhou li zhushu* 26:19b).

[162] See "Pin li" (*Yi li zhushu*, 8:84b).

[163] Geng Chutong 耿楚侗 (fl. 1582) commented, "Zi Gong was motivated to dispense with the sheep with his care for the ritual as well. His care, however, was expressed in an intense manner so that he ended up seeming to care about the sheep" (Unknown source).

[164] See *Rites of Zhou*, "Si zunyi 司尊彝" (*Zhou li zhushu*, 20:3a).

[165] They claimed that the lords ignored the mandate of the Son of Heaven on the one hand and on the other turned their backs on the responsibility to protect the people.

presents the announcement of the day issued by the Son of Heaven to his ancestors and then provides his subjects with it. The second phase is the court's reception at the ancestral shrine, in which the lord offers a sacrifice of hogs and sheep to the forefathers and the founder. The third phase is the observation of the first day, in which the lord listens to his ministers at the Great Shrine regarding the state affairs relevant to the time of the first day.

Of these three phases, the first can be omitted, whereas the second and the third cannot. If the second phase is omitted, a state cannot perform the monthly sacrificial ritual for the ancestors, so the state's ritual protocols diminish to the same level as that of the commoners; if the third phase is omitted, one hundred officials cannot receive the ruler's command, and accordingly all the government affairs will come apart. When taking into consideration this potentially disastrous result, a state is unable to evade the ritual even for one month. How could it remain relaxed as if nothing had happened for 130 years? Therefore, the classic says, "In the leap months, they do not present the announcement of the first day to their ancestors. However, they still have the court's reception at the ancestral shrine" (*Zuo zhuan zhushu*, 18:5b). With this record it becomes evident that the court's reception cannot be omitted even when the announcement of the first day has already been omitted. The classic also says, "Summer, the fifth month: The state of Lu did not follow the ritual of observing the first day four times" (20:1a). With this record, it becomes clear that from the sixth month the state of Lu resumed the ritual and continued until the end of the year without omitting the administration of the ritual. Then is it acceptable to say that "from the time of Duke Wen, the state of Lu stopped following the ritual of observing the first day," when the classic never mentioned it? If Zheng's theory was correct, the classic should have said, "Summer, the fifth month: The state of Lu began not to follow the ritual from this month." Why did it merely say, "Summer, the fifth month: The state of Lu did not follow the ritual of observing the first day four times?"

In addition, the sheep for the announcement of the first day must be the same sheep as the one for the court's reception at the shrine. If they dispensed with the sheep, when they had no reason to prepare two sheep for the two phases, respectively, it would mean that the court's reception was also abolished. Now, even minor clerks with poor salaries are capable of offering a sacrifice for the ritual of observing the first day. Imagine that a dignified state of one thousand chariots, having offered the Jiao sacrifices to Heaven and the Di sacrifice to their ancestors amid its glittering culture and civilization, abolishes the ritual for 130 years. Is this acceptable in principle?

I also want to ask a question. Which of the classics supports the argument that sacrifices for the sacrificial rituals are called *xiyang*? In his commentaries on the three *Rites* and the *Analects* of Lu, Zheng Xuan promptly commented, "Raw sacrifices are called *xi*" whenever he came across the character *xi*. Could this definition possibly have been what *Er ya* gave to us or what Du Lin 杜林 (fl. 30) and Xu Shen 許慎 (58–147)

explained to us? I have never seen such an explanation. "Pin li" contains expressions like "a set of steamed ox, hog, and sheep," "two sets of raw [腥] ox, hog, and sheep," and "two sets of raw sacrifices [餼]." In the annotation on these terms, Zheng Xuan commented, "Raw sacrifices are called *xi*" (*Yi li zhushu*, 8:13a). This comment is still acceptable. However, how can the character *xi* uniformly refer to raw sacrifices in all the writings of the nine branches and one hundred schools beyond this record?

In my reading of the ancient classics, it is evident that this character usually refers to certain edible things to offer to guests. Examples of this meaning are found in "Pin li," "Pin yi 聘義," "Si yi 司儀," and "Zhang ke 掌客"; by reading these sources, one may be able to understand that meaning. In addition, the following is recorded in some classical texts: "When Duke Xiang of Shan [單襄公, r. c. 589–574 BCE] went to the state of Chen, the state chef did not send any food [餼];"[166] "Zi Han fled to the state of Jin. Shu Xiang offered him food [餼] for one hundred people."[167] "Huang Wuzi 皇武子 told a man of Qin 秦, 'Provisions [餼] and livestock ran out.'"[168] "Zifu Jingbo 子服景伯 (fl. 492–480 BCE) said to Zi Gong, 'In the gathering of the feudal lords, the proprietor of the meeting location offers something edible [餼]'" (*Zuo zhuan zhushu*, 59:6a).[169] These are the grounds for the meaning of *xi*.

The character *xi* can also be used for three meanings other than "something edible to treat guests to": military provisions, one's salary, and relief food, as seen in the following: "The crown prince of Zheng soundly defeated the troops of Rong 戎. The lord of Qi fed his soldiers with food [餼];"[170] "Duke Chu of Jin [晉出公, r. 474–452 BCE] returned from Linqiu 廩丘. The lord of Jin sent [餼] Zangshi 臧石 a living ox."[171] These excerpts are pertinent to the meaning of military provisions. *Constant Mean* says, "Match their rations [餼] with their work" (*Zhong yong zhangju*, 17a); *Guanzi* says, "Many of the assistants to the magistrate and deputy officials do not have salaries [餼] gained from the field" (*Guanzi*, 9:17a). These excerpts are pertinent to the meaning of salary. *Record of Rites* says, "Widowers, widows, orphans, and old people without offspring are always secured with food for living [餼];"[172] *Zuo's Commentary* also records: "The duke of Qin helped relieve [餼] a famine in the state of Jin with grain."[173] These excerpts are

---

[166] See *Guo yu* (*Guo yu*, 2:13a).
[167] See *Zuo's Commentary* (*Zuo zhuan zhushu*, 41:43b).
[168] See the final year of the reign of Duke Xi (*Zuo zhuan zhushu*, 16:21b).
[169] In the sixth year of the reign of Duke Huan, the great officials of the feudal lord were dispatched to defend the state of Qi. The lord of Qi fed them some food [餼] (*Zuo zhuan zhushu*, 5:30b); in the fourteenth year of the reign of Duke Huan, the duke had a meeting at the state of Cao. The lord of Cao sent some food [餼] (6:25b).
[170] See *Zuo's Commentary* (*Zuo zhuan zhushu*, 5:30b).
[171] See the twenty-fourth year of the reign of Duke Ai (*Zuo zhuan zhushu*, 60:26b).
[172] See "Wang zhi" (*Li ji zhushu*, 13:32a).
[173] See the fifteenth year of the reign of Duke Xi (*Zuo zhuan zhushu*, 13:20a). In the twenty-ninth year of the reign of Duke Xiang, *Zuo's Commentary* also says, "[On experiencing a disease among the people] Zi Pi 子皮 of Zheng fed them with grain" (*Zuo zhuan zhushu*, 39:8b).

pertinent to the meaning of relief food.[174] Then why would it be necessary to render *xi* as raw sacrifices? Actually, there is one more term related to the character *xi*. In "Pin li," rice, millet, hay, and straw are all regarded as *xi*. In this case, it refers to fodder. *Guo yu* records: "Zifu's wife wore clothes made of coarse hemp, and the fodder [餼] for his horse was no more than the foxtails of weeds" (*Guo yu*, 4:19a). This means that something for feeding horses was called *xi*. In ancient times, people named anything uncooked, whether grain or meat, which was used to offer to guests as *xi*. And as time passed, all kinds of edible things provided for others came to be called *xi*. Therefore the *Outer Commentary* [*Guo yu*] records: "The state chef provides meals; the warehouse keeper sends out edible things [餼]" (2:15b). In accord with this definition, even things for feeding horses came to be called *xi*.

This is an explanation of the original definition of *xi*. Unfortunately, Zheng Xuan stuck to its definition as "raw sacrifices," due to which sacrifices for the sacrificial ritual were eventually called *xiyang*. In extensive reading of the nine classics, can anyone find a case in which the sacrificial offerings, in the rituals for the Jiao sacrifice, ancestors, the land god, the grain god, mountains, rivers, and one hundred spirits, are necessarily called *xi*? Decisively, there is no such case. Why is it so? It is because you cannot treat your ancestors as guests, or entertain spirits, in the same way you feed the soldiers, or regard the solemn shrines as places in which to provide relief food. All in all, what do *gao shou* and *xiyang* mean? I claim that *xiyang* refers to the sheep for feeding guests.

With regard to this, "Chunguan, Taishi 大史" records: "The Great Scribe announces the first day to the enfeoffed states" (*Zhou li zhushu*, 26:19b). When he was about to promulgate it, he paid visits to the states. Then how could the states not feed him according to the rituals for guests? At the time of Zi Gong, however, the Way of Zhou had waned more seriously, and accordingly, the Great Scribe of the king could not pay visits to the states to promulgate the announcement of the first day. Yet the officers of ritual administration were still in charge of the sheep for the Great Scribe, overseeing their nourishment and nutrition and thereby wasting the fodder. On seeing this, Zi Gong wanted to dispense with the sheep.

Alas! The practice of promulgating the announcement of the first day had endured for a long time. "Yao dian" records: "[Yao let his officials] observe the sun, the moon, the stars, and the constellations so as to make known respectfully the time to be used by people" (*Shang Shu zhushu*, 1:8b). The work of tilling in the spring, harvesting in the fall, weeding in the summer, and storing in the winter was also commanded by the Son of Heaven. Even in the Xia, this law was preserved, which can be attested to by "Xia xiaozheng 夏小正," which has been transmitted to us.[175] Even in

---

[174] A line of a poem in *Poetry* reads: "Lament these widowers and widows" (*Mao Shi zhushu*, 18:2b). On this, Zheng Xuan commented, "This poem conveys a wish to provide them with relief food [餼]" (18:2b). Another poem reads: "The government became lax with all in its distribution" (25:57a). On this, Zheng Xuan commented, "Relief food was insufficient" (25:57a).

[175] "Yong bing 用兵," in *Da Dai Li ji*, records: "At the time of King Jie of Xia and King Zhou of Shang, their calendars deviated from the normal standard, and accordingly the star Sheti 攝提 lost its direction. Thus they did not announce the first day to the feudal lords" (*Da Dai Li ji*, 11:9a).

the nasty Qin, they wrote one chapter called "Yue ling" and proclaimed it to all under heaven. All of these are the old decrees relevant to the announcement of the first day. At the time of Duke Wen, this law had not yet perished, so they did not announce the first day in the leap months, regarding which Confucius left a record in *Spring and Autumn*. When it came down to the last days of Lu, the king's envoys did not arrive, so the sheep for serving them became useless. Regardless, if they had eventually dispensed with the legacy of the king, it would have ceased permanently. This is the reason that Confucius uttered his lamentation. Is Zheng's theory harmonious with principle?[176]

* * *

Dasan's disagreement with the old and new commentaries, which are entirely based on Zheng Xuan's comments on the main passage and other records relevant to it, arose from his belief that it was unlikely that the state of Lu never observed the ritual of the first day of the month, one of the most significant Confucian rituals, for 130 years, following its last administration by Duke Wen. It seemed especially unlikely in view of the fact that the state of Lu was famed for its preservation of Confucian rituals and music and that even a low-ranking official would observe some of the rituals for the first day of the month. Dasan found a clue in Mao Qiling's argument for a way to overcome the old and new commentaries: Mao criticized the old and new commentaries because he thought they narrowly depended on Zheng Xuan's comments without referring to other classics. Mao further insisted that the performance of the announcement of the first day should be distinguished from the observation of the rituals of the first day in which the ruler discusses urgent matters with his ministers in order to issue administrative orders—an opinion Dasan accepted.

Dasan's interpretation, however, differs from Mao's in many aspects. First, Dasan regarded the announcement of the first day and the court's reception at the ancestral shrine as two separate rituals, whereas Mao believed that they occurred simultaneously. Second, Dasan did not agree with Zheng Xuan's allegation that after the period of Duke Wen, the state of Lu stopped observing the entire ritual of the first day, whereas Mao accepted that claim. Third, Dasan thought it excusable for a feudal state not to perform the announcement of the first day when the Zhou court could not send the king's envoy to supervise it, whereas Mao did not discuss this matter. Fourth, according to Dasan the character *xi* refers to something edible and prepared for guests—not raw sacrifices, which is the definition Zheng Xuan gave the term and Mao accepted.

---

[176] According to *Rites of Zhou*, the office of the Great Scribe is constituted of two low-level great officials and four upper-level low-ranking officials; the office of Lesser Scribe is constituted of eight middle-level low-ranking officials and sixteen low-level low-ranking officials (*Zhou li zhushu*, 17:19a).

Fifth, Dasan eventually asserted that the sheep Zi Gong wished to dispense with was *xiyang*—the sheep that the state of Lu was feeding to treat the king's envoy anytime he arrived—and not the one prepared for the court's reception, because in his view the state of Lu could not omit the reception for which the sheep was required.

Although all commentators agreed that this passage contains Confucius's lamentation about his time, to Dasan this passage especially conveys Confucius's sorrow over the irresistible decline of the Zhou culture, while to others it displays Confucius's criticism of the violation of ritual propriety by Lu. In this chapter, Dasan does not raise direct questions to Zhu Xi because Zhu Xi just adopted the old commentaries. At any rate, he presents a new interpretation, so that it is listed in "Overview of Original Meanings."

3.18 The Master said, "The full observance of ritual propriety in serving one's lord: people deem this flattery."

子曰; 事君盡禮, 人以爲諂也.

3.18.1 Grounds

1) Kong Anguo commented, "At the time those who served their lords often failed to abide by ritual propriety. Thus people tended to consider those who followed it flatterers."

3.18.2 Arguments

1) I question Master Zhu as follows:
    The old commentaries related the expression "the full observance of ritual propriety in serving one's lord" not only to Confucius but to others. *Lun yu jizhu*, however, argued that it was pertinent to Confucius's deeds.

* * *

In this chapter, *Lun yu jizhu* invokes Cheng Yi's admiration for Confucius's virtue, which he thought could be observed in Confucius's modest criticism of his contemporaries: "If another person were to discuss an issue of this sort, he would have said, 'My full observance of ritual propriety in serving my lord: the petty people deem this flattery.' However, Confucius's remark was not born out of resentment. The sage's Way is unrestricted and his virtue is enormous, as is evident here" (*Lun yu jizhu*, 2:6b). Dasan followed the old commentary probably because Cheng Yi's comment seems speculative.

3.19 Duke Ding asked, "How should a lord command his ministers? How should a minister serve his lord?" Confucius replied, "A lord should command his ministers with ritual propriety. A subject should serve his lord with wholeheartedness."

定公問; 君使臣, 臣事君, 如之何? 孔子對曰; 君使臣以禮, 臣事君以忠.

3.19.1 Grounds

1) Kong Anguo commented, "Duke Ding is a posthumous title for a lord of the state of Lu."[177]
2) Dazai Jun commented, "Ji Huanzi ousted Duke Zhao, so Duke Zhao eventually died at Qianhou 乾侯. This implies that Ji Huanzi violated the morals of a subject in an extreme manner. Duke Ding succeeded the throne as the younger brother of Duke Zhao and became anxious about his position. Thus he asked this question."

3.19.2 Arguments

1) Xing Bing argued, "If a lord were not to follow ritual propriety, the subjects would also spare themselves the effort to be wholehearted."[178]
   In respect to this, Dongjian 東澗 [Yan Ruoqu] contested: "In discussing the father's benevolence and the son's filial piety, if one links these virtues with 'if,' the entire meaning becomes distorted" (Kun xue ji wen, 7:16a).

* * *

What Yan Ruoqu criticized about Xing Bing's view was that wholeheartedness, like the unconditional moral obligation of filial piety, was to be imposed on the subjects unconditionally. In other words, it was normative and not contingent on the lord's actions. By introducing Yan's view, Dasan indicates that he accepted this perspective of deontological ethics.

3.20 The Master said, "The Guanju is joyful but not provocative; it is sad but not hurtful."

子曰; 關雎, 樂而不淫, 哀而不傷.

---

[177] Xing Bing commented, "According to 'Lu shi jia 魯世家,' 'Duke Ding, whose name was Song 宋, was the son of Duke Xiang and the younger brother of Duke Zhao. According to Shi fa, those who gave comfort to the people and were very considerate were given the title 'Ding.'"
[178] Yin Hejing 尹和靖 (fl. 1126–1127) also argued, "The lord and the subjects are associated through rightness. Thus if a lord commands his subjects with ritual propriety, the subjects will serve their lord with wholeheartedness" (Lun yu jizhu, 2:6b).

3.20.1 Grounds

1) I supplement as follows: The Guanju here refers to the three poems led by the Guanju ode.[79] Even when indulging in the music of lutes, small and large, bells, and drums, one does not lose respect. This is to be joyful but not provocative. Even when ascending a hill on the back of an emaciated horse, one does not sorrow long. This is to be sad but not hurtful.

3.20.2 Arguments

1) In my investigation, *Zuo's Commentary* records: "When Mushu 穆叔 (d. 537 BCE) went to the state of Jin . . . [t]he Viscount of Jin offered him a banquet. . . . [M]usicians sang the three poems led by 'Wenwang 文王' and then sang another three poems led by 'Lu ming 鹿鳴.' "[80] Likewise, ancient people usually presented poems by lumping together three poems and marking them with the title of the first poem. Thus "the Guanju" here includes the first poem Guanju ode, the Getan 葛覃 ode, and the Juaner 卷耳 ode. The Guanju ode is joyful but not provocative; the Getan ode is fatiguing but not resentful;[81] and the Juaner ode is sad but not hurtful. If the reader appreciates these poems by incorporating the comments of Jizi and Confucius, their meaning will stand out by itself. The Juaner ode reads: "I hope that I may not have to think of him long. . . . I hope that I may not have to sorrow long" (*Mao Shi zhushu*, 1:44a). Isn't this what is meant by "sad but not hurtful?"

2) Xing Bing argued, "The Preface of *Poetry* said, '[The Guanju ode] expresses sympathy for a virtuous lady and is thoughtful of a virtuous and talented man without showing an attitude of undermining the good.' " I would refute this.

    For detail, see my "Seo-am ganghak gi."

* * *

According to "Seo-am ganghak gi," Dasan's record of an academic meeting held at Seo-am in 1795, his unique understanding of the term "Guanju" came from Yi Sam-hwan. Yi, a nephew of Yi Ik, who heralded the Practical Learning, was the eldest participant in the meeting and a renowned scholar among his contemporaries. He argued, "In ancient times, people lumped together three poems when they discussed lyrical poems. Thus 'Zhou nan 周南,' which contains the local lyrical poems of Zhou, presents three poems—the Guanju ode, the Getan ode, and the Juaner ode—together. 'Shao nan 召南' also presents three poems—the Quechao 鵲巢 ode, the Caipan ode 采蘩, and the Caiping

---

[79] For more details, see the following discussion.
[80] See the fourth year of the reign of Duke Xiang (*Zuo zhuan zhushu*, 29:23b–24a).
[81] This is a comment by Jizi 季子 from Yanling 延陵 [季札].

采蘋 ode—together.... [I]n my view, the expression 'joyful but not provocative' fits the tune of the Guanju ode; the expression 'sad but not hurtful' fits the tune of the Juaner ode" ("Seo-am ganghak gi," 465c). Actually, Yi's view was formed in response to Dasan's inquiry into the nature of the Guanju: in the inquiry, Dasan suspected that the expression "sad but not hurtful" had nothing to do with the content of the Guanju ode. Thus, in a sense, the unique interpretation of the term "Guanju," which is listed in "Overview of Original Meanings," originated from Dasan's own critical mind.

Introducing Yi's view, Dasan wished to supplement it: he offered additional evidence for the conventional practice of grouping three poems together and unearthed a prototypical passage of appreciation for the Getan ode, the second poem in the Guanju trio, from a record in *Zuo's Commentary*. In this record, Jizi (576–484 BCE), a prince of the state of Chu, left a lengthy appraisal of the major poems of *Poetry*, which he had had an opportunity to listen to during his diplomatic visit to the state of Lu. Thanks to a historian's record of his appraisal, it became known as the earliest comment on the lyrical poems of *Poetry*. Even though it is debatable whether the expression "fatiguing but not resentful" pertains exclusively to the Getan poem, since Jizi describes the entirety of "Zhou nan" and "Shao nan" with this phrase (see *Zuo zhuan zhushu*, 39:14a), Dasan's attempt to supplement Yi's view shows that his knowledge of the Confucian classics became profound in the years after his participation in the academic meeting at Seo-am.

3.21 Duke Ai asked Zai Wo about the altar of the land god. Zai Wo replied, "The sovereign of the Xia used pine; the lord of the Yin used cypress; the lord of the Zhou used chestnut, meant to make the people fearful." On hearing this, the Master said, "Things that are done, I do not speak about; things that are accomplished arbitrarily, I do not remonstrate about; things that are past, I do not blame."[182]

哀公問社於宰我. 宰我對曰; 夏后氏以松, 殷人以柏, 周人以栗, 曰使民戰栗. 子聞之曰; 成事不說, 遂事不諫, 既往不咎.

3.21.1 Grounds

1) Master Zhu commented, "Zai Wo was Confucius's disciple, whose name was Yu 予."[183]

---

[182] In the editions of Zhang Yu 張禹 (d. 5 BCE), Bao Xian, and Zhoushi 周氏 [周生烈], *wen she* 問社 ("asked about the altar of the land god") appears as *wen zhu* 問主 (asked about the spiritual wooden tablet in the altar of the land god).

[183] Xing Bing commented, "According to *Shi ji*, 'Zai Wo's adult name was Zi Wo 子我'" (*Shi ji*, 67:7b). Zheng Xuan commented, "[He was] a man of Lu" (67:7b). For more information, see the following passage.

2) Kong Anguo commented, "In general, when a state erected the altar of the land god following its establishment, it planted trees most suitable for its soil.[184] Ignorant of the real implications of the practice, Zai Wo fabricated a theory to contend that the Zhou's adoption of chestnut [栗] was 'meant to make the people fearful [栗].'"

3) Master Zhu commented, "*Zhanli* 戰栗 ('fearful') is a term that describes people who feel fear. In ancient times, the government often executed people at the altar of the land god. Zai Wo based his theory on this practice."

4) I supplement as follows: *Sui* 遂 means to accomplish things arbitrarily.[185] Zai Wo wished to compel his lord to show majesty and aspire for valor. Therefore Confucius criticized him.

3.21.2 Arguments

1) Zhao De 趙惪 (fl. 1328) argued, "In the fifth year of the reign of Duke Ding, the lord of Lu pledged an oath with the three Huan to the Zhou altar of the land god and then with the people to the Bo altar of the land god. Thus the two altars of Lu were the places to summon the people to alert them. In the fourth year of the reign of Duke Ai, a fire broke out at the Bo altar. I suspect that Duke Ai asked this question with some concerns stemming from the fire at the Bo altar" (Unknown source). I would refute this as follows:

   If so, why did Duke Ai and Zai Wo converse only on the meaning of the Zhou altar on the fire at the Bo altar?

2) Kong Yingda argued, "In this passage of the *Analects*, the character *hou* 后 ('sovereign') is only applied to the founder of the Xia. In this regard, *Baihu tong* records: 'King Yu [the founder of the Xia] received the kingly authority through a simple bow [to appreciate the concession of the position] that came exclusively to be called *hou*.' The reason the founders of the Yin and the Zhou were called *ren* 人 ('lord') is that people [人] eventually returned to them, impressed with their practice of humanity and rightness."[186] I would refute this as follows:

   In "Zhou yu," the crown prince Jin 晉 (565–549 BCE) said, "When Bo Yu 伯禹 [King Yu] finished dredging the rivers, the great Heaven commended him for his deeds. Because of this, all under heaven was entrusted to him. He was also granted the clan name Si 姒 and the family name You Xia 有夏. On Yu's obtaining of all under heaven, he continued to use his family name [Xia] as the title of his dynasty. Thus he came to be called 'the sovereign of the Xia [夏后氏]'" (*Guo yu*, 3:9a–b).[187]

---

[184] Xing Bing commented, "The Xia capital Anyi 安邑 was suitable for growing pine; the Yin capital Bo 亳 was suitable for growing cypress; and the Zhou capitals Feng 豐 and Hao 鎬 were suitable for growing chestnut. Each dynasty planted the tree suitable for its soil."

[185] *Changes* says, "The wife does nothing by herself [遂]" (*Zhou Yi zhushu*, 6:29b). *Gongyang's Commentary* also says, "The great officials do not accomplish things by their own will [遂]" (*Chunqiu Gongyang zhuan zhushu*, 5:8a).

[186] See Kong's scholium on "Tangong" (*Li ji zhushu*, 6:16a).

[187] My second elder brother said, "Ancient people were artless and simple. When they obtained all under heaven, they continued to use the original official title that they received as viscounts or dukes, without separately creating the title of the dynasty. It was not until the time of King Tang that they

3) He Xiu argued, "*Song* 松 ('pine') is here synonymous with *rong* 容 (appearance). [The purpose of] the adoption of this tree was to have people worship the god by imagining its appearance. It implies that the Xia people would adopt the human-based calendar [the Xia calendar]; *bai* 柏 ('cypress') is here synonymous with *po* 迫 (to approach). The adoption of this tree was to have people get close to the god without parting away. It implies that the Yin people would adopt the earth-based calendar [the Yin calendar]; *li* 栗 ('chestnut') connotes the meaning of trembling that portrays the august and reverence-inspiring look. It implies that the Zhou people would adopt the heaven-based calendar [the Zhou's calendar]."[188] *Er ya yi* also records: "According to Xu Xun's 徐鉉 (916–991) theory ... [w]hen its shield cracks, the chestnut dangles dangerously from the tree—this is an image provoking fear" (*Er ya yi* 爾雅翼, 10:8a). I would refute these as follows:

Since there were always six categories of Chinese characters, it has been possible to create a character by emulating [諧] an existing character's sound. When people gave a name to things in the past, they frequently used this method. In accordance with this practice, Confucius said, "Humanity [*ren*] refers to being human [*ren*]" (*Zhong yong zhangju*, 14b), and "To rule [*zheng*] is to correct [*zheng*]" (*Lun yu jizhu*, 12:17). It was also this method that Zai Wo used when he rendered *li* as "fearful." As a fruit, on the other hand, the chestnut is as hard and rigid as jade, so the temper of a rigid person is also described with this character *li*. An expression in "Yu shu 虞書," "tolerant but rigid [*li*]" (*Shang Shu zhushu*, 2:36b), is an example of this meaning. Indeed, being respectful and diligent often leads to the mindset of self-control. Thus people also use this character [*li*] to indicate this mindset [齊栗]. In its excessive form, it amounts to a fearful mindset. This transformation of the meaning of a character is related to the category of the phonetic loan characters [假借], among the six categories. He Xiu's theory originated from Zai Wo. Similarly, in their discussion of the classics, Han Confucians contested: "The paulownia tree [桐] refers to conformity [同]" (*Yi li zhushu*, 13:60b); "the bamboo tree [竹] refers to grief [蹙]" (*Baihu tongyi*, B:64a);[189] "[according to Liu Xiang] the mulberry tree [桑] refers to loss [喪]" (*Yu ding peiwen yunfu* 御定佩文韻府, 99D:56b). Their far-fetched and interpolated arguments had no limit. All of them, however, are distortions of learning.

4) For a classical text on the discussion here, see "Da si tu," in *Rites of Zhou*, which says, "The head minister of the masses identifies the number of feudal states and fiefs inside the imperial domain and creates boundaries

---

created a title for the dynasty to distinguish themselves from viscounts and dukes. As a result, in the pre-Qin writings, the names of the sovereigns prior to the sovereign of the Xia uniformly included the suffix *shi* 氏. After the Yin and the Zhou, the names of the rulers included the suffix *ren*."

[188] See He's annotation in the second year of the reign of Duke Wen in *Gongyang's Commentary* (*Chunqiu Gongyang zhuan zhushu*, 13:6b–7a).

[189] This remark is related to the funeral cane.

for the imperial domain by building ditches and barriers. He establishes the sanctum of the land god and grain god, in which he plants trees as the field lords.[190] In doing so, he uses the variety of tree most suitable for the soil[191] and eventually adopts the tree's name for the name of the sanctum and the field that surrounds it" (*Zhou li zhushu*, 10:3a).[192] Also see "Fengren 封人" (12:15a) and a scholium on the passage from "Da si tu" above by Jia Gongyan, which says, "The expression 'to plant the field lords' in the 'Da si tu' means that they planted trees within the registered field and regarded it as the field lords."

In my view, the land god and grain god were in the first place the earth spirits,[193] like Hou Tu 后土 or Hou Ji 后稷. In the sacrificial rituals for the earth spirits, they were coupled with the former sages, such as Julong 句龍 or Zhou Qi 周棄. Besides the earth spirits and the former sages, people planted a tree for the so-called field lord and regarded it as the symbol of the spirit to whom all fields belong. In remote antiquity, people followed this convention, and the sages did not discard it in their compliance with the ancient systems. "Meishi 媒氏," in *Rites of Zhou*, records: "Legal disputes that stem from relationships between males and females are held at the altar of the grain god of the previous dynasty" (*Zhou li zhushu*, 14:22b). In accordance with this, the early Confucians mentioned: "Duke Shao heard a legal dispute at the altar of the crab apple tree" (*Zuo zhuan zhushu*, 32:19a). Later uses of terms such as the altar of the chestnut-leaved oak[194] or the altar of the elm[195] are all remnants of the ancient customs.

5) For a classical text that contains various names of trees for spirits, see *Baihu tong* (*Baihu tongyi*, A:19b–20a).

6) I explore the textual differences as follows:

Xing Bing argued, "In the Zhang Yu, Bao Xian, and Zhoushi editions, the main passage reads: 'Duke Ai asked Zai Wo about the wooden tablet [主].' Some early Confucians deciphered this as referring to the spiritual wooden tablet in the royal ancestral shrine[196] or the tree that was to be regarded as the spiritual tablet in the altar of the grain god." Huang Kan also argued: "The *Analects* with Zheng Xuan's commentary states, 'Duke Ai asked about the wooden tablet.'" For more classical texts on this assertion, see Lu Deming's comment (*Jingdian shi wen*, 24:4b, 4); Kong Yingda's scholium on a passage in the second year of the reign of Duke Wen in *Zuo's Commentary* (*Zuo zhuan zhushu*, 17:11b, 6); Yichuan's [Cheng Yi] comment

---

[190] This means that they regarded the trees as the lords of the field.

[191] Zheng Xuan commented, "For example, they include the pine tree, cypress, and chestnut tree" (*Zhou li zhushu*, 10:3a).

[192] Zheng Xuan commented, "When the pine tree was planted, they named the field 'the field of the pine tree sanctum'" (*Zhou li zhushu*, 10:3a).

[193] For this meaning, see "Da Zongbo."

[194] See *Zhuangzi* (*Zhuangzi zhu* 莊子注, 2:15a).

[195] See *Han shu* (*Qian Han shu*, 25-A: 19a).

[196] Du Yuankai 杜元凱 [Du Yu] and He Xiu accepted this meaning in their interpretation of *Spring and Autumn*.

(*Er Cheng yishu*, 21-B:1b, 4); and Wang Yinglin's comment (*Kun xue ji wen* 7:11b, 4–5). In respect to this issue, Mao Qiling argued: "In the *Analects* from Qi, *she* 社 ('the land god') appears as zhu 主 (spiritual tablet). The spiritual tablet in the sanctum of the land god is made of stone, not wood.[197] When people discussed the system of spiritual tablets in the Tang dynasty, they relied on *Lüshi Chunqiu* and Zheng Xuan's interpretation of the term, which is in harmony with the wording in the *Analects* from Qi" (*Lun yu jiqiu pian*, 2:8a).

According to my investigation, Zhang Yu, Viscount Anchang 安昌, studied the theory of the *Analects* from Qi. However, the *Analects* from Qi is full of errors and is not worthy of discussions.

* * *

In this chapter, the reader again sees Dasan's critical and rational stance against superfluously speculative theories. He rebuts Zhao De's theory because it is not consistent with the narrative of the main passage; he disproves Kong Yingda's theory on the grounds that it contradicts what is recorded in a more reliable source; he dismisses He Xiu's and Xu Xun's theories because they are far-fetched; he questions Mao Qiling's theory, at least in part, because it is dependent on a dubious text, the *Analects* from Qi (Dasan's interpretation here was partially influenced by Mao's theory). In support of his rejection of these theories, Dasan referred to the *Analects, Guo yu,* and *Rites of Zhou.*

As seen here, it is Dasan's unyielding principle to draw conclusions in his research on the basis of contexts and narratives of the classical texts—not on sources whose authenticity can hardly be proven. Given that he wrote *Noneo gogeum ju* while in exile, far away from the geographical core of Korean academia, not to mention that of Chinese academia, he must have had limited access to their vast collections of Chinese documents, though he was allowed to use the secluded personal library of one of his family members. In other words, it is likely that he had no means of scrutinizing all the claims that were suggested by scholars who had more access to libraries containing research materials. It would have been inevitable for him to rely only on the more authentic texts that were available, even with such scant resources. However, this point should not be taken to mean that his circumstances forced him to join the academic trend of legitimism. Rather, his gravitation toward the classical sources matches his aspiration to become a legitimate interpreter of the Confucian teachings. Accordingly, he believed that it had become a common academic trend of Han Confucianism to propose excessively speculative arguments, which he considered an abuse of academic freedom. Hence, his excoriation of Han scholars in his comment of this

---

[197] Since the sanctum of the land god has no roof and thereby no shrine to enshrine the wooden spiritual tablet, they used the stone spiritual tablet.

chapter: "Their far-fetched and interpolated arguments had no limit. All of them, however, are distortions of learning."

3.22 The Master said, "Guan Zhong's capacity was small indeed!" Someone said, "Was Guan Zhong frugal, then?" The Master replied, "Guan Zhong married three women and did not assign his house officials multiple duties related to his house's affairs. How can he be considered frugal?" Someone said, "Did Guan Zhong know ritual propriety, then?" The Master replied, "Only the lords of the states can fence the gate with a screen; Guan fenced the gate with a screen too. Only the lords of the states can have a stand for returning drinking cups to promote a relationship with another lord; Guan had this stand too. If Guan knew ritual propriety, who does not know it?"

> 子曰; 管仲之器小哉! 或曰; 管仲儉乎? 曰; 管氏有三歸, 官事不攝, 焉得儉?
> 然則管仲知禮乎? 曰; 邦君樹塞門, 管氏亦樹塞門, 邦君爲兩國之好有反坫,
> 管氏亦有反坫. 管氏而知禮, 孰不知禮?

3.22.1 Grounds

1) Master Zhu commented, "Guan Zhong refers to the great official of Qi whose name was Yiwu 夷吾."

2) I supplement as follows: *Qi xiao* 器小 ("capacity is small") means that his receptiveness is limited.

3) Bao Xian commented, "*Sam gui* 三歸 ('married three women') refers to marrying three women with different surnames. Noble ladies' marriages are called *gui*."[198]

4) I supplement as follows: To take over one's responsibility for certain tasks as a favor for him is called *she* 攝 ("appoint his house officials multiple duties").[199]

5) Bao Xian commented, "The lord of the state naturally has much business and employs separate officers for each office. The great officials, however, appoint their house officials multiple duties. At the time, each of Guan Zhong's house officials occupied a separate office. This cannot be considered frugal."

---

[198] Huang Kan commented, "According to ritual propriety, the feudal lord marries nine women from three states in one marriage: one woman from the largest state becomes his legitimate wife, and her niece and younger sister, called niece-in-law and sister-in-law, accompany her to become his concubines. Besides this, two women from two different states become his maid-wives [媵]. These maid-wives are also accompanied by their niece [niece-in-law to the lord] and sister [sister-in-law to the lord]. Since three women from each of the three states are engaged in this marriage, the number of women amounts to nine. Great officials' marriages do not involve other states. However, they marry three women within the state: one becomes his wife and the other two become his concubines as niece-in-law and sister-in-law."

[199] A passage in the second year of the reign of Duke Cheng in *Zuo's Commentary* reads: "I have taken over [攝] this office to fill a vacant position" (*Zuo zhuan zhushu*, 25:17b).

6) I supplement as follows: *Shu* 樹 ("screen") is here synonymous with *bing* 屏 (folding screen);[200] *sai* 塞 ("fence") is synonymous with *bi* 蔽 (to cover).

7) Zheng Xuan commented, "The lord of people separates inner quarters from outer quarters by the gate. For this, he places a screen at the gate to intercept others' views."

8) I supplement as follows: *Hao* 好 ("to promote the relationship") means that neighboring states attempt to improve their relationships through meetings.

9) I supplement as follows: *Fandian* 反坫 ("a stand for returning drinking cups") refers to a tool for returning drinking vessels, which was made of clay. It was placed between two pillars.[201]

10) Zheng Xuan commented, "According to the ritual of offering wine, the host and the guest are to return the drinking cups by placing them on the stand when they finish drinking."

3.22.2 Arguments

1) For classical texts on the discussion here, see *Zhanguo ce* 戰國策, which says, "Lord Wen of the Zhou [東周文君, r. 259–249 BCE] fired Ji 籍, the Master of Construction, and appointed Lü Cang 呂倉 to the office of prime minster. The people of the Zhou were displeased and said: 'The lord of Song constructed his pavilion by depriving the people of the farming time. The people criticized him, but no loyal ministers came forward to cover his fault. Whereupon Zi Han resigned from the post of prime minister and became Si gong 司空 [the head official of construction].[202] So the people came to criticize Zi Han [for the construction of the pavilion], considering the lord favorably. Duke Huan of Qi [齊桓公, r. 685–643 BCE] had a crowd of ladies at court to the extent that there were seven hundred residence halls for ladies. The people of Qi criticized him. Whereupon Guan Zhong intentionally married three women from three different families to cover Duke Huan's fault,[203] so that he himself received the people's blame'" (*Zhanguo ce*, 1:5b); Mao Qiling's comment on this record (*Lun yu jiqiu pian*, 2:2a, 2–6); "Li yue zhi 禮樂志," in *Han shu* (*Qian Han shu*, 22:14a, 1–2); "Huo zhi liezhuan 貨殖列傳 [食貨志 in all editions of *Noneo gogeum ju*]" (*Shi ji*, 129:3b, 1); "Gongsun Hong zhuan 公孫弘傳," in *Han shu* (*Qian Han shu*, 58:7a).

   Owing to these grounds, in my view, it is evident that *san gui* refers to marrying three women.

---

[200] According to *Er ya*, "The folding screen is called *shu*" (*Er ya zhushu*, 4:8a).
[201] They called it *fandian* to distinguish it from other stands such as *chongdian* 崇坫 or *sidian* 食坫.
[202] Si gong was the primary supervisor of public construction. According to *Zuo's Commentary*, "Zi Han himself held a whip and beat the people to finish the construction" (*Zuo zhuan zhushu*, 33:11b).
[203] Bao Biao 鮑彪 (fl. 1156) commented, "Noble ladies' marriages are called *gui*, and men's marriages, *jia* 家. This passage means that Guan Zhong married three women" (*Baoshi Zhanguo ce zhu* 鮑氏戰國策注, 2:12b).

2) For discussion on the textual differences here, see *Shuo yuan* by Liu Xiang 劉向 (77–6 BCE) (*Shuo yuan* 說苑, 11:3a, ll. 1–5); *Da Ming yitong zhi* 大明一統志, which says, "The Pavillion of *Sangui* in Yanzhou 兖州 prefecture of Shangdong 山東 is located two *li* miles west of Dong'a 東阿 county. Guan Zhong is known to have constructed it" (quoted in *Rongo kokun gaiden*).

On these records, Mao Qiling explained, "Liu Xiang, the author of *Shuo yuan*, found that *Zhanguo ce* recorded both episodes of Zi Han and Guan Zhong at the same place, which uniformly pertain to the minister's endeavor to cover the faults of his lord. He also noticed that the expression *san gui* was not clearly connected to the vocabulary for marriage [娶]. Finally, he suspected that they shared the same story. He confused the state of Qi with the state of Song, Guan Zhong with Zi Han, and marrying women with constructing a pavilion, and dared to change the character for men's marriage [家] to the character for pavilion [臺].[204] . . . [S]omeone said, '[Guan Zhong's] pavilion of *san gui* was constructed and named after his marriage with three women. In the past, people often constructed a pavilion to commemorate a person's marriage. In *Poetry*, Duke Xuan of Wei [衛宣公, r. 718–700 BCE] constructed a new pavilion when marrying a lady from the state of Qi; in *Zuo's Commentary*, Duke Zhuang of Lu [魯莊公, r. 693–661 BCE] constructed a pavilion that stretched out to the residence of Dangshi 黨氏 when marrying Meng Ren 孟任.' The allegation that Guan constructed a pavilion, however, is groundless, so this explanation cannot be accepted" (*Lun yu jiqiu pian*, 2:12a–13a).

In my view, Duke Huan's care for Guan Zhong enabled him to have a secure life to the end and did not change until the last moment. If *Shuo yuan*'s narrative is true, Duke Huan might have divested Guan Zhong of his power during the early years of Guan Zhong's success. The theory of *Shuo yuan* is not worth an introduction.

3) I question Master Zhu as follows:

Master Zhu argued, "This part[205] only points to Guan Zhong's lavishness, while the part that follows portrays him as ignorant of ritual propriety due to his violation of it. I am afraid that the theory of Guan Zhong's marriage with three women is not acceptable" (*Zhuzi yu lei*, 25:41a). In my view, the subjects and concubines are similar to one another in nature. "Not assigning the house officials multiple duties for one's house's affairs" and "preparing concubines and maid-wives with various family names"[206] are the same thing. If they are related to the matter of violating ritual propriety, both of them are related to the matter; if they are related to the matter of lavishness, both of them are related to the matter; if they are related to the

---

[204] *Shuo yuan* records: "Guan Zhong constructed a pavilion so as to receive the people's blame" (*Shuo yuan*, 11:3a). The phrase "to receive the people's blame" derives from *Zhanguo ce*.

[205] This refers to the first part of the main passage.

[206] "Qu li" contains a passage that says, "[When a family sends its female offspring to the Son of Heaven, the envoy should state that] I have prepared the hundred families" (*Li ji zhushu*, 5:37b).

matter of being ignorant of ritual propriety, both of them are related to the matter. Why should giving house officials separate responsibilities constitute lavishness but marrying women with various family names constitute a violation of ritual propriety? I am afraid that the old commentary is more persuasive.

4) Huang Kan argued, "Although the lords of the states can marry three women from three states, their governments should deal with one family."[207] I would refute this as follows:

Duke Zhuang of Wei (r. 757–735 BCE) married a woman from the state of Qi, who was later known as Zhuang Jiang 莊姜, and then married again women from the state of Chen, who were later known as Dai Gui 戴嬀 and Li Gui 厲嬀.[208] When Zhuang Jiang got married, two other women from Qi accompanied her; when Dai Gui got married, two other women from Chen also accompanied her.[209] No historical documents testify that all these women had the same family name. Thus it is proven here that the legitimate wife and concubines do not necessarily have the same family name.[210]

5) Jin Lüxiang argued, "The school of mathematicians holds a theory for constructing pavilions with *san gui*" (*Lun yu jizhu kaozheng*, 2:5a). I would refute this.

6) For a classical text that supports the meaning of *fandian* ("a stand for returning drinking cups), see "Jiao tesheng" (*Li ji zhushu*, 25:20b, 2) and Zheng Xuan's comment on it (25:20b, 3–7).

7) For a classical text that mentions Guan Zhong's small capacity, see *Xin xu*, by Liu Xiang (*Xin xu* 新序, 4:2a, 6–7).

In my view, the remark in *Mencius*, "[Guan Zhong's] accomplishments were as low as you know" (*Mengzi jizhu*, 2A:1), also conveys the same message. For another classical text on this topic, see "Xian zhi 先知," by Master Yang (*Lun yu jizhu daquan*, 3:37b, 7–8).

* * *

One of the differences between Dasan's and Zhu Xi's readings of this passage, which is crucial but hard to notice, concerns their understandings of the character *xiao* 小 ("small capacity"). According to Dasan, it implies that Guan Zhong's receptiveness was limited; to Zhu Xi, in contrast, it implies that "he did not know the way of sages and great learning" (*Lun yu jizhu*, 2:7a). In other words, Dasan believed that it simply alluded to the quantitative limitation of Guan Zhong's merits in that he was only partially successful, whereas

---

[207] This means that although the woman from the largest state becomes the legitimate wife and the others from smaller states become the maid-wives, only women from the states that share the same family name can become the maid-wives.

[208] See *Zuo's Commentary* (*Zuo zhuan zhushu*, 2:15a).

[209] One of them was Li Gui.

[210] Zang Xuanshu of Lu took his wife's niece as his concubine. This shows that great officials originally had a maid-wife.

Zhu Xi related it to Guan Zhong's lack of the moral quality in order to present the neo-Confucians' generic criticism of meritorious subjects. That Dasan's mere agreement with Bao Xian's comment is listed in "Overview of Original Meanings," which Zhu Xi refuted, may point to Dasan's persistent objection to the neo-Confucian evaluation of Guan Zhong.

Guan Zhong is a controversial figure in the Confucian tradition. He surrendered to Prince Xiaobai 小白, who killed Guan Zhong's lord, Prince Jiu 糾 (d. 685 BCE), after a series of bloody struggles over the throne of the state of Qi and finally took the throne for himself as Duke Huan. Guan Zhong was appointed prime minister of the state, and thanks to his devotion and statesmanship, Duke Huan was so successful that he became known as one of the five powerful and meritorious lords of the Spring and Autumn period. Aware of Guan Zhong's disloyalty to his lord, Confucius's disciples Zi Lu and Zi Gong blamed Guan Zhong for undermining Confucian virtues. However, Confucius rebuked them and praised Guan Zhong for his merits (see 14.17 and 14.18).

Cheng Yi and Zhu Xi actually did not agree with Confucius's endorsement of Guan Zhong. Zhu Xi was reluctant to recognize Guan Zhong: "Although Guan Zhong was not a person of humanity, he practiced the virtue of humanity, as he benefitted human beings" (*Lun yu jizhu*, 7:13b). Cheng Yi took a more rigid stance and declined to accept him at all: "Suppose that Duke Huan was a younger brother and Prince Jiu was an older brother. Then, Guan Zhong's initial support for Prince Jiu was right, and Duke Huan should be regarded as having usurped the state and killed his older brother. If so, Duke Huan would be an enemy to Guan Zhong. If [Confucius] endorsed his service for Duke Huan only in light of his later merits, isn't this endorsement tantamount to thoroughly devastating virtue and thus leaving widely open the possibility of disloyal riots, which would be repeated for one thousand generations?" (7:14a)

Interestingly, it is on this issue that Dasan criticizes Cheng Yi and Zhu Xi most severely in *Noneo gogeum ju* (for more details, see his comment on 14.18). Even in his question to Zhu Xi here, Dasan shows that he intended to mitigate Zhu Xi's criticism of Guan Zhong by defining the act of "marrying three women" as a mistake of lavishness, not a crime in violation of ritual propriety. As a matter of fact, Dasan believed that the record of *Zhanguo ce* was closer to the truth than that of *Shuo yuan*—which implies that Dasan might have excused Guan Zhong's "mistake" because the misbehavior was aimed at covering Duke Huan's fault, an act of loyalty to the lord. Dasan thought that they were tied to one another through mutual trust of this sort, so that Guan Zhong could enjoy his life.

3.23 The Master, talking to the Chief Music Master of Lu on music, said, "Music can be readily understood. In the beginning, it rises with an ensemble of the eight sounds. As it proceeds, it flows in harmony, distinction, and succession and thus on to the conclusion."[211]

子語魯大師樂曰; 樂其可知也. 始作翕如也, 從之, 純如也, 皦如也, 繹如也, 以成.

3.23.1 Grounds

1) I supplement as follows: *Taishi* 大師 ("the Chief Music Master") refers to the head of all music masters.[212] Low-level great officials assumed the position.[213] *Zuo* 作 ("it rises") is here synonymous with *qi* 起 (to rise); *cong* 從 ("as it proceeds") is here synonymous with *sui* 隨 (to follow);[214] *cheng* 成 ("the conclusion") refers to the end of the musical performance.
2) Master Zhu commented, "*Xi* 翕 ('an ensemble of sounds') in here synonymous with *he* 合 (to collect)."
3) I supplement as follows: The eight sounds in ensemble are called *xi*;[215] being harmonious in unity is called *chun* 純 ("harmony");[216] when tones are clear and distinct, it is called *jiao* 皦 ("distinction");[217] flowing continuously like a long thread is called *yi* 繹 ("succession").[218] In the beginning, the sound of music develops gradually, so it rises in an ensemble of sounds; as the musical performance goes on, music is played in a more rapid tempo, so it flows on in harmony, distinction, and succession to its conclusion. These are expressions to describe the sound of music.

3.23.2 Arguments

1) Xing Bing argued, "Taishi refers to Da si yue 大司樂 (Head of the Office of Music) of the Zhou." I would refute this as follows:
   Taishi is the Chief Music Master.
2) He Yan argued, "*Cong* should be rendered as *zong* 縱 (to release). This means that after the five sounds have already been played, musicians set all sounds free as though releasing something." I would refute this as follows:
   Court music cannot tolerate the free release of all sounds. In it, once the first movement has been played, the second movement follows it. *Cong* is here synonymous with *chen* 趁 (to follow).

* * *

---

[211] *Cong* 從 ("as it proceeds") should be read in the level tone.
[212] He is the overseer of the bell master, the musical-stone master, the reed instrument master, and the pipe master.
[213] According to *Rites of Zhou*, two low-level great officials were appointed to the office.
[214] One of the previous passages says, "He puts his words into action first; he utters his words after [從] the action" (*Lun yu jizhu*, 2:13).
[215] A line in "Xiao ya" reads: "Brothers are already in harmony [翕]" (*Mao Shi zhushu*, 16:24a).
[216] This means that no unnecessary sound interferes.
[217] This is He Yan's comment.
[218] *Shuo wen* says, "*Yi* refers to spooling off threads" (*Shuo wen jie zi*, 13-A: 1b).

In He Yan's view, court musicians are allowed to play their instruments, after the first movement, without restraining their emotions. His rendition of *cong*, according to which it is synonymous with *zong*, may have caused rigid Confucians to wince because for them it usually connoted the state of being lax. Musicians' performances of the court music in He's interpretation resembled today's symphonies, which Dasan would have likely regarded as disharmonious with the actual court music of Joseon that he experienced. The Confucian ritual music, including the court music, has been well preserved in Korea. Consistent with Dasan's explanation, it never becomes too dramatic because it is designed to subdue one's emotional impulses while one listens to it.

Dasan followed Zhu Xi's view on the meaning of *xi*: it refers to an ensemble of sounds. However, Zhu Xi thought that the ensemble was created with five sounds, while to Dasan it refers to an ensemble of eight sounds. As Dasan mentions in his comment on the ancient music (see *Sangseo gohun*, 59:c), the eight sounds actually indicate the eight different musical instruments that produce eight distinct sounds. In comparison, the five sounds signify the traditional five scales. Dazai Jun also commented that the ensemble was made with the eight instruments probably because he intended to oppose Zhu Xi's comments whenever possible and because the term "the eight sounds" appeared in "Shun dian 舜典" (*Shang Shu zhushu*, 2:27a)—one of the most ancient Confucian documents—before the concept of the five sounds was formed.

3.24 The warden of the land god's altar at Yi requested an audience with the Master, saying, "Whenever a noble person comes here, I never fail to obtain an audience with him," whereupon the followers presented him. Emerging from the audience, he said, "My fellows! Why should you be concerned about your master's loss of office? All under heaven has endured a long time without the Way. Heaven would employ your master as a wooden alarm bell."

儀封人請見曰; 君子之至於斯也, 吾未嘗不得見也. 從者見之. 出曰;
二三子, 何患於喪乎? 天下之無道也久矣, 天將以夫子爲木鐸.

3.24.1 Grounds

1) Zheng Xuan commented, "Yi probably refers to a town of the state of Wei."[219]
2) I supplement as follows: "The warden" was an official who supervised the boundary of the land god's altar.[220]

---

[219] Xing Bing commented, "*Zuo's Commentary* records: 'The Viscount of Wei entered Yiyi 夷儀.'"
[220] Master Zhu commented, "He might have been a person who was worthy but himself withdrew to a low government post."

3) Master Zhu commented, "'A noble person' refers to one of the worthies at the time. The warden sought to be introduced to the Master by saying that he was never denied an interview by the worthies."

4) Bao Xian commented, "'The followers' refers to the disciples of Confucius who attended him."

5) Master Zhu commented, "*Xian zhi* 見之 ('presented him') means that the followers helped the warden have an audience with the Master.[221] *Sang* 喪 means that one loses one's government post and leaves the state. A sentence in *Record of Rites*, 'When one loses one's office [喪], he would rather become poor,'[222] shows the same use."

6) Kong Anguo commented, "A wooden alarm bell [木鐸] is rung when administrative commands are released."[223]

7) Master Zhu commented, "The wooden alarm bell was used when officials patrolled the streets. This implies that Heaven let Our Master lose his post so that he could disseminate his teachings while traveling in the four directions."[224]

3.24.2 Arguments

1) Kong Anguo argued, "[The warden's remarks mean] why should you be concerned that Confucius's holy virtue would be ruined in the near future? Heaven will commission Confucius to create laws and institutions so that he can reign supreme under heaven." I would refute this as follows:

Kong's comment seems to consist of flattery and lacks evidence.[225] It sounds uncouth and ugly and is inferior to the new interpretation by Master Zhu. *Jiang* 將 ("would") here is a particle.[226] The phrase "Heaven would employ" conveys the warden's conjecture about Heaven's mind. It is unnecessary to connect the character *jiang* to a real upcoming event. Regardless, Fu Guang 輔廣 (fl. 1205–1207) and Chen Li are attached to the old theory [suggested by Kong]. Isn't this an error?[227] In my view, [this passage means that] since all under heaven lacks the Way, Heaven would have Our Master illuminate the Way. Why does this interpretation cause a contradiction [between *sang* ("your master's loss of office") and the expression "Heaven would employ your master"]?

---

[221] *Xian* 見 should be read as *xian* (to have an audience with), not *jian* (to see).
[222] See "Tangong" (*Li ji zhushu*, 8:9a).
[223] Xing Bing commented, "*Duo* 鐸 is a bell. Its tongue is made of either metal or wood. In regard to military affairs they ring the metal alarm bell; in regard to civil affairs they ring the wooden alarm bell." Qi Lüqian 齊履謙 (fl. 1321) commented, "The wooden alarm bell has a metal mouth and a wooden tongue; a metal alarm bell has a wooden mouth and a metal tongue" (*Lun yu jizhu daquan*, 3:42a).
[224] *Zuo's Commentary* quotes a passage from *Xia shu* 夏書 that says, "The messenger patrolled the streets, ringing the wooden alarm bell" (*Zuo zhuan zhushu*, 32:28b).
[225] Confucius eventually could not obtain a position.
[226] A line of a poem in "Zheng feng 鄭風" reads: "O [將] Shu 叔, do not try to hunt again" (*Mao Shi zhushu*, 7:10a).
[227] Chen Li argued, "Later theory does not strictly match the meaning of the character *sang* and the phrase 'All under heaven has endured a long time without the Way'" (*Lun yu jizhu daquan*, 3:42b).

In my view, in ancient times when a man lost his post and left a state, the mourning rituals were applied to all things related to him. Thus "Qu li" says, "When a great official or a low-ranking official leaves a state, he prepares a platform after crossing the border to face the state and performs the weeping ritual for his departure. He wears a plain upper garment, a plain lower garment, and a plain cap. He removes hems from his clothes, puts on a pair of shoes without decorations, covers his chariot with a sheet of plain dog hide, rides a horse with an untrimmed mane, does not cut his nails, and does not perform the premeal ceremony. Only after three months pass does he return to wearing normal clothes" (*Li ji zhushu*, 4:17a). Mencius's remark "When Confucius passed three months without a lord to serve, he condoled with himself" (*Mengzi jizhu*, 3B:8) is also pertinent to this practice. Duke Mu of Qin [秦繆公, r. 659–621 BCE] said to Chong'er 重耳 [晉文公], "The period of one's lacking a government post [喪] should not last long"; Uncle Fan [舅犯, fl. 657–651] said, "Those who have lost their government post [喪] do not have anything to treasure." Chong'er also said, "I have lost my position [喪], and my father died." *Record of Rites* says, "If a man loses his government post [喪], he becomes unconcerned about his residence."[228] The sentence—"Why should you be concerned about your Master's loss of office"—also implies that Confucius lost his office and left the state.

* * *

Dasan identifies the "warden" as an official who supervised the boundary of the land god's altar. This is an understanding unique from that of all other major commentators, who argued that it referred to an official in charge of supervising the boundary of an enfeoffed land. Even though he does not provide the source of his rendition here, it derives from his perception of the way to establish a state in ancient times (see *Sangseo gohun*, 94:a).

It is noticeable that he frowns on Kong Anguo's groundless "flattery" of Confucius precisely because it contradicted Confucius's actual life. Kong's comment may convey the perception Han scholars generally had of Confucius, according to which Confucius was often portrayed as having mysterious powers. The neo-Confucians' belittlement of Han Confucianism partly stemmed from their objection to the sort of mystification and exaggerated sanctification of Confucius that Han scholars practiced. In that respect, Dasan was on the same page as neo-Confucians.

3.25 The Master said of the Shao, "Absolutely beautiful, and absolutely yielding the good!" He said of the Wu, "Absolutely beautiful, but not absolutely yielding the good!"

子謂韶, 盡美矣, 又盡善也. 謂武, 盡美矣, 未盡善也.

---

[228] All these excerpts are from "Tangong" (*Li ji zhushu*, 9:12b–13a; 10:26a).

3.25.1 Grounds.

1) Kong Anguo commented, "The Shao is Shun's music;[229] the Wu is King Wu's music."[230]

2) I supplement as follows: *Shan* 善 ("yielding the good") should be read as a verb, as in the expressions "yielding the good for the world" and "yielding the good for the custom."[231] "Beautiful" is here a word to describe the beauty when a project begins.[232] "Yielding the good" is an expression that conveys that the project has finished excellently.[233] Shun succeeded Yao and passed his throne to Yu so that his reign had no flaws from beginning to end. Thus his music was absolutely beautiful and absolutely yielded the good.[234] Meanwhile, seven years after King Wu obtained all under heaven, he met his demise. Accordingly, the recalcitrant people of Yin were still disobedient, and the rituals and music failed to thrive yet. Thus his music was absolutely beautiful but did not yield the good. Music generally symbolized achievements. So whereas the Shao had nine chapters, the Wu had only six chapters. This is what the expression "not absolutely yielding the good" means.

3.25.2 Arguments

1) Kong Anguo argued, "Owing to his holy virtue, Shun gained the king's authority through a concession. Thus his music was absolutely good. King Wu conquered all under heaven to obtain his position. Thus his music was not absolutely good."[235] I would refute this as follows:

Kong Anguo suggested that we read *shan* as a word opposite to *e* 惡 (evil) as in the term *shan e* (good and evil). In general, "good" is compared to "evil," and thus, if something is not absolutely good, it will eventually return to evil. "Good" and "evil" are always in contrast, like *yin* and *yang* or black and white. If something does not belong to *yang*, it belongs to *yin*; if something is not close to white, it is close to black. Nothing is in between *yin* and *yang*, belonging to neither *yin* nor *yang*; nothing is in between black and white, being close to neither black nor white. If it is said that King Wu's music was not absolutely good, there must be remnants of the root of evil in it, which have not been totally removed. Imagine an earthen pot. Even though all parts are in good shape, when a small hole creates a leak, it will

---

[229] "Yu shu" says, "The Performance of Xiao Shao 簫韶 is finished in nine chapters" (*Shang Shu zhushu*, 4:20b).

[230] *Rites of Zhou* says, "They dance the Tai Wu dance" (*Zhou li zhushu*, 22:13b).

[231] *Changes* says, "He yields the good for the world but does not boast of his merits" (*Zhou Yi zhushu*, 1:19a). It also says, "The noble person maintains his excellent virtue to yield the good for the custom" (9:12a).

[232] *Changes* says, "His inner personality is beautiful, so its beauty diffuses over his four limbs" (*Zhou Yi zhushu*, 2:11a).

[233] *Mencius* says, "Yield the good for its consequences." [This saying is not found in *Mencius*.]

[234] This means that it yielded the good for its consequences.

[235] Xing Bing argued, "Attacking one's lord as his subject, although it is a response to Heaven's order and an acceptance of the people's request, is inferior to succeeding the throne through a bow of appreciation for the concession of power. Thus King Wu's music was not absolutely good."

eventually be destroyed. Imagine a person. Even though every aspect is in good shape, when a little evil is not removed, he will end up being an evil person. This signifies the fundamental demarcation between good and evil.

The affairs of Tang and Wu are not a small topic of morality. If they are regarded as good it means that they were amazingly good; if they are regarded as evil it means that they were amazingly evil. It does not make sense in principle to assume that they preserved the greater good but could not escape from a little evil. If someone preserves the greater good but cannot escape from a little evil, he is apparently not a sage. If someone is not a sage, he will eventually return to the great evil. How can an ambiguous perception be tolerated here?

King Wu would not be the only person affected by this ambiguous perception. It was King Wen who laid a foundation for the conquering of King Wu; it was the Duke of Zhou who accomplished this task. If King Wu is said to be not absolutely good, such blame and accusation cannot be directed only to King Wu in a way matching principle. As a result, King Wen and the Duke of Zhou must be regarded as not absolutely good as well. This is not a minor issue because in this interpretation, the three sages in a school will uniformly latch onto the great dishonor. Even three-feet-high children know that Confucius was definitely not at all dissatisfied with King Wen and the Duke of Zhou. When it is obvious that he kept his deep reverence for King Wen and the Duke of Zhou in his mind, if he were to say that he had some reservations about King Wu, would King Wu not feel resentment?

According to *Zuo's Commentary*, Ji Zha 季札 had a chance to observe the Zhou's music.[236] After appreciating a performance of the Shao Huo 韶濩 dance, he commented, "It still hints at a feeling of shame against the virtue."[237] Early Confucians held on to this remark so tightly that they eventually gibed, "The affairs of Tang and Wu have deserved a bit of blame from the beginning." As a matter of fact, when Mei Ze forged "Zhonghui zhi gao 仲虺之誥," he dared to create this sentence: "It still hints at a feeling of shame against the virtue." Contradicting what this sentence relates, Ji Zha commented after he watched a performance of the Tai Wu dance, "How beautiful! The Zhou's culture was indeed efflorescent" (*Zuo zhuan zhushu*, 39:26b). As seen here, with regard to King Wu's music, he was very positive without showing any criticism. So was it possible for Ji Zha to criticize King Tang's music only when he recognized the beauty of King Wu's music? The allegation that *Zuo's Commentary* is often groundless and exaggerated is germane in this respect.

In conclusion, Confucius never connected discussion of music to his evaluation of people; he never connected his discussion of the Shao and the Wu to his views on Shun and Wu. "Yielding the good" or "not

---

[236] See the twenty-ninth year of the reign of Duke Xiang (*Zuo zhuan zhushu*, 39:19b–27b).
[237] This comment is about Tang's music (*Zuo zhuan zhushu*, 39:26b).

yielding the good" pertains to the evaluation of the sounds and features of music. In general, music with nine chapters is dedicated to those who have accomplished more merits, as seen in Nine Yuan 淵 or Nine Shao; in contrast, music with six chapters is dedicated to those who have not accomplished as much merit as other sages have, as seen in Six Ying 英 or Six Wu. Is Confucius's remark "not absolutely yielding the good" not relevant to this?

2) Gu Yanwu argued, "Ji Zha commented on King Wen's music and said, 'Beautiful! However, it still hints at a sense of resentment.' The true meaning of Confucius's remark 'the Wu was not absolutely yielding the good' can be understood in light of this comment. The remark '[King Wen's virtue] has not penetrated into all under heaven'[238] refers to the music of King Wen that 'still hints at a sense of resentment'; the remark 'King Wu met his demise when all under heaven did not fully enjoy the peace'[239] refers to the music of King Wu that is 'not absolutely yielding the good.' *Record of Rites* says, 'Music symbolizes achievements.' During his reign, King Wu punished King Zhou, sentenced him to death, and conquered the Yan 奄 [Yin]. It took him three years to punish the ruler of the Yin to death, and the script of the adorned tortoise still says, 'There was great difficulty in the western lands.' Indeed, the recalcitrant people of the Yin continued to cause turmoil. In comparison with Shun's era, in which he could administer his state at will, how different they were! Therefore the Tai Wu music, although it was composed by the Duke of Zhou, could not reach the level of music enjoyed in a peaceful age in which the world has totally changed and people's customs have been transformed according to ideals. The time of sages is not subject to men's abilities"[240] *(Re zhi lu,* 7:2b–3a).

In my view, Gu's understanding is accurate.

3) Ogyu argued, "Of the various pieces of music transmitted to future generations, some are preserved intact while others are damaged. The intact music is absolutely good. Thus when Our Master listened to music in the state of Qi, he could forget about the taste of meats. The damaged

---

[238] See *Mencius* (*Mengzi jizhu*, 2A: 1).

[239] See "Feng Shan shu 封禪書," in *Shi ji* (*Shi ji*, 28:9a).

[240] Liu Rujia 劉汝佳 (1610–1663) argued, "Whether one succeeds to the throne through a bow of appreciation for the concession of power or one obtains all under heaven through conquering is a matter of the sages' time. Had Shun reigned in the world of Wu, he would have conquered it as well. Confucius said, 'Tang and Yu conceded the throne to the virtuous ministers. The sovereign of the Xia [King Yu] and the founders of the Yin and the Zhou transmitted it to their sons. The principle of rightness in all these cases, however, was the same' (*Mengzi jizhu*, 5A:6). Taking action in compliance with human inborn nature or to return to it both hinge on differences between people. As for the achievements, however, they are the same. In some cases, it is possible to take action that is harmonious with inborn nature and Heaven's principle; in other cases, one should try to reverse the situation to return to inborn nature. A dispute about which music is better with a focus on their methods is not different from the comment '[Yu's music is better than King Wen's music] because the rope that hangs the big bell of King Wen's orchestra onto its holder is about to be cut [due to King Wen's frequent use of the bell]'" (quoted in *Re zhi lu*, 7:3a).

music is not absolutely good. Thus when Our Master discussed music with Bin Moujia 賓牟賈, he could not maintain his theory to the end." I would refute this as follows:

If music is damaged, how can it be called "absolutely beautiful"?

* * *

Dasan stresses that *shan* should be read as a verb, meaning "yielding the good." By this he means that King Wu's rule was good enough in nature but its accomplishments had limits because King Wu died before his mission could be completed. He died only seven years after he assumed the throne, not because he was short on morality but because it was his destiny. Similarly, in Dasan's view, King Wu applied the Confucian principles to his reality in a more aggressive way merely because his times were different from those of King Wen. It is still possible to insist—as Kong Anguo, Xing Bing, and Zhu Xi did—that even in Dasan's understanding, King Wen and the Duke of Zhou were better than King Wu. Whereas other commentators' judgments on their standing were informed by King Wu's disloyalty to a superior and his use of violence, however, Dasan accepted hierarchy among them simply because some accomplished less while others accomplished more. In other words, his evaluation of the historical figures is centered on their merits, not their strict adherence to Confucian norms. Consistent with this perspective, Dasan persistently refuted the neo-Confucian disclaimers about King Wu.

> In my view, this theory [of Fan Zuyu] that Confucius frequently honored the great virtue of Taibo and King Wen was intended implicitly to satirize King Wu. . . . [W]hen it comes to the issue of moral duty, can even King Wen be said sincerely to abide by it? According to the law during the period of King Yao, King Shun, and the Three Dynasties, only the Son of Heaven held a capital area as large as one thousand square *li*, whereas the dukes in the upper ranks were allowed to possess only one hundred square *li*. However, King Wen [as a duke of the Yin] possessed two-thirds of all under heaven. How could this be said to fulfill moral duty? . . . [C]onfucius must have had no intention to deprecate King Wen and the Duke of Zhou: is there any reason only to deprecate King Wu? (*Noneo gogeum ju*, 231a–b)

As Dasan advises, the reader should not overlook the significance of this discussion of King Wu. This discussion provides a crucial hint about his stance on many subtle political disputes between political powers that were active during the Joseon dynasty: monarchical hegemony versus bureaucratic hegemony, meritocracy versus rule by virtue, moral consequentialism versus deontological ethics, circumstantial consideration of morals versus normative consideration of morals, and so on. Dasan might have denied that he belonged to any one side in these disputes because he wished to achieve syntheses in his thinking and also believed that sages integrated all good things into their singular lives: for instance, in his view, King Wu was meritorious and thereby virtuous, or vice versa. However, it is possible for the reader to position Dasan with respect to these convoluted disputes, owing to his clear statements on how to evaluate King Wu, which should be combined with his understanding of Guan Zhong (see 3.22).

Earlier commentaries contain nothing like Dasan's interpretation of *shan*, so it is listed in "Overview of Original Meanings," although it was inspired by Gu Yanwu's insightful observation, as Dasan makes evident in his long quotation of Gu's opinion here.

3.26 The Master said, "Not lenient when occupying a high position, not respectful when participating in rituals, not sorrowful when condoling with mourners—what could I admire about these people?"[241]

子曰; 居上不寬, 爲禮不敬, 臨喪不哀, 吾何以觀之哉?

3.26.1 Grounds

1) I supplement as follows: "Occupying a high position" means that one assumes the position of the ruler or a local governor; "participating in rituals" means that one practices all rituals with others, whether they be auspicious or ominous; "condoling with mourners" means to condole with the mourners by performing the ritual weeping. The sentence "What could I admire about these people" means that those people are not worth observing.[242]
2) For classical texts relevant to this passage, see *Da Dai Li ji* (*Da Dai Li ji*, 4:10a, 4–8) and "Qu li" (*Li ji zhushu*, 3:8a, 1; L7).

---

[241] *Lin* 臨 ("condoling with") should be read in the departing tone.
[242] Dazai Jun commented, "Probably because there existed such a person as described here, Confucius derided him."

CHINESE GLOSSARY

Abang gangyeok go 我邦疆域考
A-eon gakbi 雅言覺非
Ahak pyeon 兒學編
Akseo gojon 樂書孤存
Anchang 安昌
An Jae-hong 安在鴻
An Jeong-bok 安鼎福
Ansan 安山
Anyi 安邑
Aphae 押海
Baek-eon si 百言詩
Baek Nam-un 白南雲
Bai gui 白圭
Baihu tong 白虎通
Baihu tongyi 白虎通義
Bangrye chobon 邦禮草本
Ban Gu 班固
Bao Biao 鮑彪
Baoshi Zhanguo ce zhu 鮑氏戰國策注
Bao Xian 包咸
Bao Ziliang 包子良
Ba yi 八佾
Bei feng 邶風
Bian zheng 辨政
Biao ji 表記
Bing Ji 丙吉
Bin Moujia 賓牟賈
Bo Yi 伯夷
Bo Yu 伯禹
Bo 亳

Buniu 不狃
Bu Shang 卜商
Byeong-in 丙寅
Cai 蔡
Cai Chen 蔡沈
Cai Mo 蔡墨
Caipan 采蘩
Caiping 采蘋
Cai Xuzhai 蔡虛齋
Cai yi 綵衣
Cang Lang 滄浪
Cao 曹
Ceng 鄫
Chai 柴
Chang 嘗
Chang'an 長安
Che 徹
Chen 陳
Cheng Fuxin 程復心
Cheng Ji 成季
Cheng Yi 程頤
Chengzi 程子
Chengzi yishu 程子遺書
Chen Kang 陳亢
Chen Li 陳櫟
Chen shu 陳書
Chibiaonu 赤熛怒
Chi Mei Wang Liang 魑魅魍魎
Choe Nam-seon 崔南善
chongdian 崇坫
Chong'er 重耳
Chu 出
Chu ci 楚辭
Chu ci zhangju 楚辭章句
Chunchu gojing 春秋考徵
Chunguan 春官
Chunqiu 春秋
Chunqiu fanlu 春秋繁露
Chunqiu Gongyang zhuan 春秋公羊傳
Chunqiu Gongyang zhuan zhushu 春秋公羊傳註疏
Chunqiu Guliang zhuan 春秋穀梁傳
Chunqiu Guliang zhuan zhushu 春秋穀梁傳註疏
Chunqiu Zuo zhuan 春秋左傳
Chunqiu Zuo zhuan zhushu 春秋左傳註疏
Chu yu 楚語

Ci 祠
Ci 賜
Cimian qifu biao 辭免起復表
Da Dai Li ji 大戴禮記
Daedong sugyeong 大東水經
Daehak gang-ui 大學講義
Daehak gong-ui 大學公義
Daehan gangyeok go 大韓疆域考
Dai Gui 戴嬀
Dai Zhen 戴震
Da Ming yitong zhi 大明一統志
Dangshi 黨氏
Dao shu 道術
Daozi 悼子
Dasan 茶山
Da she 大射
Da she yi 大射儀
Da si tu 大司徒
Da si yue 大司樂
Da Wang Shangshu shu 答王尙書書
Daxiaozong tongshi 大小宗通釋
Daxue yanyi 大學衍義
Daxue zhangju 大學章句
Da ya 大雅
Da Yu mo 大禹謨
Dazai Jun 太宰純 (太宰春台)
Dazhuan 大傳
Da Zongbo 大宗伯
Di 狄
Di 禘
Diao 調
Diguan 地官
Di Ku 帝嚳
Ding 定
Diqiu 帝丘
Dizi liezhuan 弟子列傳
Dongjian 東澗
Donglou 東樓
Dongping Xianwang zhuan 東平憲王傳
Dong Zhongshu 董仲舒
Duanmu 端木
Du Du zhuan 杜篤傳
Du Fu 杜撫
Dui 兌
Du Kuai 杜蕢

Du Lin 杜林
Du Mo 杜橆
Du Xin zhuan 杜歆傳
Du Yu zhuan 杜預傳
Du Yu 杜預
Du Yuankai 杜元凱
Er Cheng quanshu 二程全書
Er Cheng yishu 二程遺書
Er ya 爾雅
Er ya yi 爾雅翼
Er ya zhushu 爾雅註疏
Eulchuk 乙丑
Fan 犯
Fan Chi 樊遲
fandian 反坫
Fang ji 坊記
Fang Mengxuan 方孟旋
Fang Xuanling 房玄齡
Fang yan 方言
Fan Ning 范甯
Fan Xu 樊須
Fan Zuyu 范祖禹
Fei 費
Feng 豐
Fengren 封人
Feng Shan shu 封禪書
Fu 黼
Fu Guang 輔廣
Fuji [夏父]弗忌
Fu Qian 服虔
Fu Sheng 伏生
Fuxi 伏羲
Gai 該
Gangjin 康津
Gao Yao mo 皋陶謨
Gaoxin shi 高辛氏
Gaoyang shi 高陽氏
Gapja 甲子
Garye jak-ui 嘉禮酌儀
Garye jilseo 家禮疾書
Geng Chutong 耿楚侗
Geng ji zhao 耕籍詔
Ge Qizhan 葛屺瞻
Getan 葛覃
Goengbo 紘父

Gojong 高宗
Gonggong 共工
Gongmok 公牧
Gongsun Ao 公孫敖
Gongsun Hong zhuan 公孫弘傳
Gongye Chang 公冶長
Gongzhong 共仲
Gongzi pu 公子譜
Goseongsa 高聲寺
Goulong 句龍
Goumang 句芒
Guai 夬
Guan 觀
Guanju 關雎
Guanren 官人
Guan Yefu 觀射父
Guanyinzi 關尹子
Guan Zhong 管仲
Guanzi 管子
Gukjo jeollye go 國朝典禮考
Gu Lun 古論
Guo 虢
Guo Pu 郭璞
Guo Qingluo 郭青螺
Guo yu 國語
Guwen Shang Shu yuanci 古文尚書冤詞
Gu Yanwu 顧炎武
Gwallye jak-ui 冠禮酌儀
Gwangmu 光武
Gwinong 歸農
Gwon Cheol-sin 權哲身
Gwon Tae-hwi 權泰彙
Gyeonggi 京畿
Gyeongse yupyo 經世遺表
Haenam 海南
Han Shi waizhuan 韓詩外傳
Han shu 漢書
Han Wei Liuzhao baisan jia ji 漢魏六朝百三家集
Han Yu 韓愈
Hao 鎬
He 紇
Heo Mok 許穆
Heuksan 黑山
Heumheum sinseo 欽欽新書
He Xiu 何休

He Yan 何晏
Hong 洪
Hong 鴻
Hong fan 洪範
Hong Hyeon-ju 洪顯周
Hou Han shu 後漢書
Hou Ji 后稷
Hou Tu 后土
Huaiyang jun Huangshi Youyu chuan ming 淮陽郡黃氏友于川銘
Huan 桓
Huangdi 黃帝
Huang Kan 皇侃
Huang-Lao 黃老
Huang Ming dazheng ji 皇明大政記
Huang Wuzi 皇武子
Huan Tui 桓魋
Hu Guang 胡廣
Hu Hong 胡宏
Hui 惠
Hui feng 檜風
Huishu 惠叔
Huo zhi liezhuan 貨殖列傳
Hutu 狐突
Hwang Sa-yeong 黃嗣永
Hwaseong 華城
Hyejang 惠藏
Hyojong 孝宗
Hyun Chae 玄采
Idam sokchan 耳談續纂
Ito Koreshada 伊藤維禎 (伊藤仁齋)
Janggi 長鬐
Jang Jiyeon 張志淵
Jegi go 祭期考
Jeongche jeonjung byeon 正體傳重辨
Jeong Gu 鄭逑
Jeong Gyu-yeong 丁奎英
Jeong Hak-yeon 丁學淵
Jeong In-bo 鄭寅普
Jeong Jae-won 丁載遠
Jeongjo 正祖
Jeongmyo 丁卯
Jeongsun 貞純
Jeong Yak-jeon 丁若銓
Jeong Yak-jong 丁若鍾
Jeong Yak-yong 丁若鏞

Ji 姬
Ji 籍
Jia Gongyan 賈公彥
Jia Kui 賈逵
Ji An 汲黯
Jiang 蔣
Jianghou 蔣侯
Jiao tesheng 郊特牲
Jiao 角
Jiao 郊
Jiaoshi dui 郊事對
Jia Yi 賈誼
Jie 桀
Ji fa 祭法
Ji Huanzi 季桓子
Jil-ui 質疑
Jimo 卽墨
Jin 晉
Jing 旌
Jingdian shi wen 經典釋文
Jin Lüxiang 金履祥
Jinsan 珍山
Jin shu 晉書
Jinsi lu 近思錄
Jin yu 晉語
Ji Kangzi 季康子
Jiong ming 冏命
Jiong 駉
Ji Pingzi 季平子
Jisun Fei 季孫肥
Jisun He 季孫紇
Jisun Shu 季孫宿
Jisun Si 季孫斯
Jisun Yiru 季孫意如
Jisun 季孫
Jitian fu 籍田賦
Ji tong 祭統
Jiu gao 酒誥
Jiu ge 九歌
Jiu 糾
Ji Wenzi 季文子
Ji Wuzi 季武子
Jixi li 旣夕禮
Ji yi 祭義
Ji You 季友

Ji Zha 季札
Jizi 季子
Joseon 朝鮮
Joseon Yukyo yeonwon 朝鮮儒教淵源
Ju 莒
Juaner 卷耳
Julong 句龍
Jun Chen 君陳
Jungyong gang-ui bo 中庸講義補
Jungyong gang-ui 中庸講義
Jungyong jajam 中庸自箴
Junren 均人
Junzi 君子
Juyeok sajeon 周易四箋
Juyeok simjeon 周易心箋
Kang gao 康誥
Kao gong ji 考工記
Kenen 蘐園
Kong Anguo 孔安國
Kong congzi 孔叢子
Kong Kui 孔悝
Kong Yingda 孔穎達
Kongzi jia yu 孔子家語
Kongzi xian ju 孔子閒居
Kongzi yan ju 孔子燕居
Ku 譽
Kuang 曠
Kui 夔
Kuiquan 逵泉
Kun 坤
Kundi gao 昆弟誥
Kun xue ji wen 困學紀聞
Jilseo 疾書
Kyujanggak 奎章閣
Langya daizui bian 琅琊代醉編
Lao Dan 老聃
Li 厲
li 理
Li 黎
Li Gao 李翺
Li Gui 厲媯
Li ji 禮記
Li ji daquan 禮記大全
Li ji zhushu 禮記註疏
Lin Fang 林放

Lingweiyang 靈威仰

Linqiu 廩丘

Li qi 禮器

Li ren 里仁

Li sao 離騷

Liu Rujia 劉汝佳

Liu Xiang 劉向

Liu Xie 劉勰

Liuzi 柳子

Li Xun zhuan 李尋傳

Li yue zhi 禮樂志

Li yun 禮運

Lü 旅

Lu 魯

Luan Zhao 欒肇

Luan 欒

Lü Cang 呂倉

Lü Dalin 呂大臨

Lu Deming 陸德明

Lü Huiqing 呂惠卿

Lu Jiashu 陸稼書

Lu Jugang 陸聚岡

Lu Lun 魯論

Lu ming 鹿鳴

Lun heng 論衡

Lun yu bijie 論語筆解

Lun yu jijie yishu 論語集解義疏

Lun yu jijie 論語集解

Lun yu jiqiu pian 論語稽求篇

Lun yu jizhu daquan 論語集注大全

Lun yu jizhu kaozheng 論語集注考證

Lun yu jizhu 論語集注

Lun yu shuoyi 論語說義

Lun yu yishu 論語義疏

Lun yu Zheng Xuan zhu 論語鄭玄註

Lun yu Zhengshi zhu 論語鄭氏註

Lun yu zhengyi 論語正義

Lun yu zhushu 論語註疏

Lüshi Chunqiu 呂氏春秋

Lu shi jia 魯世家

Lu song 魯頌

Lu Xiangshan 陸象山

Lü xing 呂刑

Lu yu 魯語

Lu zhi Jiao Di bian 魯之郊褅辯

Maengja yo-ui 孟子要義

Maessi Sangseo pyeong 梅氏尙書平

Mao Chang 毛萇

Mao Dake 毛大可

Mao Qiling 毛奇齡

Mao Shi zhushu 毛詩註疏

Ma Rong 馬融

Ma Zhou 馬周

Meishi 媒氏

Mei Ze 梅賾

Meng 蒙

Meng Ren 孟任

Mengsun 孟孫

Meng Wubo 孟武伯

Meng Xizi 孟僖子

Meng Yizi 孟懿子

Meng Zhuangzi 孟莊子

Mengzi jizhu daquan 孟子集注大全

Mengzi jizhu 孟子集注

Mengzi zhu 孟子注

Mengzi zhushu 孟子註疏

Minbo ui 民堡議

Ming shi 明史

Ming Taizu wenji 明太祖文集

Mingtang wei 明堂位

Min Zi Qian 閔子騫

Miyong 美鏞

Mo Di 墨翟

Mongmin simseo 牧民心書

MoSi gang-ui 毛詩講義

Mozi 墨子

Mu 穆

Mubo 穆伯

Mujin 戊辰

Mun Il-pyeong 文一平

Mu shi 牧誓

Mushu 穆叔

Naju 羅州

Nam-in 南人

Nan 難

Nangong Jingshu 南宮敬叔

Nan Rong 南容

Nanwu cheng 南武城

Ningwuzi 甯武子

Nok-am Gwon Cheol-sin myoji myeong 鹿庵權哲身墓誌銘

Noneo gogeum ju 論語古今註
Noneo sucha 論語手箚
Nügung 女宮
Ogyu Nabematsu 荻生雙松 (荻生徂徠)
Oh Guk-jin 吳國鎭
Ohak ron 五學論
Pan Yue 潘岳
Pi 噽
Pin li 聘禮
Pin yan 賓筵
Pin yi 聘義
Pin zhi chu yan 賓之初宴
Pungsan 豊山
Qi 啓
Qi 杞
Qi 棄
Qian 乾
Qian Han shu 前漢書
Qianhou 乾侯
Qian kun 乾坤
Qi ao 淇奧
qi cui 齊衰
Qi Lun 齊論
Qi Lüqian 齊履謙
Qin 秦
Qing dafu xiaozhuan zan 卿大夫孝傳贊
Qingmiao 清廟
Qu Boyu 蘧伯玉
Qu Dao 屈到
Quechao 鵲巢
Qu li 曲禮
Qu Yuan 屈原
Ran Qiu 冉求
Ran You 冉有
Ren Fan 任昉
Re zhi lu 日知錄
Rong 戎
Rongo kokun 論語古訓
Rongo kokun gaiden 論語古訓外傳
Ruan Yuan 阮元
Rulin zhuan 儒林傳
Rushou 蓐收
Ru xing 儒行
Sa-am 俟菴
Sa-am seonsaeng yeonbo 俟菴先生年譜

Sado 思悼

Sammija jip 三眉子集

Sammija 三眉子

Sangfu xiaoji 喪服小記

Sangrye oepyeon 喪禮外編

Sangrye sajeon 喪禮四箋

Sangseo gohun 尚書古訓

Sangseo jiwon rok 尚書知遠錄

Sang-ui jeolyo 喪儀節要

Sangzhang 喪杖

San shu 三恕

Sarim 士林

Sarye gasik 四禮家式

Seo-am ganghak gi 西巖講學記

Seo-in 西人

Seonggyungwan 成均館

Seongho 星湖

Seo Yong-bo 徐龍輔

Shan 單

Shanfu 山甫

Shanfu 膳夫

Shang Shu 尚書

Shang Shu daquan 尚書大傳

Shang Shu guwen shuzheng 尚書古文疏證

Shang Shu zhushu 尚書註疏

Shao 召

Shao 韶

Shaohao 少皥

Shao Huo 韶濩

Shao Kangjie 邵康節

Shao nan 召南

Shaowei 少微

Shao yi 少儀

She yi 射儀

Shen Cheng 申棖

Shen Cunzhong 沈存中

Shengnong 神農

Shengzhi 聖治

Sheti 攝提

Shi er bian 示兒編

Shi fa 謚法

Shi guanli 士冠禮

Shi hunli 士昏禮

Shi huo zhi 食貨志

Shi ji 史記

Shi ji jijie 史記集解
Shijing 詩經
Shi jizhuan 詩集傳
Shi Kuang 師曠
Shi qi 釋器
Shi ren 碩人
Shi sangli 士喪禮
Shisanjing zhushu 十三經注疏
Shi tian 釋天
Shi wen 釋文
Shu 叔
Shu 蜀
Shujing jizhuan 書經集傳
Shu jizhuan 書集傳
Shuliang He 叔梁紇
Shun dian 舜典
Shun 舜
Shuo wen jie zi 說文解字
Shuo wen 說文
Shuo yuan 說苑
Shusun Bao 叔孫豹
Shusun Tong 叔孫通
Shusun 叔孫
Shu Xiang 叔向
Shu Ya 叔牙
Si 姒
Si 斯
sidian 食坫
Si gong 司空
Sigyeong gang-ui bo 詩經講義補
Sigyeong gang-ui 詩經講義
Siku quanshu 四庫全書
Silhak 實學
Sima fa 司馬法
Sima Qian 司馬遷
Sima Rangju 司馬穰苴
Simgyeong milheom 心經密驗
Sin Hag-yu gagye 贐學游家誡
Singan hoe 新幹會
Sinhae 辛亥
Sinji 薪智
Sinjoseon sa 新朝鮮社
Si qiu 司裘
Si yi 司儀
Si zunyi 司尊彝

Si shu gai cuo 四書改錯

Si shu jiangyi kunmian lu 四書講義困勉錄

Si shu shengyan 四書賸言

Si shu shengyan bu 四書賸言補

Si shu wu jing jiangyi 四書五經講義

Sohak ji-eon 小學枝言

Sohak jucheon 小學珠串

Song Xiangfeng 宋翔鳳

Song Zijing 宋子京

Sun 損

Sui shu 隋書

Sukjong 蕭宗

Sun Chuo 孫綽

Sun Jihe 孫季和

Sun Yi 孫奕

Su Zixi 蘇紫溪

Su Ziyou 蘇子由

Tai Bo 泰伯

taiji 太極

Taiping yulan 太平御覽

Tai Shi 大史

Taishi 泰誓

Taiwang 太王

Tai Wu 大武

Tak-ong 擇翁

Tan 潭

Tang 湯

Tangong 檀弓

Tao Xia 大夏

Tao Yuanming 陶淵明

Teng 滕

Tianguan 天官

tianli 天理

Tianwen zhi 天文志

Tinglin 亭林

ti-yong 體用

Tuogao 橐皋

Waihunag 外黃

Waiqi shi jia 外戚世家

Wan 萬

Wang Chong 王充

Wang Fengfu 王豐甫

Wang Ji 王季

Wangjian ji 王儉集

Wang Lizhen 王利貞

Wang Shiqian　王時潛
Wang Shu　王恕
Wang Shu　王肅
Wang Wujiu　王无咎
Wang Yangming　王陽明
Wang Yinglin　王應麟
Wang Yuangui zhuan　王元規傳
Wang zhi　王制
Wei　衛
Wei feng　衛風
Wei guwen Shang Shu　僞古文尚書
Wei Liaoweng　魏了翁
Wei Linggong　衛靈公
Weisheng　尾生
Wei Wenjing　魏文靖
Wei Xiang　魏相
Wei Zhao　韋昭
Weizi zi ming　微子之命
Weizi　微子
Wen　文
Wenbo　文伯
Wen Kong　問孔
Wenwang　文王
Wenwang guanren　文王官人
Wenwang shizi　文王世子
Wen xin diao long　文心雕龍
Wenxuan zhu　文選注
Wenyange　文淵閣
Wenyuange Siku quanshu　文淵閣四庫全書
Wenzi　文子
Won-ui chonggwal　原義總括
Wu　吳
Wu　武
Wu'an　武安
Wu Cheng　吳程
Wufeng　五峰
wuji　無極
Wu Jiamo　吳嘉謨
Wu Wuzhang　吳無障
Wu yi　無逸
Wu Yu　吳棫
Wuzi　武子
Xi　僖
Xi　熙
Xia　夏

Xia 袷

Xiaguan 夏官

Xiahou Zhan 夏侯湛

Xiahou Zhan zhuan 夏侯湛傳

Xiang 湘

Xiang 相

Xiang 襄

Xiang 象

Xiang dafu 鄉大夫

Xiangshan yulu 象山語錄

Xian ju fu 閒居賦

Xiang she li 鄉射禮

Xiang Yu benji 項羽本紀

Xian zhi 先知

Xiaobai 小白

Xiaojing zhushu 孝經註疏

Xiaojing 孝經

Xiaoshan 蕭山

Xiao Shao 簫韶

Xiao shi 小師

Xiao Si kou 小司寇

Xiao xu 小胥

Xiao ya 小雅

Xiao Zongbo 小宗伯

Xia shi 夏時

Xia shu 夏書

Xia xiaozheng 夏小正

Xi ci zhuan 繫辭傳

Xi Dan 姬亶

Xihe 西河

Xihe ji 西河集

Xing Bing 邢昺

Xingfang shi 形方氏

Xin shu 新書

Xin Tang shu 新唐書

Xin xu 新序

Xiu 修

Xuan 宣

Xuanming 玄冥

Xuanyuan 軒轅

Xu Dongyang 許東洋

Xue 薛

Xue Han 薛漢

Xue ji 學記

Xu Fenpeng 徐奮鵬

Xu Hong 徐紘
Xu Jingan 許敬菴
Xunzi 荀子
Xu Shen 許慎
Xushi bijing 徐氏筆精
Xu Shicheng 許石城
Xu xiu Siku quanshu 續修四庫全書
Xu Xuan 徐鉉
Xu Xuanhu 徐玄扈
Xu Xun 徐巡
Xu Zhongshan 徐仲山
Yan 奄
Yan Chouyou 顏讎由
Yan Du zhuan 延篤傳
Yang Hu 陽虎
Yang Shengan 楊升菴
Yang Shi 楊時
Yang Zhu 楊朱
Yangzi 揚子
Yangzi 楊子
Yan Hui 顏回
Yanling 延陵
Yan Qianqiu 閻潛丘
Yan Ruoqu 閻若璩
Yan Shigu 顏師古
Yan tie lun 鹽鐵論
Yan Yan 言偃
Yan yi 燕義
Yan Yuan 顏淵
Yao dian 堯典
Yao Jiheng 姚際恒
Yao Lifang 姚立方
Yao yue 堯曰
yehak 禮學
Yeokhak seo-eon 易學緒言
Yeolsu 洌水
Yeolsu jeonseo 洌水全書
Yeongjo 英祖
Yeoyudang jeonseo 與猶堂全書
Yeoyudang jeonseo boyu 與猶堂全書補遺
Yeoyudang jip 與猶堂集
Yeoyudang 與猶堂
Ye song 禮訟
Ye-ui mundap 禮疑問答
Yi 易

Yi 李
Yi 毅
Yi-a sul 爾雅述
Yi Byeok 李蘗
Yichuan 伊川
Yi Ga-hwan 李家煥
Yi Gang-hoe 李綱會
Yi Geon-bang 李建芳
Yi Hwang 李滉
Yi Ik 李瀷
Yi Ji 益稷
Yi li 儀禮
Yi li zhushu 儀禮註疏
Yin 嚚
Yin 殷
Yin 隱
Ying 英
Yin Hejing 尹和靖
Yiru 意如
Yi Sam-hwan 李森煥
Yiwu 夷吾
Yiyi 夷儀
Yong 雍
Yong bing 用兵
Youli 羑里
You Ruo 有若
Yousi ce 有司徹
You Xia 有夏
Youzi 有子
Youzhou shi Futu song 幽州石浮圖頌
Yu 予
Yu 虞
Yuan Liaofan 袁了凡
Yuan Xian 原憲
Yuan 淵
Yuchang 鬱邑
Yu ding Kangxi zidian 御定康熙字典
Yu ding peiwen yunfu 御定佩文韻府
Yue ji 樂記
Yue ling 月令
Yue Ming 說命
Yue Yi zhuan 樂毅傳
Yue 礿
Yue 籥
Yue 說

Yueming 說命
Yue shi 樂師
Yufu 羽父
Yu Hyeong-won 柳馨遠
Yun 尹
Yun Dan 尹傳
Yun Dong 尹侗
Yun Seon-do 尹善道
Yun Yong-kyun 尹瑢均
Yupian 玉篇
Yushan 余山
Yu shu 虞書
Yuxiong 鬻熊
Yu zao 玉藻
Zairang 宰讓
Zai Wo 宰我
Zang 臧
Zangshi 臧石
Zeng 鄫
Zeng Shen 曾參
Zengzi zan 曾子贊
Zeng Zhe 曾皙
Zengzi ben xiao 曾子本孝
Zengzi daxiao 曾子大孝
Zengzi li shi 曾子立事
Zengzi 曾子
zhan cui 斬衰
Zhan Qin 展禽
Zhang Dingsi 張鼎思
Zhang ke 掌客
Zhang Lei 張耒
Zhangke 掌客
Zhang Qixian 張齊賢
Zhanguo ce 戰國策
Zhang Xuanshu 臧宣叔
Zhang Yu 張禹
Zhao 昭
Zhao Boxun 趙伯循
Zhao De 趙悳
Zhaohun fu 招魂賦
Zhao Qi 趙岐
Zhaoxiang 朝享
Zheng Duanjian 鄭端簡
Zheng feng 鄭風
Zheng Sinong 鄭司農

Zheng Xuan 鄭玄
Zheng 鄭
Zhenji 鍼季
Zhen lu 振鷺
Zhen Xishan 眞西山
Zhen yu 振羽
Zhen Yu 甄宇
Zhenzi 貞子
Zhenzi zan 曾子贊
Zhezong 哲宗
Zhixin relu 知新日錄
Zhong 重
Zhongdou 中都
Zhonghui zhi gao 仲虺之誥
Zhong Ni 仲尼
Zhong Ni yan ju 仲尼燕居
Zhong Qingfu 仲慶父
Zhongsun Heji 仲孫何忌
Zhongsun Mie 仲孫蔑
Zhongsun Zhi 仲孫彘
Zhong Yingqi 仲嬰齊
Zhong yong 中庸
Zhong yong zhangju 中庸章句
Zhongzhong 衆仲
Zhou Dunyi 周敦頤
Zhou Fuxian 周孚先
Zhou gao 周誥
Zhou 周
Zhou 紂
Zhou li 周禮
Zhou li zhushu 周禮註疏
Zhou nan 周南
Zhou Qi 周棄
Zhou Shenglie 周生烈
Zhoushi 周氏
Zhou shu 周書
Zhou song 周訟
Zhou Yi zhengyi 周易正義
Zhou Yi zhushu 周易註疏
Zhou yu 周語
Zhou Yuangong ji 周元公集
Zhouzhi Qiao 舟之嬌
Zhu 柱
Zhuang Jiang 莊姜
Zhuangzi zhu 莊子注

Zhuansun Shi 顓孫師

Zhuanxu 顓頊

Zhu-Chen 朱陳

Zhurong 祝融

Zhu Si 洙泗

Zhu Xi 朱熹

Zhuzi 朱子

Zhuzi daquan 朱子大全

Zhuzi yu lei 朱子語類

Zi Chan 子産

Zi Chi 子遲

Zi dao 子道

Zifu Jingbo 子服景伯

Zi Gong 子貢

Zi Han 子罕

Zijia Ju 子家駒

Zi Lu 子路

Zi Pi 子皮

Ziqi 子期

Zi Qin 子禽

Zi Si 子思

Zi Wo 子我

Zi Xia 子夏

Zi yi 緇衣

Zi You 子有

Zi You 子游

Zi Yu 子輿

Zi Yuan 子淵

Zi Zhang 子張

Zuo zhuan 左傳

BIBLIOGRAPHY

A. Collections

Dasan haksul munhwa jaedan 茶山學術文化財團. *Jeongbon Yeoyudang jeonseo* 定本 與猶堂全書. Dasan haksul munhwa jaedan, 2012.

Minjok munhwa chujin hoe 民族文化推進會. *Hanguk munjip chonggan* 韓國文集 叢刊. Seoul: Minjok munhwa chujin hoe, 1989–2011.

Taiwan shangwu yinshuguan 臺灣商務印書館. *Wenyuange Siku quanshu* 文淵閣四庫 全書. Taipei: Shangwu yinshuguan, 1983.

Unokichi Hattori 服部宇之吉; Giichirō Seki 關儀一郎. *Nihon meika Shisho chūshaku zensho* 日本名家四書註釋全書. Tokyo: Tōyō Tosho Kankōkai, 1922–30.

B. Books by Dasan (Jeong Yak-yong) in Jeongbon Yeoyudang jeonseo

Abang gangyeok go 我邦疆域考 (vol. 32)

A-eon gakbi 雅言覺非 (vol. 5, 66–150)

Akseo gojon 樂書孤存 (vol. 23)

Chunchu gojing 春秋考徵 (vol. 14)

Daedong sugyeong 大東水經 (vol. 33)

Daehak gang-ui 大學講義 (vol. 6, 147–164)

Daehak gong-ui 大學公義 (vol. 6, 67–146)

Garye jak-ui 嘉禮酌儀 (vol. 22, 227–252)

Gyeongse yupyo 經世遺表 (vols. 24, 25, 26)

Heumheum sinseo 欽欽新書 (vols. 30, 31)

Idam sokchan 耳談續纂 (vol. 5, 151–177)

Ilbon go 日本考 (vol. 37, 469–566)

Jungyong gang-ui bo 中庸講義補 (vol. 6, 281–400)

Jungyong jajam 中庸自箴 (vol. 6, 225–280)

Juyeok sajeon 周易四箋 (vols. 15, 16)

Maengja yo-ui 孟子要義 (vol. 7)

Maessi Seo pyeong 梅氏書平 (vol. 13)

Magwa hoetong 麻科會通 (vol. 34)

Minbo ui 民堡議 (vol. 37, 352–404)

Mongmin simseo 牧民心書 (vols. 27, 28, 29)

Munheon bigo gan-o 文獻備考刊誤 (vol. 5, 28–66)
Noneo gogeum ju 論語古今注 (vols. 8, 9)
Pungsu jip-ui 風水集議 (vol. 22, 323–390)
Sangrye oepyeon 喪禮外篇 (vol. 21)
Sangrye sajeon 喪禮四箋 (vols. 18, 19, 20)
Sangseo gohun 尚書古訓 (vols. 11, 12)
Sangseo jiwon rok 尚書知遠錄 (vol. 37, 567–739)
Sang-ui jeolyo 喪儀節要 (vol. 22, 49–226)
Sigyeong gang-ui 詩經講義 (vol. 10)
Simgyeong milheom 心經密驗 (vol. 6, 193–224)
Sohak ji-eon 小學枝言 (vol. 6, 165–192)
Sohak jucheon 小學珠串 (vol. 5, 178–250)
Yeokhak seo-eon 易學緒言 (vol. 17)
Ye-ui mundap 禮疑問答 (vol. 22, 253–322)

C. Classical Texts Cited

Ban Gu 班固. *Baihu tongyi* 白虎通義 (vol. 850 of SKQS).

Ban Gu 班固. *Qian Han shu* 前漢書 (vols. 249–251 of SKQS).

Bao Biao 鮑彪. *Baoshi Zhanguo ce zhu* 鮑氏戰國策注 (vol. 406 of SKQS).

Cai Chen 蔡沈. *Shujing jizhuan* 書經集傳 (vol. 58 of SKQS).

Cheng Hao 程顥; Cheng Yi 程頤. *Er Cheng yishu* 二程遺書 (vol. 698 of SKQS).

Chen Tingjing 陳廷敬; Zhang Yushu 張玉書. *Yu ding peiwen yunfu* 御定佩文韻府 (vols. 1011–1028 of SKQS).

Chen Tingjing 陳廷敬; Zhang Yushu 張玉書. *Yu ding Kangxi zidian* 御定康熙字典 (vols. 229–231 of SKQS).

Dai De 戴德. *Da Dai Li ji* 大戴禮記 (vol. 128 of SKQS).

Dazai Jun 太宰純. *Rongo kokun gaiden* 論語古訓外傳. Edo [Tokyo]: Kobayashi Shinbē, 1745.

Du Yu 杜預; Kong Yingda 孔穎達. *Chunqiu Zuo zhuan zhushu* 春秋左傳註疏 (vols. 143–144 of SKQS).

Fang Xuanling 房玄齡. *Jin shu* 晉書 (vols. 225–226 of SKQS).

Fan Ning 范甯; Yang Shixun 楊士勛. *Chunqiu Guliang zhuan zhushu* 春秋穀梁傳註疏 (vol. 145 of SKQS).

Fan Ye 范曄. *Hou Han shu* 後漢書 (vols. 252–253 of SKQS).

Fu Sheng 伏生. *Shang Shu daquan* 尚書大傳 (vol. 68 of SKQS).

Guan Zhong 管仲; Fang Xuanling 房玄齡. *Guanzi* 管子 (vol. 729 of SKQS).

Guo Pu 郭璞. *Er ya zhushu* 爾雅註疏 (vol. 221 of SKQS).

Guo Xiang 郭象. *Zhuangzi zhu* 莊子注 (vol. 1056 of SKQS).

Gu Yanwu 顧炎武. *Re zhi lu* 日知錄 (vol. 858 of SKQS).

Han Ying 韓嬰. *Han Shi waizhuan* 韓詩外傳 (vol. 89 of SKQS).

Han Yu 韓愈; Li Gao 李翺. *Lun yu bijie* 論語筆解 (vol. 196 of SKQS).

He Xiu 何休; Xu Yan 徐彥. *Chunqiu Gongyang zhuan zhushu* 春秋公羊傳註疏 (vol. 145 of SKQS).

He Yan 何晏. *Lun yu jijie* 論語集解 in *Lun yu zhushu* 論語註疏 (vol. 195 of SKQS).

He Yan 何晏; Xing Bing 邢昺. *Lun yu zhushu* 論語註疏 (vol. 195 of SKQS).

Huang Kan 皇侃. *Lun yu jijie yishu* 論語集解義疏 (vol. 195 of SKQS).

Huan Kuan 桓寬. *Yan tie lun* 鹽鐵論 (vol. 695 of SKQS).

Hu Guang 胡廣. *Li ji daquan* 禮記大全 (vol. 122 of SKQS).

Hu Guang 胡廣. *Lun yu jizhu daquan* 論語集注大全 (vol. 205 of SKQS).

Hu Guang 胡廣. *Mengzi jizhu daquan* 孟子集注大全 (vol. 205 of SKQS).

Hu Kuang 胡爌. *Shi yi lu* 拾遺錄 (vol. 858 of SKQS).

Jeong Gyu-yeong 丁奎英. *Sa-am seonsaeng yeonbo* 俟菴先生年譜. Seoul: Jeongmun sa, 1984.

Jia Yi 賈誼. *Xin shu* 新書 (vol. 695 of SKQS).

Jin Lüxiang 金履祥. *Lun yu jizhu kaozheng* 論語集注考證 (vol. 202 of SKQS).

Kong Anguo 孔安國; Kong Yingda 孔穎達. *Shang Shu zhushu* 尚書註疏 (vol. 54 of SKQS).

Kong Fu 孔鮒. *Kong congzi* 孔叢子 (vol. 695 of SKQS).

Lei Li 雷禮; Fan Shouji 範守己; Tan Xisi 譚希思. *Huang Ming dazheng ji* 皇明大政記. Shanghai: Shanghai gu ji chu ban she, 2002.

Li Shan 李善. *Wenxuan zhu* 文選注 (vol. 1329 of SKQS).

Liu Xiang 劉向. *Shuo yuan* 說苑 (vol. 696 of SKQS).

Liu Xiang 劉向. *Xin xu* 新序 (vol. 696 of SKQS).

Liu Xie 劉勰. *Wenxin diaolong* 文心雕龍 (vol. 1478 of SKQS).

Lü Buwei 呂不韋. *Lüshi Chunqiu* 呂氏春秋 (vol. 848 of SKQS).

Lu Deming 陸德明. *Jingdian shi wen* 經典釋文 (vol. 182 of SKQS).

Lu Jiuyuan 陸九淵. *Xiangshan yulu* 象山語錄 (vol. 1156 of SKQS).

Lu Longqi 陸隴其. *Sishu jiangyi kunmian lu* 四書講義困勉錄 (vol. 209 of SKQS).

Luo Yuan 羅願. *Er ya yi* 爾雅翼 (vol. 222 of SKQS).

Mao Heng 毛亨; Zheng Xuan 鄭玄; Kong Yingda 孔穎達. *Mao Shi zhushu* 毛詩註疏 (vol. 69 of SKQS).

Mao Qiling 毛奇齡. *Lun yu jiqiu pian* 論語稽求篇 (vol. 210 of SKQS).

Mao Qiling 毛奇齡. *Sishu gai cuo* 四書改錯. In vol. 165 of *Xu xiu Siku quanshu* 續修四庫全書. Shanghai: Shanghai guji chubanshe, 1995–2002.

Mao Qiling 毛奇齡. *Si shu shengyan* 四書賸言 (vol. 210 of SKQS).

Mao Qiling 毛奇齡. *Si shu shengyan bu* 四書賸言補 (vol. 210 of SKQS).

Mao Qiling 毛奇齡. *Xihe ji* 西河集 (vols. 1320–1321 of SKQS).

Ouyang Xiu 歐陽脩. *Xin Tang shu* 新唐書 (vols. 272–276 of SKQS).

Qu Yuan 屈原; Wang Yi 王逸. *Chu ci zhangju* 楚辭章句 (vol. 1062 of SKQS).

Sima Qian 司馬遷. *Shi ji* 史記 (vols. 243–244 of SKQS).

Sima Qian 司馬遷; Pei Yin 裴駰. *Shi ji jijie* 史記集解 (vols. 245–246 of SKQS).

Sun Yi 孫奕. *Shi er bian* 示兒編 (vol. 864 of SKQS).

Su Xun 蘇洵. *Shi fa* 諡法 (vol. 646 of SKQS).

Wang Bi 王弼; Han Kangbo 韓康伯; Kong Yingda 孔穎達. *Zhou Yi zhushu* 周易註疏 (vol. 7 of SKQS).

Wang Chong 王充. *Lun heng* 論衡 (vol. 862 of SKQS).

Wang Shu 王肅. *Kongzi jia yu* 孔子家語 (vol. 695 of SKQS).

Wang Yinglin 王應麟. *Kun xue ji wen* 困學紀聞 (vol. 854 of SKQS).

Wei Zhao 韋昭. *Guo yu* 國語 (vol. 104 of SKQS).

Wei Zheng 魏徵. *Sui shu* 隋書 (vol. 264 of SKQS).

Xing Bing 邢昺. *Lun yu zhengyi* 論語正義 in *Lun yu zhushu* 論語註疏 (vol. 195 of SKQS).

Xuanzong 玄宗; Xing Bing 邢昺. *Xiaojing zhushu* 孝經註疏 (vol. 182 of SKQS).

Xu Bo 徐𤊹. *Xushi bijing* 徐氏筆精 (vol. 856 of SKQS).

Xun Kuang 荀況. *Xunzi* 荀子 (vol. 695 of SKQS).

Xu Shen 許慎. *Shuo wen jie zi* 說文解字 (vol. 223 of SKQS).

Yang Xiong 揚雄. *Fang yan* 方言 (vol. 221 of SKQS).

Yao Hong 姚宏; Gao You 高誘. *Zhanguo ce* 戰國策 (vol. 406 of SKQS).

Yao Silian 姚思廉. *Chen shu* 陳書 (vol. 260 of SKQS).

Zhang Fu 張溥. *Han Wei Liuzhao baisan jia ji* 漢魏六朝百三家集 (vols. 1412–1416 of SKQS).

Zhao Qi 趙岐; Sun Shi 孫奭. *Mengzi zhushu* 孟子註疏 (vol. 195 of SKQS).

Zhen Dexiu 眞德秀. *Daxue yanyi* 大學衍義 (vol. 704 of SKQS).

Zheng Xuan 鄭玄; Jia Gongyan 賈公彥. *Yi li zhushu* 儀禮註疏 (vol. 102 of SKQS).

Zheng Xuan 鄭玄; Jia Gongyan 賈公彥. *Zhou li zhushu* 周禮註疏 (vol. 90 of SKQS).

Zheng Xuan 鄭玄; Kong Yingda 孔穎達. *Li ji zhushu* 禮記註疏 (vols. 115–116 of SKQS).

Zheng Xuan 鄭玄; Ma Guohan 馬國翰. *Lun yu Zhengshi zhu* 論語鄭氏註. Changsha: Changsha Lang huan guan, 1883.

Zhou Dunyi 周敦頤. *Zhou Yuangong ji* 周元公集 (vol. 1101 of SKQS).

Zhu Xi 朱熹. *Daxue zhangju* 大學章句 (vol. 197 of SKQS).

Zhu Xi 朱熹. *Lun yu jizhu* 論語集注 (vol. 197 of SKQS).

Zhu Xi 朱熹. *Mengzi jizhu* 孟子集注 (vol. 197 of SKQS).

Zhu Xi 朱熹. *Zhong yong zhangju* 中庸章句 (vol. 197 of SKQS).

Zhu Xi 朱熹. *Zhuzi yu lei* 朱子語類 (vols. 700–702 of SKQS).

Zhu Yuanzhang 朱元璋. *Ming Taizu wenji* 明太祖文集 (vol. 1223 of SKQS).

D. Modern Works

Ames, Roger T; Rosemont, Henry. Jr. *The Analects of Confucius: A Philosophical Translation*. New York: Ballantine Publishing Group, 1998.

Baker, Donald L. "The Use and Abuse of the Sirhak Label: A New Look at Sin Hu-dam and His *Sohak byon*." *Gyohoesa yongu* 3 (1981): 183–254.

Bang, In. "Danguk dae bon *Juyeok sajeon* yeongu 단국대본 주역사전 연구." *Dasan hak* 17 (2010): 7–44.

Brooks, Bruce E; Brooks, Taeko A. *The Original Analects: Sayings of Confucius and his Successors*. New York: Columbia University Press, 1998.

Cheon, Gwan-u. "Joseon hugi silhak ui gaenyeom jaeron 조선후기 실학의 개념 재론." In *Hanguksa ui jaebalgyeon* 한국사의 재발견, ed. Cheon Seoul: Iljo-gak, 1974, 107–185.

Choe, Ik-hwan. *Silhak pa wa Jeong Dasan* 實學派와 丁茶山. 1955. Reprint, Seoul: Cheongnyeon sa, 1989.

Choe, Ik-hwan. "*Yeoyudang jeonseo* reul dokham 여유당전서를 독함 (15)." *Dong-A Ilbo*, February 1939, 3.

Choi, Byonghyon. *Admonitions on Governing the People*. Berkeley: University of California Press, 2010.

Gardner, Daniel K. *Zhu Xi's Reading of the Analects: Canon, Commentary, and the Classical Tradition*. New York: Columbia University Press, 2003.

Han, U-geun. "Yijo Silhak ui gaenyeom e daehayeo 이조 실학의 개념에 대하여." *Jindan hakhoe* 15 (Seoul: Jindan hakhoe, 1958): 25–46.

Han, Yeong-u, et al. *Dasi, Silhak-iran muet-inga* 다시, 실학이란 무엇인가. Seoul: Pureun yeoksa, 2007.

Hinton, David. *The Analects*. Washington, DC: Counterpoint, 1998.

Hong, I-seop. *Jeong Yak-yong ui jeongchi gyeongje sasang yeongu* 丁若鏞의 政治經濟思想 研究. Seoul: Hanguk yeongu doseogwan, 1959.

Huang, Chichung. *The Analects of Confucius*. New York: Oxford University Press, 1997.

Im, Hyeong-taek. "Jeong Yak-yong ui Gangjin yubaegi ui gyoyuk hwaldong gwa geu seonggwa 정약용의 강진 유배기의 교육 활동 과 그 성과." In *Silsa gusi ui Hanguk-hak*, ed. Im Hyeong-taek. Seoul: Changbi, 2000, 399–434.

Im, Hyeong-taek. *Silsa gusi ui Hanguk hak* 實事求是의 韓國學. Seoul: Changbi, 2000.

Jang, Dong-u. "*Yeoyudang jeonseo* jeongbon sa-eop eul wihan pilsabon yeongu—gyeongjip eul jungsim euro 여유당전서 정본 사업 을 위한 필사본 연구—경집을 중심으로." *Dasan hak* 7 (2005): 251–289.

Jang, Dong-u. "*Yeoyudang jeonseo* pilsabon e gwanhan gochal 여유당 전서 필사본에 관한 고찰." *Dasan hak* 15 (2009): 119–138.

Jang, Ji-yeon. *Joseon Yukyo yeonwon* 朝鮮儒敎淵源. Seoul: Hoedong seogwan, 1922.

Jeong, Gyu-yeong. *Dasan-ui han pyeongsaeng: Sa-am seonsaeng yeonbo* 俟菴先生年譜. Trans. Jae-so Song. Paju: Changbi, 2014.

Jeong, In-bo. *Damwon munrok* 薝園文錄 4 in vol. 5 of *Damwon Jeong In-bo jeonjip* 薝園鄭寅普全集. Seoul: Yonsei University Press, 1983.

Jeong, In-bo. "Dasan seonsaeng ui saeng-ae wa sasang 다산 선생의 생애와 사상." In *Damwon gukhak sango*. Seoul: Mungyo sa, 1955, 70–108.

Jeong, In-bo. "Yu-ilhan jeongbeopga Jeong Dasan seonsaeng seoron 유일한 정법가 정다산 선생 서론 (1)." *Dong-A ilbo*, September 1934, 10.

Ji, Du-hwan. "Joseon hugi Silhak yeongu ui munjejeom gwa banghyang 조선후기 실학연구의 문제점과 방향." *Daedong gojeon yeongu* 3 (1987): 103–148.

Jo, Seong-eul. Yeoyudang jip *ui munheonhak jeok yeongu—siyul mit jammun ui yeondae gojeung-eul jungsim euro* 여유당집의 문헌학적 연구—시율 및 잡문의 연대 고증을 중심으로. Seoul: Hye-an, 2004.

Kim, Bo-reum. "*Yeoyudang jip* eseo *Yeoyudang jeonseo* ro 여유당집에서 여유당전서로." *Jindan hakbo* 124 (2015): 207–234.

Kim, Bo-reum. "*Yeoyudang jip* seongnip e gwanhan gochal 여유당집 성립에 관한 고찰." *Dasan hak* 18 (2011): 197–235.

Kim, Eon-jong. "*Yeoyudang jeonseo boyu* ui jeojakbyeol jinwi munje e daehayeo 여유당전서 보유의 저작별 진위 문제에 대하여 (1), (2), and (3)." *Dasan hak* 9 (2006): 123–175; *Dasan hak* 10 (2007): 305–331; *Dasan hak* 11 (2007): 321–353.

Kim, Eon-jong. *Jeong Dasan Noneo gogeumju woneui chonggwal gojing* 丁茶山論語古今註原義總括考徵. Taipei: Xuehai Publishing, 1988.

Kim, Jun-seok. "Yu Hyeong-won ui byeonbeop gwa silliron 유형원의 변법과 실리론." *Dongbang hakji* 72 (Seoul: Yonsei University, 1995).

Kim, Mun-sik. "*Yeoyudang jeonseo* gyeongjip cheje ui geomto 여유당전서 경집 체제의 검토." *Dasan hak* 5 (2004): 385–411.

Kim, Yeong-ho. "*Yeoyudang jeonseo* ui *text* geomto 여유당전서의 텍스트 검토." In *Jeong Dasan yeongu ui hyeonhwang* 정다산 연구의 현황, ed. Han U-geun et al. Seoul: Min-eum sa, 1985, 11–41.

Lau, D. C. *The Analects*. Harmondsworth; New York: Penguin Books, 1979.

Legge, James. *Confucian Analects, the Great Learning, and the Doctrine of the Mean*. New York: Dover, 1861. Reprint, 1973.

Palais, James. *Confucian Statecraft and Korean Institutions: Yu Hyŏngwon and the Late Chosŏn Dynasty*. Seattle: University of Washington Press, 1996.

Park, Hong-sik. "Ilje ganggeomgi Jeong In-bo, An Jae-hong, Choe Ik-hwan ui Dasan yeongu 일제강점기 정인보, 안재홍, 최익한의 다산 연구." *Dasan hak* 17 (2010): 45–93.

Setton, Mark. *Chŏng Yagyong: Korea's Challenge to Orthodox Neo-Confucianism.* Albany: State University of New York Press, 1997.

Sin, Yong-ha. "19 segi mal Jang Ji-yeon ui Dasan Jeong Yak-yong ui balgul 19세기말 장지연의 다산 정약용의 발굴." *Hanguk hakbo* 29, no. 1 (2003): 2–21.

Slingerland, Edward G. *Confucius Analects: With Selection from Traditional Commentaries.* Indianapolis, IN: Hackett, 2003.

Song, Jae-so. "Dasan hakdan yeongu seoseol 다산학단 연구 서설." *Dasan hak* 12 (2008): 7–24.

Soothill, William Edward. *The Analects of Confucius.* Yokohama: Fukuin, 1910.

Waley, Arthur. *The Analects of Confucius.* London: G. Allen & Unwin. 1938.

Watson, Burton. *The Analects of Confucius.* New York: Columbia University Press, 2007.

Yi, Eul-ho. *Dasan gyeonghak sasang yeongu* 茶山經學思想研究. Seoul: Eul-yu munhwa sa, 1966.

Yi, Ji-hyeong. *Noneo gogeum ju* 論語古今註 (vols. 1–5). Seoul: Sa-am, 2010.

Yi, U-seong. "Chogi Silhak gwa Seongnihak ui gwangye 초기실학과 성리학의 관계." *Dongbang hakji* 58 (Seoul: Yonsei University, 1988): 15–22.

Yi, U-seong. "Silhak yeongu seoseol 실학연구서설." *Silhak yeongu immun* 실학연구입문, ed. Yeoksa hakhoe. Seoul: Iljo-gak, 1973, 1–17.

Yu, Gwon-jong. "Jeong Yak-yong ui dgwa cheolhak sasang 정약용의 경전 해석과 철학사상." In *Hanguk Yuhak sasang daegye* 한국유학사상대계, vol. 3. Andong: Hanguk gukhak jinheungwon, 2005, 385–398.

INDEX